ROUTLEDGE HANDBOOK OF QUEER DEVELOPMENT STUDIES

Around the world lesbian, gay, bisexual, trans, intersex and queer (LGBTIQ) individuals are subjected to violence and intimidation based on their real or perceived sexuality, gender identity or expression. With those most at risk of human rights violations often living in areas of low economic development, questions of sexuality, gender identity, and expression have become a significant area of research within the field of development studies. The *Routledge Handbook of Queer Development Studies* is the first full length study of queer development studies, collecting the very best in research from around the world. Topics for discussion include:

- Queering policy and planning in development
- Queer development critique and queer critiques of development
- Global LGBTIQ rights
- Queer social movements and mobilizations

The *Routledge Handbook of Queer Development Studies* is an essential guide for scholars, upper level students, practitioners and anyone with an interest in global analyses of sexualities, gender identities, and expressions.

Corinne L. Mason is an Associate Professor of Gender and Women's Studies and Sociology at Brandon University, Canada. Mason is the author of *Manufacturing Urgency: Violence against Women and the Development Industry*, and her work can be found in *Feminist Formations*, *International Feminist Journal of Politics* and *Feminist Media Studies*.

The Routledge International Handbook Series

A full list of titles in this series is available at: https://www.routledge.com/Routledge-International-Handbooks/book-series/RIHAND

Recently published titles:

The Routledge International Handbook of Consumer Psychology
Edited by Cathrine V. Jansson-Boyd, Magdalena J. Zawisza

The Routledge International Handbook of Sandplay Therapy
Edited by Barbara A. Turner

The Routledge International Handbook of Sexual Addiction
Edited by Thaddeus Birchard and Joanna Benfield

The Routledge International Handbook of Forensic Psychology in Secure Settings
Edited by Jane L. Ireland, Carol A. Ireland, Martin Fisher, Neil Gredecki

The Routledge International Handbook of Critical Positive Psychology
Edited by Nicholas J. L. Brown, Tim Lomas, Francisco Jose Eiroa-Orosa

The Routledge International Handbook of Sexual Addiction
Edited by Thaddeus Birchard, Joanna Benfield

The Routledge International Handbook of Self-Control in Health and Well-Being
Edited by Denise de Ridder, Marieke Adriaanse, Kentaro Fujita

The Routledge International Handbook of Psychosocial Epidemiology
Edited by Mika Kivimaki, David G. Batty, Ichiro Kawachi, Andrew Steptoe

The Routledge International Handbook of Human Aggression: Current Issues and Perspectives
Edited by Jane L. Ireland, Philip Birch, Carol A. Ireland

The Routledge International Handbook of Jungian Film Studies
Edited by Luke Hockley

ROUTLEDGE HANDBOOK OF QUEER DEVELOPMENT STUDIES

Edited by Corinne L. Mason

LONDON AND NEW YORK

First published 2018
by Routledge
2 Park Square, Milton Park, Abingdon, Oxon OX14 4RN

and by Routledge
711 Third Avenue, New York, NY 10017

Routledge is an imprint of the Taylor & Francis Group, an informa business

British Library Cataloguing-in-Publication Data
A catalogue record for this book is available from the British Library

Library of Congress Cataloging-in-Publication Data
Names: Mason, Corinne L., editor.
Title: Routledge handbook of queer development studies / edited by Corinne Mason.
Description: First Edition. | New York : Routledge, 2018. | Includes bibliographical references and index.
Identifiers: LCCN 2017040568 (print) | LCCN 2017042230 (ebook) | ISBN 9781315529530 (eBook) | ISBN 9781138693753 (hardback)
Subjects: LCSH: Queer theory. | Sexual minorities – Civil rights. | Gay liberation movement.
Classification: LCC HQ76.25 (ebook) | LCC HQ76.25 .R68 2018 (print) | DDC 306.76/6-dc23
LC record available at https://lccn.loc.gov/2017040568

ISBN: 978-1-138-69375-3 (hbk)
ISBN: 978-1-315-52953-0 (ebk)

Typeset in Bembo
by HWA Text and Data Managemement, London

CONTENTS

Contents

Contents

CONTRIBUTORS

Dennis Altman AM is an Emeritus Professor of Politics at LaTrobe University, Australia, and author of 13 books, most recently *The End of the Homosexual* (2013) and (with Jon Symons) *Queer Wars* (2016). He was awarded the Simon and Gagnon Award for career contributions to the field of sociology of sexualities by the American Sociological Association's Section on Sexualities 2013, and has been President of the AIDS Society of Asia and the Pacific, and on the Governing Council of the International AIDS Society.

Niharika Banerjea is an Associate Professor in Sociology at the School of Liberal Studies, Ambedkar University, Delhi, India. Her research and teaching interests lie in the areas of sexualities, gender, sexuality and development, transnational feminisms, social justice activisms, qualitative methods and collaborative ethnographies. She is part of the transnational participatory project, Making Liveable Lives: Rethinking Social Exclusion, with activists and academics in India and the UK. An academic–activist, Niharika is also associated with Sappho for Equality, the activist forum for lesbian, bisexual women and transmen rights.

Kath Browne is a Professor in Human Geography at the University of Brighton, UK. Her research interests lie in sexualities, genders and spatialities. She works on the transnational participatory project, Making Liveable Lives: Rethinking Social Exclusion, with activists and academics in the UK and India. Her work engages with lesbian, gay, bisexual and trans (LGBT) equalities, lesbian geographies, gender transgressions and women's spaces. She works with Catherine Nash and Andrew Gorman Murray on understanding transnational resistances to LGBT equalities. She has authored international, interdisciplinary journal publications, co-wrote with Leela Bakshi *Ordinary in Brighton: LGBT, Activisms and the City* (2013), and *Queer Spiritual Spaces* (2010), and co-edited *The Routledge Companion to Geographies of Sex and Sexualities* (2016) and *Lesbian Geographies* (2015).

Ashley Currier is an Associate Professor of women's, gender and sexuality studies at the University of Cincinnati, USA. She is the author of *Out in Africa: LGBT Organizing in Namibia and South Africa* (2012). Her research has appeared in *Australian Feminist Studies*, *Critical African Studies*, *Feminist Formations*, *Gender & Society*, *GLQ*, *Mobilization*, *Politique Africaine*, *Qualitative*

Sociology, Signs: Journal of Women in Culture and Society, Social Movement Studies, Studies in Law, Politics, and Society and *Women's Studies Quarterly*. She is working on a book manuscript about the politicization of homosexuality in Malawi and another project examining mobilization around marriage equality in Kentucky (USA).

Petra L. Doan is a Professor in the Department of Urban and Regional Planning at Florida State University, USA. She has lived, worked and conducted research in sub-Saharan Africa (Togo, Burkina Faso, Côte d'Ivoire, Mali and Botswana) and the Middle East (Jordan and Egypt). In addition, for the past 15 years she has explored planning issues related to the lesbian, gay, bisexual, trans and queer (LGBTQ) community. She has edited two books: *Queerying Planning: Challenging Heteronormative Assumptions and Reframing Planning Practice* (2011) and *Planning and LGBTQ Communities: the Need for Inclusive Queer Space* (2015). She also has published in *Gender, Place, and Culture, Women's Studies Quarterly, Environment and Planning A*, the *Journal of Planning Education and Research, Progressive Planning* and the *International Review of Urban and Regional Research*.

Peter Drucker (PhD Columbia 1994) is a Fellow of the International Institute for Research and Education in Amsterdam, the Netherlands, teaching and writing on global political economy and lesbian, gay, bisexual, trans, intersex and queer (LGBTIQ) studies. He is the editor of the anthology *Different Rainbows* (2000) on same-sex and transgender identities in the global South, and the author of *Warped: Gay Normality and Queer Anti-Capitalism* (2015).

Andil Gosine is an Associate Professor in Art and Politics at the Faculty of Environmental Studies, York University, UK. His research, writing and arts practices explore imbrications of ecology, desire and power.

Neville Hoad is an Associate Professor of English and Women's and Gender Studies at The University of Texas at Austin, USA. He is the author of *African Intimacies: Race, Homosexuality and Globalization* (2007) and co-editor (with Karen Martin and Graeme Reid) of *Sex & Politics in South Africa: Equality/Gay & Lesbian Movement/the Anti-Apartheid Struggle* (2005). He is currently working on a book project about the literary and cultural representations of the HIV/AIDS pandemic in sub-Saharan Africa, in addition to a sequel to *African Intimacies* entitled *Erotopolitics: Africa, Sovereignty, Sexuality*.

Christine M. Klapeer is a transdisciplinary political theorist anchored in the field of gender, queer, postcolonial and decolonial studies as well as in materialist feminisms. In her current research project, Queer(s) in Development, she is engaged with the ambivalent role of development institutions as new arenas for (transnational) lesbian, gay, bisexual, trans, intersex and queer (LGBTIQ) politics. Her third book *Queer G(r)ifts. Development Politics, LGBTIQ Rights and the Trajectories of Transnational Queer Solidarity* is in preparation. Christine received her doctorate from the University of Innsbruck, Austria, and has been teaching feminist political theory, gender, postcolonial, queer and critical development studies at various universities, including the University of Vienna and the CEU in Budapest. She currently holds a position in Gender/Queer Studies at the University of Bayreuth, Germany.

Amy Lind is Mary Ellen Heintz Professor and Head of the Department of Women's, Gender, and Sexuality Studies. She is the author of *Gendered Paradoxes: Women's Movements, State Restructuring, and Global Development in Ecuador* (2005), and editor of four volumes, including *Development, Sexual Rights and Global Governance* (2010) and *Feminist (Im)mobilities in Fortress(ing) North America: Rights, Citizenships and Identities in Transnational Perspective* (2013, co-edited with Anne Sisson Runyan, Patricia McDermott and Marianne Marchand). Her new book, *From Nation to Plurination: Resignifying State, Economy and Family in Ecuador* (with Christine Keating), addresses the cultural, economic and affective politics of Ecuador's postneoliberal Citizen Revolution.

Marcus McGee is an independent researcher formerly affiliated with the Social Sciences Division at the University of Chicago, USA. His ethnographic work focuses on the interplay of political violence, mass mediation, and embodiment in Latin America and particularly Mexico.

Nyx McLean is a non-binary queer academic researcher interested in lesbian, gay, bisexual, transgender, intersex, asexual and queer (LGBTIAQ) Pride within the context of post-apartheid South Africa with a specific focus on queer identities and assimilation. Their research work includes exploring how the role of the Internet and its digital environments may enable social change and the production of counter publics with a specific focus on sexual identities, gender expression and marginalised identities. Their previous research has included exploring transgender and lesbian identities' use of the Internet; considering digital as enabling queer counter publics; the digital as providing a feminist future for queer African women; and marginalised desires and the Internet. They have served as board member for South Africa's first and oldest transgender organisation, Gender DynamiX.

Ariel G. Mekler is pursuing a PhD in Political Science at the City University of New York, USA. She received her master's in Global Affairs from New York University where her academic and field research focused largely on peacebuilding methods and lesbian, gay, bisexual, trans, intersex and queer (LGBTIQ) human security measures. While working as a graduate intern with USAID's Inaugural LGBT Policy Unit, Ariel helped to support the first ever LGBT Vision for Action initiative. Her current research examines the intersection of LGBTIQ considerations, security concepts, political violence and international relations, specifically analyzing how these macro level systems impact the lived experience of LGBTIQ populations worldwide.

Elizabeth Mills is a lecturer in the Department of Social Anthropology, at Sussex University, UK. Working predominantly in South Africa, her research lies at the interface of medical and political anthropology. She has researched and published on a range of topics including sexuality, gender, posthumanist performativity, the politics of science and medicine, emergent forms of biosociality, and precarity and the post-apartheid state.

Robert C. Mizzi is an Assistant Professor in the Faculty of Education at the University of Manitoba, Canada. His research focuses on transnational sexual and gender minority educators and their work and welfare in different educational contexts. He has published in journals such as the *Journal of Homosexuality*, *Development in Practice* and the *Journal of Studies in International Education*. Robert's most recent book is co-edited with Tonette Rocco and Sue Shore and is entitled *Disrupting Adult and Community Education: Teaching, Learning, and Working in the Periphery* (2016). Visit www.robertmizzi.com to learn more about Robert's work.

Julie Moreau is an Assistant Professor of Political Science and Sexual Diversity Studies at the University of Toronto, Canada. Her research on queer politics focuses on lesbian, gay, bisexual, trans and queer (LGBTQ) social movements, political participation and citizenship. Her work appears in *New Political Science*, *Space and Polity*, *Journal of Lesbian Studies*, *Mobilization: An International Journal* and several edited collections. She is currently working on a book manuscript entitled *After Equality: Organizing Lesbian Citizenship in South Africa and Argentina*, which examines the strategic construction of sexual identities in contexts of legal equality, and a collaboration on LGBTQ political participation in the 2016 US presidential election.

Nick J. Mulé, PhD is an Associate Professor in the School of Social Work at York University in Toronto, Canada where he teaches policy, theory and practice. He is also seconded to the School of Gender, Sexuality and Women's Studies. His research interests include the social inclusion/exclusion of lesbian, gay, bisexual, trans and queer (LGBTQ) populations in social policy and service provision and the degree of their recognition as distinct communities in cultural, systemic and structural contexts. He also engages in critical analysis of the LGBTQ movement and the development of queer liberation theory. He has co-edited *LGBTQ People and Social Work: Intersectional Perspectives* (2015), *Queering Social Work Education* (2016) and *The Shifting Terrain: Nonprofit Policy Advocacy in Canada* (2017). A queer activist for many years, Nick is the founder, past chairperson and currently member at large of Queer Ontario. In addition, he is a psychotherapist in private practice serving LGBTQ populations in Toronto.

Jonathan Symons is a Senior Lecturer in International Relations at Macquarie University, Sydney, Australia. Jon's research interests include both global environmental politics and also the international politics of sexuality. He is co-author (with Professor Dennis Altman) of *Queer Wars: The New Global Polarization over Gay Rights* (2016).

Maria Tonini has a PhD in Gender Studies from Lund University, Sweden. Her doctoral thesis explored the ambiguities of recognition from the perspective of young queer people in India. Currently, she works as a postdoctoral researcher at the South Asian Studies Network, Lund University. In her current project, she combines her interests in gender and sexuality studies, South Asia and recognition by analysing Indian men's rights activists' online communities as expressions of perceived misrecognition.

Chloé Vaast is a Gender Advisor at the Royal Tropical Institute (KIT), Amsterdam, the Netherlands. She received her master's degree in Gender and Development from the Institute of Development Studies (IDS), University of Sussex, UK. Chloé is a former gender consultant at the Sexuality, Poverty and Law programme at IDS, EngenderHealth in New York City, as well as CIFOR (Center for International Forestry Research) in Indonesia and Burkina Faso.

Matthew Waites, PhD is a Senior Lecturer in Sociology at the University of Glasgow., UK He is author of *The Age of Consent: Young People, Sexuality and Citizenship* (2005) and co-editor (with Corinne Lennox) of *Human Rights, Sexual Orientation and Gender Identity in the Commonwealth: Struggles for Decriminalisation and Change* (2013). He is co-editor with Patricia Hynes, Michele Lamb and Damien Short, of three special issues on sociology and human rights, including issues of the *International Journal of Human Rights* in 2010 ('Sociology and Human Rights: New Engagements') and 2012 ('New Directions in the Sociology of Human Rights'), and a special issue of *Sociology* ('The Sociology of Human Rights') in 2012. He also co-edited (with Kelly Kollman) 'The Global Politics of LGBT Human Rights' special issue of *Contemporary Politics* (2009). A recent article in *Sociological Review* is titled 'LGBTI Organisations Navigating Imperial Contexts: The Kaleidoscope Trust, the Commonwealth and the Need for a Decolonizing, Intersectional Politics' (2016).

Chamindra Weerawardhana is the LGBTQIA (lesbian, gay, bisexual, transgender, queer, intersex and asexual) Officer and Acting Secretary of the Labour Party in Northern Ireland. She is also a Director of Venasa, Sri Lanka's premier transgender network and a board member of Sibéal, the Irish Feminist and Gender Studies Network. She is a researcher at Queen's University Belfast, where she is the first trans woman to hold a research appointment.

Zahele Muholi (front cover photo) is a visual activist and photographer born in 1972 in Umlazi, Durban, and living in Johannesburg. They co-founded the Forum for Empowerment of Women (FEW) in 2002, and in 2009 founded Inkanyiso (www.inkanyiso.org), a forum for queer and visual (activist) media. Muholi's self-proclaimed mission is 'to re-write a black queer and trans visual history of South Africa for the world to know of our resistance and existence at the height of hate crimes in SA and beyond'. They continue to train and co-facilitate photography workshops for young women in the townships. Muholi studied Advanced Photography at the Market Photo Workshop in Newtown, Johannesburg, and in 2009 completed an MFA: Documentary Media at Ryerson University, Toronto. In 2013 they became an Honorary Professor at the University of the Arts/Hochschule für Künste Breme

ACKNOWLEDGEMENTS

I am deeply grateful to every contributor in this volume for allowing me to collect and curate this book. In many ways, this collection represents a conversation I was interested in having with scholars about where queer theory, queer inquires, and queer scholars/ship fit into the field of development studies. My hope is that this collection further opens up this conversation in the field, and elsewhere, about the critical nature of the chapters found within these pages, but also the significance of the 'sexuality turn' in development more broadly.

The trust of authors to publish their work is an honour that I take very seriously. All errors are my own.

I developed the idea for this book during my time as a Visiting Fellow in the Institute of Development Studies (IDS) at the University of Sussex in spring 2015. I am especially thankful to my IDS supervisor Elizabeth Mills, and to the Faculty of Arts at Brandon University for financially supporting this fellowship opportunity.

I am also very grateful to Cynthia Weber for taking the time to discuss this collection and helping me to see this project clearly at the International Feminist Journal of Politics conference in 2016.

Thank you to Routledge editors Leila Walker and Helena Hurd for their support in publishing this collection, even as the goalpost moved a few times to accommodate contributions and the birth of my child. Thank you to Amber Christensen who organized the final edits and proofs of this collection.

Foundational chapters in this collection have been previously published in the *Institute of Development Studies Bulletin* (with printing and distribution support from Swedish International Development Cooperation Agency), *Contemporary Politics*, *Development in Practice* and *Postcolonial Studies*. Thank you for granting me the permission to reprint material here.

On personal note, thank you to my partner Rune Breckon for their unwavering support.

INTRODUCTION TO *ROUTLEDGE HANDBOOK OF QUEER DEVELOPMENT STUDIES*

Corinne L. Mason

In official remarks for the 2011 Recognition of International Human Rights Day, former US Secretary of State Hillary Clinton announced that $3 million would be placed into a new Global Equality Fund to fight global lesbian, gay, bisexual, and transgender (LGBT) discrimination. Echoing her words at the Fourth United Nations Conference on Women in Beijing (1995) where she declared "women's rights are human rights," Clinton pronounced that "gay rights are human rights, and human rights are gay rights" (Clinton 2011). According to the Human Rights Campaign (HRC 2015a), this speech at the United Nations (UN) Human Rights Council in 2011 "broke the gay glass ceiling" and ushered in a new era for transnational LGBT rights.

The human rights of lesbian, gay, bisexual, transgender, intersex, and queer (LGBTIQ) individuals are violated around the world. LGBTIQ people are attacked, kidnapped, raped, and murdered based on their real or perceived sexuality, gender identity, and/or expression. They face social, political, and economic exclusion and marginalization. In one third of the world's countries, LGBTIQ people can be arrested and jailed, and in five countries they may be executed for engaging in same-sex relationships and acts (UN 2013). As of 2015, seventy-six countries around the world criminalize consensual same-sex relationships (UN Human Rights Council 2015). According to a 2013 report published by the International Lesbian, Gay, Bisexual, Trans and Intersex Association (ILGA), countries that are (sometimes interchangeably) labeled Third World, developing, underdeveloped, or Global South are considered the most homophobic and transphobic globally. Worldwide mappings of pride and prejudice[1] function as a grid of interpretation, where global inequalities are mapped along evolutionary timelines, and where homophobia is represented as "backward" and can be overcome through all the benefits that development and globalization have to offer. In the words of Dan Savage (2011), "it gets better" for the underdeveloped world. Forays into what we might now call "homo-tolerance" (Klapeer in this volume) is relatively untrodden territory for major players in the development industry, but as Lavinas Picq and Theil (2015) maintain, there is now international salience of sexual and gender discrimination in domestic contexts.

The "Homosexual Question," to use Rahul Rao's term (2014), is a new marker of modernity, where campaigns, images, and news stories of LGBT rights and sexual minority activism globally circulate to mark "a temporal phase of wider acceptable of LGBT rights and conjuring up visions of progress" (200). For Jasbir Puar (2011), the Woman Question "how do you treat your women?" has been replaced by "how well do you treat your homosexuals?" (139). And while gender continues to be an essential focus of development policy and programming, and gender-based analyses remain indispensable, sexuality, gender identity, expression, and sex characteristics analyses (SOGIE/SC)[2] sophisticate and complicate development's understanding of structural, systemic, and interpersonal inequality and the promotion of human rights globally.

And although Hillary Clinton is said to have ushered in a new era of global LGBT rights with her 2011 human rights speech, academics, practitioners, and activists concerned with questions of development, foreign policy, migration, social movements, and human rights have long been concerned with questions of SOGIE/SC. As early as 2000, (then) IDS researcher Susie Jolly asked, "What use is queer theory to development?" To date, research in the area of SOGIE/SC analyses, LGBTIQ rights, and development has proliferated but remains disjointed at best, with scholars working on issues of global LGBTIQ rights, homophobia, transphobia, social movements, human rights, international relations, and global governance within subfields and disciplinary silos.

The objective of the *Routledge Handbook of Queer Development Studies* is to name and locate a home for queer scholars and/or queer scholarship in order to situate, ground, and collect the queerly diverse voices, methods, frameworks, and political and activist commitments in the field of development studies, and also make room for queer investigations of development. In conversation with Queer International Relations scholar Cynthia Weber at the International Feminist Journal of Politics conference in 2016, I came to better understand my intention to publish this reader.[3] In this conversation, we agreed that what development means is different to different people, and what queer means is different to different people. We established that a handbook of queer development studies should take stock of the history of scholars working in the field, and leave space for foundational and emergent contestations, contradictions, fractures, and debates about queer-ness, queer theory, and development. While acknowledging the past, in the moment we discussed the publication of this handbook, I was sure that there was a rising interest and activity of scholars, practitioners, and activists doing queer development studies now that needed to be showcased.

My aim in editing the *Routledge Handbook of Queer Development Studies* is threefold; i) to define a field of inquiry to trace some of the historical field-building by scholars (who may or may not have had "queer development studies" as a field in mind); ii) to hold space for critical dialogues and interdisciplinary exchanges, many of which may transpire within these pages; and iii) to invite new or under-heard scholars, activists, and practitioners into the conversation.

In the section that follows, I briefly trace some important histories in the making of this field. This brief review of literature is not complete, nor is it meant to be read as the only way of historicizing the field. Rather, here, I offer a mapping of initial ideas and key debates in the field, which are further picked up and expounded throughout the text.

A brief review of literature

While it is impossible to account for the entirety of scholarship that has led to a sustained and sophisticated conversation on LGBTIQ rights, SOGIE/SC, queer studies, and development, it is important to briefly summarize some of the foundational scholarship that has made it possible for me to publish this handbook and to offer the concept of "queer development studies" as a field of inquiry.

One of the central research hubs for questions of sexuality and development, and a key history to trace in the development of this field, has been the Institute of Development

Studies (IDS) housed at the University of Sussex. In 2000, Susie Jolly outlined queer theory's use to development studies through canonical scholars Judith Butler, Eve Sedgwick, Leo Bersani, David Halperin, Johnathon Dollimore, and Alan Sinfield, ultimately landing on the definition of queer through Halperin:

> queer is by definition whatever is at odds with the normal, the legitimate, the dominant. There is nothing in particular to which it necessarily refers. It is an identity without essence.
>
> *(as cited in Jolly 2000: 2)*

She suggests throughout this discussion paper for IDS that queer does not only challenge sexual norms, but also other kinds of norms, which could and should include a challenge to "development norms," specifically materialism and the sex–gender division too often present in gender and development theory and practice (2). As Jolly (2000) maintains, gender and development experts already had the frameworks of analysis and experience to include sexuality rights in their work even though many were not actually engaging with these questions at the time.

Following this foundational discussion paper, the IDS published an in-house *IDS Bulletin* on the topic of sexuality and development in 2006. Edited by Andrea Cornwall and Susie Jolly, the Bulletin entitled "Sexuality Matters," focused on what development scholars perceived as a "'silence' in the mainstream of development: sexuality" (1). Cornwall and Jolly argued that while mainstream development organizations had undergone a social-turn away from a purely economic focus to a more thoughtful consideration of human development and rights, sex and sexuality was "treated as a health issue, or disregarded altogether as a 'luxury'" and that "sexuality barely features in development debates" (1). "Sexuality Matters" features papers from the "Realising Sexual Rights" workshop held at the Institute of Development Studies in 2005, and the publication made the case for taking sexuality seriously in development, publishing the work of key scholars and activists including, but not limited to, Sonia Corrêa, Andil Gosine, Kate Sheill, Alain Greig, and Jaya Sharma.[4] This *IDS Bulletin* and corresponding workshop was one of the first in development studies scholarship to make space for studies of sexual and gender minorities, and queer theory, in the field.

Ten years later, amidst a proliferating interest in the relationship between queer studies and development, Amy Lind's collection *Development, Sexual Rights and Global Governance* (2010) emerged as a foundational text by bringing together scholars and practitioners working in the area of sexuality rights and development.[5] In this collection, authors tackle theoretical and ethnographic inquiries about how "people's intimate lives are tied up with state and neoliberal governmentalities" (4). Lind's (2010) collection maps the ways in which development institutions remain heteronormative even while sexual and gender minorities are both the "beneficiaries" of development in the Global South and also the "experts" of development as queer employees (see for example Gosine 2010). Both "que(e)rying" development frameworks, and "queering" development intuitions and discourses, Lind's collection offers "queer development studies" a strong foundation on which to build.

Lind's (2010) collection sets the groundwork for this handbook, but so too does a myriad of research on diverse sexualities and genders. Until recently, the development industry has largely focused on gender and sexuality as separate from sexual orientation and desire. According to editors Jolly, Cornwall, and Hawkins (2013) of the book *Women, Sexuality and the Political Power of Pleasure*, there is a tendency on the part of development to assume that that pleasure has no place in the industry when there are more pressing concerns. Questions of sexuality have instead too often focused on violence and disease, especially in relation to sexual violence, conflict, and the global HIV/AIDS pandemic. While sexual orientation, gender identity, and expression were not explicitly identified as central to questions of desire and pleasure in this book, it lays important introductory work on the subject of desire, and its centrality, rather than peripheral relation, to development.

In addition to the lack of focus on desire, the absence of attention paid to questions of sexuality have been taken up by development scholars through a vital and sustained critique of the heteronormativity of development. In this research, scholars reveal the many ways in which development policy and programs rely on heteronormative frameworks, and also outline the major gaps in understanding sexuality and sexual orientation as it relates to gender issues (see Bedford 2009; Lind 2009; Bergeron 2009, 2010). Focused on the level of the household, these scholars pay specific attention to the ways in which development organizations such as the World Bank rely on "proper heteronormativity" to fulfill neoliberal economic prescriptions toward national growth (Bedford 2009). According to Bedford's (2009) research on heterosexism in development, organizations too often consider "gender mainstreaming" narrowly as empowering women to work, while at the same time relying on the heteronormative household (men, women, and children) in new ways to survive the retrenchment of social safety nets under neoliberal economic prescriptions of development. Heteronormativity is also explored by influential collections including *Queer African Reader* (2014) edited by Sokari Ekine, which claims space for queer African writers to disrupt hegemonic narratives of blanket homophobia across the continent, and Marc Epprect's (2008) *Heterosexual Africa? The History of an Idea from the Age of Exploration to the Age of AIDS*, which traces how Africa was constructed as a "homosexual-free zone" and the consequences of this stereotype.

Beyond heterosexism, a scholarly focus on global LGBTIQ rights has brought with it critiques of the Western imperialism and globalization of English language descriptions of SOGIE/SC, the acronym LGBTIQ, and the globalization of gay language (Leap and Boellstorff 2004) and the manipulation and utilization of "LGBT rights" language to obtain funding at the level of local and grassroots agitations for change (Currier 2012). Additionally, studies take seriously the ways in which global homophobia is mapped onto the poorest nations in the world (Rao 2014), leaving these spaces open to Western intervention and development expertise (Massad 2002; Amar 2013), and also how political homophobia is mobilized in post-colonial contexts (Weiss and Bosia 2013). Scholars critical of queer theory's US- or Eurocentrism take issue with how representations of LGBT people center the Western world, but also how the "third world" and its subjects are always already queer subjects (Kapoor 2015). Using the terms "pinkwashing," "homonationalism," and "sexual exceptionalism," Jasbir Puar's (2007) foundational scholarship on queer transnationalism investigates the ways in which Western nations are able to transcend the violence of empire while exporting and policing LGBT rights globally. "Transnational queer critique," as coined by Desai, Bouchard, Detournay (2011) is another theoretical offering that expands on transnational feminisms to map power differentials between LGBTIQ people globally. Echoed by both queer theorists and international scholars, including Weber (2014, 2016), Sjoberg (2012), Marchand and Runyan (2011), the transnational is queer as requires a queer analytic.

As I hope this collection makes clear, there has been a "sexuality turn"[6] in development. There is an entire field of study about non-conforming sexualities and genders in development, of which some are represented in this collection. While the above overview of literature does not do justice to the deeply sophisticated and broad spectrum of scholarship that falls under the umbrella of queer development studies, this introductory chapter brings attention to some of the key concerns in the field, including the "queering" and "que(e)rying" of development (Lind 2010), which has been over and again suggested and argued for (see Jolly 2000; Lind and Share 2003, 2010; Gemmerli 2009; and Klapeer in this volume), but for whatever reason, has not yet gained traction in the mainstream of the field of development studies, and has yet to see sustained engagement by the development industry.[7]

This is not to suggest that development institutions have not changed the ways that they approach questions of sexuality and gender minority rights, but that individuals with non-normative and "colonial non-conforming" (Native Youth Sexual Network 2015) sexualities, gender identities, expressions, and sex characteristics continue to be the latest, and at times most contentious, subjects or "clients" of development, to use Escobar's (1995) phrase.

Que(e)r(y)ing the industry

While the development industry continues to be heteronormative and cisnormative, mainstream development organizations and foreign aid apparatuses are now explicitly addressing LGBTIQ rights, at least discursively. For example, in 2015, the United States announced a special envoy for LGBT rights following a State of the Union address in which President Barak Obama explicitly tied development objectives to national security by claiming that protecting gender and sexual minority rights globally would "make us all safer." Former US National Security Advisor Susan Rice announced a $4 million partnership between the US Agency for International Development (USAID) and the National Gay & Lesbian Chamber of Commerce (NGLCC) to encourage and support LGBT business owners and entrepreneurs in developing countries (PR Newswire 2014). According to Rice, "America's support for LGBT rights is not just a national cause but it's also a global enterprise" (The White House 2014). For Justin Nelson, the co-founder and president of NGLCC:

> We know the best way to break down barriers is to use the common language of business to expand minds and create opportunities. Trade and commerce creates jobs everywhere and more must be done to ensure our trading partners don't suffer from discrimination. We are grateful to the Obama Administration and USAID for working with us to ensure everyone can participate in our increasingly global economy.
>
> *(PR Newswire 2014)*

In 2013, the UN launched a Free and Equal campaign focused on the human rights of LGBT people globally, a far cry from UN Secretary-General Kofi Annan once claiming "this is not something the organization should get involved in" (Deen 2003: 3–4). Maybe most surprisingly, the World Bank published its first report on the cost of homophobia in 2014 (Lee Badgett 2014); subsequently, the organization began the process of reviewing their safeguards to standardize protection mechanisms for LGBT people in all major projects (HRC 2014). The president of the organization recently announced that it would "cut off lending to projects in developing countries that could endanger LGBT rights" (*Pink News* 2016). At the 2016 *Economist*'s conference "Pride and Prejudice," he stated:

> In 2014 the Ugandans had passed a law, and it was quite a bit more draconian than a lot of the laws that exist: it said homosexuality would be punished with life imprisonment, but it became a requirement that anyone who suspects others of homosexuality had to report that also… Right at that moment we were about

to approve a $90 million loan to support health clinics in Uganda… I worked as a doctor, and this is an important issue for me… but we looked carefully and we found out that it was possible that active discrimination could happen in these clinics, and because of the requirement to report homosexual behaviour, gay men and women could go to these clinics… and we could actually endanger people from the LGBTI community, so we had to stop that loan.

(Pink News 2016)

As the World Bank began to analyze its safeguards to better protect LGBT people, a lead advocate for LGBT rights within the organization, and president of the World Bank's LGBT employee group, Fabrice Houdart, was investigated for allegedly leaking the safeguard documents. Interestingly, in 2010, Houdart became GLOBE's president at the same time as the World Bank had added Parents and Friends of Ex-Gays & Gays—a Virginia gay reparative therapy group—to the 250 charitable organizations it encourages Bank employees to donate portions of their salaries to (HRC 2010; PFOX 2016). In 2011, Houdart publicly come out in the organization. He has been personally targeted after vocally criticizing the World Bank president and his senior management team for awarding bonuses to senior employees at a time of cutbacks at the organization (Hudson 2015). More precisely, Chief Financial Officer Bertrand Badré, whom Kim had hired and put in charge of budget cuts, received a nearly $100,000 bonus on top of his $379,000 salary (Rice 2016). President Kim has been busy with what Andrew Rice of *Foreign Policy* (2016) calls an internal "structural adjustment: a top-to-bottom reorganization of the bank"; he announced a cut of $400 million in administrative expenses, and eliminated about 500 jobs. Badré, ultimately, gave up the bonus after numerous "town halls" were held and Kim announced a no-retaliation policy due to a "climate of fear" within the organization. A year later, Locke Lord, a law firm that reviewed the mishandling of a $1 billion loan from China, the subject of a whistle-blowing blog post by Houdart, investigated the leak of the Bank's draft safeguards; investigations are normally done internally (Feder 2015). Houdart "sits at the intersection of two employee movements seeking to transform the 70-year old development giant: one against the Bank restructuring, and the other pushing for broader attention to the human rights impact of its lending" (Feder 2015). Such occurrences call for serious interrogation of discursive support for social inclusion for LGBTIQ individuals, how queer employees are positioned within development institutions, and the kinds of radical queer activism which are im/possible in the mainstream of the development industry. Theorists of queer development, such as Pia Laskar (2014), use the term "homotransnationalism"—a modification of Jasbir Puar's trailblazing concept of homonationalism—to call for further investigations into the collusion of neoliberal capital, LGBTIQ rights, and progressive narratives of development. It is not just the ever-changing landscape of queer theory, including transnational foci, that suggests that this is a moment to call, again, for the que(e)r(y)ing of development. The shift to large-scale campaigns, new policy, funding structures, and a programming focused on non-normative gender and sexualities opens up a range of possibilities for new lines of academic inquiry. This shifting, changing landscape of the development industry suggests that queer development studies is ripe for engagement.

Why queer development studies?

In the midst of burgeoning research on global LGBTIQ rights and SOGIE/SC analyses, and an industry that is paying attention to LGBTIQ identities and experiences, a field of study devoted to this topic has yet to be named or curated, until this point. The *Routledge Handbook of Queer Development Studies* brings together selected research of scholars who helped to build the foundation for queer development studies as a field alongside new research that is que(e) r(y)ing development. This handbook has been made possible by the persistence of scholars, practitioners, and activists claiming, quite rightly, that development must take LGBTIQ human rights seriously, that gender analyses must extend to include gender identity and expression, that heteronormativity hurts development, and that queering development is an important theoretical interruption of ongoing processes and powers. The scholarship that laid the groundwork for this collection is both vast and vital. And while some of this early work in the field appears in this text, much this reader holds space for emerging theories and theorists. In this handbook, each part includes one foundational work followed by an original chapter by authors who situate their own work in various histories of the field, understanding, commitments to, and challenges of, development and diverse delineations of "queer," including as non-normative sexual, gender, and political identifications and scholarly method.

In 2000 Susie Jolly's asked "what use is queer theory to development?" and while almost a decade has passed, this questions remains most relevant and is at the heart of this handbook. To expand on this foundational question, this collection also asks:

- How is queer theory changing development?
- What does queer theory have to say to development studies now, and does development theory have to say to queer theory?
- How are queer theory, queer and trans theorists, queer and trans practitioners, and SOGIE/SC analyses altering development studies and challenging the development industry?
- How might scholars use the field of queer development studies to approach the study of development, to make space for marginalized theories, theorists, identities, and experiences?
- How might scholars use this newly coined field to challenge norms of development and mainstream paradigms?

In many ways, the contributions to this handbook answer these and other questions. They also pose and answer theoretical and empirical questions I have not, and map various disjunctive trajectories that this field-defining collection makes possible.

Outline

In this introduction, I review four major que(e)ries in the field of queer development studies, and by reviewing one foundational work in this topical or thematic area, I outline where contributors to this collection make their point of entry into these debates and dialogues. The four que(e)ries are as follows:

1 Queering policy and planning
2 Queer development critique
3 Global LGBTIQ rights
4 Aiding queer mobilizations?

Part I: Queering policy and planning

The foundational text (Chapter 1) of Part I is Peter Drucker's (2009) "Changing families and communities: an LGBT contribution to an alternative development path" originally published in *Development in Practice*. In it, Drucker argues that because discussions about LGBT people often focus on the question of citizenship, their socio-economic rights and role in development are ignored or obscured in heterosexist and neoliberal paradigms. Charting neoliberal economic globalization as processes that intersect with sexuality and gender, Drucker illustrates how economic inequality increases cultural and class tensions which leads to both the marketization of gay and lesbian citizenship, and alternative community and family formations of gender non-conforming people. Since development policy primarily focuses on the public sphere of the economy, when it does pay attention to private life, it imagines the heterosexual, nuclear family as linchpins of economic growth. Drucker claims that transgender people, in particular, build and rely upon alternative families and social and economic safety nets as they navigate exclusions, discrimination, and violence that do not fall neatly into development imaginings of nuclear families. For Drucker, "Queering development, beginning with queering grassroots social movements and queering the politics of global justice, will require re-imagining the economy, development, and the relationship between the global North and South" (p. 27). Such a re-imagination of development, transnational power relations, and global markets marks Drucker's scholarship as ground-breaking in the field of queer development studies. His focus on heteronormativity, and exclusions that occur because of the lack of attention paid to non-heteronormative family and community structures, is an important place to start this edited collection. Authors in this part pick up themes of heterosexism and heteronormativity, in particular, and calls to queer development in policy and planning.

In Chapter 2, Robert C. Mizzi sheds light on the tensions of queering educational practices in development. Employing multivocal autoethnography, Mizzi offers a window into the experiential through unpacking tension and complications that arise for sexual and gender minorities when forming student–educator relationships and the tensions of critical thinking and liberatory educational models in professional development and outcome-based educational settings. Claiming that "train-the-trainer" approaches in education for international development are problematically heteronormative and cisnormative, Mizzi challenges dominant narratives of expertise of Westerner's "doing" development, and links educator–student relationships to post-development and post-colonial concerns about systemic and structural power relations, including colonial continuities. Using the example of his own experience as a Canadian, cisgender male, sexual minority, adult educator in Kosovo, Mizzi challenges how "train-the-trainer" methods may leave heteronormative and cisnormative behaviors intact as trainers occupy a position of authority as "official representatives" of the international educator, while, simultaneously, local trainers are positioned as a cultural culprit of perpetuating cisnormativity, heteronormativity, and/or queer phobias. Mizzi's concern with where and how sexual and gender minorities are positioned within the "doing" of international development is a key question in the queering of development.

Furthering the dialogue of cis and heteronormativity, Chapter 3 by Petra L. Doan challenges development planning. Focusing on resistance by donors to include and support LGBT populations, Doan's chapter explores how discursive support for LGBT rights in development at large are upended by the political and religious leanings of donors, specifically evangelical Christian donors from the United States. Using queer theory, Doan asks whether institutions, including the UN and Western governments, specifically the United States, can implement LGBT-inclusive development planning when heteropatriarchy is entrenched in their national machineries and institutions. When city planners and municipal officials fail to plan for the presence of gay neighborhoods in the United States, for example, how can one expect Western development "experts" to export LGBT-inclusive planning efforts? Such apprehensions about the implications of hetero and cissexism in Western or Global North donorship are essential to the task of queering processes and planning.

In Chapter 4, Chloé Vaast and Elizabeth Mills investigate the "Leave no one behind" core principle of the Sustainable Development Goals (SDGs). Taking this principle to task, the authors maintain that inequality and poverty can only be eradicated if development directly and explicitly engages with individuals and communities who are marginalized because of their sexual orientation, gender identity, and expression (SOGIE). Focusing on the harms of social exclusion, Vaast and Mills explain how sexual and gender minorities are marginalized at the institutional and infrastructural level, especially where services to address poverty do not attend to the specificities of life for sexual and gender minorities. As development organizations plan for a post-2015 development era, Vaast and Mills warn that current Sustainable Development Goals run the risk of further marginalizing those who face social exclusions on the basis of their sexuality and gender.

Part II: Queer development critique

Part II begins with Neville Hoad's (2010) "Arrested development or the queerness of savages: resisting evolutionary narratives of difference" (originally published by *Postcolonial Studies*). With the addition of a new and reflective preface, Hoad's influential text (Chapter 5) sets the stage for queer development critique. By framing theoretical interventions in the collection through Hoad's work, my intention is to bring to the fore critical interventions into theories and representations of global queerness. In this well-known and highly cited text, Hoad challenges discourses of development's perpetuation of race, gender, nation, and class tropes emerging in the context of imperialism and neo-imperialism. Hoad's meticulous mapping of evolutionary constructions of "the homosexual"—Darwinian, Freudian, and Foucauldian—grounds this part's contributions to dialogues on transnational sexual and gender difference. In his new preface, he thoughtfully considers where his arguments about developmental narratives of difference might now land within recent queer and critical race dialogues, especially those offered by transnational queer, queer of color, and Indigenous queer critiques (see for example Ferguson 2004; Puar 2007; Rifkin 2012). Such a critical reflection of his own work pushes queer development studies scholars to more carefully engage with queer critical race and Indigenous queer theory, which opens up new lines of inquiry and political commitments in the field. By considering how the development industry's emergent interest in SOGIE/SC analyses and the wide-scale criminalization of sexual and gender minorities in the underdeveloped world, Hoad's revisit of his early and foundational work holds space for fresh, critical, and queer theoretical reflections on colonial non-conforming sexualities and gender identities and expressions within the context of development discourses.

In Chapter 6, Christine M. Klapeer investigates the "discursive explosion" on the topic of LGBTIQ rights and development aid, and the way in which LGBTIQ rights have become central to development discourse and politics. Claiming that the development industry has seen a multiplication of handbooks, manuals, guidelines and research reports on LGBTIQ rights in development, discursive constructions of queer development by international donors and development agencies mean that sexual and gender minorities from the Global South and East participate tactically by adhering to and manipulating languages of development institutions. Concerned by how LGBTIQ identities and communities become intelligible objects of development, Klapeer frames her intervention into queer development from a post-colonial and what she calls "radical" development studies perspective. She asks: "How do these new LGBTIQ-inclusive development frameworks become entangled with (established) developmental governmentalities, particularly with racialized processes of (sexual) othering?" (p. 104). In doing so, Klapeer answers Hoad's call to question representations of sexual and gender difference in development discourses (Chapter 5 in this volume)—what she calls a "homo-developmentalist lens"—with specific attention paid to questions of racialization, queer transnational critique, and challenges to development as a solution to global LGBTIQ inequalities.

Chapter 7, "Decolonising development work: a Transfeminist perspective" by Chamindra Weerawardhana closes Part II by challenging racialized, gendered, and sexualized power and practice in development. A truly intersectional analysis of development and its normative functioning, Weerawardhana maintains that questions of gender and sexuality, especially challenges to cisnormativity and heteronormativity in development, necessarily requires a decolonial and critical race analysis of the Eurocentricity of development and its colonial roots. Beginning her chapter with an experience of observing the currency of whiteness and Western-ness in relation to development "expertise," Weerawardhana offers transfeminist-of-color epistemologies and transfeminist theory to development studies, a juncture that has not seen much engagement. Calling into question "limitations of queer liberalism and homo-righteous imperatives," in development, such as the UN's 2030 SDGs, she points out how a supposedly "queer" focus on LGBTIQ rights in development has not actually excavated the entrenched cisnormative gender binary. The SDGs refer to women's rights, but specifically target cisgender women's rights leaving transgender women and gender plural people out of stated development goals. It is not only development objectives that are trans-formed by Weerawardhana's chapter; she challenges who takes up space as development experts by using her own experience in development circles to illuminate how cis-ness continues to be essential to the professional success of development practitioners, even in "queer" or LGBTIQ-focused spaces.

Part III: Global LGBTIQ rights

The foundational text in Part III is Mathew Waites' (2009) "Critique of 'sexual orientation' and 'gender identity' in human rights discourse: global queer politics beyond the Yogyakarta Principles," originally published in *Contemporary Politics* (Chapter 8). Waites is critical of the concepts of sexual orientation and gender identity in human rights discourses. Focusing on the Declaration of Montreal (2006) and the Yogyakarta Principles (2007), Waites carefully outlines how issues of sexual orientation and gender identity function in international human rights law and at the UN. In thinking about how these concepts are both restrictive and generative, Waites employs Sara Ahmed (2006) to think through the ways bodies and identities are orientated through such language, and Judith Butler's (1990) concern with the narrowing of bodies, identities, desires, and experiences to intelligibility. Waites suggests that the mainstreaming of the concepts of sexual orientation and gender identity produce a gender and sexuality matrix that is concretized by the uninterrupted deployment of this language. Ultimately, he argues that these terms are necessary to use in human rights claims and contestations, but that they must be simultaneously challenged.

In Chapter 9, Ariel G. Mekler considers the mainstreaming of sexual orientation and gender identity, but also gender expression, and sex characteristics. In this chapter, Mekler's concern is with the United Nations Development Programme's (UNDP) conceptualization of human security in relation to LGBTIQ individuals. Focusing on structural and systemic oppressions and marginalizations of sexual and gender minorities, Mekler explains how the three major components of human security as defined by UNDP —the freedom from fear, the freedom from want, and the freedom to live with dignity—must include measures of economic security, food security, health security, environmental security, personal security, community security, and political security for LGBTIQ populations. Concerned with the mainstreaming of SOGIESC in human rights, security, and international development, Mekler challenges development to recognize lived experiences and account for interlinked vulnerabilities to human insecurity that are specific to LGBTIQ communities.

In Chapter 10, Niharika Banerjea and Kath Browne undertake a queer-feminist examination of development discourses which explicitly label, or function in such a way as to label, some nations as "forward" and other as "backward" on the basis of LGBTIQ rights as legal protections or criminalization. Arguing that development too often narrows questions of gender to motherhood (which serves to heteronationalize women in development) and questions of sexuality to HIV/AIDS, the authors argue that sexuality, gender identity, and expression is conceptualized as a social problem demanding state intervention, instead of a complex, and yet basic, part of one's livelihood. Employing Judith Butler's (2004) concept of a livable life, Banerjea and Browne theorize how a livability lens, rather than purely legal or economic analyses, can help development move beyond hierarchies and generalized mappings of homo/transphobia in their conceptualization of LGBTIQ rights. For the authors, development must stop equating legislative protections with livability; while it may make life more livable for some, there must be an effort to better understand what they phrase the "interplays of legislation and liveabilities" when conceptualizing LGBTIQ rights (p. 176).

Following que(e)ries of mainstreaming LGBTIQ rights and SOGIE/SC analyses at the international level, Dennis Altman and Jonathan Symons (Chapter 11) add questions of aid conditionality to this part's concern with discourses of human rights and security. For Altman and Symons, the clapback against successes of the LGBT movement in various parts of the world has resulted in an international polarization. They conceptualize violence against LGBT individuals and anti-homosexual laws as evidence of an increasing repression of LGBT rights at the same time as a global movement toward equality and recognition is popularized. More specifically, the support of the United States under the Obama Administration, in addition to European and Latin American powers, for LGBT human rights and protections for individuals on the basis of their sexual orientation and gender identity (SOGI) has sharply divided governments transnationally. Russia and "an Islamic bloc", in particular, claim such rights are counter to religious and cultural traditions and reject the mainstreaming of SOGI protections in international laws. Further questioning the language of human rights, Altman and Symons challenge the prevailing notion that international protections are the most effective way of ensuring the safety and security of those who fail to live up to heterosexist norms globally.

Part IV: Aiding queer mobilizations?

The final part of this handbook is devoted to research on queer mobilizations at the level of grassroots organizing, civil society, and non-governmental organizations. Since questions of funding structures and aid packages, but also autonomy, frame the chapters in this part, the foundational text is Andil Gosine's (2015) "Rescue, and real love: same-sex desire in international development" published by the Institute for Development Studies Sexuality and Development Programme. In this chapter (Chapter 12), Gosine reflects on how sexuality, and particularly homosexuality, was invisibilized in development fifteen years ago. By comparison to critiques of the mainstreaming of LGBTIQ rights and SOGIE/SC analyses that comprise this handbook, Gosine reminds readers that international organizations have historically failed to see the relevance of including LGBTIQ issues in their work. The consequence of this change from invisibility to (hyper)visibility is illuminated by Gosine's analysis of the World Bank's unexpected participation in advocacy for sexual minorities. He claims that development resources are too often made available for rescue projects that are self-motivated, including justifying the continued existence of national organizations through a reorientation of their efforts toward the global. Questioning the ways in which LGBTIQ rights are folded into neoliberal capitalism, Gosine is critical of how the complexity of desire—what he call "real love"—is narrowed and consumed by development. Connecting back to Robert C. Mizzi's (Chapter 2) analysis of "train-the-trainer" education for international development, Gosine questions the flow of "expertise" from development organizations to local levels. Following Gosine's call to queerly orient knowledge production and flows of expertise, this part is devoted to research that centers localized queer mobilizations aimed at social transformation and radical change.

Marcus McGee's chapter "Queer paradise: development and recognition in the Isthmus of Tehuantepec" (Chapter 13) challenges the representations and co-optations of local sexual and gender dissidents in development discourses. McGee focuses on the case of the muxe of Juchitán, a group of indigenous people in Oaxaca, Mexico, who have found favor in the development industry, and whose image is used to bolster support for a variety of policies and projects in their name. Understood as a third gender, McGee argues that this group experiences unprecedented levels of tolerance in their local communities, which runs counter to dominant narratives that position sexual and gender minorities as victims of culture and tradition in the Global South. Complicating this hegemonic narrative, McGee shows how muxe identity, and advocacy politics around muxe people, is depicted as progressive and at the forefront of progressive LGBT equality, while this group is concurrently positioned as a nostalgic and primitive pre-colonial gender identity. McGee's intensive ethnography is a welcome diversion from primarily discursive and textual analyses in this volume. McGee pairs interviews with people who identify as muxe with documentary and media analysis, and carefully examines how muxe people understand and manipulate development's representations of third gender people in Mexico.

In Chapter 14, Julie Moreau and Ashley Currier provide a critical investigation into donorship and the effect of funding structures on LGBT movement organizations and activism activities in Malawi and South Africa. Focusing specifically on Northern donors' direct funding to African LGBT organizations, the authors claim that new forms of hetero and homonormativity arise in relation to funding. Like McGee, Moreau and Currier offer ethnographic research conducted in Malawi and South Africa about what they call a "queer dilemma" of Northern funding trickling into Southern LGBT movements. The authors describe this dilemma as the paradox between the perception that LGBT activism in Africa is too heavily influenced by the requirements of donors, and the reality of LGBT organizations being vulnerable to homophobic criticism by organizations in other local social movements. Thinking through NGOization, especially the professionalization of LGBT organizations, Moreau and Currier offer insight into the complications of aiding queer social movements.

Connected to the question of Western influence on LGBTIQ movements in the Global South, Nick J. Mulé's chapter "Politicized priorities: critical implications for LGBTQ movements" (Chapter 15) takes seriously the plight of LGBTQ asylum seekers in the context of development and global aid apparatuses. For Mulé, developed LGBTQ movements can function as a yardstick to measure a nation's relative progressiveness in relation to inclusivity of LGBTQ rights. Calling into question homonormative agendas, this chapter questions the ways in which development narratives too often fall into the trap of teleological models, where representations of progression and regression are uncritically accepted. According to Mulé, transnational systems of power create conditions in which some individuals become asylum seekers or refugee claimants but host land LGBTIQ movements rarely diversify to reflect newcomer experiences or address global homophobias and transphobias beyond homonationalist political agendas.

Further challenging dominant narratives that equate de/criminalization of homosexuality with progressiveness and regressiveness, Maria Tonini's "Circumscribed recognition: creating a space for young queer people in Delhi" (Chapter 16) also explores questions of normativity, but does so in such a way as to make room for young queer voices that desire a form of normalcy that comes with social and political recognition. Since the re-criminalization of same-sex sexuality in 2013 in India (following its decriminalization in 2009) the significance of legal recognition of sexual minorities has been fiercely debated. In this chapter, Tonini investigates how recognition is experienced by young queer people (16–25 year olds) living in Delhi. Focusing on a grassroots queer youth group called "Niral Club," she explores the impact of spaces that are formed to provide solidarity and leisure activities, and specifically a sense of normalcy for queers. Using the concept of "circumscribed recognition" Tonini explicates the too often accepted binary of radical/normative or activist/assimilated as a way to describe queer social movements and identities. In doing so, her ethnographic research offers a glimpse into the lives of young queers navigating social, affective, political, and legislative realities in Delhi.

The last chapter in this volume is entitled "Disrupting Joburg Pride: exploring the depoliticisation of Africa's first Pride march" written by Nyx McLean. In it (Chapter 17), they offer a provoking analysis of the disruption of Joburg Pride in 2012 by the One in Nine Campaign, which called for one minute of silence for black queer victims of violence. In the context of political disruptions of pride by activists transnationally (most notably Black Lives Matter in the North American context) and couched in history of die-ins and political funerals staged by activists transnationally at the height of the HIV/AIDS epidemic, this chapter explores the backlash against the One in Nine Campaign for politicizing Joburg Pride, which has seen increasing commercialization and apoliticization since the 1990s. Using a mixed method of oral histories and media analysis, McLean argues that in the interest of projecting an image of the LGBTIAQ community to commercial sponsors, and a transnational audience who expect a particular form of homotolerance from South Africa given its legislative protection of queers, Joburg Pride has excluded black queer experiences, especially their disproportionate experiences of hate crimes, from the narrative of LGBTIAQ life in Johannesburg. This final chapter offers an entry point for further studies in queer development to think through transnational connections and solidarities between racialized queer experiences in the Global North and Global South to disrupt simplistic global mappings of countries with pride (and expertise) and those with prejudice (requiring rescue).

Notes

1 Pride and Prejudice is the name of a conference organized by *The Economist* in 2016. According to the website, Pride and Prejudice "is a global LGBT conference and initiative that will

catalyse fresh debate on the economic and human costs of discrimination against the LGBT community." In 2016, and again in 2017, conferences were held in Hong Kong, New York, and London.
2 In this handbook, authors use a variety of acronyms to shorten the language of sexual orientation, gender identity, expression, and sex characteristics. The most common usages in this text are SOGI and SOGIE, but SOGIESC is used by Ariel Mekler. This addition of "sex characteristic" to the acronym is important, even if less popular, to make space for intersex rights and analyses which pay attention to the experiences of intersex populations. Like SOGIE/SC, authors in this volume use a mixture of LGBT, LGBTIQ, and LGBTIAQ to refer to diverse sexualities, gender identities, and expressions.
3 I am thankful to Cynthia Weber for this mentoring session.
4 See http://www.ids.ac.uk/publication/sexuality-matters (accessed September 22, 2017) for a complete table of contents.
5 Upon writing the Postscript for this reader, Amy Lind informed me that she and Susie Jolly were writing their earliest works at the same time, and while their queer curiosities were very similar, they did not know each other. In fact, many of the scholars working in this area, and uncited here, were working on these issues in locations other than IDS. Lind reminded me that while conversations were surely unfolding at IDS, conversations were also happening elsewhere. This clarification points to the diversity of scholars working on these issues, and also to the disconnection of scholars at the time. Connections, of course, have since been made, and this reader attempts to pull scholars even closer together by establishing a field of study.
6 In 1995, Jan Nederveen Pieterse introduced the idea of a "cultural turn" in development, reflecting a wider turn in social sciences to questions of discourse and power. I use "sexuality turn" as a shorthand to reference the turn to questions of SOGIE/SC in development.
7 For the purposes of this introduction, I use the term "development industry" as defined by Andil Gosine (Chapter 12 in this volume) who claims it "is an unstable amalgam of many different actors often working in support of, sometimes against, each other's interests: governments, international agencies like the World Bank and International Monetary Fund, non-governmental organizations of feminists, environmentalists, human rights activists or religious fundamentalists, health institutions, social service workers, economists, doctors, lawyers, educators and more."

References

Amar, P. 2013. *The Security Archipelago: Human-Security States, Sexuality Politics, and the End of Neoliberalism*. Durham, NC: Duke University Press.
Ahmed, Sara. 2006. *Queer Phenomenology: Orientations, Objects, Others*. Durham, NC: Duke University Press.
Bedford, Kate. 2009. *Developing Partnerships: Gender, Sexuality and the Reformed World Bank*. Minneapolis, MN: University of Minnesota Press.
Bergeron, Suzanne. 2009. "Interpretive analytics to move caring labor off the straight path." *Frontiers: A Journal of Women's Studies* 30, no.1: 55–64.
Bergeron, Suzanne. 2010. "Querying feminist economics' straight path to development." In *Development, Sexual Rights and Global Governance*, edited by A. Lind, pp. 54–64. London: Routledge.
Butler, Judith. 1990. *Gender Trouble: Feminism and the Subversion of Identity*. New York: Routledge.
Butler, Judith. 2004. *Undoing Gender*. New York: Routledge.
Clinton, Hillary. 2011. "Recognition of International Human Rights Day." http://www.state.gov/secretary/rm/2011/12/178368.htm (accessed December 11, 2015.).
Cornwall, Andrea and Jolly, Susie. 2006. "Sexuality matters." *IDS Bulletin* 37.5.
Currier, Ashley. 2012. *Out in Africa: LGBT Organizing in Namibia and South Africa*. Minneapolis, MN: University of Minnesota Press.
Deen, T. 2003. "Human rights: U.N. in debt to gays and lesbians," Inter Press Services New Agency. October 14.
Desai, Jinga, Bouchard, Danielle, and Detournay, Diane. 2011. "Disavowed legacies and honorable thievery: the work of the 'transnational' in feminist and LGBTQ studies." In *Critical Transnational*

Feminism Praxis, edited by Amanda Lock Swarr and Richa Nagar, pp. 46–54. New York: SUNY Press.

Duffy, Nick. 2016. "World Bank 'won't fund' projects in developing countries that endanger LGBT people." *Pink News*. March 3. http://www.pinknews.co.uk/2016/03/03/world-bank-wont-fund-projects-in-developing-countries-that-endanger-lgbt-people/ (accessed September 22, 2017).

Ekine, Sokari. 2014. *Queer African Reader*. Oxford: Pambazuka Press

Epprect, Marc. 2008. *Heterosexual Africa? The History of an Idea from the Age of Exploration to the Age of AIDS*. Athens, OH: Ohio University Press.

Escobar, Arturo. 1995. *Encountering Development: The Making and Unmaking of the Third World*. Princeton, NJ: Princeton University Press.

Feder, Lester J. 2015. "LGBT employee leader under investigation at World Bank." *Buzzfeed News*. April 9. https://www.buzzfeed.com/lesterfeder/lgbt-employee-leader-under-investigation-at-world-bank?utm_term=.niJ6AAN5o#.xn0zXXKA5 (accessed September 22, 2017).

Ferguson, Roderick A. 2004. *Aberrations in Black: Toward a Queer of Color Critique*. Minneapolis, MN: University of Minnesota Press.

Gemmerli, Tobias. 2009. "Queering development – incorporating sexuality: the problem of heteronormativity in the development paradigm." Unpublished paper. http://ps.au.dk/fileadmin/Statskundskab/Dokumenter/subsites/Uland/QUEERING_DEVELOPMENT_INCORPORATING_SEXUALITY.pdf (accessed September 22, 2017).

Gosine, Andil. 2010. "World Bank's GLOBE: Queers in/queering development." In *Development, Sexual Rights and Global Governance*, edited by A. Lind, pp. 67–85. London and New York: Routledge.

Hudson, D. 2015. "LGBTI advocate investigated by World Bank: Fabrice Houdart describes his treatment as an 'ordeal.'" *Gay Star News*. http://www.gaystarnews.com/article/lgbti-advocate-investigated-world-bank-fabrice-houdart-describes-his-treatment-'ordeal'13041/ (accessed May 1, 2015).

Human Rights Campaign (HRC). 2010. "HRC to World Bank: Remove PFOX from your community connections campaign." December 8. http://www.hrc.org/press/hrc-to-world-bank-remove-pfox-from-your-community-connections-campaign (accessed September 22, 2017).

Human Rights Campaign (HRC). 2014. "Revising World Bank safeguard policy." http://www.hrc.org/resources/entry/revising-world-bank-safeguard-policy (accessed July 15, 2015).

Human Rights Campaign (HRC). 2015a. "Op-Ed: Obama's state of the union marks milestone for LGBT movement." http://www.hrc.org/blog/entry/op-ed-obamas-state-of-the-union-marks-milestone-for-lgbt-movement (accessed May 15, 2015).

Human Rights Campaign (HRC). 2015b. "Revising World Bank safeguard policy." Resources. http://www.hrc.org/resources/entry/revising-world-bank-safeguard-policy (accessed July 3, 2015).

Institute of Development Studies. 2005. "Realising sexual rights." Event: International Workshop. Wednesday September 28 – Friday September 30. Brighton, UK.

International Lesbian, Gay, Bisexual, Trans and Intersex Association (ILGA). 2013. "Lesbian and gay rights in the world." http://old.ilga.org/Statehomophobia/ILGA_Map_2014_ENG.pdf (accessed May 15, 2015).

Jolly, Susie. 2000. "What use is queer theory to development?" Queering Development Seminar Series. IDS Discussion Paper. Institute for Development Studies. Brighton, UK.

Jolly, Susie, Cornwall, Andrea, and Hawkins, Kate. 2013. *Women, Sexuality and the Political Power of Pleasure*. London: Zed Books.

Kapoor, Ilan. 2015. "The queer Third World" *Third World Quarterly*, 36, no. 9:1611–1628.

Laskar, Pia. 2015. "The illiberal turn: aid conditionalis and the queering of sexual citizenship." *Lambda Nordica* no. 1: 86–100.

Lavinas Picq, Manuela and Thiel, Markus. 2015. *Sexualities in World Politics: How LGBTQ Claims Shape International Relations*. London: Routledge.

Leap, William and Boellstorff, Tom. 2004. *Speaking in Queer Tongues: Globalization and Gay Language*. Chicago, IL: University of Illinois Press.

Lee Badgett, M.V. 2014. "The cost of homophobia and the exclusion of LGBT people: A case study of India." The World Bank. http://www.worldbank.org/content/dam/Worldbank/document/SAR/economic-costs-homophobia-lgbt-exlusion-india.pdf (accessed October 19, 2016).

Lind, Amy, and Jessica Share. 2003. "Queering development: institutionalized heterosexuality in development theory, practice and politics in Latin America." In *Feminist Futures: Re-imagining Women,*

Culture and Development, edited by Kum-Kum Bhavnani, John Foran and Priya A. Kurian, pp. 55–73. London: Zed Books.

Lind, Amy. 2009. "Governing Intimacy, Struggling for Sexual Rights: Heteronormativity in the Global Development Industry." *Development* 52, no. 1: 34–42.

Lind, Amy. 2010. *Development, Sexual Rights and Global Governance*. London and New York: Routledge.

Marchand, Marianne H. and Runyan, Anne Sisson. 2011. *Gender and Global Restructuring: Sightings, Sites, and Resistances*. London: Routledge.

Massad, Joseph. 2002. "Re-Orienting Desire: The Gay International and the Arab World." *Public Culture* 14, no. 2: 361–385.

Native Youth Sexual Health Network. 2015. Twitter. https://twitter.com/NYSHN/status/600025622107291649 (accessed July 5, 2015).

PFOX (Parents and Friends of Ex-Gays & Gays). 2015. "Get to know PFOX." http://www.pfox.org (accessed September 22, 2017).

Pieterse, Jan Nederveen. 1995. "The cultural turn in development: questions of power." *The European Journal of Development Research* 7, no. 1: 176–192.

PR Newswire. 2014. "Ground-breaking partnership between National Gay & Lesbian Chamber of Commerce and USAID to create opportunities for LGBT entrepreneurs in developing countries." *PR Newswire*. June 26. http://www.prnewswire.com/news-releases/ground-breaking-partnership-between-national-gay--lesbian-chamber-of-commerce-and-usaid-to-create-opportunities-for-lgbt-entrepreneurs-in-developing-countries-264802561.html (accessed September 22, 2017).

Puar, Jasbir K. 2007. *Terrorist Assemblages: Homonationalism in Queer Times*. Durham, NC: Duke University Press.

Puar, J. K. 2011. "Citation and censorship: The politics of talking about the sexual politics of Israel." *Feminist Legal Studies* 19, no 2: 133–142.

Rao, Rahul. 2014. "Queer questions." *International Feminist Journal of Politics* 16, no. 2: 199–217.

Rice, Andrew. 2016. "How the World Bank's biggest critic became its president." *The Guardian*. 11 August 2016. https://www.theguardian.com/news/2016/aug/11/world-bank-jim-yong-kim (accessed 22 April 2017).

Rifkin, Mark. 2012. *The Erotics of Sovereignty: Queer Native Writing in the Era of Self-Determination*. Minneapolis, MN: University of Minnesota Press.

Savage, Dan. 2011. *It Gets Better: Coming Out, Overcoming Bullying, and Creating a Life Worth Living*. New York: Plume Press.

Sjoberg, Laura. 2012. "Toward trans-gendering international relations?" *International Political Sociology* 6, no. 4: 337–354.

State of the Union. 2015. "Remarks by the President in State of the Union Address." http://www.whitehouse.gov/the-press-office/2015/01/20/remarks-president-state-union-address-january-20-2015 (accessed January 22, 2015).

The Economist. 2016. "Pride and prejudice." Event. https://events.economist.com/events-conferences/americas/pride-and-prejudice-2016/ (accessed September 22, 2017).

The White House. 2014. "Remarks by National Security Advisor Susan E. Rice at the White House forum on global LGBT human rights." Office of the Press Secretary. June 24. https://obamawhitehouse.archives.gov/the-press-office/2014/06/24/remarks-national-security-advisor-susan-e-rice-white-house-forum-global- (accessed September 22, 2017).

United Nations. 2015. "Free and equal." https://www.unfe.org/ (accessed January 23, 2015).

United Nations – Human Rights Council. 2011. "Discriminatory laws and practices and acts of violence against individuals based on their sexual orientation and gender identity." Retrieved from http://www.ohchr.org/Documents/Issues/Discrimination/A.HRC.19.41_English.pdf

United Nations High Commissioner for Human Rights and reports of the Office of High Commissioner and the Secretary-General. 2015. Report of the Office of the United Nations High Commissioner for Human Rights. GA HRC/29/23., 29th sess., Agenda items 2 & 8. "Discrimination and violence against individuals based on their sexual orientation and gender identity." 4 May 2015. http://www.ohchr.org/EN/HRBodies/HRC/RegularSessions/Session29/ A/HRC/29/23. Documents/A_HRC_29_23_en.doc (accessed 7 June 2016).

Weber, C. 2014. "From queer to queer IR." *International Studies Review* 16, no. 4: 596–601.

Weber, C. 2016. *Queer International Relations: Sovereignty, Sexuality, and the Will to Knowledge*. Oxford: Oxford University Press.

Weiss, M.L. and Bosia, M.J. 2013. *Global Homophobia: States, Movements, and the Politics of Oppression*. Urbana, IL: University of Illinois Press.

PART I

Queering policy and planning

1

CHANGING FAMILIES AND COMMUNITIES

An LGBT contribution to an alternative development path[1]

Peter Drucker

In recent years the international institutions that dominate international development policy have given increasing attention to issues that are not narrowly economic, including in particular gender issues and democratic participation (referred to more often under the rubric of 'good governance'). Non-economic issues are also important to those in the global justice movement challenging neoliberal orthodoxy. LGBT (lesbian/gay/bisexual/transgender) issues have, however, most often been addressed through such categories as citizenship, less often as directly related to alternative development strategies.

In fact LGBT people have the potential to play a significant role in formulating and implementing an alternative path to sustainable and equitable development. Mobilization and self-organization of those who suffer most directly from neoliberalism, though no panaceas, are indispensable to creating, let alone implementing, alternative development strategies. Self-organization; including LGBT self-organization, needs to take place in the most basic units of society—families and communities—so as to counter policies imposed from above by the state and capital. This makes it important to understand the role of gender and sexuality in the ways families and communities are structured and the ways family and community intersect with the state and economy.

Neoliberalism: the heteronormative dimension

The economic policies that have been imposed virtually worldwide since the early 1980s are generally summed up in the phrase 'neoliberal globalization'. The economic harm that neoliberal globalization has done is now widely recognized. Less widely recognized are the ways in which neoliberal globalization is heteronormative.

Heteronormativity means the ways in which heterosexuality is institutionalized, 'both explicitly (by excluding LGBT people from the analysis) and implicitly (by assuming that all people are heterosexual...)' (Lind and Share 2003, 57). Neoliberalism has changed the forms heteronormativity takes as it has changed the forms of gender oppression.

Under capitalism the family has served as a mechanism both for inculcating hierarchical and authoritarian social relations and for reproducing the labour force through women's unpaid labour (Seccombe 1993, 5–20; Coontz 1988, esp. 287–365). The reproduction of heteronormativity has facilitated both of these basic functions of the capitalist family. However, neoliberalism in many ways undermines the direct and obvious domination of wives and daughters by husbands and fathers and the Fordist gender regime, under which men in the 1950s and '60s had a privileged position in the wage labour market and women in many families a correspondingly constricted sphere in the home (Brenner 2003, 78–79). Neoliberalism may thus be undercutting the heteronormative family's effectiveness as a site for inculcating traditional authoritarian hierarchies. But it reinforces the family's role as a site where basic needs are met in privatized ways. By imposing cuts in social spending— education, health care, childcare—since the 1980s, structural adjustment programmes in underdeveloped countries have displaced the costs of social reproduction even more onto women in the family (Barbosa et al. 1994, 8–9). Wherever LGBT people are excluded from or marginalized in families, they must struggle harder to have their basic needs met.

The enduring strength of women's and lesbian/gay movements and the difficulty of rolling back many of their non-economic achievements complicated the victories of pro-market forces in the 1980s and '90s. Women's and lesbian/gay equality have become steadily more established as political commonplaces (in rhetoric if not in reality) at the same time that once widespread redistributive economic policies have been dismissed as outmoded. Alongside the global economy, the idea has also spread that there is now a 'global gay' (a term problematized by Dennis Altman in e.g. 2003) or 'globalization of sexual identity' (Wright 2000, 107, as cited in Lind and Share 2003, 65–66).

In fact many of women and LGBT people's gains are delayed effects of battles that were fought in the 1970s, based on the dynamic of a different regime of capital accumulation, a different relationship of forces between labour and capital and a different social climate (Went 2000, 89–90). The link between emancipation and globalization is thus in part an optical illusion. The illusion helps obscure gender and sexual aspects of 'really existing globalization'.

Varieties of heteronormativity

Focusing on sexual globalization also risks obscuring the different forms of heteronormativity under neoliberalism in different social formations. In developed capitalist countries since the Second World War, geographical displacement, rising wages, the development of a welfare state and legal victories have redefined the heterosexual norm from a strict taboo on 'the love that does not speak its name' to a situation where LGBT people are considered 'abnormal' more in a statistical than in a pathological sense—and in the sense that they are still more or less marginal to the family institutions through which society reproduces itself (D'Emilio 1983). This process of redefining the heterosexual norm has not been uniformly replicated in underdeveloped countries, however. First, pre-colonial and pre-capitalist sexual cultures had extraordinarily rich and varied forms of same-sex sexuality to begin with, in some cases expressed in open, socially accepted forms of same-sex identity in historical periods when 'sodomites' were still being burned alive in Europe. With the arrival of colonialism and capitalism, these varied indigenous sexual cultures combined with different modes of insertion into the world market to produce widely divergent heterosexual norms.[2]

This article cannot give much sense of the richness of the process (see Drucker 1996, 75–101). It can only cite a few examples of the different results that different modes of capitalist underdevelopment—along with colonialist, populist, fundamentalist and communalist ideologies and laws and other factors—have helped produce. In the Arab world, particularly low levels of women's participation in the labour force have helped perpetuate harsh conditions of 'compulsory heterosexuality' for women and lesbian invisibility (Khayatt 1996; Rich 1983, 183–185; Lind and Share 2003). In Caribbean regions whose role in the world economy has never fully recovered from the abolition of slavery and poverty is endemic among Afro-Caribbean women, forms of sexual and emotional bonding among women co-exist with heterosexual family patterns in which men are less than central (Wekker 1999). In much of South and Southeast Asia, pre-colonial forms of transgender have been incorporated into a domestic and global sexual market (Oetomo 1996; Altman 2000, 141–142, 149–150). In some of the most industrialized areas of the underdeveloped world, such as South Africa and the Southern Cone, by contrast, LGBT cultures resembling those of developed countries have become somewhat more prominent (Gevisser 2000; Green 1999).

A second set of reasons why the heterosexual norm has not been redefined in the same way in underdeveloped countries as in developed ones is the comparatively lower levels of working-class wages in underdeveloped countries, comparatively weaker welfare states and high levels of inequality. These have all helped ensure a great variety of forms of heteronormativity in much of the underdeveloped world. In particular, forms of same-sex sexuality identified as 'lesbian' or 'gay' tend more on average to be characteristic of middle-class layers of the population in many countries, while transgender often tends to be more prevalent among poor and working-class people (Carrier 1975, 120–121; Mejía 2000, 49; Oetomo 1996, 265, 268; Boellstorff 2005).

Third, heteronormativity takes different forms in different contexts, including within the same social formations, depending on whether or not existing families and communities bend to accommodate different forms of LGBT sexuality and identity. In underdeveloped countries people tend to be more dependent on their families and communities, even in big cities, where networks based on kinship, ethnicity and region of origin are often crucial to day-to-day survival. This means that breaking with families or communities is often harder to do, and has more drastic consequences when it occurs.

Sometimes LGBT people therefore seek and find ways to continue to take part in pre-existing family and community networks, and even incorporate same-sex partners into them. The often central role of religious and/or ethnic 'tradition'[3] in families' and communities' ideological discourses can complicate this process of incorporation; sometimes for example same-sex partners are just tacitly accepted as 'friends' (Chou 2000, 196–197). Another option—often the only one available to transgender people in many countries—is to join alternative families and communities of sexual dissidents. In many cases these sexually dissident communities are economically very marginal, confined to the informal sector and sometimes the sex trade.

Neoliberal globalization has compounded the divergences and inequalities that uneven capitalist development had helped produce. It 'reinforces and reproduces inequalities' (Mtewa 2003, 39). In the underdeveloped world specifically, the rise in economic inequality been accompanied by increased cultural tensions and class differences within both established and emerging LGBT communities (Fernández-Alemany 2000 and Babb 2001, cited in Lind and Share 2003, 60), including sexual divergences. On the one hand, commercial gay scenes and the disproportionately middle-class lesbian/gay communities oriented towards them have consolidated and expanded. On the other hand, various sexually dissident communities, such as increasingly militant transgenders in much of Latin America and South and Southeast Asia, have become more visible and vocal.

LGBT people in the underdeveloped world have been fighting, socially and sometimes even politically, on one or both of two different fronts. More and more of them have begun to fight against prejudice and repression, which have been fuelled by the dislocation of societies all over the world with the collapse of Fordist-based social and political orders, in the underdeveloped world often meaning populist or nationalist 'socialist' regimes relying on import-substitution development strategies. At the same time many LGBTs have been trying to resist pressures to claim them for a homogeneous, middle class-dominated lesbian/gay community.

Casualization of wage labour and the growth of the informal sector in the underdeveloped world under neoliberal globalization have included the growth of the sex trade. Economic internationalization has included the rise of international sex tourism, in two directions: the arrival of tourists from developed countries taking advantage of cheap sex for sale, and the arrival in developed countries of sex workers. Undocumented immigrants form a high proportion of sex workers in many European countries; transgender people form a high-proportion of same-sex sex workers almost everywhere. Wholesale exclusion of transgender people from most sectors of formal employment is one reason for this.

Queering families and communities

The sexual dimension of neoliberal globalization has never received much explicit attention in official development policy. The international financial institutions have been enthusiastic proponents of tourism as a source of hard currency for countries like Thailand, but usually without acknowledging the major part that sex tourism plays in it. Transgender people and others who do not fit into normative gender and sexual categories, even within the increasingly normative categories of lesbian/gay identity, are voiceless and invisible as a rule in the official discourse of development.

Official development policy tends to focus on the public sphere of the economy, and turn its gaze away from aspects of life defined as private. To the extent it does pay attention to the public implications of private life, it usually sees the heterosexual, nuclear family as a useful contributor to as well as a beneficiary of market-based economic growth.

Admittedly, liberal feminism has had an impact on the World Bank's conception of the heterosexual nuclear family. A proper family is assumed to facilitate women's autonomous participation in the market economy as well as men's, and women are assumed to benefit from autonomous economic activity by becoming more equal inside the family. But the reality that people in underdeveloped countries live on a mass scale outside the domain of proper heterosexual families, just as they live on a mass scale outside the formal market economy, is assumed to be a mess to be tidied away over time, rather than a potential basis for choosing other options than those foreseen in neoliberal economic or social theory. A 1994 World Bank policy paper acknowledged for example that barriers to economic participation by women with children are 'less onerous in countries where extended families predominate' but noted that the 'cost-effectiveness' of 'alternative childcare arrangements' 'has yet to be evaluated' (World Bank 1994, 38, 48). This kind of tunnel vision helps account for what Kleitz calls the 'incapacity of development theory to imagine a functional role for sexual minorities' and helps ensure that 'queer women and non-traditional heterosexual women remain invisible' (Lind and Share 2003, 69).

The biases of international financial institutions and aid agencies in developed countries in defining 'family' can have unfortunate effects, not only on LGBT people but on all those whose well-being is linked up with support from extended or unconventional family and community networks. Neoliberal economists' inclination to see increases in economic well-being as the result of individuals' insertion into a market economy, with only a basic domestic support structure behind them, in fact does scant justice to the social strategies that enable people in underdeveloped countries to survive and, sometimes, improve their lives. Especially with the cutbacks in publicly provided education, health care and social benefits as a result of structural adjustment programmes, people's dependence on extended family and friendship networks to sustain them in times of sickness, disability, childhood, old age or other periods of dependency has become all the greater. Pressure from neoliberal institutions to give up existing patterns of subsistence and barter economics and rely more on market-derived income has left people more vulnerable to the periodic crises that are endemic to a neoliberal economy.

Patterns of subsistence, barter, and collective and communal mutual aid remain particularly important in various ways for LGBT people in underdeveloped countries. Those who are most excluded from formal employment and existing family structures, particularly transgender people, rely very much on their own self-created and -sustaining community and family structures for protection against violence and persecution and for economic survival. One unpublished Peruvian study showed, for example, that femme lesbians supported their butch partners when the butches could not find either 'female' or 'male' jobs (cited in Lind and Share 2003, 73n15).

In Asian regions that are or once were predominantly Hindu, transgender networks can fill niches in caste hierarchies. Indian *hijras* and other South and Southeast Asian transgender groups with traditional identities in their cultures gain a high proportion of their income, alongside prostitution, from their traditional roles as entertainers in various kinds of festivities. The more commercialized an economy becomes, the more such transgender entertainers tend to be incorporated into capitalist tourist and entertainment industries, as is the case for example with Thai *kathoeys*. But in the absence of legal regulation or conventional trade union organization, transgender community networks remain important in carving out and defending their economic niche and negotiating their remuneration.

The spread of AIDS has also highlighted and increased the role of LGBT community networks in securing health care for their members. In most underdeveloped regions LGBT access to commercial or official health care has been anything but automatic. In country after country existing LGBT networks have been crucial to securing care for seropositive people, not only through political battles but also through ongoing, day-to-day service provision (see e.g. Schifter 1989).

Alongside the economic role of alternative or separate LGBT family and community structures, there is also a molecular process—a process that is at work neighbourhood by neighbourhood, family by family or even individual by individual—of queering existing families and communities. The role of existing families in providing room and board to its members' same-sex partners has already been mentioned. Even less visibly, women who live more or less in a separate women's sphere of domestic labour and household production bond with each other in all sorts of emotional and erotic ways (Rich 1983, 192–193). As long as women's intimate relationships with each other take place privately and beyond men's field of vision, they can be entirely compatible with traditional and even conservative family ideology. But if and when women begin to speak publicly about their ties with each other inside existing families, a queering process gets under way, which need not have any explicit sexual component but *can* include a sexual and/or affectional dimension.

Social and particularly political mobilization by women can foster female solidarity and bonding, for example when women cooperate in public to get fuel or water or milk for their children or health services (such as abortion or contraception), or to resist genital mutilation of their daughters. The movements' sexist adversaries often recognize the queer potential of female bonding, and lesbian-bait the movements in order to thwart them. Activist women react all too often by stressing their own heterosexuality and femininity, marginalizing, rendering invisible or excluding the lesbians and bisexuals among them. The same heterosexist dynamic can be at work in women's informal and communal production networks, which facilitate women's survival when they are excluded from or disadvantaged in formal economies (Lind and Share 2003, 61, 64). But the potential to replicate heteronormativity exists alongside a potential for queering. Cultural factors, personal ties and conscious choices can all help determine which potential wins out.

The processes of queering existing families and communities and of building and sustaining distinctive LGBT families and communities come together when LGBT and other families and communities intersect. This requires overcoming the stigmas and taboos that mark off separate LGBT networks. Non-gay-identified 'men who have sex with men' (MSMs) in many underdeveloped countries often recoil from any possibility of being linked to the family and social networks of the transgender men they have sex and sometimes sexual relationships with, in defence of their own masculinity and for fear of losing their status within 'their own' families. The most minimal signs of respect and recognition for transgender people, their families and communities can be major steps forward in queering their broader societies. Breakthroughs are most likely in times of major social transformation, as for example when the breakdown of South African apartheid also helped break down barriers for social participation by LGBT people and some South African MSMs (such as Zulu *injongas*) became willing to be publicly identified with LGBTs (McLean and Ngcobo 1994, 164–165).

Queering families, communities and larger societies lays bare the socially constructed, ideological character of gender, family and sexual structures. People can then begin to pose questions, not so much about what is 'natural' or 'what is part of our culture' as about what kinds of networks best meet their material, social, emotional and sexual needs. Networking and organizing can begin to trump biology. This means that development should focus not just on women but also on all 'those who lose out from not fitting into gender norms/ sex categories' (Jolly 2000). This can be the starting point for 'redefining identities outside reproduction and the family', which so far 'remains mostly untouched' by official development policy (Kleitz 2000).

Self-organization and social demands

Today in most societies the prevailing family and community structures are organized in ways that maintain and perpetuate male domination of women, heteronormativity and other inequitable social relations. As a result, families and communities often exert a conservatizing influence in society, in rich countries as well as poor ones, even where poor and working people mobilize in large numbers against the dominant economic policies. Sustained and transformative social mobilization requires changes at the family and community level, so as to transform conservatizing influences into emancipatory ones. This means that family and community structures dictated by ideology and tradition need to be modified starting from the dynamics of struggle and self-organization.

The way neoliberal globalization sets working people at opposite corners of the earth in cutthroat competition with each other throws up barriers to self-organization. Nevertheless discontent with their fate under neoliberalism, combined with the upheavals and questioning resulting from economic restructuring, have spurred the subaltern actors within traditional families and communities—women and LGBTs—to organize themselves in many underdeveloped countries.

Self-organization of LGBT people, though encountering even greater resistance and taking place on a more modest scale than women's self-organization, has a similar potential to help bring about needed changes at the grassroots. Self-organization by women and LGBTs, whether in separate women's or LGBT spaces or in existing institutions, always risks replicating or mimicking existing relations of domination as long as such inequitable relations prevail in the larger society. But they can also pose a challenge to the habits and organizational forms of traditionally straight male-dominated, gender normative and heteronormative trade unions and movements for economic and social change (Duggan 1997).

A discourse of rights, while a valuable tool for sexual emancipation in the underdeveloped world, needs to be thoroughly fleshed out in order genuinely to empower the great majority of poor and working LGBTs. Speaking of LGBT civil rights or legal sexual rights—that is, the absence of persecution or discrimination—is necessary but insufficient. Sexual rights need to be linked concretely to social and economic rights in an alternative development discourse, as they are in LGBT people's lives.

Until now LGBT organizations in the underdeveloped world have often felt they had to focus on the basic fight against persecution, for dignity and civil rights. Social movements fighting for housing, education and welfare programmes, on the other hand, have rarely shown any awareness of the presence of LGBT people among those on whose behalf they are fighting, or the specific importance of their demands for sexual emancipation. Queering the social movements is an enormous task that remains to be tackled in underdeveloped (and developed) countries: asserting the right of same-sex couples to housing, for example, and the right of LGBT youth to independent incomes and safety and dignity at school.

One social movement that has been visibly queered to a great extent in many underdeveloped countries is the grassroots movement for health care, in particular for people with HIV/AIDS. Soon after the founding of ACT UP New York in 1987 and of similar ACT UP groups in other North American cities, the direct action movement against AIDS began to demonstrate its internationalist spirit and potential.[4] During the same years LGBT organization in a number of underdeveloped countries laid the basis for grassroots queer health care movements, in some cases creating embryonic LGBT movements or organizations in countries where they had never existed before. This was the case for example in Costa Rica in 1987 (Schifter 1989) and a number of Southeast Asian countries as well as Zimbabwe. A striking case was the cooperation that took place between LGBT activists with the ministry of health in Sandinista Nicaragua (Randall 2000, 96–97).

Like women's activism, AIDS activism in the underdeveloped world has since been embraced by international development agencies and financial institutions, with contradictory results. Aid from international agencies, health ministries and private foundations turned many struggling AIDS activist groups into well-established non-governmental organizations (NGOs) in the 1980s (Lind and Share 2003, 56). The result has in general been an ongoing tension between their founders' impulses for sexual emancipation and pressure from donors to tone down the message. Some organizations' degree of success in challenging both heteronormativity and the power of major multinational corporations is all the more remarkable.

AIDS activists internationally joined in Durban, South Africa, in July 2000 to denounce the international financial institutions and their policies of trade liberalization as responsible for the 'millions [who] have died of AIDS and tens of millions … infected with HIV' (ACT UP 2000). The apogee so far of grassroots queer HIV/AIDS activism has probably been reached with South Africa's Treatment Action Campaign (TAC). TAC built on earlier links between LGBT and anti-apartheid activism to put the ANC government under pressure and eventually win an unprecedented (though still inadequate) degree of access to HIV drugs for poor and low-income people in an underdeveloped country. Even more impressive if possible, TAC became a central player in the fight against drug patents in the hands of pharmaceutical multinationals and against 'intellectual property rights', a key point in the 'free trade' agenda of international neoliberalism. It has been an outstanding example of the queering of the global justice agenda.

Queering from within social movements has its potential limitations. Grassroots social movements have the advantage that the people with the most urgent and direct stake in change have a close relationship to them, but the disadvantage that their social base can put them under pressure to achieve quick results. This can come at the expense of long-term, fundamental sexual and social change. As a result, in LGBT as in feminist movements, grassroots groups can become 'primarily *advocates for* rather than *mobilizers of* their constituency' (Brenner 2003, 81). There are risks of bureaucratization, dependence on donors and subordination of transgender people and other sexual minorities. The best safeguard is to build strong links between social movements with solid, active LGBT bases and radical political movements.

Sex and the social forums

LGBT activists have found allies as well as adversaries in battles to queer the movements over the past decade in some of the NGO gatherings that debate the directions taken by international civil society. Explicit recognition for lesbians was initially included in the Action Platform of the Fourth World Conference on Women in Beijing in 1995, for example, only to be dropped from the final document. Ecuadorian and Brazilian delegates at the UN World Conference Against Racism in Johannesburg in 2001 backed calls to fight discrimination based on sexual orientation, which the preparatory Dakar African NGO Forum also took up, while others resisted (Mtewa 2003, 37–38, 41–42). LGBT activists have seized the opportunities provided by these gatherings to network and highlight the links between sexual emancipation and global justice, for example in the fight against the Free Trade Area of the Americas (GLBT South-South Dialogue 2003b). LGBTs from the underdeveloped world have pushed these same links at international LGBT gatherings (GLBT South-South Dialogue 2003a).

The World, regional, national and local Social Forums are a particularly interesting laboratory for observing developments in broader global justice movements. Compared with traditional social organizations and political parties, the Social Forums offer a space where diverse movements 'can meet and exchange, in a much less hierarchical way than in the past' (Rousset 2005). The Forums are seen explicitly as spaces for 'horizontal solidarities', cross-cutting the usual boundaries between issues and currents. This has made it easier for sexual issues to get a hearing.

There has been a significant though uneven level of LGBT participation in the Social Forum process. Much of the greatest progress has been made at Latin American Social Forums, notably at the second World Social Forum in Porto Alegre, Brazil, in 2002, and again at the third Porto Alegre Forum in 2003, where thousands of people passed through the LGBT space. An even bigger breakthrough took place at the World Social Forum in Mumbai in 2004, where thousands of transgender *hijras* processed through the streets and made their presence felt in the tents where discussions took place. Unfortunately their presence was not translated into LGBT representation at the level of the World Social Forum's International Council or other central bodies of the Social Forum process. The problem may be in large part that LGBT organizations in underdeveloped countries lack the solid structures and finances of the biggest NGOs, trade unions and movements that play the biggest roles in and especially between Forums.

A queer agenda for participation

On the basis of the initial experiences with LGBT self-organization around global justice themes, some specific LGBT contributions can be put forward to a global justice agenda. Some ideas involve an LGBT contribution to conceiving participatory democracy and its importance for equitable development. Others identify sexual dimensions to apparently purely socio-economic demands, around such issues as health care, housing, a social safety net and workers' rights.

Full and equal LGBT participation in development requires overturning at least two major barriers: gender- and heteronormative definitions of who gets to participate, and definitions of citizenship that do not take enough account of social and cultural difference. LGBTs have had an explicit place in 'thematic assemblies' on issues of 'social inclusion' in the participatory budget process in Porto Alegre and several other Brazilian cities (Bruce 2003, 98–99). This remains an isolated example, however. Participatory development programmes engaging with the informal sector need to include transgender people and LGBT actors in the sex trade.

LGBT participation will require that LGBT people be seen, heard and acknowledged. The formal democracies that have become more common in recent decades in Latin America and other parts of the underdeveloped world still have little or no meaning for millions of the excluded, including homeless people, street children and transgender people. Talk of democratic governance or participatory development rings hollow as long as these people's lives are ruled and sometimes destroyed by the whims of police, paramilitaries or thugs. Challenges to homophobia and particularly lesbophobia are crucial to overcoming repression of and violence against women and many others, which are still endemic worldwide (Kleitz 2000).

A queer agenda for economic empowerment

Queering development, beginning with queering grassroots social movements and queering the politics of global justice, will require re-imagining the economy, development, and the relationship between the global North and South. Along the way specific demands must be reformulated on a range of economic issues so as to reflect the experience, needs and creativity of LGBT people.

The politics of health care is the best example so far of the queering of a grassroots social movement. LGBT people, particularly those who are seropositive or at risk of seroconversion, have a high stake in insisting that 'consumers' of health care must have a decisive voice in its provision. They understand from their own experience how crucial it is that health care is considered a right, not a commodity. The fight against pharmaceutical multinationals and the rest of the global medical industry is based on the insistence that the human right to health care prevail over 'intellectual property rights' and the right to profit.

A similar process of queering can take place with other economic demands. LGBT people have a specific stake for example in winning recognition in practice of the human right to housing, since physical space is a precondition for the flourishing of human sexuality and relationships. Decent and affordable housing for poor and low-income people, an important goal in itself, must take account of the diversity of the families and communities they belong to. Similarly, the fight against youth poverty and for economic independence for young people must take account of the specific importance of this demand for LGBT young people.

The response of governments to such demands, when it is not simply denial and repression, is often that 'the money just isn't there' to implement such demands. This smokescreen needs to be blown away. LGBT people along with others need to highlight the frightful contrast between the relatively small sums needed to treat AIDS and other deadly diseases worldwide (according to a 1994 United Nations estimate, US $5–7 billion a year for ten years) (Toussaint 1999, 238–239) and the gargantuan amounts that go every year to underdeveloped countries' debt service ($340 billion in 2002) and military spending ($1.04 trillion in 2004).

Refracting an alternative development programme through the prism of all the queer demands that have been added to the global justice agenda, and the queer demands that still need to be formulated and accepted, will doubtless change it drastically. Calls for 'deglobalization', and particularly for 'subjecting the private sector and the state to constant monitoring by civil society' (Bello 2000; cf. Bond 2003), requires bearing in mind what movements and communities have not usually been included in 'civil society'. Queering concepts like democracy, civil society and community would involve rethinking them in basic ways. LGBT movements themselves do not yet know how this queering process can proceed or where it will end up. Inevitably, LGBT movements will be rebuilt and restructured as, like labour and other social movements, they come gradually to grips with a transformed global context.

Acknowledgements

This chapter was originally published by Taylor & Francis Ltd as Peter Drucker (2009) Changing Families and Communities: An LGBT Contribution to an Alternative Development Path, *Development in Practice* Vol. 19, No. 7 (Sep., 2009), pp. 825–836 and is reproduced here by permission of the publisher.

Notes

1 Thanks to Amy Lind and Alan Sears for comments on an earlier version of this article.
2 This does not mean that the possibility of LGBT cultures depends on a society's level of economic development. For an analysis of the roles that indigenous sexual cultures, capitalist development, state repression, medicine, cultural globalization, religion and politics play in shaping same-sex identities, see Drucker 2000, 9–41.
3 Often in fact the traditions in question are inventions of the 19th or 20th centuries, as many African 'tribal' traditions are as well (see Ranger 1992, 211–262). African presidents like Zimbabwe's Robert Mugabe for example learned that homosexuality is 'un-African' as part of their Christian mission educations.
4 The global justice movement is indebted to the LGBT movement for creative forms of direct action that ACT UP used from 1987 on to protest against policies around the AIDS epidemic, drawing in its turn on earlier experiences of civil rights, peace and anti-nuclear movements. Beginning in Seattle in 1999 many similar tactics spread around the world, though ironically LGBT people have not often been very visible in global justice actions (Shepard and Hayduk 2002).

References

ACT UP. 2000. "Treatment for all … now!" http://www.actupny.org/reports/durban-access.html

Altman, Dennis. 2000. "The emergence of gay identities in Southeast Asia." In *Different Rainbows*, edited by Peter Drucker, pp. 137–156. London: Millivres/GMP.

Altman, Dennis. 2003. "Neo-colonialism or liberation: Who invented the 'global gay'?" *Queer Zagreb*.

Babb, Florence E. 2001. *After Revolution: Mapping Gender and Cultural Politics in Nicaragua*. Austin, TX: University of Texas Press.

Barbosa, Mariela et al. (1994) "Introduction: Women and economic integration." In *Women's Lives in the New Globalization Economy*, edited by Penny Duggan and Heather Dashner. Amsterdam: IIRE.

Bello, Walden. 2000. "From Melbourne to Prague: the struggle for a deglobalized world." http://www.corpwatch.org

Boellstorff, Tom. 2005. *The Gay Archipelago: Sexuality and Nation in Indonesia*. Princeton, NJ: Princeton University Press.

Bond, Patrick. 2003. "'Deglobalisation'? Sure, but what's next?" *Green Left Weekly Online*. http://www.greenleft.org.au/2003/527/30818

Brenner, Johanna. 2003. "On feminism and global justice." *New Politics* 9, no. 2: 78–87.

Bruce, Iain. 2003. *The Porto Alegre Alternative: Direct Democracy in Action*. London/Amsterdam: Pluto Press/IIRE.

Carrier, Joseph. 1975. "Urban Mexican male homosexual encounters," Ph.D. dissertation, Irvine, CA: University of California.

Chou, Wah-shan. 2000. "Individual strategies for *tongzhi* empowerment in China." In *Different Rainbows*, edited by Peter Drucker, pp. 193–206. London: Millivres/GMP.

Coontz, Stephanie. 1988. *The Social Origins of Private Life: A History of American Families 1600–1900*. London: Verso.

D'Emilio, John. 1983. "Capitalism and gay identity." In *Powers of Desire: The Politics of Sexuality*, edited by Ann Snitow, Christine Stansell and Sharan Thompson., pp. 100–116. New York: Monthly Review Press.

Drucker, Peter. 1996. "'In the tropics there is no sin.'" *New Left Review* 218: 75–101.

Drucker, Peter. 2000. "Introduction: Remapping sexualities." In *Different Rainbows*, edited by Peter Drucker, pp. 9–41. London: Millivres/GMP.

Duggan, Penny. 1997. *The Feminist Challenge to Traditional Political Organizing*, Working Paper no. 33 Amsterdam: IIRE.

Fernández-Alemany, M. 2000. "Negotiating gay identities: The neoliberalization of sexual politics in Honduras." Paper presented at the 2000 Congress of the Latin American Studies Association, Miami, FL, March.

Gevisser, Mark. 2000. "Mandela's stepchildren: Homosexual identity in post-apartheid South Africa." In *Different Rainbows*, edited by Peter Drucker, pp. 111–136. London: Millivres/GMP.

GLBT South-South Dialogue. 2003a. "South-South recommendations, ILGA 20th World Conference (Rome, July 2000)." In *Globalization: GLBT Alternatives*, edited by Irene León and Phumi Mtewa, pp. 87–89. Quito: GLBT South-South Dialogue.

GLBT South-South Dialogue. 2003b. "Declaration on the Free Trade Area of the Americas (FTAA)." In *Globalization: GLBT Alternatives*, edited by Irene León and Phumi Mtewa, pp. 95–97. Quito: GLBT South-South Dialogue.

Green, James N. 1999. *Beyond Carnival: Male Homosexuality in Twentieth-Century Brazil*. Chicago, IL: University of Chicago Press.

Jolly, Susan. 2000. "What use is queer theory to development?" Institute for Development Studies, discussion paper. http://www.ids.ac.uk/ids/pvty/qd/qd2000.html

Khayatt, Didi. 1996. "The place of desire: Where are the lesbians in Egypt?". unpublished paper

Kleitz, Gilles. 2000. "Why is development work so straight?" Discussion Paper for Queering Development Seminar Series. Brighton: Institute for Development Studies. http://www.ids.ac.uk/ids/pvty/qd/qd2000.html

Lind, Amy and Jessica Share. 2003. "Queering development: Institutionalized heterosexuality in development theory, practice and politics in Latin America." In *Feminist Futures: Re-Imagining Women, Culture and Development*, edited by Kum-Kum Bhavnani, John Foran and Priya Kurian, pp. 55–73. London: Zed Books.

McLean, Hugh and Linda Ngcobo. 1994. "Abangibhamayo bathi ngimnandi (Those who fuck me say I'm tasty): Gay sexuality in Reef townships." In *Defiant Desire: Gay and Lesbian Lives in South Africa*, edited by Mark Gevisser and Edwin Cameron, pp. 158–185. Johannesburg: Ravan Press.

Mejía, Max. 2000. "Mexican pink." In *Different Rainbows*, edited by Peter Drucker, pp. 43–55. London: Millivres/GMP.

Mtewa, Phumi. 2003. "GLBT visions for an alternative globalization." In *Globalization: GLBT Alternatives*, edited by Irene León and Phumi Mtewa, pp. 35–48. Quito: GLBT South-South Dialogue.

Oetomo, Dédé. 1996. "Gender and sexual orientation." In *Fantasizing the Feminine in Indonesia*, edited by Laurie J. Sears, pp. 259–269. Durham, NC: Duke University Press.

Randall, Margaret. 2000. "To Change Our Own Reality and the World: A Conversation with Lesbians in Nicaragua." In *Different Rainbows*, edited by Peter Drucker, pp. 91–109. London: Millivres/Prowler.

Ranger, Terence. 1992. "The invention of tradition in Colonial Africa." In *The Invention of Tradition*, edited by Eric Hobsbawm and Terence Ranger, pp. 211–261. Cambridge: Cambridge University Press.

Rich, Adrienne. 1983. "Compulsory heterosexuality and lesbian existence." *Powers of Desire: The Politics of Sexuality*, edited by Ann Snitow, pp. 177–204. New York: Monthly Review Press.

Rousset, Pierre. 2005. "The World Social Forum: A new framework for solidarities." In *Bandung 2005: Rethinking Solidarity in Global Society*, edited by Darwis Khudori, pp. 139–143. Yogyakarta: Ghadjah Mada University/Yayasan Pondok Rakyat.

Schifter Sikora, Jacob. 1989. *La Formación de una Contracultura: Homosexualismo y Sida en Costa Rica*, San José: Guayacán.

Seccombe, Wally. 1993. *Weathering the Storm: Working-Class Families from the Industrial Revolution to the Fertility Decline*. London: Verso.

Shepard, Benjamin and Ronald Hayduk. 2002. *From ACT UP to the WTO: Urban Protest and Community Building in the Era of Globalization.*; London: Verso.

Toussaint, Eric. 1999. *Your Money or Your Life! The Tyranny of Global Finance*. London/Dar es Salaam: Pluto/Mkuki na Nyota.

Wekker, Gloria. 1999. "What's identity got to do with it?" In *Female Desires: Same-Sex Relations and Transgender Practices across Cultures*, edited by Evelyn Blackwood and Saskia E. Wieringa, pp.119–138. New York: Columbia University Press.

Went, Robert. 2000. *Globalization: Neoliberal Challenge, Radical Responses*. Amsterdam/London: IIRE/Pluto Press.

World Bank. 1994. *Enhancing Women's Participation in Economic Development*. Washington, DC: World Bank.

Wright, Timothy. 2000. "Gay organizations, NGOs and the globalization of sexual identity: The case of Bolivia." *Journal of Latin American Anthropology* 5 no. 2: 89–111

2

TROUBLING HETERO/ CISNORMATIVE EDUCATIONAL PRACTICES IN INTERNATIONAL DEVELOPMENT

Robert C. Mizzi

Despite its complexity, a goal of educating adults is to generate personal, social, and organizational change (Spencer 2006). Adult learning can be informal (without structure and has some degree of spontaneity), formal (with structure and in an organized space), or non-formal (various learning situations, but lacks formal organization or credential) (Merriam, Caffarella and Baumgartner 2007). Learners or educators in international development can be either aid workers or aid recipients, and a part of a grassroots development project or a staff member that is a part of a larger intergovernmental aid agency (Logue 2001). The learner often has contact with an international, Western-educated educator who is considered an "expert" in a certain field and therefore in a dominant position of power (Mizzi and Hamm 2013). Education in an international development context straddles both adult education (AE) and human resource development (HRD) subfields.

On one hand, AE practice in international development promotes participatory engagement and critical thinking of adult learners, community engagement, culturally relevant content, and a deconstruction of international adult educator positionality and of a Western-oriented curriculum (Berkvens, Kalyanpur, Kuiper and Van den Akker 2012; Mizzi and Hamm 2013). AE engages critical pedagogy so that, as Freire and Macedo (1987) write, one can "read the word and the world" that constructs a social hierarchy, question why this order remains in place, and begin to re-conceptualize a more equitable society. Learning is considered a cultural and social activity in AE, and with that, there are expectations for adult educators to include relevant perspectives in their classrooms via curricula, teaching practices, and other forms of engagement (Guy 1999). An example of AE practice in international development is the Canada-based Coady Institute, which uses a community-based approach to educate leaders in development on how to tackle global challenges (Coady Institute n.d.).

On the other hand, HRD is the educational process that aims for people to improve their performance for the betterment of an organization (Watkins and Marsick 2014). Common approaches of HRD in international development include pre-departure orientations, train-the-trainer programs, professional development, individualized learning, and organizational development services, such as (re)training and direct employee intervention programs (Johnson and Thomas 2006; Logue 2001; Pasteur and Scott-Villiers 2004). Hinton and Groves (2004) state that "International development practice is currently based on a linear outcome-oriented perspective, which focuses on individual institutions within the system to a degree that excludes attention to the relationships among actors" (5). This top-down approach to international development draws on Western HRD practice (Hinton and Groves 2004) and privileges and prizes Western, masculinist knowledge (Andersson and Auer 2005; Hinton and Groves 2004; Kothari 2002). Gronemeyer (1992) argues that Western control of international development is designed to affirm accomplishments and secure standards achieved in the West. Education often functions as the conduit to make these moves, despite, as Waisbord (2006) writes, the "training is not always adjusted to job expectations and demands in the workplace" (231). For example, without serious consideration of the complexity of educational practice, more training is recommended to "solve the problem" of resistors and activists who participated in the 2004 revolt against international control of Kosovo (Heinemann-Grüder and Grebenschikov 2007). HRD may then be deployed as the means to expect conformity with Western agendas. Recently, there has been growing interest in critical HRD, whereby power and privilege are questioned and experiences of marginalization are examined in hopes of generating a more equitable workplace (Fenwick 2014; Sambrook 2014). This emergent perspective of HRD has some promise to shape workers and workplace learning involved with international development through, for example, engaging social movements as a bridge to HRD (see Callahan 2013).

Having defined these two primary forms of educating adults (AE and HRD), the purpose of this chapter is to unravel the tensions of engaging education in international development and point out some of the difficulties for sexual and gender minority subjects. I use the term "sexual and gender minority" (SGM) as a catchall to include lesbian, gay, bisexual, or transgender (LGBT) persons, or persons with same-sex sexualities or gender variance in general. I continue this chapter with analyzing the international development, sexuality, and education context and offer an autoethnographic vignette of an educational exercise from the perspective of being a Canadian, cisgender male, sexual minority, adult educator in Kosovo. I then analyze this vignette and question the effects on SGM subjectivity through the following themes: (1) deployment of the train-the-trainer approach, (2) a pedagogical aim to establish close student–educator relationships, and (3) establishment of a hetero/cisnormative educational space. My analysis aims to demonstrate how educating adults is a complex and power-filled activity, which means that educational participants, pedagogies, and policies cannot be standardized with the view to facilitate or rescue development. Queer development studies can deconstruct this standardization and its (hetero/cis)normative assumptions, and proffer educational spaces where SGM subjectivities, knowledges, and performances can flourish.

International development, sexuality, and education

The presence and practices of international aid workers working in the global South are critiqued by scholars in international development as being riddled with power differentials that favor aid workers and suppress local counterparts. Aid workers, donors, and diplomats tend to mismanage relations with local people according to their own rules and purposes without much consideration of the practices and knowledges of the people with whom they work (Crossley and Holmes 2001; Escobar 1992). Escobar (1992) explains:

> institutional practices such as project planning and implementation...give the impression that policy is the result of discrete, rational acts and not the process of coming to terms with conflicting interests, a process in which choices are made, exclusions effected, and worldviews imposed. There is an apparent neutrality in identifying people as "problems", until one realizes first, that this definition of "the problem" has already been put together in Washington or some capital city of the Third World, and second, that problems are presented in such a way that some kind of development programme has to be accepted as the legitimate solution.
>
> *(140)*

Given international development's use of education to generate change, it is no great leap that a "development programme" in this context could very well involve educational policy or practice. There are then two observable themes here in Escobar's contribution: distance (between cultures) and determination (to avoid alternative approaches to engagement). Both themes suggest a form of otherness whereby "problem" identities are managed by distant decision-making authorities to contain culture. Kapoor (2008) continues with these two themes and contributes an espousal of "culture" and "policy" in a way that perpetuates otherness. Culture may become an object of policy when people speak about culture, write about culture, show pictures about culture, and create debates about culture. In actual fact though, Kapoor (2008) argues that culture has very little involvement with the process of policy-making. Policy-making then becomes a "technical and institutional-laden process" that systematizes culture according to certain words, images, and beliefs (Kapoor 2008, 19). For example, while pre-departure orientations may advise international workers to be conscious of visible and invisible layers of culture, culture remains a peripheral concept in constructing pre-departure orientations (Mizzi 2014; Mizzi and O'Brien-Klewchuk 2016).

While it is important to critically reflect on culture in order to re-conceptualize what it means to be an aid worker, we also cannot simply ignore colonizing and social histories in educational contexts. Ignoring colonizing and social histories means excluding discussion on how dominant perceptions of race, gender, and sexuality influenced the education of adults over time. For example, English (2004) reported how Western, female, adult educators involved with international development felt dislocated, disconnected, and displaced in their classrooms because they came from a white, Western, world that has a history of colonizing communities. In effect, they were continually negotiating a complex mix of identity and culture by mingling their past experiences with their present work circumstance.

Given that pre-mid-1990s aid workers are portrayed as ceasing to operate as individuals (Watson 1996), more recent research indicates that sexual minority aid workers experience social, historical, and political tensions (Gosine 2010; Jolly 2011; Mizzi 2013; Wright 2000). Excluding SGM identities and perspectives in education may be symptomatic of a larger structural issue that regulates sexuality as a taboo topic, and excludes discussions about sexuality, for example, as being pleasurable (Jolly 2007), an aspect of human identity and behavior (Mizzi 2013), or as a preventative measure against gender-based violence (Hayhurst, MacNeill, Kidd, and Knoppers 2014).

International development represents a conflicted space for education, as it creates a work context where principles of AE and HRD are both present. Watkins and Marsick (2014), through citing Habermas, explain the relationship between the two sub-fields: "there is a tension that can never be resolved between "the system," that is core to the essence of organizations, and the "life-world," or the holistic experiences of people from which life's meaning is constructed" (47). The tense relationship between AE and HRD in international development became apparent when I was the director of Queer Peace International, which was a Canadian non-governmental organization (NGO) that engaged global South SGM communities through AE. In one meeting with leaders of another Canadian NGO, I was discussing the ways in which the education of adults is delivered in an African country through international development. Coming from a stronger AE background, I was aware of the work of African adult education scholar Julius Nyerere (1978), who writes,

> if adult education is to contribute to development, it must be a part of life – integrated with life and inseparable from it. It is not something which can be put into a box and taken out for certain periods of the day or week – or certain periods of a life. And it cannot be imposed: every learner is ultimately a volunteer, because, however much teaching he is given, only he can learn.
>
> *(29)*

Yet, leaders of this particular NGO had a different perception, asking me to explain why an international aid worker would want to promote critical thinking and connect content to life experience when learners only want a "PowerPoint presentation." Having normative assumptions that learners are passive receptacles that lack relevant backgrounds, ambitions, and experiences minimize potential for student growth and achievement. Normative assumptions of the learner also has implications for SGM learners, or persons that learn queerly (i.e., learn through non-normative ways), who may wish to question heteronormative practices and policies in society, analyze the history of African homosexuality, and offer perspectives on content based on their life experiences and cultural knowledge.

If (hetero/cis)normative assumptions occupy the educational experience and "good" education is perceived as privileging accountability over social justice (Smith 2013), then SGM learners and SGM educators will once again face exclusion in a social space. The problem is that despite international development being reliant on Western educational approaches to facilitate change, it continues to ignore urgent calls to include SGM perspectives in international AE (Hill 2013) and international HRD (Gedro, Mizzi, Rocco and van Loo 2013). These scholars argue for SGM inclusion on the grounds of advancing social cohesion, knowledge of sociocultural realities, and different perspectives on content. SGM acceptance functions as a boundary marker for international development through education, where there is an appreciation of the benefits of education as a means to exchange information and enhance skills, but not in a way that promotes being and becoming SGM. Positioning SGM acceptance as boundary marker is risky business, as it (1) serves notice to other "controversial" identities and topics that they too may be considered as unworthy for inclusion in educational practice, (2) devalues and silences being and becoming SGM within "official" development discourse, and (3) causes education to fall into its traditional patterns of SGM exclusion and reject recent gains made that promote inclusivity in scholarship and practice.

Below is a multi-vocal autoethnographic vignette that shares further insight as to where tension exists when same-sex sexuality, education, and international development occupy the same space. Autoethnography is a qualitative research approach that allows researchers to tell their institutional or relational story as a means to reclaim a marginalized space and to assert agency (Ellis and Bochner 2000). There is a self-reflective element to autoethnography that allows for the researcher to offer and learn from the experience. I apply a multi-vocal method to the following autoethnographic vignette as means to highlight the competing and contradictory narrative voices within the researcher and to visualize some tensions and vulnerabilities of being a sexual minority in a hetero/cisnormative, international development workspace (Mizzi 2010). This multi-vocal approach also allows for greater conceptualization of whole-person inclusivity to show how being SGM is shaped by other facets of identity and by context.

A sexual minority teacher educator in Kosovo

An Albanian project assistant/translator, Burim, and I arrive in our company 4x4 green Toyota Jeep at a local elementary school in a rural village at approximately 9:30am. I have been in Kosovo for less than a month and already I am jumping into assignments such as the one we are currently working on: to provide individual mentorship on student-centred instruction to each member of our 32 teacher trainers.

Foreigner Voice: Since my arrival, I have grown to enjoy working with Burim. He has taken the time to explain a great deal of history, culture, language, and everything else about Kosovo to me. I appreciate how he presents "both sides" of the story. Other than a quick conversation with a senior team member, I never really had much of a pre-departure orientation, so Burim's mentorship became quite valuable to me.

Educator Voice: If there is anything about my job that I enjoy most is the fact that I continually meet with teachers to discuss pedagogy. Both Burim and I enjoy these opportunities because we receive a rare glimpse into what is happening in Kosovar schools and in professional development seminars for teachers. Even though we both realize that we cannot possibly observe all teaching experiences, we receive, through these brief encounters, some clue as to how practices with student-centred teaching are coming along.

I hop out of the Jeep and slowly opened the old steel door to the white, box-like, concrete school. Today is the day we were meant to watch a trainer teach a lesson to his grade four students and to provide "mentorship."

Minority Voice: At some level, I know what it is like to live in fear, but I don't know what it is like to be hunted (although sexual and gender minorities indeed have lived this type of life). One aspect I can definitely connect with teachers is how their feelings of dissidence as ethnic minorities can be similar to my feelings of dissidence as a gay man, but I fall short at understanding their contextual realities.

Youth Voice: I hope they don't discount me because of my age. I'll have to work overtime to prove myself.

Homophobic Control/Cultural Awareness Voice: Don't forget to lower your voice. Keep arms by your side. Choose your words carefully. Luckily, translation provides opportunities to think carefully and to remember these steps. Feminine Robert = Weak, Deviant Robert = Zero respect from my students.

Educator Voice: I find the word mentorship problematic because it connotes a one-way educator–learner relationship. Often in these consultations I would find myself being mentored by the way the teachers use student-centred teaching.

The classroom has about three large windows directly ahead of us that shed light on more drawings that are taped on the walls around the room. All of the desks are in small group formation and, despite the blackboard falling off the wall, it is clean with only a few announcements written on the board. Adnan comes over to me to say hello to me and to greet me in traditional Albanian style by grazing the side of his face against mine. I normally do not initiate the Albanian male-to-male greeting because I am not Albanian, but I certainly reciprocate if someone invites me into this long-standing ritual between men. "Nice to see you again, Robert," he says in clear English. Adnan's gentle disposition immediately puts me at ease and reminds me of our previous meetings where he brought the same genuine welcome and respect.

Educator Voice: I think Adnan is one of our strongest trainers. I've seen him in my workshops instructing teachers and now I am going to see him teach his class.

Counter-voice: Why do we use the term "trainers" to refer to our teachers who facilitate professional development workshops for their colleagues? The term is problematic in the sense that it inherently privileges trainer knowledge over *other* types of knowledges. Essentially, where does the relationship between trainer and colleagues begin and where does it end in this context?

Authority Control Voice: How should I position myself here? I don't want to seem like an expert but I feel compelled to share something. I feel more of a professional obligation to speak, yet my sensitive side wants to listen.

Adnan reports that his school director wants to sit in on his teaching as well. Having a school director sit in on a classroom observation and mentorship session is a sign of respect towards having an international expert in the school. I realize that he is not coming to evaluate Adnan, but to show his respect towards me. Nonetheless, I begin to feel somewhat nervous for Adnan so I downplay my visit so that he will feel less worried. This sensitivity to learner safety and comfort is a part of adult education practice.

We sit together at the back of the room and wait for the bell to signal the children to return to their classroom and for the school director to arrive.

"Adnan, how is your family?" I ask, thinking that the question might be an appropriate cultural gesture. In Kosovo, asking about family is considered to be a very respectful beginning to a conversation.

"Oh, good. The new baby is doing very well, but crying a lot at night."

"It must be difficult to be up most of the night plus teaching."

"Plus my job at the shop," Adnan replies, reminding me that Kosovar teachers normally have two or three jobs because of the low teacher's salary. "Yeah, it is tough, but I'm okay. How are you? How's the education project?"

"We're fine. We are visiting a lot of teacher trainers in their school classrooms now so it is good to have a visit with each of you individually and see you teach." Burim quickly checks if Adnan understands and he nods. Both Burim and I smile at Adnan. "Your English is excellent, Adnan," I compliment.

"Thank you, but I must practice some more, I…" The bell interrupts the conversation and within what seems like a few seconds the classroom is filled with 38 grade four students and a rushing old school director! I stand up to greet him in Albanian language and he seems impressed, and he sits down next to me on my right. Burim sits on my left so that he can whisper the translation into my ear. Class begins.

After successfully teaching a highly interactive and student-centred lesson, Adnan accompanies Burim and me to a café where we can talk about the lesson and share further ideas for professional development. He is open to my feedback and explains his decisions with such pedagogically-rich insights. It is no surprise why he is one of our top teacher trainers and someone who I have developed a great amount of respect for.

One week later, I receive an opportunity to meet with Adnan again during our monthly meeting with our entire team of teacher trainers. We have rented a large conference room in a hotel in Pristina where our 32 trainers arrive to learn and discuss new pedagogy. Having a safe and comfortable atmosphere to openly share our ideas is an important step due to the history of dismantled teaching for Albanians in Kosovo. Plus, such an atmosphere sets the tone for how professional development meetings for teachers should take place.

I am eager to see my students again and to facilitate a seminar around the topic of forms of assessment. I've been planning this workshop with Burim over the past week so I am interested in finding out how the teacher trainers will respond. If it is successful, I will include the topic in the revision of our textbook on student-centred instruction. In some way, the teacher trainers act as my focus group for feedback on our suggested topics. If they do not find the topic useful, I trust them to communicate to me what kind of revisions might be needed to either successfully adapt the topic to Kosovar contexts or to ditch the topic altogether.

I stand by the entrance way as the teacher trainers slowly enter. They greet me in Albanian, English, or occasionally in German or French languages. I notice that Adnan scurries past the queue, which is not out of the ordinary because he wants to secure a seat next to his friends. My thoughts are generally more about getting the seminar started and making sure everyone feels comfortable.

Burim and I begin the seminar with our usual administrative tasks. I go through the agenda slowly so that Burim can translate everything at ease.

Educator Voice: I must remember to have Burim start the session next time. I'm not really needed yet.

Homophobic Control Voice: Deep voice, hands by my side…

Authority Control Voice: I really hope this session goes well. Last time we met they became somewhat upset that we had to stop paying them to attend these seminars and ask them to voluntarily attend. Let's hope this issue doesn't re-surface!

Cultural Awareness Voice: Don't mention the conflict.

We begin the workshop on assessment and notice that some of the trainers are taking notes while others are simply listening to Burim. Of course, some are whispering to each other. Teaching adults can sometimes be no different than teaching children. People, adult or not, learn at different times and in different ways. Hopefully I can hook some of them back with my next exercise.

I provide the trainers with several different case studies that need an assessment of some kind, and they can choose from the various assessment strategies we've introduced or invent some of their own. After assigning the group task, I begin to circulate the room. I realize that I can only understand a little of their group conversations, but I enjoy watching them work. If anyone has a question, we seem to get through it in broken English/Albanian or by calling over Burim for translation.

Reflective Voice: I reflect on power in this scenario. Johnson-Bailey and Cervero (1998) refer to power dynamics in the adult education classroom when they write, "When adults, learners and teachers enter classrooms they bring with them their positions in the hierarchies that order the world, including those based on race, gender, class, sexual orientation and disability" (390). These positionalities, then, shape learning and classroom behaviours that an educator must navigate through (Johnson-Bailey and Cervero 1998). I wonder what role context plays in this social dynamic – and how to work with context in a meaningful way?

I decide to stop by Adnan's group. I have a significant rapport with his colleagues and I know they would welcome a visit. Quite a few of them speak English so that makes it easier for me to communicate with them. I slowly approach the group and people notice that I'm heading in their direction. Because Adnan's back is to me, I gently put my hand on Adnan's shoulder so that I don't startle him. "How's it going?" I gently probe the group. Adnan immediately turns around, staring directly at me, and abrasively commands, "Don't touch me." I take a step back in disbelief that he reacted with such a sharp tone, and it is evident that my facial expression changes from positive curiosity to a concerned puzzlement. I was never good at hiding my facial reactions, especially when something out of the ordinary catches me by surprise. Why would he say such a thing? Should I have not touched his shoulder? Adnan quickly turns back around to speak with his group who also seem stunned at his reaction. He ignores my presence.

Homophobic Control Voice: I think he knows, or at least deeply suspects, that I am gay. Perhaps he read about my volunteer work on the gay Kosovo website? This encounter reminds me of Pharr (1997), who writes that when SGM people experience questionable acts of rejection or marginalization, they have good reason to assume that these acts could be based on homo/transphobia and sexual stigma given their history of persecution.

Gender Voice: Perhaps he does not like to have men touch him on his shoulder? I need to consider where I put my hands. I also need to consider that perhaps he might be overtired because he is taking care of his infant son most of the night.

Educator Voice: I am still at a loss. I don't think our mentoring went poorly last week nor do I think anything was said that would have been controversial to a point that I would be shut out in such a way. How am I going to navigate through this with so many probabilities? Normally I would speak to the student about such an outburst, but I'm not sure how that will go over since I will need Burim to help with translation.

    Counter-voice: As an educator, I can't help but to feel very saddened by Adnan's reaction. I have high hopes for all the trainers and to see one of our strongest react in this way just reminds me of the differences that we all share. Dialogue about respecting differences does not always lead to the eradication of prejudice.

Safety Voice: I am so tired of hiding and evading personal questions and comments and being on guard. My identity is connected to the classroom community. I'm wearing down. If I felt more comfortable in this classroom then perhaps I would feel more confident in my interactions here.

Foreigner/Reflective Voice: There is no evidence that points towards a probable cause for Adnan's outburst and yet I immediately pinned this episode against homophobia. Does working in a foreign culture cause one's vulnerability, in my case my sexuality, to inform emotions? Can an educator lose objectivity when there is a heightened tension around her/his vulnerability? While I suspect many educators would have felt disjointed by Adnan's response, I recognize that, as an international adult educator, I need to be continually thinking about how my students perceive me and my teaching. In other words, because of the cultural and linguistic differences, I need to work harder to ensure that a respectful educator–learner relationship is formed. If the teacher trainers do not positively respond to my teachings, then adopting the teaching reforms will occur at a somewhat slower pace. Adult learning is so relational in nature that it serves no good to be insensitive to my student's feelings. However, I am left feeling exposed and disappointed as a result of what had transpired between Adnan and me. Even though the same dilemma might have presented itself in Canada, I feel as though the rules of engagement with students and colleagues change here because (1) I am outside of my home country and can't immediately access social policy and programs, family and friends for protection, support and solutions, and (2) I am working in a culture of violence, fear and instability and need to be constantly on my guard.

I felt the need to consult with Burim in order to feel accepted once again. I wonder if touching a man's shoulder is culturally taboo among men. Somewhat to my relief, Burim denies that it was a case of cultural miscommunication and that same-sex touch in this manner is completely acceptable. He concludes by brushing off the incident and saying, "Eh, don't worry about it."

Learner/Gender Voice: Yet these words do not soothe my worries but reiterate a hyper-masculine ideal that, because I am a man, I should not be concerned with emotional reactions of other men. One thing is clear: my *safe* and *comfortable* classroom isn't that safe and comfortable for me.

Learner/Safety/Authority Control Voice: I wish I had the institutional support to guide me through this situation. I do not recall anyone ever telling me the steps that I could take if I had a difficult or challenging time in the workplace or classroom.

Learner/Safety Voice: I feel very much trapped, alone and like a failure in this situation. Everything that I know about adult education isn't pointing me to the right response. In fact, if I followed what Freire and others have recommended by building dialogue with my adult learners, I might have created a much larger difficulty than I could manage. I cannot communicate my feelings because of the potential negative repercussions with the rest of the class and my job. I feel compelled to protect my employer's ambitions to re-construct Kosovar teaching practices as a priority over my own comfort level.

Educator Voice: I am still the educator who is training this group, including Adnan. He is going to have to acknowledge me on some level if he is going to continue on with his professional development. There is still some power I hold here.

Homophobic Control Voice: [Silence.]

It is heart-wrenching for me, as a sensitive educator who cares deeply about his students, not to be able to inquire with Adnan about his problem with me. But the risk for exposure of my own sexuality is too great. As a result, Adnan, one of our star pupils, has effectively shut down his relationship with me, which impacts his growth potential and causes me to further regulate my interactions with students.

There are three themes present in the above vignette. First, train-the-trainer is a commonly employed educational model in contexts such as international development that means to develop a cohort of trainers of certain subject matter. In this model, a worker trains an elite group of trainers, and then that group of trainers trains their colleagues without interference of the lead trainer. The trainer curriculum is often standardized so that it can be used across communities and contexts (Piskurich 2008).

As illustrated, the train-the-trainer approach can be problematic for SGM identities and perspectives. Power is transferred from the international to the local trainer, assumes that the trainer is a normative figure who is impervious to being challenged, has all the right answers, is not a learner, and is positioned as the new "expert" in the room. The trainer may very well continue to model hetero/cisnormative behaviors observed in the international educator, and there will be little room to challenge this value because the trainer is an "official representative" of the international agency. This model removes the educator from assuming responsibility if learning goes awry, and re-positions the local trainer as the culprit in perpetuating (hetero/cis)norms that stifle inclusion efforts. For the international educator, there can be a heavy expectation to maintain the status quo as to what kinds of knowledge are passed onto the trainer, especially for those educators who have precarious work situations and who may not wish to "rock the boat." If the international aid worker is immersed in a hetero/cisnormative work situation, and there is little space given to explore queerness, then educational processes are bound by the rules of this work situation as well. There is little re-conceptualization of educational roles and practices when the train-the-trainer approach is utilized, and the trainer/trainee power differential remains intact.

Second, having a close student–educator relationship is meant to support adult learning and development. This close relationship supports students openly asking questions, educators sharing their backgrounds and experiences, dismantling power differentials in the classroom, and both identifying and addressing barriers to student success. Educators tell autobiographical stories, for example, as a means to strengthen this relationship (Brookfield 1995).

The above vignette suggests otherwise, and that a close relationship may only take place in organizational contexts that support plurality of ideas and identities. There are links (such as, teaching practices) that connect educational spaces, work culture, and organizational rules, and these links create a difficult balance between work requirements and personal values. Student–educator relationships are culturally bound and organizationally structured, and by that a close relationship may not be entirely possible or desirable. In contexts where SGM exclusion is rife, expanding on the notion of close relationships may be helpful, whereby the educator generates closeness with other kinds of relationships, such as building closeness with a curriculum that engages SGM perspectives, with educational policy that supports SGM inclusion, or with local SGM activists and educators.

Third, while it is entirely unknown if Adnan based his reactions on homophobia, on other gendered or professional reasons, or as a side-effect to employing instrumentalist and technocratic approaches in international development, there are concerns that still unfold for the SGM educator when working in a hetero/cisnormative space. A starting point can be moving beyond only naming "sexual orientation" or "gender identity" in human rights or social development education and, rather, interrogating (1) the cultural positioning of sexuality and gender differences in curriculum, policy, administration, and pedagogy and (2) examining the effects of compulsory, cisgender heterosexuality in a diverse society. Raising awareness to marginalizing encounters of homo/transphobia, hetero/cisnormativity, and hetero/cissexism in conjunction with sexism, racism, ableism, classism and so forth shows how SGM marginalization affects everyone, and not just those with non-normative sexualities and genders. The above vignette offers one implication of where a heteronormative work situation can create anxiety for SGM educators, and quite possibly SGM learners, to a point where thoughtful engagements become risky endeavors. In light of working in hetero/cisnormative international development, SGM workers must be constantly on guard for troubling encounters, or continually adopt activist orientations despite the consequences. When local stakeholders (e.g., SGM activists) and international educators work together to create an inclusive learning space, then conversations and spaces that embrace sexuality and gender and other forms of difference can hopefully come from a place of mutual respect and openness.

Concluding thoughts

Working in a hetero/cisnormative, international space has drawbacks for SGM workers and participants. It requires assertive SGM staff members to reveal their non-normative sexual and gender identities and to ask for information relevant to their lives. Individuals who are not so confident or who may be questioning their sexuality may remain silent and, effectively, miss out on receiving helpful information. The absence of sexual and gender diversity (1) disregards the potential for critical and creative discussions on how sexuality and gender is understood everywhere, (2) causes sexual and gender minorities to be seen as predatory because they must search for important legal, social, and cultural information that has been excluded from official programs and policies, and (3) produces a knowledge gap that can result in aid workers overstepping cultural boundaries around sexuality differences. The danger is that when there are reported encounters with violence or harassment of any kind, training becomes the knee-jerk solution to the crises, and with that comes heavy expectations for education to "fix" the situation, despite the act of educating adults being a complex activity.

As Kapoor (2008) reminds us, policy and culture need to work together if change processes are to be relevant. International development may benefit more from a necessary wider organizational assessment and systems change that incorporates not only SGM perspectives, but those cultural perspectives that often sit in the periphery. A deconstruction of "training" and other educational processes can point to how adult teaching, learning, and leading is a complex, power-filled process, and can take place both internal and external to structured educational events. This systems change approach may create an equitable and inclusive experience of educating adults in international development.

References

Andersson, Krister, and Auer, Matthew. 2005. "Incentives for contractors in aid-supported activities." In *The Samaritan's dilemma: The political economy of development aid*, edited by Clark Gibson, Krister Andersson, Elinor Ostrom, and Sujai Shivakumar, pp. 160–171. Oxford: Oxford University Press.
Berkvens, Jan, Kalyanpur, Maya, Kuiper, Wilmad, and Van den Akker, Jan. 2012. "Adult learning and professional development in a post-conflict area: The case of Cambodia." *International Journal of Educational Development* 32: 241–251.
Brookfield, Stephen. 1995. *Becoming a critically reflective teacher*. San Francisco, CA: Jossey-Bass.
Callahan, Jamie. 2013. "'Space, the final frontier': Social movements as organizing spaces for applying HRD." *Human Resource Development International* 16, no. 3: 298–312.

Coady Institute. (n.d.). "About us." Coady. http://coady.stfx.ca/coady/ (accessed September 9, 2016).

Crossley, Michael, and Holmes, Keith. 2001. "Challenges for educational research: International development, partnerships and capacity building in small states." *Oxford Review of Education* 27, no. 3: 395–409.

Ellis, Carolyn, and Bochner, Arthur. 2000. "Autoethnography, personal narrative, reflexivity: Researcher as subject." In *Handbook of qualitative research*, edited by Norman Denzin and Yvonna Lincoln, pp. 733–768. Thousand Oaks, CA: Sage.

English, Leona. 2004. "Third space/identity montage and international adult educators." In *Reimagining comparative education*, edited by Peter Ninnes and Sonja Mehta, pp. 225–240. London: Routledge-Falmer.

Escobar, Arturo. 1992. "Planning." In *The development dictionary: A guide to knowledge as power*, edited by Wolfgang Sachs, pp. 132–145. London: Zed Books.

Fenwick, Tara. 2014. "Conceptualizing critical HRD (CHRD): Tensions, dilemmas and possibilities." In *The Routledge companion to human resource development*, edited by Rob Poell, Tonette Rocco, and Gene Roth, pp. 113–123. New York: Routledge.

Freire, Paulo, and Macedo, Donaldo. 1987. *Literacy: Reading the word and the world*. South Hadley, MA: Bergin and Garvey.

Gedro, Julie, Mizzi, Robert C., Rocco, Tonette, and van Loo, Jasper. 2013. "Going global: Professional mobility and concerns for LGBT workers." *Human Resource Development International* 16, no. 3: 282–297.

Gosine, Andil. 2010. "The World Bank's GLOBE: Queers in/queering development." In *Development, sexual rights and global governance*, edited by Amy Lind, pp. 67–85. New York: Routledge.

Gronemeyer, Marianne. 1992. "Helping." In *The development dictionary: A guide to knowledge as power*, edited by Wolfgang Sachs, pp. 53–69. London: Zed Books.

Guy, Talmadge. 1999. "Culture as context for adult education: The need for culturally relevant adult education." *New Directions for Adult and Continuing Education* 82: 5–18.

Hayhurst, Lyndsay, MacNeill, Margaret, Kidd, Bruce, and Knoppers, Annelies. 2014. "Gender relations, gender-based violence and sport for development and peace: Questions, concerns and cautions emerging from Uganda." *Women's Studies International Forum* 47: 157–167.

Heinemann-Grüder, Andreas, and Grebenschikov, Igor. 2007. "Security governance by internationals: The case of Kosovo." In *Security sector reconstruction and reform in peace support operations*, edited by Michael Brzoska and David Law, pp. 31–46. London: Routledge.

Hill, Robert. 2013. "Queering the discourse: International adult education and learning." In *Learning with adults: A reader*, edited by Peter Mayo, pp. 87–98. Rotterdam: Sense.

Hinton, Rachel, and Groves, Leslie. 2004. "The complexity of inclusive aid." In *Inclusive aid: Changing power and relationships in international development*, edited by Leslie Groves and Rachel Hinton, pp. 3–19. London: Earthscan.

Johnson, Hazel, and Thomas, Alan. 2006. "Individual learning and building organizational capacity for development." *Public Administration and Development* 27: 39–48.

Johnson-Bailey, Juanita, and Cervero, Ronald. 1998. "Power dynamics in teaching and learning practices: An examination of two adult education classrooms." *International Journal of Lifelong Education* 17, no. 6: 389–399.

Jolly, Susie. 2007. *Why the development industry should get over its obsession with bad sex and start to think about pleasure*. IDS Working Paper 283. Brighton, UK: IDS

Jolly, Susie. 2011. "Why is development work so straight? Heteronormativity in the international development industry." *Development in Practice* 21, no.1: 18–28.

Kapoor, Ilan. 2008. *The postcolonial politics of development*. New York: Routledge.

Kothari, Uma. 2002. "Feminist and postcolonial challenges to development." In *Development theory and practice: Critical perspectives*, edited by Uma Kothari and Martin Minogue, pp. 35–51. New York: Palgrave.

Logue, Ann. 2001. "Trainer: Will travel." *Training and Development* 46–49. April.

Merriam, Sharan, Caffarella, Rosemary, and Baumgartner, Lisa. 2007. *Learning in adulthood: A comprehensive guide* (revised edn). San Francisco, CA: Jossey-Bass.

Mizzi, Robert C. 2010. "Unravelling researcher subjectivity through multivocality in autoethnography." *Journal of Research Practice* 6, no.1. Article M3. Retrieved from http://jrp.icaap.org/index.php/jrp/article/view/201/185.

Mizzi, Robert C. 2013. "'There aren't any gays here': Encountering heteroprofessionalism in an international development workplace." *Journal of Homosexuality* 60, no. 11: 1602–1624.

Mizzi, Robert C. 2014. "Troubling preparedness: Investigating the (in)visibility of LGBT concerns within pre-departure orientations." *Development in Practice* 24, no. 2: 286–297.

Mizzi, Robert C., and Hamm, Zane. 2013. "Canadian community development organizations, adult education and the internationalization of a pedagogical practice." In *Building on critical traditions: Adult education and learning in Canada*, edited by Tom Nesbit, Susan Brigham, Nancy Taber, and Tara Gibb, pp. 342–352. Toronto: Thompson Educational Publishing.

Mizzi, Robert C., and O'Brien-Klewchuk, Angela. 2016. "Preparing the transnational teacher: A textual analysis of pre-departure orientation manuals for teaching overseas." *Human Resource Development International* 19, no. 4: 329–344.

Nyerere, Julius. 1978. "'Development is for man, by man, and of man': The declaration of Dar es Salaam." In *Adult learning, a design for action: A comprehensive international survey*, edited by Budd Hall and J. Roby Kidd, pp. 27–36. Toronto: ICAE.

Pasteur, Katherine, and Scott-Villiers, Patta. 2004. "Minding the gap through organizational learning." In *Inclusive aid: Changing power and relationships in international development*, edited by Leslie Groves and Rachel Hinton, pp. 181–198. London: Earthscan.

Pharr, Suzanne. 1997. *Homophobia: A weapon of sexism*. Berkeley, CA: Chardon Press.

Piskurich, George. 2008. "Off-the-shelf materials." In *ASTD handbook for workplace learning professionals*, edited by Elaine Beich, pp. 283–292. Alexandria, VA: ASTD.

Sambrook, Sally Anne. 2014. "Critical HRD." *Handbook of human resource development*, edited by Neil Chalofsky, Tonette Rocco, and Michael Lane Morris, pp. 145–163. Hoboken, NJ: Wiley.

Smith, Kevin. 2013. "Covert critique: Critical pedagogy 'under the radar' in a suburban middle school." *International Journal of Critical Pedagogy* 4, no. 2: 127–146.

Spencer, Bruce. 2006. *The purposes of adult education: A short introduction*. Toronto, ON: Thompson Educational Publishing.

Waisbord, Silvio. 2006. "When training is insufficient: Reflections on capacity development in health promotion in Peru." *Health Promotion International* 21, no. 3: 230–237.

Watkins, Karen, and Marsick, Victoria. 2014. "Adult education and human resource development: Overlapping and disparate fields." *New Horizons in Adult Education and Human Resource Development* 26, no. 1: 42–54.

Watson, Keith. 1996. "Is small still beautiful in educational consulting and advisory work?" In *Consultancy and research in international education: The new dynamics*, edited by Lene Buchert and Kenneth King, pp. 193–200. Bonn: NORRAG.

Wright, Timothy. 2000. "Gay organizations, NGOs, and the globalization of sexual identity: The case of Bolivia." *Journal of Latin American Anthropology* 5, no. 2: 89–111.

3

QUEERYING DEVELOPMENT PLANNING

Recognizing needs and identifying vulnerable populations in Africa

Petra L. Doan

The issue of lesbian, gay, bisexual, transgender, and queer (LGBTQ) populations in the context of international development planning and institutions has not been well explored. The broader field of development studies has taken up this challenge, but planning continues to lag behind. This chapter aims to fill that gap by examining several examples from sub-Saharan Africa. In particular, the chapter explores some of the resistance to adopting more inclusive LGBTQ approaches to development planning from within the Western donor nations, and in particular from the evangelical community in the United States. In addition, the chapter considers the ways this resistance to LGBTQ inclusion is echoed in part by religious and political leaders in some sub-Saharan nations. Finally, the chapter considers the difficulties of planning for a vulnerable sub-population when identity categories are not stable and are colored by evolving understanding and expressions of sexuality and gender identity.

Two working papers (Anyamele et al. 2005; Jolly 2010a) have provided an important glimpse into shifting donor policy vis-à-vis the importance of recognizing the presence of and differential needs of LGBTQ populations. The first argued that it was essential to address the issue of men who have sex with men and women who have sex with women in order to get a handle on the HIV/AIDS problem. Both papers recognized that the marginalized status of LGBTQ people in many countries of the Global South made it urgent to provide development assistance to ameliorate their situation. Joseph (2010) also argued that HIV/AIDS work is essential to urban planning because much of the infected population lives and works under conditions of informality in the South African context.

In addition, two books have opened the door to a wider discussion of the place of LGBTQ issues within the field of human rights and development (Cornwall et al. 2008; Lind 2010). Cornwall et al. highlighted the fact that much development activity and policy has occurred in a highly heteronormative context, which has for the most part effaced sexuality from nearly all discussions of development policy. They maintained that "for mainstream development sex is treated as a health issue, to be dealt with by experts in disease prevention and health promotion" ignoring the pleasure and intimacy components of sexuality that are why most people engage in sexual relationships (5). Accordingly it is necessary to shift the conceptualization of sexuality from that of a negative problem to that of a positive force that makes some people's lives quite frankly bearable. Jolly (2010b) argued forcefully that development agencies need to get over their obsession with sex as negative (women as victims of bad sex and men as perpetrators of bad sex) and face the reality that sex is often about pleasure for people who are terribly marginalized. Lind (2010) suggested that development agencies too often view the family as a heteronormative construction and fail to consider the wide range of living situations in which non-normative people in the Global South are found. Development policy that has ignored these situations has often gone awry.

Several recent high-level policy statements have signaled broader recognition of LGBTQ issues. The United Nations Human Rights Council (UNHRC) has recently adopted a policy document that explicitly incorporates LGBTQ populations under the human rights umbrella, further adding to international support for sexual minorities (see UNHRC Report of November 2012). In the US context, former President Barack Obama issued a memorandum to all heads of agencies and departments emphasizing the importance of international initiatives to advance LGBTQ human rights (Obama 2011). In response, former Secretary of State Hillary Clinton issued a statement in December 2011 that LGBTQ rights are human rights. These statements marked a definitive shift in US foreign policy regarding the importance of considering LGBTQ populations. While on the surface such high visibility support is a huge step forward, the realities on the ground are much more complex. This chapter uses a queer theory perspective to ask whether institutions (the UN) and governments (the US and other Western powers) who are themselves supported by the heteropatriarchy (Elder 1995) can ever implement development policies that address the needs of the vast array of sexual minorities and gender identities across the globe. A queer lens necessarily critiques the notion that progress in terms of legislative recognition is sufficient. Rather Oswin (2014) suggests that queer theory

> interrogates heteronormativity beyond the heterosexual–homosexual binary and points out that the march of progress always entails the pitting of the properly domestic against the queer, even when gays and lesbians make it in from the margins. It details queerness as a stranding in a state of arrested development, as a constitutive casting out from the normal, the natural and the national.
>
> *(Oswin, 2014, 416)*

A variety of questions about development planning follow from this queer perspective. Does international recognition of LGBTQ rights as human rights really change the climate for planning at the local level, improving the lives of people whose various identities have resulted in their marginalization from mainstream society? Can such sweeping statements of "rights" really countermand the bias and oppression embedded in Western Judeo-Christian culture, as well as in post-colonial regimes in Africa? When hateful and discriminatory legislation has been adopted or is under consideration in places like Uganda, is it helpful for Western diplomats to use the "bully pulpit" to lecture sovereign nations about domestic policy? Does the adoption of constitutional protections for LGBTQ people in South Africa really provide protection for groups working at ground level to change conditions that enable LGBTQ people to live more openly and free from discrimination?

The consequences of lack of support for LGBTQ people in the Global South are clearly high. A recent World Bank report (Anyamele et al. 2005) noted that LGBTQ populations faced severe discrimination in most of these countries. Specific consequences include eviction from family homes and neighborhoods, loss of jobs, discrimination in health care, and high levels of violence including violence perpetrated by the police. These are familiar lists to LGBTQ activists and scholars working in Western contexts but it is rare to hear development agencies addressing these kinds of problems explicitly, though this trend may be shifting (Jolly 2011). For example, a recent report by consultants to the United Nations Development Programme (UNDP) highlighted that full social inclusion of transgender individuals is sorely lacking and yet must be seen as a critical element in the global fight against HIV/AIDS (Divan et al. 2016).

The queer theory perspective permits us to identify the struggles for full inclusion as a form of disciplinary discourse that Michel Foucault (1978) would clearly recognize. In the context of planning issues within the United States, there are real issues linked to heteronormative resistance to recognizing and protecting LGBTQ spaces (Doan 2011). For example, in Atlanta planners and municipal officials failed to identify and plan for the presence of a gay neighborhood, resulting in the redevelopment of the area and the loss of many LGBTQ businesses (Doan and Higgins 2011). In North America there is an ongoing struggle to find ways to plan for inclusive LGBTQ spaces (Doan 2015).

In the Global South the problem is further complicated by the need to unpack both long-standing colonial as well as neo-colonial and neo-liberal influences. The anti-LGBTQ policies that some scholars and development practitioners in the West find so hateful are frequently a result of colonial regimes that attempted to discipline sexuality as a means of controlling "native" populations. Colonial administrators often used urban planning to create a "cordon sanitaire" around the administrative hub of the city to protect themselves from being infected by the "dangerous customs" and "perverse behaviors" of the long time inhabitants of these countries (King 1990; Njoh 2009; Beeckmans 2013). Stoler (1989) describes the set of racist and class specific values that drove "colonial distinctions of difference, linking fears of sexual contamination, physical danger, climatic incompatibility, and moral breakdown" (636) of European colonizers. These same regimes colluded with evangelical missionaries to "civilize" and bring religion to the heathens in the hopes of saving their souls, but also disciplining their behaviors.

Sub-Saharan Africa has been much in the news in the past few years regarding issues of sexual orientation and gender identity and, as such, it provides a useful lens through which to examine this delicate problem of how to make development planning more inclusive of LGBTQ populations, thereby ensuring basic justice, social welfare, and economic opportunity of this marginalized community. The question that will be addressed in this chapter is what are the implications of these changes for development planning efforts around the globe, but especially in the Global South?

The practical realities of developing more inclusive policies and programs must be cognizant of the deep-seated resistance to this change and take note of the very real constraints to progress in this area. These constraints can be divided into three general areas: 1) resistance to LGBTQ-inclusive policies on the part of conservative forces in the United States, 2) resistance to LGBTQ-inclusive policies from conservative forces in the Global South, and 3) difficulties in identifying LGBTQ populations in the context of overt hostility, violence, and evolving identities. The intent here is not to dissuade development practitioners from engaging with these issues, but in keeping with good planning processes it is essential to survey the threats to moving forward before developing a clear plan for improvement.

Resistance to LGBTQ-inclusive policies within the United States

One reason for the failure of development agencies to embrace issues of non-normative sexuality and gender is that there are still very intense levels of resistance to LGBTQ issues within social conservatives in the West, and especially in the United States. Since development agencies and non-governmental organizations (NGOs) are ultimately dependent upon the largesse of governments and charitable donors, they inevitably shy away from controversy, enabling a kind of difficult silencing of development workers around this issue. For instance, in November 2012 I participated in a panel on LGBTQ issues in development planning that occurred just prior to the US general election in the state of Ohio. Unfortunately one of the panelists was unable to join the panel because her superiors at the United States Agency for International Development (USAID) decided that talking about LGBTQ issues in development planning was too sensitive. At the last minute she was told that she could not present her work on building networks and strengthening LGBTQ civil society in Africa. Perhaps the closely contested national election in 2012 triggered this decision to "silence" a senior staff member because the conference was held in the key swing state of Ohio. Whatever the reason for the rescinded travel permission, this situation is one example of the kind of silencing that constrains wider debate and discussion within the US context. The election of Donald Trump in November 2016 makes the issue of support for LGBTQ rights even more fraught.

Although polls show a majority of Americans now are in support of LGBTQ people and the Supreme Court decision in favor of same-sex marriage, there are still many people for whom LGBTQ issues remain a hot button issue. In other Western countries development organizations and NGOs face similar pressure, creating a kind of collective silencing of discussion about policies to address the discrimination and violence faced by LGBTQ people in the Global South.

Resistance to LGBTQ-inclusive policies within the Global South

Another challenging component of resistance to LGBTQ development policies is from anti-LGBTQ groups within the Global South. These groups include government officials, church leaders, and some local NGOs whose pronouncements about the venality of gays and lesbians are often quite shocking. The Zimbabwean President, Robert Mugabe, is perhaps the most outspoken opponent of gays and lesbians on the continent. A recent Zimbabwean newspaper article provides the following quote:

> In 1995, government shut down a book exhibit by Galz [Gays and Lesbians Zimbabwe] at the Harare International Book Fair after which Mugabe declared: "Homosexuals are worse than dogs and pigs; dogs and pigs will never engage in homosexual madness; even insects won't do it."
>
> *(Zhangazha 2015)*

While this is the most visible and often repeated quote from an African leader, it exemplifies resistance to LGBTQ inclusion from a range of other perspectives. Scholars who have looked at these claims find them deeply flawed. Epprecht (2008) provides a closer reading of anthropological reports and field notes, suggesting that sexuality is as diverse in Africa as in any other continent and that the claim that homosexuality does not exist in Africa is patently false.

What is the source of this resistance? It is very important for development planners wishing to engage with this issue to reflect on this discourse. The history of colonial interventions with regard to the sexuality of African peoples has been extremely negative. Tamale (2011) argues that colonial powers used misconceptions about primitive African sexuality to "other" and subjugate African women and men. "Through religion and its proselytizing activities, Africans were encouraged to reject their previous beliefs and values and adopt the 'civilised ways' of the whites" (16). Tamale goes on to describe Western researchers with "a voyeuristic, ethno-pornographic obsession with what they perceived as exotic (read perverse) African sexual cultures … The standard approach was to view these sexual cultures as primitive, bizarre and dangerous and apply a knee-jerk reflex to 'fix' them" (19).

Given that religion was often the tool for colonial control, it is understandable that it also became a mechanism for maintaining the post-colonial status quo. Sadgrove et al. (2012) argue that homosexuality has been illegal in Uganda since the colonial period, under British legislation outlawing "carnal knowledge" that might undermine the colonialist order. Epprecht (2008) provides convincing evidence that the colonial regimes and the African elites who replaced them used a Foucaultian discourse of heteronormativity to try to efface any forms of deviant sexuality. Is it any wonder then that current African leadership now shies away from another group of Western "invaders" telling them what to do with regard to their intimate lives? But upon closer examination, much of the support for this anti-LGBTQ policy may in fact also have its roots in current Western homophobia. The Ugandan situation provides some useful insights.

The consequences of the Ugandan Anti-Gay Bill

The case of the Ugandan Anti-Gay Bill introduced in 2009 is a rich illustration of this process at work. Ugandan MP David Bahati introduced this bill to criminalize homosexuality and make serial homosexuality punishable by death (see Gettleman 2010; Sadgrove et al. 2012). When British Prime Minister David Cameron and US Secretary of State Hillary Clinton both complained and threatened to reduce development assistance if such a law was passed, a Ugandan presidential advisor reported the government's outrage at Western interference. "That fellow [Mr Cameron] said the same thing. Now this woman [Clinton] is interfering. If the Americans think they can tell us what to do, they can go to hell" (Chothia 2011). The bill has been subsequently amended to change the penalty to life in prison and the amended bill was passed in 2013 and signed into law in 2014.

There is a strong link between the US evangelical movement and the instigators of the "anti-gay bill" that was passed by the Ugandan legislature. A meeting including both US and Uganda evangelical leaders held in Uganda prior to the introduction of this bill in October 2009 was the stimulus for the passage of this bill. At this meeting US evangelicals described the "gay agenda" of sodomizing young boys to convert Ugandan children to homosexuality (Gettleman 2010). It appears that only those interest groups, such as these evangelicals, that align with themselves with local leadership are allowed to have such significant influence on domestic policy in Uganda.

A useful example is provided by Hoad's (2007) description of the alliance forged between ultra-conservative US Anglicans and their African allies before the 1998 Lambeth Conference of Anglican Bishops. The intent of this effort was to organize against what they saw as the "pro-gay" agenda of more liberal Anglicans. US Bishop Barbara Harris, the first black woman Bishop, suggested that one of the key differences resulting in divergent policy was the exercise of the near absolute authority wielded by African diocesan bishops. Harris goes on to say, the vitriolic, fundamentalist rhetoric of some African, Asian and other bishops of color, who were in the majority, was in my opinion reflective of the European and North American missionary influence propounded in the Southern Hemisphere during the 18th, 19th and early 20th centuries.

(As cited in Hoad, 2007, 64)

Sadgrove et al. (2012) suggested that within the worldwide Anglican Community, African Bishops continued to hold a firm line against any movement that is more inclusive of gay ordination, refusing to allow openly gay Bishop Gene Robinson to be seated at the Lambeth Conference in 2008. Furthermore, Anglican Archbishop Peter Akinola of Nigeria has the support of US churches opposed to the ordination of gay bishops and sent a letter highly critical of LGBTQ issues to the Archbishop of Canterbury (Kaoma 2012).

Returning to the case of Uganda, the central issue is that passage of the anti-gay bill has created a situation that remains critical for the LGBTQ population. Ugandan authorities appear bent on displaying a kind of necropolitics (Mbembe 2003) towards LGBTQ individuals to demonstrate their ability to control who lives and who dies. For example, the murder of David Kato (Rice 2011; BBC News 2011), one of the organizers of SMUG – Sexual Minorities Uganda – after he was outed as gay in the Ugandan tabloid press, was an egregious example of necropolitics. Furthermore, Peters (2016) described the ways that deeply embedded fears of being outed have had very serious consequences on Ugandan transgender women infected with HIV. In response, some LGBTQ Ugandans fled to Kenya (Igunza 2015), though their situation in that neighboring country was also precarious. In this highly charged atmosphere, it is extremely difficult to undertake rational planning of inclusive development measures. Clearly there is an urgent need for donor agencies to step up their work to provide assistance and support to this highly vulnerable population, but many LGBTQ Ugandans refused to stay in the initial refugee camp set up for them by the Kenyan authorities, further complicating the task of identifying the most vulnerable (Zomorodi 2016). Expectations of swift resettlement to more supportive Western countries have been deflated and many of this vulnerable community continue to wait both in camps and in Nairobi.

The consequences of including LGBTQ equality in South Africa's Constitution

South Africa illustrates a different situation where instead of legislation intended to harm LGBTQ people, the constitution contains an equality clause intended to protect them. However, as the following case illustrates, constitutional protection may not provide sufficient protection in the absence of more widespread support. The passage of South Africa's 1994 Constitution with a progressive equality clause with the Bill of Rights that enshrined the right of non-discrimination based on sexual orientation provided hope to many LGBTQ people across Africa. Van Zyl (2005) argues that the adoption of South Africa's Constitution validated the citizenship of queer South Africans and yet

has undoubtedly changed many people's perceptions about themselves, and given them a possibility for "respectability"… However, apart from the creation of new black elites the dynamics of economic power have remained mostly unaltered for the majority of South Africans – whites (12% of the population) still earn more than half of the country's income.

(Van Zyl, 2005, 26–27).

Just as inclusion in the constitution does not ensure full economic participation for black and colored people, it also does not fully protect LGBTQ people. Constitutional protections may provide a measure of legitimacy for LGBTQ individuals in South Africa, but the equality clause has done little to diminish homophobia in many areas of the country. There is considerable resistance from some policy-makers and government leaders to passing legislation that would protect South Africans from continuing anti-LGBTQ violence because some leaders accept that "homophobic victimization is an endemic part of the South African landscape" (Nel and Judge 2008, 19). Ratele (2006) suggests that violence against women and lesbians is linked to the ways that "power both defines and shields the transgressions of those who wield authority in society" (60). Furthermore, a report prepared for the Institute of Development Studies in the UK suggests that "the prejudice expressed by national leaders in South Africa towards those who do not follow the codes of hetero-normative patriarchy authorizes the violence of those who rape and murder lesbian women" (Lewin et al. 2013, 25). It is hardly surprising that corrective rapes still happen to lesbians in South Africa with alarming frequency (Fihlani 2011).

The gap between what is written in the constitution and the actual practice of homophobia by some individuals presents challenges to development planners seeking to ensure the safety of LGBTQ individuals. Van Zyl (2011) suggests that not all identities are recognized and therefore protected.

> In this process of (re)fashioning heterosexual patriarchal "African" identities, collective identities relating to different gender and sexual norms are effectively erased from the equality clause—for example, queers, female-headed households, unmarried mothers, pregnant teenagers, and people living with HIV and AIDS— remaining at the margins of society and denied full citizenship.
>
> *(Van Zyll, 2011, 351)*

The task of planning for these disparate groups in the South African context is in fact quite challenging. Tucker's excellent monograph (2009) on visibility and invisibility among different racial groups within the queer community problematizes the notion that there is a single LGBTQ community. In her study of three organizations involved in marketing Cape Town as a queer vacation mecca, Oswin (2005) notes that the "link between visibility and tolerance is tempered by the recognition that these organizations have limited reach in a gay and lesbian community severely divided, particularly along class and race lines" (575). Western derived concepts frequently used in planning strategies for LGBTQ communities such as gayborhoods are also not very helpful since poor, black gay men are unlikely to find acceptance in what are usually considered "white leisure spaces" (Visser 2013). The situation in South Africa demonstrates the ongoing struggle to de-link homophobia and hetero-nationalism wrapped up in the post-colonial necropolitics described by Mbembe (2003). It is critical to recognize that even in South Africa, colonial and post-colonial homophobia are intricately linked making it essential to increase the visibility of the ways that "same-sex practices disturb and threaten gendered relations of reproduction, and systems of social regulation of reproduction" (van Zyl 2005, 32).

Difficulties in identifying LGBTQ stakeholders

Hillary Clinton's announcement that LGBT rights are human rights was at once very welcome and very problematic. One commentator suggested that the $3 million in grants to advance LGBTQ rights on the African continent was taken by conservatives as proof positive of their argument that the West is imposing its own sexual values by investing huge sums of money (Kaoma 2012). Clearly, overt development assistance to LGBTQ groups will be subjected to attacks both from within donor countries and by groups within countries receiving foreign assistance, making LGBTQ-inclusive development policies very difficult to implement. Such difficulties do not mean that inclusive policies should be ignored, but development planners must recognize the conflicted nature of these efforts as they move forward.

Gender and sexuality in Africa, as everywhere, are highly contextual and spatially contingent. Simple categories are not terribly functional. Even the identities of gay and lesbian, which to most Americans seem quite clear, are Western constructions that are not always accepted in the African context. Not that men don't have sex with men and women don't have sex with women, but the Western-based identities are problematic. As previously noted, the long history of Westerners imposing gender and sexual regimes upon Africans makes this particularly difficult. For instance, Ifi Amadiume (1987) described the penetration of large parts of Africa by Christian missionaries under the protection and often outright sponsorship of colonial authorities that was incredibly destructive of traditional religious practice and undermined non-Western conceptions of gender and sexuality. Amadiume (1987) argues that missionaries among the Igbo people of Nigeria provided schools that only "Christians" could attend and used this mechanism to undermine traditional understandings of gender roles and religious practice. Furthermore, most of the children educated in these schools were men, further entrenching male dominance and eroding the long-standing status of women in the area, and especially gender roles which were not understood by Western Christians. Notable among these were the Ekwe title which enabled a woman to become a "female husband" and marry other women. Another key traditional gender role – a "male daughter" who in the absence of sons was able to inherit her father's land and property – was also undermined.

While these non-normative gender roles (or non-normative within the Judeo-Christian tradition) are not described as what would today be termed sexual orientation, they do raise interesting questions about the nature of the relationship between these female husbands and their wives. Amadiume (1987) argues passionately that such women should not be understood as lesbian, but this appears to be another case of an African scholar refusing to label Africans with the Western identity of "lesbian" at the same time omitting any discussion of their sexual relations.

Another group of people in Nigeria that seem to be part of the queer community are the Yan Daudu whose non-normative sexuality transcends easy categorization (Gaudio 2009). These individuals exhibit feminine characteristics, call themselves by special women's names, usually entertain men, and have sexual relations with men, but some also clearly identify as Muslim and have made the Haj to demonstrate their adherence to the tenets of their religion.

In the South African context, there are also very clear tensions over variations in gender identity. Schwenke (2010) suggests that in much of Africa trans people are frequently "disempowered victims of a society and a government that humiliates, ridicules, ignores, or all too commonly treats them with extreme violence and rejection" (187). Accordingly, many flee their native countries for the relative safety of places like South Africa where the Alternation of Sex Description and Sex Status Act of 2003 provides some legal benefits to transgender and intersex individuals. However, Sibusiso Kheswa (2014) notes that South Africa is not really a safe haven for gender non-conforming people from elsewhere in Africa, because they are unable to change their sex status given their immigrant non-citizen status. Furthermore, because of social stigma many transgender Africans are "currently invisible in epidemiological research, and they are almost certainly being ignored" (Jobson et al. 2012, 161). Some gender non-conforming individuals live in a place of in-between as shown by the following quote.

> I am an in-between and a beyond. I exist between normalized binaries and beyond those binaries. An in-between: something that does not quite sit in very well and when it does sit, it is somewhere between a pair of shorts and a pair of trousers Too long to be shorts, not long enough to be trousers, like badly fitted harem pants. This is the in-between world of belonging and not quite belonging.
>
> *(Musang 2014, 49)*

A key question for development planners and practitioners working in the area of LGBTQ rights is how do you identify a sub-population that is well hidden and is already experiencing severe discrimination? USAID's recent project evaluation guidance document (USAID 2011) required all development project papers to explore the impacts of the projects on LGBTQ stakeholders. On the surface this new guidance seems an important step forward, but is enormously complicated in reality. In the US context, we do a very poor job of identifying LGBTQ stakeholders to urban development projects (see the previously cited Atlanta example in Doan and Higgins 2011). How then can we expect that temporary project consultants flown into a country to write a project proposal will have any understanding of the actual impacts on local LGBTQ populations in Africa?

The answer is clearly that without careful ties to local LGBTQ community groups this undertaking is simply not possible. Support for local LGBTQ networks is therefore essential to developing inclusive projects. Nyanzi (2013) argues that in spite of the anti-homosexuality bill in Uganda, activism among LGBTQ Ugandans is rising.

> Swimming against the homophobic tide driven by African national and religious leaders, self-identified homosexual men, women and transgender people actively carve out new spaces and reclaim old terrains in which they enact non-heteronormative sexualities. They simultaneously claim their dual identities as African Ugandans and homosexual individuals.
>
> *(Nyanzi 2013, 963)*

The task for development planners is to find ways of supporting these efforts.

Similarly, Theron and Kgositau (2015) provide a rich description of a new trans archive that is developing in South Africa that aims to document the history of trans people in Africa as well as their struggles to achieve legal recognition in the face of homophobic and transphobic attitudes. Both authors were associated for a time with a highly dynamic trans group (Gender DynamiX), and they note that since "the founding of Gender DynamiX, followed by the mushrooming of new organizations in 2008 and 2009, a number of gains have been accomplished" (581). Kheswa (2014) describes a more recent role of Gender DynamiX as helping asylum-seeking immigrants who have fled to South Africa because they were targeted for violence or imprisonment in their home countries because of their identity, but in reality they have woefully inadequate resources to undertake this work. Once again it seems hugely important for development planners to first identify and then listen to what these vulnerable groups see as the most critical issues for their communities. Once the issues are well understood, then specific measures to strengthen indigenous planning capacity and development policy-making might be useful.

Conclusions: urgency of finding and supporting queer African voices

Anyamele et al. (2005) suggest that strengthening LGBTQ groups in Africa is vital to the safety of this population. Currier (2010) suggests that local African groups like Behind the Mask in the South African context and elsewhere may be the way forward. Local LGBTQ groups exist but are inadequately funded and have been largely ignored as part of the plethora of civil society groups that often receive foreign assistance. This trend is changing, but levels of funding and overall support need to be dramatically increased. Such groups exist and are the best way of reaching groups that are otherwise virtually invisible. With effective support such groups also may be able to take counter-measures in what has become an ongoing struggle for autonomy. The suit by SMUG against David Lively, one of the pastors who attended the meeting in Uganda that incited the anti-gay bill (BBC News 2012), was recently remanded due to lack of standing although the judge found that considerable harm had been done by Lively to people in Uganda.

The increasing donor interest in supporting transgender programming may be partly responsible for the inclusion of transgender in LGBTQ organizing in Namibia and South Africa (Currier 2015). However, Currier cautions against dismissing the resulting programs since even "hastily assembled programs might be better than the alternative: no services or resources for transgender and gender-variant constituents" (110). In this case some intervention may be better than none, but still not sufficient. Husakouskaya (2017) argues that even with this increased attention the needs of transgender internal migrants within South Africa are not adequately addressed.

Development planners must be acutely aware that visibility can be extremely dangerous, as is made crystal clear by David Kato's murder (BBC News 2011). Another meeting of Ugandan LGBTQ activists held in June 2012 at a local hotel was shut down by the police, and the government minister in charge of the raid announced that 38 Ugandan organizations would be banned for "promoting homosexual behavior" (Smith 2012).

So there remains a very real question about how development planners can move this agenda forward. It is indeed a very delicate path, but the fragility of this highly charged territory does not mean we should continue to silence ourselves about the needs on the ground. In other circumstances academics opposed to human rights policies in various difficult contexts have banded together to take action in support of colleagues who for a variety of reasons must work behind the scenes or "behind the mask." Clearly greater emphasis on building international networks to support and sustain local LGBTQ activists would be helpful. Funding from development agencies to support institution building within individual countries and across continents is part of the picture, but unlikely to be sufficient. Support for networking among larger groupings of scholars and activists is also likely to be an important way of ensuring that conversations happen and this problem is not placed on the back burner or in some dark closet until the political atmosphere seems more conducive.

References

Amadiume, Ifi. 1987. *Male Daughters, Female Husbands: Gender and Sex in an African Society*. London: Zed Books.

Anyamele, C, Lwabaayi, Nguyen T, Binswanger, H. 2005. *Sexual Minorities, Violence, and AIDS in Africa*. Africa Region Working Paper Series, No. 84. Washington, DC: The World Bank.

BBC News. 2011. "Uganda gay rights activist David Kato killed," January 27, http://www.bbc.co.uk/news/world-africa-12295718

BBC News. 2012. "Uganda gay group sues US minister over anti-gay bill," March 15, http://www.bbc.co.uk/news/world-us-canada-17387887

Beeckmans, L. 2013. "Editing the African city: reading colonial planning in Africa from a comparative perspective," *Planning Perspectives*, 28, no. 4: 615–627.

Chothia, F. 2011. "Gay rights: Africa, the new frontier," BBC Africa, 7 December 2011. Available at: http://www.bbc.com/news/world-africa-16068010

Cornwall, A, Correa, S, Jolly, S. (eds.) 2008. *Development with a Body: Sexuality, Human Rights and Development*. London: Zed Books.

Currier, A. 2010. "Behind the mask: developing LGBTI visibility in Africa." In *Development Sexual Rights and Global Governance*, edited by Amy Lind, pp. 155–168. London: Routledge.

Currier, A. 2015. "Transgender invisibility in Namibian and South African LGBT organizing," *Feminist Formations*, 27, no. 1: 91–117.

Divan, V, Cortez, C, Smelyanskaya, M, Keatley, J. 2016. "Transgender social inclusion and equality: a pivotal path to development," *Journal of the International AIDS Society*, 19, no. 2, http://dx.doi.org/10.7448/IAS.19.3.20803

Doan, PL. (ed.). 2011. *Queerying Planning: Challenging Heteronormative Assumptions and Reframing Planning Practice*. Farnham: Ashgate.

Doan, PL. (ed.). 2015. *Planning and LGBTQ Communities: the Need for Inclusive Queer Space*. London: Routledge.

Doan, P, Higgins, H. 2011. "The demise of queer space? Resurgent gentrification and the assimilation of LGBT neighborhoods," *Journal of Planning Education and Research*, 31, no. 1: 6–25.

Elder, G. 1995. "Of moffies, kaffirs, and perverts: male homosexuality and the discourse of moral order in the apartheid state." In *Mapping Desire*, edited by David Bell and Gil Valentine, pp. 56–65. New York: Routledge.

Epprecht, M. 2008. *Heterosexual Africa?: The History of an Idea from the Age of Exploration to the Age of AIDS*. Athens, OH: Ohio University Press.

Fihlani, P. 2011. "South Africa's lesbians fear 'corrective rape'," BBC News, Cape Town, June 29, 2011, http://www.bbc.co.uk/news/world-africa-13908662

Foucault, M. 1978. *The History of Sexuality, Volume 1: An Introduction*. Robert Hurley, trans. New York: Random House.

Gaudio, RP. 2009. *Allah Made Us: Sexual Outlaws in an Islamic African City*. Chichester, UK: John Wiley & Sons.

Gettleman, J. 2010. "Americans' role seen in Uganda anti-gay push," *The New York Times*, January 3, 2010, http://www.nytimes.com/2010/01/04/world/africa/04uganda.html?_r=1

Hoad, N. 2007. *African Intimacies: Race, Homosexuality, and Globalization*. Minneapolis, MN: University of Minnesota Press.

Husakouskaya, N. 2017. "Queering mobility in urban Gauteng: transgender internal migrants and their experiences of 'transition' in Johannesburg and Pretoria," *Urban Forum*, 28: 91–110.

Igunza, E. 2015. "Gay Ugandans regret fleeing to Kenya," BBC Africa, 10 November 2015. Available at: http://www.bbc.com/news/world-africa-34764968

Jobson, G, Liesl, A, Theron, B, Kaggwa, JK, Kim, H-J. 2012. "Transgender in Africa: invisible, inaccessible, or ignored?" *SAHARA-J: Journal of Social Aspects of HIV/AIDS* 9, no. 3: 160–163.

Jolly, S. 2010a. "Poverty and sexuality: what are the connections?" Study commissioned by the Swedish International Development Agency, http://www.sxpolitics.org/wp-content/uploads/2011/05/sida-study-of-poverty-and-sexuality1.pdf

Jolly, S. 2010b. "Why the development industry should give up its obsession with bad sex and start to think about pleasure." In *Development Sexual Rights and Global Governance*, edited by Amy Lind, pp. 23–38. London: Routledge.

Jolly, S. 2011. "Why is development work so straight? Heteronormativity in the international development industry," *Development in Practice*, 21, no. 1: 18–28.

Joseph, S. 2010. "Tackling informality: why HIV/AIDS needs to be a critical component of urban development policies," *Urban Forum*, 21: 85–105.

Kaoma, K. 2012. "Exporting the anti-gay movement: how sexual minorities in Africa became collateral damage in the U.S. culture wars," *The American Prospect*, April 24, http://prospect.org/article/exporting-anti-gay-movement

Kheswa, S. 2014. "Negotiating personhood: what it's like being transgender in South Africa." In *Reclaiming Afrikan: Queer Perspectives on Sexual and Gender Identities*, curated by Zethu Matabeni, pp. 67–70. Athlone, South Africa: Modjaji Books.

King, Anthony D. 1990. *Urbanism, Colonialism and the World Economy: Cultural and Spatial Foundations of the World Urban System*. London: Routledge.

Lewin, T, Williams, K, Thomas, K. 2013. "A progressive constitution meets lived reality: sexuality and the law in South Africa," Institute of Development Studies Evidence Report 7. Brighton: IDS. https://opendocs.ids.ac.uk/opendocs/bitstream/handle/123456789/2705/ER7%20Final%20Online.pdf?sequence=1&isAllowed=y

Lind, A. (ed.). 2010. *Development, Sexual Rights and Global Governance*. New York: Routledge

Mbembe, JA. 2003. "Necropolitics," translated by Libby Meintjes, *Public Culture*, 15, no. 1: 11–40.

Musang, Neo. 2014. "In time and space." In *Reclaiming Afrikan: Queer Perspectives on Sexual and Gender Identities*, curated by Zethu Matabeni, pp. 49–55. Athlone, South Africa: Modjaji Books.

Nel, J, Judge, M. 2008. "Exploring homophobic victimization in Gauteng, South Africa: issues, impacts and responses," *Acta Criminologica: Southern African Journal of Criminology*, 21, no. 3: 19–36.

Njoh, AJ. 2009. "Urban planning as a tool of power and social control in colonial Africa," *Planning Perspectives*, 24, no. 3: 301–317.

Nyanzi, S. 2013. "Dismantling reified African culture through localised homosexualities in Uganda," *Culture, Health & Sexuality*, 15, no. 8: 952–967.

Obama, B. 2011. "International initiatives to advance the human rights of lesbian, gay, bisexual, and transgender persons," The White House: presidential memorandum, https://obamawhitehouse.archives.gov/the-press-office/2011/12/06/presidential-memorandum-international-initiatives-advance-human-rights-l

Oswin, N. 2005. "Researching 'gay Cape Town' finding value-added queerness," *Social & Cultural Geography* 6, no. 4: 567–586.

Oswin, N. 2014. "Queer time in global city Singapore: neoliberal futures and the 'freedom to love'," *Sexualities*, 17, no. 4: 412–433.

Peters, MM. 2016. "'They wrote "gay" on her file': transgender Ugandans in HIV prevention and treatment," *Culture, Health & Sexuality*, 18, no. 1: 84–98.

Ratele, K. 2006. "Ruling masculinity and sexuality," *Feminist Africa: Special Issue on Subaltern Sexualities*, 6: 48–63.

Rice, Xan. 2011. "Ugandan gay rights activist David Kato found murdered," *The Guardian*, January 27, http://www.guardian.co.uk/world/2011/jan/27/ugandan-gay-rights-activist-murdered

Sadgrove, J, Vanderbeck, RM, Andersson, J, Valentine, G, Ward, K. 2012. "Morality plays and money matters: towards a situated understanding of the politics of homosexuality in Uganda," *The Journal of Modern African Studies*, 50: 103–129.

Schwenke, C. 2010. "Empowerment and transgender," *Development*, 53, no. 2: 187–190.

Smith, D. 2012. "Uganda bans 38 organizations accused of 'promoting homosexuality'," *The Guardian*, June 20, http://www.guardian.co.uk/world/2012/jun/20/uganda-bans-organisations-promoting-homosexuality

Stoler, A. 1989. "Making empire respectable: the politics of race and sexual morality in 20th-century colonial cultures," *American Ethnologist: Journal of the American Ethnological Society*, 16, no. 4: 634–660

Tamale, S. (ed.). 2011. *African Sexualities: A Reader*. Cape Town: Pambazuka Press.

Theron, L, Kgositau, TR. 2015. "The emergence of a grassroots African trans Archive," *TSQ: Transgender Studies Quarterly*, 2, no. 4: 578–583.

Tucker, A. 2009. *Queer Visibilities: Space, Identity, and Interaction in Cape Town*. Chichester, UK: Wiley-Blackwell.

UNHRC. 2012. *Born Free and Equal: Sexual Orientation and Gender Identity in International Human Rights Law*. United Nations. Human Rights Council. HR/PUB/12/06

USAID. 2011. *Project Evaluation Guidance*. Washington, DC: US Agency for International Development.

Van Zyl, M. 2005. "Shaping sexualities – per(trans)forming queer." In *Performing Queer: Shaping Sexualities 1994-2004 – Volume One*, edited by Mikki Van Zyl and Melissa Steyn, pp. 19–36. Roggebaai, South Africa: Kwela Books.

Van Zyl, M. 2011. "Are same-sex marriages unAfrican? Same-sex relationships and belonging in post-apartheid South Africa," *Journal of Social Issues*, 67, no. 2: 335–357.

Visser, G. 2013. "Challenging the gay ghetto in South Africa: time to move on?" *Geoforum*, 49: 268–274.

Zhangazha, W. 2015. "Mugabe comes face-to-face with gays," *Zimbabwe Independent*, November 27, 2015, https://www.theindependent.co.zw/2015/11/27/mugabe-comes-face-to-face-with-gays/

Zomorodi, G. 2016. "Responding to LGBT forced migration in East Africa," *Forced Migration Review*, 52: 91–93.

4

GENDER, SEXUALITY AND DEVELOPMENT

Avenues for action in a post-2015 development era

Chloé Vaast and Elizabeth Mills

The recently adopted Sustainable Development Goals (SDGs) reflect a hard-won global consensus, at a policy level, that poverty is multidimensional and that any sustained response to multidimensional poverty should be grounded in a human rights approach to ensure that no one is excluded from the benefits of development. The commitment to eradicating exclusion and marginalization is reflected in the language of the SDGs, as they call for development to 'leave no one behind'. This recent commitment in international development reflects a longstanding argument made by development practitioners that, "[i]t is no longer possible to ignore discrimination, inequality and social exclusion and their developmental consequences" (Cornwall and Jolly 2006, 1).

> Yet when it comes to the economic, social, political and human rights implications of sex and sexuality, there is a silence at the heart of mainstream development. Consigned to being treated as a health issue, or disregarded altogether as a "luxury", sexuality barely features in development debates.
>
> *(Ibid., 1)*

Cornwall, Corrêa and Jolly (2008) go on to argue that inclusive and meaningful development is one that has 'a body'; this requires a conceptual expansion in which approaches to inequality go beyond describing sexual and gender norms and towards unpacking and addressing social and power relations as they are embodied (see also Jolly 2000). Despite building a case for this argument over a decade ago with a global network of colleagues around the world in the groundbreaking text *Development with a Body*, Cornwall, Corrêa and Jolly's case still stands: development policy and practice continue to approach sexuality and gender through a heteronormative lens.

We draw on this legacy of research in gender, sexuality and development, with an aim to understand and address the mechanisms of 'social exclusion' in the post-2015 development era. We consider social exclusion as it operates, first, at a societal level, reinforced through punitive laws and cisnormative policies; and second, at an institutional and infrastructural level, often through the absence of services that can address multidimensional poverty among sexual and gender minorities. We conducted a systematic policy and literature review of 65 empirical studies that documented linkages between social exclusion and poverty among sexual and gender minorities. In this chapter we apply these findings to the SDG framework in order to advance a sexual orientation, gender identity and expression (SOGIE)-sensitive development framework, in which no one is 'left behind'.

Social exclusion: a relational process of marginalization

Development is a process through which an individual, a community or a nation can progress economically, socially, culturally, psychologically and spiritually. The centre of any development is the human being, and human wellbeing is the ultimate goal of development.... All this calls for a broader perspective on development policies and programs through which the nexus of poverty, discrimination and environmental degradation can be addressed. It points to the need of understanding the increasingly complex drivers of persistent poverty at societal and ecological margins.

(von Braun and Gatzweiler 2014, 11)

René Lenoir, who published 'Les Exclus: Un Francais sur dix' in 1974, originally used the term 'the excluded' to refer to the poor, the disabled, the suicidal, the elderly, abused children, drug addicts, single parents, and other marginalized individuals (Haan 1998; Sen 2000; Silver 1994). As a concept, 'social exclusion' gained momentum in French policy discourse during the 1980s (Haan 1998; Silver 1994) and was later adopted by other European counties within the context of social funding and anti-poverty programmes (Haan 1998; Kabeer 2005; Silver 1994). Those using the term 'social exclusion' preferred it to 'poverty', as the former term is not charged with the same stigma as the latter (Estivill 2003). Social exclusion was considered as a framework for in-depth analysis of the social, economic and political causes and consequences of poverty, beyond income inequality alone (Fraser 2010; Jackson 1999).

While conceptualization of social exclusion has diversified over the past three decades, it has generally been understood as the 'opposite of social integration' or inclusion (Estivill 2003; Haan 1998; Silver 1994). In analysing the exclusion of queer people[1] in international policy, as represented by the SDGs, it is useful to understand social exclusion as a relational process through which people become excluded in societies. For this purpose we draw on the definition of social exclusion provided by Estivill (2003, 19):

Social exclusion may therefore be understood as an accumulation of confluent processes with successive ruptures arising from the heart of the economy, politics and society, which gradually distances and places persons, groups, communities and territories in a position of inferiority in relation to centres of power, resources and prevailing values.

While the term itself suggests that exclusion is 'social', theorists have described how social exclusion operates in at least three interlinked spheres, extending beyond the social to include economic and political spheres. The social aspect of exclusion is characterized by rupture: the disturbance or, one could say, the 'queering' of the dominant, mainstream, socially and culturally acceptable values (Estivill 2003). Political exclusion refers to those who cannot or are not allowed to enjoy and exercise their rights. Economic exclusion refers to access to and ownership of resources. These various types of exclusion are related and the degree to which people can participate fully in all these spheres indicates the extent to which certain individuals and groups are excluded (Kabeer 2005). As Kabeer (2005) explains, social exclusion functions by 'locking out' individuals and groups (marginalized on the basis of caste, gender, or sexuality, for example) and limiting their participation in social, economic and political spheres of life. Their exclusion is not only predicated on who they are (i.e. subjectively experienced understandings of self) but on how they are categorized by others (i.e. externally applied and often quite narrow identity categories). Therefore, according to Kabeer, social exclusion is fundamentally related to ones' actual and/or perceived identity:

> A "social exclusion" perspective draws attention to the overlap between these different experiences of disadvantage, in other words, to the experience of those individuals and groups who, in addition to their poverty, face discrimination by virtue of their identity, undermining their capacity to participate in the economic, social and political functionings of their society on equal terms.
>
> *(Ibid. 2005, 3)*

Social exclusion therefore refers to the marginalization from the social, political and economic spheres at various levels in societies (individual, institutional, societal). The causes of exclusion are broader than the lack of material resources; they are also embedded in cultural and social processes that stigmatize, 'distance' (Estivill 2003) or 'lock out' (Kabeer 2000) specific groups of individuals.

Understanding exclusion as a process offers greater leverage for identifying points to halt this process and work towards a more inclusive approach to complete wellbeing through development. In exploring social development as a process, Estivill (2003) and Kabeer (2000) argue that there is a level of 'chronic' or 'hard core' exclusion: this entails unequal access to and participation in socio-economic life, and this form of exclusion is operationalized through institutions that in turn create radical disadvantage (Estivill 2003; Kabeer 2000, 2005). As Kabeer (2005) notes, this type of exclusion systematically marginalizes specific individuals or groups, because of who they are and who they are perceived to be. We argue that a person's sexual orientation and/or gender identity and/or expression are characteristics that contribute to their positioning in the 'hard core' type of social exclusion.

From the Millennium Development Goals to the SDGs: the exclusion of SOGIE-related issues

While the Millennium Development Goals (MDGs) brought the global community together to address poverty from the beginning of the millennium, the goals failed to acknowledge poverty's multidimensional, dynamic and relational properties. The MDGs were criticized for prioritizing consensus, and in doing so, for failing to build on hard-won commitments for women's rights in the years preceding the Millennium Summit (Fehling, Nelson, and Venkatapuram 2013; Fukuda-Parr 2016; Kabeer 2015). An example is the dual omission of the commitment to combat violence against women (Kabeer 2015; Stuart and Woodroffe 2016) and to provide reproductive health services to all (Fehling et al. 2013). In addition to the main goals themselves, the goal-specific indicators and targets were criticized for focusing on individual behavior change as a key component for advancing transformation over substantive (and often more complex) measures to address structural forms of inequality that reinforce marginalization linked to gender and sexuality (Gabizon 2016; Stuart and Woodroffe 2016). Human rights practitioners and academics have also criticized the MDGs for not consistently integrating human rights principles throughout goals and targets with regards to equality and non-discrimination (Fukuda-Parr 2016).

It is no secret: sexuality has been and remains a battleground within the United Nations (UN) human rights system (Saiz 2004). Given the focus on consensus and 'buy in' by member states, it was not possible to include in the MDGs measures that would address social exclusion among sexual and gender minorities (Palmary and Nunez 2009). As we go on to discuss, this concern to establish consensus among member states also shaped the formation of the SDGs: many member state representatives held conservative views of both gender and sexuality, with some representing states that had ratified laws criminalizing lesbian, gay, bisexual, transgender, queer and intersex (LGBTQI) populations.

On September 25th of 2015, over 150 UN member states adopted the new framework for the post-2015 development agenda: the Sustainable Development Goals. Building on the MDGs, the scope of the SDGs is significantly larger. The new goals promote a broad spectrum of environmental, social and economic sustainable development agendas (Fukuda-Parr 2016; Galati 2015) that are founded on the principles of human rights (Razavi 2016) and aimed at fulfilling the overall commitment that 'no one will be left behind'. Differing from the process of the MDGs, the SDGs were created through a wide consultation with academics, citizens, scientists, civil society organizations and the private sector from across the globe (Bradshaw 2015; Gabizon 2016; Razavi 2016).

While an extensive consultation process fed into the finalization of the SDGs, the final 'in print' version elides the complex process and the extremely fraught contestations that have resulted in the silencing of some voices and the amplification of others. Unlike the process leading to the MDGs, international and national civil society engaged in the SDGs process through multiple arenas, including through the Addressing Inequalities Networked Alliance (AINA), and the global consultation on addressing inequalities, moderated by the UN High Commissioner for Human Rights and ARC International. The AINA consultation revealed an overwhelming consensus around the need for a rights-based, people-centered post-2015 agenda featuring a self-standing global goal on inequalities, with a particular focus on gender- and sexuality-based inequalities.

Similarly working to amplify the voices of sexual and gender minority groups in the UN, a joint statement was issued by the SOGIE Caucus during the 47th Session of the Commission on Population and Development (CPD47).[2] This statement strongly criticized attempts to silence the debate on SOGIE human rights during CPD47. The statement drew particular attention towards the significant violence, stigma and discrimination that people with diverse sexual orientation, gender identities and expressions experience around the world, calling for SOGIE inclusion and recognition. Linking to the post-2015 framework even more directly, on March 21st, 2014 the Lesbian, Bisexual and Trans Caucus and Allies at the 58th Commission on the Status of Women (CSW) issued a statement out of frustration with SOGIE issues being considered 'too controversial' at the CSW, and demanding the inclusion of SOGIE in the CSW process.[3] The statement received overwhelming support and was signed by over 70 organizations and more than 20 individuals. The LBT Caucus and Allies later decided to update the statement into one of the most comprehensive manifestos, published April 1st, 2014, demanding the inclusion of SOGIE in the post-2015 development agenda.[4] Despite the level of support of the statement, the overall concluding document of the 58th CSW did not mention anything in regards to sexual orientation, gender identity or expression (Kabeer 2015).

Revealing a pronounced unwillingness to 'hear' the many joint statements among civil society organizations and some member states, the final version of the SDGs also fails to acknowledge social exclusion on the basis of sexual orientation, gender identity and expression. Due to contestations, especially from African and Arab states, weaker and less specific language on gender and sexuality was included with no acknowledgement of the existence of LGBTQI people (Fukuda-Parr 2016; Gabizon 2016; Kabeer 2015). In the SDG outcome document, 'other status' is mentioned twice: once under Goal 10.2, 'Reducing Inequality', in regards to empowerment and inclusion for all, and again under 'The New Agenda' in paragraph 19 with reference to the promotion and protection of human rights. The inclusion of 'other status' is considered as a partial victory by those advocating for LGBTQI rights, who adapt the meaning of 'other' to include SOGIE-related issues (Goetz and Jenkins 2016; Mills 2015; Stuart and Woodroffe 2016). The aim of 'leave no one behind' is meaningful in acknowledging that people face inequalities beyond income alone (Stuart and Woodroffe 2016). However, by not recognizing specific barriers that LGBTQI people face and their exclusion, the SDGs are still leaving some people behind.

The case for a SOGIE-sensitive development framework

As outlined above, while the SDGs do not use the term 'social exclusion', the interlinked nature of the targets and indicators indicate recognition of poverty as multidimensional. The SDGs note the importance of combating inequality within and among countries by creating sustainable economic growth and promoting social inclusion, and they reaffirm the importance of human rights. Specifically, the SDG framework acknowledges that socially excluded groups are those groups who are in dire need of inclusion, protection and tailored measures to address poverty's multidimensionality (Mills 2015; Stuart and Woodroffe 2016). Despite including progressive language on social inclusion and acknowledging the importance of 'leaving no one behind', the SDGs fail to engage in any meaningful way with the lived reality of LGBTQI people. This is not an inadvertent oversight. This failure to 'name' those people and groups that experience 'hard core' exclusion, like LGBTQI people, is an explicit denial of their equal right to participate in the social, economic and political dimensions of development across all levels of society. This failure to acknowledge LGBTQI people as those people in dire need of inclusion and protection thus invisibilizes their experiences of discrimination and exclusion.

In order to bring these experiences to light, the following section presents findings from a comprehensive review of all studies in which social, economic and political exclusion has impacted the lives of LGBTQI people around the world. We argue that the invisibilization of SOGIE-related discrimination at an international level can reinforce a process of social exclusion across all levels of society, from the global to the local. In doing so, those actors involved in perpetuating social exclusion, by adopting cisnormative assumptions in their development programmes for example, remain invisible too, and they are not held accountable to the broader public. In order to interrupt this process through which social exclusion becomes entrenched through the very actions of those actors (like governments and donors) ostensibly committed to equality for all, we make a case for creation of a SOGIE-sensitive development framework.

As noted in the introduction, the findings discussed below were generated through a systematic policy and literature review of social exclusion related to SOGIE. The literature review included 65 articles, limited to English-language publications from the previous ten years (2005–2014) on SOGIE issues from Africa, Asia, Latin America and the Middle

East. Individual searches on sexuality using specific key terms were matched against terms representing the 17 proposed (at the time of the search) Sustainable Development Goals.

There are a number of limits to the findings presented below. First, the findings cannot and do not represent a comprehensive or cross-cutting analysis of the relationship between sexuality, gender identity and development. We recognize that empirical data on the various forms of exclusion faced by sexual and gender minorities, especially those in the Global South, is limited (Badgett, 2014; Badgett, Nezhad, Waaldijk, and van der Meulen Rodgers 2014). Second, the exclusion of sexual and gender minorities has historically been examined in relation to development within the context of health inequality, and this focus continues to shape much literature in the field of sexuality, gender identity and development. In fact, the most accessible data on sexual minorities comes from HIV programmes (Cornwall and Jolly 2006; Jolly 2000; Mills 2015) frequently focusing on men who have sex with men (MSM) and transgender women (Badgett 2014; Badgett et al. 2014; S. Baral, Sifakis, Cleghorn, and Beyrer 2007; S. D. Baral et al. 2013; Cáceres, Aggleton, and Galea 2008; Gosine 2009; Khosla 2009; Mills 2015). Overall, we found substantially more studies on sexual orientation and development compared to literature on gender identity, gender expression and development. This bias is noteworthy and is reflected in the findings below; it is also the focus of an upcoming article by the first author on gender identity and trans rights in development discourse. We believe the relationship between social and economic exclusion and those marginalized on the basis of their gender identity and expression is enormously under-explored and warrants greater focus in future studies.

While the findings presented in this chapter hold these limitations, they also offer important empirical evidence to support key development actors working to ensure that development addresses, rather than entrenches, social exclusion particularly among LGBTQI people. The findings draw on the terms used by respective authors (variously queer, lesbian, gay, trans, LGBT, LGBTQI, SOGIE) to recognize the sensitivity of context-appropriate language and in order to maintain the integrity of the referenced studies.

Addressing multidimensional poverty: SDG 1 (Poverty), SDG 8 (Economic Growth and Opportunity) and SDG 10 (Inequality)

> Violations of sexual rights create a negative cycle of limited opportunities in education which compound limited opportunities in employment caused by discrimination. Together these result in weaker capacities and poverty.
>
> *(Armas 2006, 24)*

With social exclusion as our lens, specifically focusing on LGBTQI people, we are reminded to look at forms of marginalization as a relational process through which people become excluded in societies. As such, studies show that there are a significant number of factors that contribute to SOGIE-related poverty, including inequalities linked to race, ethnicity, gender and location among others (Badgett, Durso, and Schneebaum 2013; Billies, Johnson, Murungi, and Pugh 2009; Prokos and Keene 2010; Thoreson 2011). These studies find that LGBTQI people with lower socio-economic status and education levels have an increased vulnerability to social stigma and discrimination; this in turn affects their opportunities for accessing employment and undermines economic security. Even when employed, studies find that workplace discrimination on the basis of sexual orientation and gender identity and expression is a major barrier to job retention and professional development (Bowleg, Brooks, and Ritz 2008; Mills 2015; Swank, Fahs, and Frost 2013).

Research conducted in Turkey on workplace discrimination found that most participants were not 'out' at their workplace because they feared verbal abuse or violence. In some cases, 'out' LGBTQI employees have been forced to pay 'penalty wages' (Botti and D'Ippoliti 2014; Drydakis 2014; Laurent and Mihoubi 2012). In other words, those who were 'out' often faced severe discrimination (sustained harassment through to repeated unwanted jokes and innuendos) as well as actual job termination and threats of violence (Ozturk 2011). Social stigma and discrimination remains present in the everyday lives of many LGBTQI individuals and communities around the world, and particularly in countries that do not have legal and policy provisions to protect them from discrimination in the employment sector. As a result many are 'locked out' of opportunities for economic growth and many struggle to access public services and other forms of social protection that can act as security nets to offset economic marginalization.

For example, qualitative research in the Philippines has examined the extent to which being queer affects the way that low-income Filipinos experience multidimensional poverty that spans economic and socio-cultural exclusion. The absence of social protection policies, in particular, has been shown to play a significant role in increasing lesbian, bisexual and transgender people's likelihood of struggling with poverty compared to heterosexual people. This is a result of creating social protection policies for heterosexual citizens, to the exclusion of all those people who hold different sexual orientations or gender identities and expressions. As a result, social policy provisions are filtered through a cissexist and homophobic lens to only apply to heterosexual marriages and related housing and welfare benefits including pensions, nuclear and biological families, and heterosexual-headed households, to name a few (Lim, Jordan, and Tangente 2013). In another study from the Philippines, interviewees said that their gender expression was a barrier to higher education and stereotypically 'queer' professions tended to be irregular as well as poorly remunerated (Thoreson 2011). The study also found that the queer participants' ability to contribute financially to the household increased the likelihood that they would be accepted socially, and within their families (*ibid.*). This is also reflected by a recent study with transgender people in Nepal. The authors found that economic wellbeing mitigates against stigma, to some extent, within families (Boyce and Coyle 2013).

While currently a rather blunt tool for guiding development policy and programming, SDG 10 has generated a great deal of contestation in the consultation period. Target 10.2 states that by "2030 empower and promote the social, economic and political inclusion of all irrespective of age, sex, disability, race, ethnicity, origin, religion or economic or other status." This target, while broad, is still ambiguous and the term 'other status' can be an entry point for SOGIE issues. A second potential entry point under this goal relates to target 10.3, which states that it aims to "ensure equal opportunity and reduce inequalities of outcome, including through eliminating discriminatory laws, policies and practices and promoting appropriate legislation, policies and actions in this regard."

Therefore all goals pertaining to justice, discrimination and protection fall under Goal 10. The legal and policy frameworks through which SOGIE discrimination is entrenched, or addressed, through development programmes would apply to this goal. Together, these studies point to a cyclical dynamic where LGBTQI people with lower socio-economic status and educational levels are more vulnerable to social stigma and discrimination, and in turn access to economic opportunities (Boyce and Coyle 2013).

Access to basic services: SDG 4 (education), SDG 11 (housing) and SDG 3 (health)

> If governments do not incorporate sexuality as an important element in their national curricula, people (and especially teenagers and young people) have less opportunity to take informed decisions regarding parenthood, sexual initiation, HIV prevention, etc.
>
> *(Armas 2006, 24)*

As noted above, SOGIE-based inequality and discrimination has marginalized LGBTQI people in various socio-economic and policy-legal aspects of their lives causing marginalization and limited access to services. In this section, we focus specifically on education, housing and health care. With respect to education among LGBTQI people, two key trends emerge: first, discrimination against people on the basis of SOGIE in educational settings contributes to premature exits from schools and universities (Mills 2015). Students who are 'out' or perceived to being LGBTQI are at higher risk of being bullied (mentally and physically) (Teixeira-Filho, Rondini, and Bessa 2011). The second trend concerns the content of sex education and broader LGBTQI awareness among teachers in education settings. Studies suggest that there is a missed opportunity for teachers (due to lack of training, discomfort with the subject or personal opinion) to discuss LGBTQI issues that could potentially improve students' health, safety and address homophobic instances within school environments (Gowen and Winges-Yanez 2014). A study in South Africa, for example, found a disconnect between the country's progressive legislation on sexual orientation and gender identity and its policies governing the content of sex education curricula. Without a uniform approach, or policy directive, to integrate education on sexual and gender diversity, the study found that teachers opted to exclude SOGIE from their lessons (DePalma and Francis 2014).

Further, even where policies exist to address social exclusion on the basis of SOGIE, social norms might continue to fuel stigma among teachers and students, deterring LGBTQI students from completing their primary, secondary or tertiary education. For example, even though Brazil has a progressive anti-homophobia, anti-transphobia education policy in place, the powerful right-wing religious lobby has effectively removed all measures to implement this policy in schools. This has been documented to negatively affect travesti, in particular (da Silva, Guerra, and Sperling 2013; Mountian 2014; Teixeira-Filho et al. 2011). In another study based on anonymous surveys in Brazil, researchers found that participants recognize that they promote hegemonic discourses of heterosexuality in their schools by threatening, or using, violence. It follows, then, that gay, lesbian and transgender people who were 'out' in their schools suffered the most severe forms of physical violence and social discrimination; this group also represented the highest number of students who reported considering suicide (Teixeira-Filho et al. 2011).

The 11th goal aims to "Make cities and human settlements inclusive, safe, resilient and sustainable." Numerous studies on 'safe settlements' have shown links between SOGIE and young LGBTQI people's safety as related to housing and, conversely, poverty and risk linked to homelessness. Given the high rates of stigma and discrimination within families around the world (Rew, Whittaker, Taylor-Seehafer, and Smith 2005), LGBTQI youth are at higher risk of homelessness, compared with heterosexual youth (Biçmen and Bekiroğulları 2014; Botti and D'Ippoliti 2014; Mills 2015; Nyanzi 2013). Further, just as heteronormative ideologies exist among staff in the education sector, as discussed above in relation to Brazil, heteronormative assumptions made by those working in the health and housing sectors have also been found to impede access among LGBTQI youth (Biçmen and Bekiroğulları 2014; Botti and D'Ippoliti 2014; Nyanzi 2013).

While positive shifts have taken place in extending the reach of HIV prevention and treatment under the MDGs, national legal and policy contexts that discriminate against SOGIE populations undermine the effective administration of these programmes by discouraging people from accessing critical health resources. There is value, then, in not only encouraging global momentum for HIV prevention and treatment, but working with those people involved in implementing these programmes – like health care workers – to sensitise them to health rights and concerns related to same sex desiring and gender variant people (Muller 2013). SOGIE-sensitive health care policies and programmes also need to extend beyond a historic focus on HIV to include mental and physical wellbeing, and essential access to health services more broadly.

These identity-based inequalities, faced by LGBTQI populations in their everyday life, occur in part as a result of social structures that systematically exclude some and privilege others. More specifically, the social exclusion faced by LGBTQI people can restrict their full participation in socio-economic life, because of who they are and who they are perceived to be, in Kabeer's (2005) terms. At a structural level, policies and laws are written from a heteronormative perspective, often inevitably perpetuating sexist and homophobic societies (Lim et al. 2013). Lack of legal recognition and rights contribute to this cycle of exclusion of LGBTQI people. Social and legal barriers to education and employment opportunities significantly impact the lower socio-economic status of LGBTQI people in comparison to their heterosexual counterparts (da Silva et al. 2013; Hull 2008; Mountian 2014; Teixeira-Filho et al. 2011).

Failing to recognize and address the discrimination experienced by sexual and gender minorities in their everyday lives will perpetuate a failure, on behalf of UN member states, in achieving fully the SDGs. To work towards inclusive development that addresses social exclusion, development actors need to shape and implement development policies that ensure: (i) that all people irrespective of their sexuality and gender identity and expression are actively protected against social, economic and political forms of discrimination; and (ii) that health, education, and social protection resources that contribute towards individual wellbeing and overall socio-economic development are made available to all those in need, leaving no one behind.

Towards a SOGIE-sensitive development era: what will it take to 'leave no one behind'?

Currently, there are 82 countries that have some form of law negatively affecting LGBTQI people. In these countries, where there is no incentive to integrate LGBTQI people into development programmes, their needs will remain invisible – in a vicious cycle – and their alienation from basic resources like health care, housing and education will continue to be under-reported and under-recognized in the international development sphere. In addition to these national-level barriers to addressing social exclusion among LGBTQI people, this chapter has shown that the current SDG framework runs the risk of entrenching rather than addressing multidimensional inequality among LGBTQI people at an international level.

While multiple dynamics intersect to create conditions of social, political and economic exclusion of LGBTQI populations, we detail two main mechanisms as they relate to policy processes at a national and international level. First, empirical studies point to the economic and social costs of national laws and policies that either actively discriminate against, or do not effectively protect, people on the basis of SOGIE (Hawkins et al. 2014; Jolly 2010; Oosterhoff, Waldman, and Olerenshaw 2014). This mechanism of discrimination, often reinforced by a dynamic interplay between state and social institutions, means that the benefits of basic development resources – like education, housing, sanitation and health care – frequently do not reach LGBTQI populations (Armas 2006; Teixeira-Filho et al. 2011). When measured in macro-economic terms, the impact of discriminatory or insensitive laws and policies also has an economic impact on the overall performance of the country's national outcomes (Badgett 2009; Bailey 2013).

The second mechanism of social exclusion relates to exclusionary development policies at an international level. These policies enable development practices through which discriminatory attitudes and practices are (inadvertently) reinforced. These practices may be shaped by global policy agendas, such as the current SDG framework, and implemented at a national level, often through donor-state or donor-civil society funding agreements. This mechanism, then, includes those actors engaged in extending the reach of global development agendas and resources (see Duffield 2002; Rivkin-Fish, Adams, and Pigg 2005). While these actors include national governments and civil society organisations as partners, linked to the first mechanism above, the dynamics of this particular mechanism points to the role of multilateral and bilateral donors that fund and implement programmes at a country level in line with the prevailing global development framework.

Critically, these development actors not only play a role in ensuring that development frameworks integrate all marginalized groups, but they are also in a position to reconfigure damaging approaches to development interventions that, for example, exclude transgender people from accessing essential health services (Sellers 2014; Shields et al. 2012), or fail to provide information on diverse sexualities, pleasure and related sexual health resources through education programmes for youth (Dunne 2007; Oduro 2012).

Together, these mechanisms draw into focus a set of development policies, programmes and actors. The first mechanism centres on state and civil society actors, and calls into focus the importance of designing and implementing national policies that effectively and constructively address multiple forms of inequality experienced by all citizens but especially by those experiencing socio-legal and economic discrimination on the basis of sexual orientation or gender identity and expression. The second mechanism moves out in scale to focus on bilateral and multilateral donors, and other international actors, that work with national governments and civil societies to implement development frameworks. National poverty-reduction frameworks are guided, to some extent, by global development frameworks; if the post-2015 framework 'leaves out' SOGIE populations, then state actors are effectively dis-incentivized from implementing SOGIE-sensitive policies in-country.

Generating inclusive strategies to address inequality for all population groups, including people who identify as queer, gay, lesbian, bisexual, transgender and intersex, is not only about taking human rights seriously, but very much about recognizing that this has positive social and economic outcomes for countries that take poverty alleviation seriously for everyone.

Notes

1 In this chapter, we use the term 'queer' to acknowledge and reflect a diverse range of sexual and gender identities that transcend narrow binaries (like male or female) and restrictive definitions (that separate gender from sexuality, or insist on fixed identities like 'gay' or 'straight'). We also use the term cognizant of the limits of labels and categories, and in an attempt to move beyond these limitations. Where we use specific terms like 'sexual minority' or 'gender minority', or

'lesbian', 'gay', or 'transgender', we do so in order to reflect the specific words used by the authors and participants of the studies discussed in this chapter.
2   The full statement is available at https://www.outrightinternational.org/content/cpd47-sogie-caucus-statement-general-discussion
3   The full Lesbian Bisexual and Trans Caucus and Allies statement is available at https://www.outrightinternational.org/content/csw58-statement-lesbian-bisexual-and-trans-caucus-and-allies
4   The full manifesto is available at https://www.outrightinternational.org/content/demanding-post-2015-development-agenda-inclusive-sexual-orientation-and-gender-identity

References

Armas, H. 2006. "Exploring linkages between sexuality and rights to tackle poverty." *IDS Bulletin* 37, no. 5: 21–26.

Badgett, M. 2009. "Bias in the workplace: consistent evidence of sexual orientation and gender identity discrimination 1998-2008." *Chi.-Kent L. Rev.*, 84: 559.

Badgett, M. 2014. *The Economic Cost of Stigma and the Exclusion of LGBT People: A Case Study of India.* Washington, DC: World Bank

Badgett, M. V., Durso, L. E., and Schneebaum, A. 2013. *New Patterns of Poverty in the Lesbian, Gay, and Bisexual Community*. Los Angeles, CA: The Williams Institute, UCLA.

Badgett, M., Nezhad, S., Waaldijk, K., and van der Meulen Rodgers, Y. 2014. *The Relationship between LGBT Inclusion and Economic Development: An Analysis of Emerging Economies*. Los Angeles, CA: The Williams Institute, UCLA.

Bailey, S. 2013. "Sexuality, and development in the Maghreb: Origins of institutionalized homophobia, and the disruption of development." Masters thesis. Brandeis University.

Baral, S., Sifakis, F., Cleghorn, F., and Beyrer, C. 2007. "Elevated risk for HIV infection among men who have sex with men in low-and middle-income countries 2000–2006: a systematic review." *PLoS Medicine* 4, no. 12: e339.

Baral, S. D., Poteat, T., Strömdahl, S., Wirtz, A. L., Guadamuz, T. E., and Beyrer, C. 2013. "Worldwide burden of HIV in transgender women: a systematic review and meta-analysis." *The Lancet Infectious Diseases* 13, no. 3: 214–222.

Biçmen, Z., and Bekiroğulları, Z. 2014. "Social problems of LGBT people in Turkey." *Procedia-Social and Behavioral Sciences* 113: 224–233.

Billies, M., Johnson, J., Murungi, K., and Pugh, R. 2009. "Naming our reality: low-income LGBT people documenting violence, discrimination and assertions of justice." *Feminism and Psychology* 19, no. 3: 375–380.

Botti, F., and D'Ippoliti, C. 2014. "Don't ask don't tell (that you're poor). Sexual orientation and social exclusion in Italy." *Journal of Behavioral and Experimental Economics* 49: 8–25.

Bowleg, L., Brooks, K., and Ritz, S. F. 2008. "'Bringing home more than a paycheck:' an exploratory analysis of Black lesbians' experiences of stress and coping in the workplace." *Journal of Lesbian Studies* 12, no. 1: 69–84.

Boyce, P., and Coyle, D. 2013. *Development, Discourse and Law: Transgender and Same-Sex Sexualities in Nepal*. IDS Evidence Report 13. Brighton: IDS.

Bradshaw, S. 2015. "Gendered rights in the post-2015 development and disasters agendas." *IDS Bulletin* 46, no. 4: 59–65.

Cáceres, C. F., Aggleton, P., and Galea, J. T. 2008. "Sexual diversity, social inclusion and HIV/AIDS." *AIDS* (London, England), 22(Suppl 2): S45.

Cornwall, A., and Jolly, S. 2006. "Introduction: sexuality matters." *IDS Bulletin* 37, no. 5: 1–11.

Cornwall, A., Corrêa, S., and Jolly, S. 2008. *Development with a Body: Making the Connections between Sexuality, Human Rights and Development*. London: Zed Books.

da Silva, D. Q., Guerra, O. U., and Sperling, C. 2013. "Sex education in the eyes of primary school teachers in Novo Hamburgo, Rio Grande do Sul, Brazil." *Reproductive Health Matters* 21, no. 41: 114–123.

DePalma, R., and Francis, D. 2014. "South African life orientation teachers: (not) teaching about sexuality diversity." *Journal of Homosexuality* 61, no. 12: 1687–1711.

Drydakis, N. 2014. "Sexual orientation discrimination in the Cypriot labour market. Distastes or uncertainty?" *International Journal of Manpower* 35, no. 5: 720–744.

Duffield, M. 2002. "Social reconstruction and the radicalization of development: aid as a relation of global liberal governance." *Development and Change* 33, no. 5: 1049–1071.

Dunne, M. 2007. "Gender, sexuality and schooling: Everyday life in junior secondary schools in Botswana and Ghana." *International Journal of Educational Development* 27, no. 5: 499–511.

Estivill, J. 2003. *Concepts and Strategies for Combating Social Exclusion: An Overview*. Geneva: International Labour Organization.

Fehling, M., Nelson, B. D., and Venkatapuram, S. 2013. "Limitations of the Millennium Development Goals: a literature review." *Global Public Health* 8, no. 10: 1109-1122.

Fraser, N. 2010. "Injustice at intersecting scales: on 'social exclusion' and the 'global poor.'" *European Journal of Social Theory* 13, no. 3: 363–371.

Fukuda-Parr, S. 2016. "From the Millennium Development Goals to the Sustainable Development Goals: shifts in purpose, concept, and politics of global goal setting for development." *Gender and Development* 24, no. 1: 43–52.

Gabizon, S. 2016. "Women's movements' engagement in the SDGs: lessons learned from the Women's Major Group." *Gender and Development* 24, no. 1: 99–110.

Galati, A. J. 2015. "Onward to 2030: sexual and reproductive health and rights in the context of the Sustainable Development Goals." *Guttmacher Policy Review* 18, no. 4. https://www.guttmacher.org/gpr/2015/10/onward-2030-sexual-and-reproductive-health-and-rights-context-sustainable-development

Goetz, A. M., and Jenkins, R. 2016. "Gender, security, and governance: the case of Sustainable Development Goal 16." *Gender and Development* 24, no. 1: 127–137.

Gosine, A. 2009. "Monster, womb, MSM: the work of sex in international development." *Development* 52, no. 1: 25–33.

Gowen, L. K., and Winges-Yanez, N. 2014. "Lesbian, gay, bisexual, transgender, queer, and questioning youths' perspectives of inclusive school-based sexuality education." *Journal of Sex Research* 51, no. 7: 788–800.

Haan, A. de. 1998. "'Social exclusion': an alternative concept for the study of deprivation?" *IDS Bulletin* 29, no. 1: 10–19.

Hawkins, K., Wood, S., Charles, T., He, X., Li, Z., Lim, A., Mountian, I., and Sharma, J. 2014. *Sexuality and Poverty Synthesis Report*, IDS Evidence Report 53. Brighton: IDS.

Hull, K. E. 2008. "Employment discrimination based on sexual orientation: dimensions of difference." In *Handbook of Employment Discrimination Research*, edited by Laura Beth Nielsen and Robert L. Nelson, pp. 167–187. New York: Springer.

Jackson, C. 1999. "Social exclusion and gender: does one size fit all?" *The European Journal of Development Research* 11, no.1: 125–146.

Jolly, S. 2000. "'Queering' development: exploring the links between same-sex sexualities, gender, and development." *Gender and Development* 8, no. 1: 78–88.

Jolly, S. 2010. "Sexuality and poverty: what have they got to do with each other?" In *Old Wineskins, New Wine: Readings in Sexuality in sub-Saharan Africa*, edited by C. Izugbara, C. C. Undie, and J. Wanjiku Khamasi, pp. 139–155. Hauppauge, NY: Nova Science Publishers.

Kabeer, N. 2000. "Social exclusion, poverty and discrimination towards an analytical framework." *IDS Bulletin* 31, no. 4: 83–97.

Kabeer, N. 2005. "Social exclusion: concepts, findings and implications for the MDGs." Paper commissioned as background for the Social Exclusion Policy Paper. London: Department for International Development (DFID)

Kabeer, N. 2015. "Tracking the gender politics of the Millennium Development Goals: struggles for interpretive power in the international development agenda." *Third World Quarterly* 36, no. 2: 377–395.

Khosla, N. 2009. "HIV/AIDS interventions in Bangladesh: what can application of a social exclusion framework tell us?" *Journal of Health, Population and Nutrition* 4: 587–597.

Laurent, T., and Mihoubi, F. 2012. "Sexual orientation and wage discrimination in France: the hidden side of the rainbow." *Journal of Labor Research* 33, no. 4: 487–527.

Lim, A. M., Jordan, C. M., and Tangente, M. G. C. 2013. *Policy Audit: Social Protection Policies and Urban Poor LBTs in the Philippines*. IDS Evidence Report 21. Brighton: IDS.

Mills, E. 2015. *'Leave No One Behind': Gender, Sexuality and the Sustainable Development Goals.* IDS Evidence Report 154. Birghton: IDS.

Mountian, I. 2014. *A Critical Analysis of Public Policies on Education and LGBT Rights in Brazil*. IDS Evidence Report 61. Brighton: IDS.

Muller, A. 2013. "Teaching lesbian, gay, bisexual and transgender health in a South African health sciences faculty: addressing the gap." *BMC Medical Education* 13, no. 1: 174.

Nyanzi, S. 2013. "Homosexuality, sex work, and HIV/AIDS in displacement and post-conflict settings: the case of refugees in Uganda." *International Peacekeeping* 20, no. 4: 450–468.

Oduro, G. Y. 2012. "'Children of the street': sexual citizenship and the unprotected lives of Ghanaian street youth." *Comparative Education* 48 no. 1: 41–56.

Oosterhoff, P., Waldman, L., and Olerenshaw, D. 2014. *Literature Review on Sexuality and Poverty.* IDS Brief Supporting Evidence Report 55. Brighton: IDS.

Ozturk, M. B. 2011. "Sexual orientation discrimination: exploring the experiences of lesbian, gay and bisexual employees in Turkey." *Human Relations* 64, no. 8: 1099–1118.

Palmary, I., and Nunez, L. 2009. "The orthodoxy of gender mainstreaming reflecting on gender mainstreaming as a strategy for accomplishing the Millennium Development Goals." *Journal of Health Management* 11, no. 1: 65–78.

Prokos, A. H., and Keene, J. R. 2010. "Poverty among cohabiting gay and lesbian, and married and cohabiting heterosexual families." *Journal of Family Issues* 31, no. 7: 934–959.

Razavi, S. 2016. "The 2030 agenda: challenges of implementation to attain gender equality and women's rights." *Gender and Development* 24, no. 1: 25–41.

Rew, L., Whittaker, T. A., Taylor-Seehafer, M. A., and Smith, L. R. 2005. "Sexual health risks and protective resources in gay, lesbian, bisexual, and heterosexual homeless youth." *Journal for Specialists in Pediatric Nursing: JSPN* 10, no. 1: 11–19.

Rivkin-Fish, M., Adams, V., and Pigg, S. L. 2005. *Sex in Development: Science, Sexuality, and Morality in Global Perspective.* Durham, NC: Duke University Press.

Saiz, I. 2004. *Bracketing Sexuality: Human Rights and Sexual Orientation: A Decade of Development and Denial at the UN.* SPW Working Papers, no. 2. Rio de Janeiro: Sexual Policy Watch.

Sellers, M. D. 2014. "Discrimination and the transgender population: analysis of the functionality of local government policies that protect gender identity." *Administration and Society* 46, no. 1: 70–86.

Sen, A. 2000. "Social exclusion: concept, application, and scrutiny." Social Development Papers No. 1. Manila, Philippines: Asian Development Bank.

Shields, L., Zappia, T., Blackwood, D., Watkins, R., Wardrop, J., and Chapman, R. 2012. "Lesbian, gay, bisexual, and transgender parents seeking health care for their children: a systematic review of the literature." *Worldviews on Evidence-Based Nursing* 9, no. 4: 200–209.

Silver, H. 1994. "Social exclusion and social solidarity: three paradigms." Discussion Paper. International Institute for Labour Studies. Geneva: International Labour Organization.

Stuart, E., and Woodroffe, J. 2016. "Leaving no-one behind: can the Sustainable Development Goals succeed where the Millennium Development Goals lacked?" *Gender and Development* 24, no. 1: 69–81.

Swank, E., Fahs, B., and Frost, D. M. 2013. "Region, social identities, and disclosure practices as predictors of heterosexist discrimination against sexual minorities in the United States." *Sociological Inquiry* 83, no. 2 : 238–258.

Teixeira-Filho, F. S., Rondini, C. A., and Bessa, J. C. 2011. "Reflexões sobre homofobia e educação em escolas do interior paulista." *Educação e Pesquisa* 37, no. 4: 725–741.

Thoreson, R. 2011. "Capably queer: exploring the intersections of queerness and poverty in the urban Philippines." *Journal of Human Development and Capabilities*, 12, no. 4: 493–510.

von Braun, J., and Gatzweiler, F. W. 2014. *Marginality: Addressing the Nexus of Poverty, Exclusion and Ecology.* Dordrecht/: Springer Open.

PART II

Queer development critique

5

ARRESTED DEVELOPMENT OR THE QUEERNESS OF SAVAGES

Resisting evolutionary narratives of difference

Neville Hoad

Preface

I would like to thank Corinne Mason for her interest in reprinting this old chestnut. In the nearly twenty years since I wrote this article, there have been significant historical changes in much of the discursive and geopolitical landscape the article was attempting to describe: most significantly the entrenchment of a right to sexual orientation and more recently gender identity in key parts of national and international public discourse—culture and law (Hoad 2016). There has also been a contested rise in criminalization legislation in several African countries—Uganda, Nigeria, the Gambia, most notably (Cheney 2009; Okoli and Halidn 2014). The development of minoritarian sexuality identities largely through the globalization of the homo/hetero binary has been met with considerable national and religious resistance, and obviously an essay which covered the same terrain today would need to engage those facts and factors.

In addition to these more discursive developments, there has also been something like "queer development" in more material registers of the term "development." While homosexual sex tourism is nothing new, and in terms of the Victorian origin narrative ruse of my essay, one need only think of Andre Gide and Oscar Wilde in Algeria and Morocco in the last decades of the nineteenth century, it is now plausible to claim a rise in global "gay" tourism at the turn of the twenty-first century (Fryer 1998; Dollimore 1987). The relation between the rise of gay neighborhoods and gentrification, ably chronicled by Sarah Schulman, has also yoked "queerness" and "development" with some material force, as has the burgeoning of studies of specific cities, from Gay New York to Queer Bangkok, an important genre for the writing of minoritarian sexual identity histories (Schulman 2012; see also Chauncey 1994; Stein 2000; Houlbrook 2006; Jackson 2011).

Secondly, while I think the central argument that I make in the article about the kinds of in/ethical narratives instantiated by evolutionary narratives holds, my thinking about the relation between materiality/contingency/history and theory/idea/example has become less certain. I can now imagine deployments of evolutionary/developmental narratives that do not necessarily replicate on the ground the problems I find in the theory. Of course, underdevelopment/dependency theory was very much around and quite vital in the original moment of writing, and to me, its absence in the thinking of developmental narratives is the greatest lacuna of the essay. The differences between what I term in the essay—the developmental narratives of difference—and the varied material practices and histories of economic under/development are sometimes so huge that the word "development" buckles and breaks, and we might need at least two different terms. I look forward to reading this anthology to see the manifold yokings of "queerness" and "development."

Thirdly, in significant ways, the historical periodizing terms of the essay need nuancing now. Neoliberalism was not yet the hegemonic designation of the present in the late 1990s, when the essay was written. "Pinkwashing" was not a quite a term in 2000, and the processes it shorthands, namely the use of "progressive" legislation and social practices on SOGI (sexual orientation and gender identity issues)—and the emergence of SOGI as a kind of replacement acronym for the proliferation of letters in LGBTQIA must be noted—as cover for the persistence of other human rights abuses and social injustices, complicate both national and international contexts.[1] The term is mostly used to describe Israel/Palestine but also applies to a range of other spaces and institutions—legal tolerance of homosexuality as condition for entry into the European union of former socialist countries, the immigration policies of ostensibly liberal democracies et al. Much, but not all, of this material and argumentation is assimilable into the assimilation into sameness argument that the essay makes in relation to developmental narratives.

Moreover, the last twenty years has seen the explosion of scholarly work on sexuality studies in relation to nationalism, race, globalization, international law, and I strongly suspect that while some of it would advance the claims of "Arrested development or the queerness of savages," much would require a qualification or nuancing of the ethical and political failures that the essay lays at the door of what it calls developmental narratives. But I hope that these nuances would qualify rather than disqualify my central argument, taking the form of "Evolutionary/developmental narratives perform violence on human differences, but…"

My essay came out two years before Joseph Massad's benchmark essay "Re-Orienting Desire: The Gay International and the Arab World" (2002) and well before its nuanced reworking as a chapter in *Desiring Arabs* (2007). That essay is often irresponsibly (and stupidly) misread or not really read at all as a piece of conspiracy theory robbing natives of their agency, when even just the redolent ironies in the term "the Gay International" should give such a claim significant pause. Massad's essay serves as a powerful caveat about the risks of making a world in one's image, especially in the unironized name of freedom, and the dangerous consequences of epistemically needing to make "gay" people in order to save them, as well as providing a cautionary tale about well-intentioned westerners gone abroad willy-nilly as members of the humanitarian industrial complex. "Re-Orienting Desire" exposes the risks of the setting to work of developmental narratives in terms of the universalisms of human rights discourses in their sexuality variants in ways that I wish I had anticipated with greater clarity in my own essay.

"Homonationalism," the neologism most closely associated with the work of Jasbir Puar and with affinities to "pinkwashing" was not yet available in the late 1990s and does useful work in describing and analyzing the effects (sometimes unwitting, sometimes cynical) of liberal notions and institutions in the multiple deployments of sexuality in an era of "the global war on terror" (Puar 2007). The term too exposes the hypocrisies of claims of sexual liberation as part of "Operation Enduring Freedom."

What has come to be known as "queer of color critique" has much to teach "Arrested development or the queerness of savages," the latter now looks like to me as privileging a scientist genealogy of race, with insufficient concern for its lived realities in multiple contexts. While much of queer of color critique is US focused, and my aspirations in the essay, were for better or worse, more global, I wish I could have read Roderick Ferguson's *Aberrations in Black: Toward a Queer of Color Critique* (2003), which articulates categories of race and sexuality/sexual difference with greater complexity and finesse than the analogies between the two that I rely on in my essay.

Indigenous Queer Studies has seen an efflorescence in the last decade, and much of it powerfully analyzes the ongoing decimation and resilience of Indigenous intimate worlds in the face of the relentless "civilizing missions" of settler colonialism in both its overtly racist and liberal multicultural guises and its antagonist anti-colonial nationalism (to start, see Rifkin 2012; Justice and Cox 2008). The specificities of settler colonialism as a comparative frame for queer work is way more developed, so to speak in 2017, than it was in 2000. T.J. Tallie's extraordinary work on the problems colonial sex and gender norms run into when they encounter Zulu intimate worlds in nineteenth-century Natal reveals the instructive convolutions of this terrain (Tallie 2012; 2013).

I wish my essay were more of a feminist essay, and here I have no excuse. Gayle Rubin's foundational essay "The Traffic in Women" (1975) uses precisely parts of the racial and civilizational archive (Morgan via Engels) that I suggest is too compromised by imperial and developmental axiomatics and still makes a continuingly vital piece of feminist theory, and Anne McClintock's *Imperial Leather* (1995) already provided a model for the theoretical and historical elaborations of the imbrications of race, class, sexuality and gender as analytic categories and lived experiences.

I remain grateful to Dennis Altman who solicited the article for *Postcolonial Studies*, and for his *Global Sex*, which set the stage for much of what followed. Given the vagaries of academic publishing, it was the fifth article I published but the second one I wrote. The central idea came from a seminar on Feminism and Psychoanalysis that I took with Gayatri Spivak, in the spring of 1993—the Freud and Irigaray bits remained unchanged from that first attempt. It was my writing sample the year on the job market when I got a job. It got me a mention in *Private Eye*'s "Pseuds Corner." I think most of it still holds, though that might be the case because perhaps the strongest arrested development is my own. You decide.

Introduction

In this essay, I argue that it should not be possible to understand the initial theories of modern male homosexual identity in the west without looking at the imperial and neo-imperial contexts of such theoretical productions.[2] I claim that the application of key tropes of Darwinian evolutionary theory permitted an imbrication of race, gender, nation and class categories in the constitution of knowledge of the body of the "invert" and subsequent "homosexual." Moreover, these evolutionary tropes persist and can be located in a range of work on "homosexuality" over the last century.[3] They can also be shown to inform work of decidedly diverging political interests. From Krafft-Ebing to Queer Theory, the language and assumptions of evolutionary theory, often displaced into contemporary discourses of development, reverberate to create a disturbing consonance between ideologies of liberation and ideologies of oppression.

The essay is part of a wider project investigating the hierarchical staging of human difference under the historical periodizings of imperialism and globalization and the attendant logics of evolution and development, respectively, and is divided into four sections. The first section considers the use of evolutionary theory in the imagining of the homosexual body at the last *fin de siècle*.[4] The second section elaborates this into a discussion of the relationship between sexuality and savagery. In the third section, I ponder what can and cannot be done with psychoanalysis in relation to hierarchical solutions to the problems of human "cultural" and sexual differences. "Developing homosexuality in the 'developing' world"—the final section—sketches the continuing vitality of these hierarchizing rhetorics of difference in current scholarship of (homo)sexuality in a global frame.

Before I begin, I need to establish the philosophical moves that enable evolutionary and/or developmental thinking, even at the risk of abstracting out of the social matrices that produce them. In defining an evolutionary narrative, I would isolate the following features: a narrative of an ultimately unified *subject*, comprising a branching hierarchy in which the manifold others of this *subject* are perceived as already incorporated into and transcended by the *subject*. This incorporation and transcendence is achieved by the temporalization of space.[5] The narrative hierarchizes difference, doing violence, by *a priori* incorporation, to the others in the constitution of the *subject*. The *subject* is constituted by progress through its various others, which are then posited as vestigial, arrested, anachronistic or degenerate. I take issue throughout with the ethics this narrative instantiates.

The specter of evolution

I take Michel Foucault's polemical assertion that "the homosexual" becomes a "species" circa 1870 as a foundational ruse, rather than as a historical fact (Foucault 1978).[6] Eve Kosofsky Sedgwick in *Epistemology of the Closet* argues that "sexuality" is a constitutive epistemological regime for modernity—

> that many of the major nodes of thought and knowledge in twentieth-century western culture as a whole are structured— indeed, fractured—by a chronic, now endemic crisis of homo/heterosexual definition, indicatively male, dating from the end of the nineteenth century.
>
> *(Sedgwick, 1990)*

While agreeing with the broad lineaments of both Foucault and Sedgwick's arguments, I wish to suggest that this "new species" and this "constitutive epistemological regime for modernity" are imbedded in a set of questions around the seductions and difficulties of asserting developmental racial difference. Knowledges of the sexual practices of colonised people, although they were frequently based on category impositions and misrecognitions, provided crucial evidence for nearly all parties engaged in turn of the century debates around what increasingly came to be called homosexuality. Before he can even utter the term, John Addington Symonds, in *A Problem in Modern Ethics* (1896), tells us:

> It confronts us on the steppes of Asia, where hordes of nomads drink the milk of mares; in the bivouac of Keltish warriors, lying wrapped in wolves' skins round their camp-fires; upon the sands of Arabia, where the Bedaween raise desert dust in flying squadrons. We discern it among the palm-groves of the South Sea Islands, in the card-houses and temple-gardens of Japan, under Esquimaux snow-huts,

beneath the sultry vegetation of Peru, beside the streams of Shiraz and the waters of the Ganges, in the cold clear air of Scandinavian winters. It throbs in our huge cities. The pulse of it can be felt in London, Paris, Berlin, Vienna, no less than in Constantinople, Naples, Teheran and Moscow. It finds a home in Alpine valleys, Albanian ravines, Californian canyons, and gorges of Caucasian mountains.

(Symonds 1896)

The "it," that Symonds is so slow to name in this panting eroticizing of the world, is found everywhere, and he mobilizes its geographic universality in an impassioned plea against its criminal status in Britain. However, "its" presence among many of the subject people of empire could be and was used as evidence that it should be further criminalized and/or pathologized, and for the same reasons and purpose was used as justification for colonizing. Unlike Symonds, I cannot beg the question of what the "it" is. A good cultural relativist would pluralize the "it," and talk about many homosexualities. This proliferation of the "its" is still dependent on an initial conceptual certainty of what the "it" is. My alternative strategy instead is, on the one hand, to attempt a radical historicizing of the category itself, by demonstrating that the idea of homosexuality is imbedded in a set of discursive networks; and, on the other hand, to stop looking for the "it" in steppes, bivouacs, palm-groves and temple-gardens and other exotic locales. Following Edward Said's Orientalism, I am less interested in the sexual practices of different peoples, but rather in how these practices are represented, imagined, indeed produced by Europeans. I ask how the "it" sits in the eye of the beholder, how it shores up, destabilizes and constitutes the gazing subject, and attendantly what possibilities it permits the gazed upon object (Said 1980).

In reading this relation of cultural and geographic otherness to homosexuality historically, I wish to stress a major intellectual reorientation—what George Stocking in Victorian Anthropology terms 'classical evolutionism' (1987). Its central feature comes to be a figuring of human cultural difference in biological terms. *Most crucially, living savages come to fill the fossil gap, through a spatialization of time written on the human body.* Johannes Fabian in his classic *Time and the Other: How Anthropology Makes its Object*, argues that the social evolutionists "discarded Time altogether" and that "the temporal discourse of anthropology as it was formed decisively under the paradigm of evolutionism rested on a conception of Time that was not only secularized and naturalized but also thoroughly spatialized." This is what allows Fabian to insist that anthropological praxis was epistemologically (not just materially or morally) linked to colonialism and imperialism. In this essay, I try to apply Fabian's analysis of temporal narratives to a figure outside of his purview, but still inflected by the discourse of the primitive, namely the male "homosexual."

The insistence on the spatialization of time in order to construe racial otherness is evident in many scientific and anthropological writings. Huxley in the 1860s claims that "the difference in the volume of the cranial capacity of the different races of mankind is far greater, absolutely than that between the lowest man and the highest ape" (Huxley 1911). Tylor settles on the Tasmanians as the living representative of the Early Stone Age, and a range of hierarchies are produced which serve to rank a variety of cultures through a study of their law, culture, religion and marriage institutions until they reach their full flower in Europe (Tylor 1894). Tylor (1874) offers the following developmental hierarchy: Australian, Tahitian, Aztec, Chinese, Italian (27). The interchangeability of the ancient and contemporaneous in the establishment of categories of race, nation, culture is neatly evidenced here, and it is easy to point to the difficulties in such hierarchies: for example, where would the Roman fit in this schema? Rather than only point to the racist incoherence of such formulations, I wish to stress their productivity; how they are mobilized and inhabited by a range of social actors.

For the paradigm of *classical evolutionism* offered a way of not only thinking through questions of human difference in the more overtly anthropological and imperial contexts, but also of thinking about social, sexual and gender differences at the center. Stocking draws out two domestic primitive types in Britain at the time—the Celtic fringe and the urban poor, citing writers who claim that "countrymen of our own are living lives worse than those of savages," and that "the race differentiated progress of the human species over the last hundred millennia is comparable to the class differentiated progress of British civilization over the last hundred years" (as cited in Stocking 1987, 219). Furthermore, the theorizing of female bodies and the creation of a male homosexual body as an object for theorizing can be seen to operate in the same discursive field.

The language of the *telos* of evolution is rife in the writings by, for and about homosexuals: in the manifestos of people so self-identified, in the sexological, psychoanalytic and anthropological documents about them, and in artistic and literary representations. At every turn one encounters terms of "arrest," "retardation," "decadence" and "degeneration," and most interestingly even assertions of a normative homosexuality tend to rework the same motifs.

Firstly, within the set of medical discourses that come to define a homosexual identity for the emerging set of European criminal codes,[7] evolutionary theories are widely deployed, drawing upon evolutionary theories of gender/the female body (the two are largely inseparable at this historical conjuncture), as well as those in the anthropological field of culture. Herbert Spencer, a key figure in the emergence of social Darwinism, argues that the evolution of the female fetus is retarded in order to keep a reserve of energy for later reproduction (as cited in Conway 1972, 140).[8] (Freud's notion of the clitoris as a vestigial penis can be seen as part of this legacy.) In Geddes, an evolutionary hierarchy of genders is used to explain the difference between the sexes right down to the level of cell metabolism, with male cell organization understood as katabolic, i.e. dissipating or spending energy in a persistent forward, expansive and adaptive drive, and female cells as anabolic, inclining to retention, storing and inertia (Geddes and Thomson 1998). The implications for subsequent psychoanalytic theories of homosexuality as arrest are obvious, despite Freud's explicit refutation of intermediate and *third sex* theories, which see the homosexual as feminized (Freud 1982, 60). Siobhan Somerville points out the racial underpinnings of these *third sex* or gender continuum models of homosexuality. Carpenter uses the racial continuum and the idea of the mixed race body as an analog for the homosexual body:

> Anatomically and mentally we find all shades existing from the pure genus man to the pure genus woman… As we are continually meeting in cities women who are one-quarter, or one-eighth male… so there are in the Inner Self, similar half-breeds, all adapting themselves to circumstances with perfect ease.
>
> *(Somerville 1994, 259)*

This use of race and gender to delineate the homosexual body is mediated through the language of evolution. Carpenter (1921) writes of the "genus man" and the "genus woman," who, along with all the stages between them and the rest of life on earth in the Darwinian schema, are "adapting themselves to circumstances."

However, evolutionary tropes are compounded, and to some extent confounded, by the representation of the homosexual as the extension of Tissot's figure of the dissipated, exhausted masturbator— the homosexual as degenerate[9] rather than retard. This trope is also frequently seen through a gendered lens—that of effeminacy. Alan Sinfield (1994) has argued that the association between effeminacy and homosexuality dates from the Wilde trials and suggests that the figure of the dandy, at least in literary representations, can embody an excess of heterosexual desire rather than its opposite prior to the Wilde scandal (27). Yet Sinfield's reading of the 1871 Boulton–Park trial makes it clear that, in certain sectors, homosexual behavior was associated with effeminacy and transvestism, even if this is not quite intelligible to the hegemonic culture at large. In the context of the American metropolis, George Chauncey (1994) in *Gay New York* provides ample evidence that the effeminate "homosexual" man (the fairy) is a recognizable figure on the streets and in the bars of certain neighborhoods by the 1890s.

Figuring effeminacy as decadence may be inflected by a developmental narrative of gender difference, where the "female" is defined reactively with reference to a male subject. For Darwin, the male is always more modified and thus more evolutionarily advanced: "The male [is] generally more modified than the female" (Darwin 1998, 221). The dandy, as a highly ornamented man, was always decadent; it takes an evolutionary ideology to make him degenerate, since in the evolutionary schema, men are only highly ornamented in primitive cultures.[10] Decadence and degeneracy, two terms frequently associated with the effeminate dandy are both developmental tropes: degeneracy implying a falling back into an earlier time, an anxious space of the past in the future, and decadence connoting a bringing into the present of some very late, perhaps never-to-be reached state, an anxious space of premature death. What the decadent/degenerate shares with the primitive is a position on the fringes of the normative evolutionary narrative. Neither figure can exist in the present. These increasingly biologized tropes of the homosexual as retard or as degenerate are refigured in the different appropriations of "savage" and Greek/idealized "homosexuality." Edward Carpenter, Richard Burton and Sigmund Freud all struggle to account for the presence of same-sex acts in cultures called backward and savage and in the valorized Greco/Roman past of Europe.

Thus, while "homosexuality" can be sustainedly connected with the primitive, evolutionary narratives come under some strain. Can the primitive and the decadent occupy the same sequential position? Can socially sanctioned "homosexuality" co-exist in the backward savages of the present and in the advanced cultures of Europe's past? What might the valence of this co-existence be? Again, it is mobilized by both sides. Reverend J. Wilson, in crusading for moral purity argues: "Rome fell, other nations are falling and if England falls, it will be this sin, and her unbelief in God, that will be her ruin" (as cited in Weeks 1977, 18).[11]

The same developmentally fraught matrix is encountered in Carpenter's expressed difficulty in incorporating the Samurai of Japan and the Dorian Greeks, alongside the Alaskan Inuit in his *Intermediate Types among Primitive Folk* (1921). The discovery and "rediscovery" of different cultural organizations of particularly male homosexuality, along the axes of both history and geography strain the evolutionary narrative, yet never entirely escape it. Symonds invokes Ancient Greece: "Here alone in history have we the example of a great and highly developed race not only tolerating homosexual passions but deeming them of spiritual value and attempting to utilize them for the benefit of society (Symonds 1896, 51).

Carpenter spreads his net much wider:

> Bearing this in mind it becomes possible to see that a great many of the customs
> we have mentioned, whether in Syria or Babylonia, or in Greece, or in Africa, or
> in North and South America, had a value quite other than that which appears at

first sight—a profound and human value—and that they represented necessary contributions towards the evolution of mankind and the expression of its latent powers. And as regards this present volume, I think we may say that among primitive folk variations of sex-temperament from the normal have not been negligible freaks, but have played an important part in the evolution and expansion of human society—that in a certain sense variations of social activity have run parallel with and been provoked by variations in same-sex temperament.[12]

Carpenter (1921) posits a gendered continuum of sexual desire, which he claims to be central to the continuing evolution of the species (170–171). In this way, he manages to mobilize cultural difference within a prevailing evolutionary paradigm to challenge (albeit in a very circumscribed way) both the homophobia and racism[13] of much evolutionist thought.

Richard Burton's "Terminal Essay" to his translation of the *Arabian Nights* in 1886 attempts to preempt charges of obscenity by making a culturally relativist argument based on the determinations of climate on same-sex passion. Burton resists the contradictions of an explicitly evolutionary narrative, disavows racial explanations and yet manages to produce male homosexuality as definitively alien to northern European peoples. He tells us that he holds pederasty to be geographical and climatic, not racial (Burton 1886, 207).

I suspect a mixed physical temperament effected by the manifold subtle influences massed together in the word climate. Something of the kind is necessary to explain the fact of this pathological love extending over the greater portion of the habitable world, without any apparent connection of race or media, from the polished Greek to the Cannibal Tupi of the Brazil.

(Burton 1886, 207)

To get round the evolutionary configuration, Burton employs a topographical one, constructing a Sotadic Zone, in which climate is seen to facilitate pathological love. This, of course, becomes entirely untenable, because the Sodatic Zone ends up including all of the Americas, Australasia, China, Japan, the Near and Middle East and the Mediterranean basin. As problematic as Burton's refutation of evolution is, it represents an attempt to think the otherness of sexual norms in terms that do not subsume the other into the self in the narrating of identity.

In significant ways, Burton's construction of a "Sotadic Zone" cannot entirely be read as counter-evolutionary because it resonates with Lamarckian notions of environment producing heritable traits—the precursor to Darwin's theory of evolution that he was at pains to refute in the *Origin of Species*. However, while the "Sotadic Zone" is clearly empirically useless, it offers an explanation that is not subject to the ethical problems of the developmental evolutionary narratives, I am discussing throughout this essay. Burton does not spatialize time. Cultural difference is understood as a function of climactic difference, not as developmental or temporal. In Fabian's terms, Burton does not confuse the category "primitive" for an object. He attempts to avoid a developmental narrative altogether. Nevertheless Burton's reduction of the social into the natural, evident in his privileging of climate as a causative factor of same-sex passion, re-inscribes this central reduction of social Darwinist thought, even though he claims no adaptive function for "homosexuality" in this organicizing of the historical. All the usual suspects in Victorian theorizing of "homosexuality" (Ellis, Carpenter, Symonds, Burton, Nordau, Krafft-Ebing) draw on notions of national, racial and cultural otherness to make arguments about what is beginning to be called "homosexuality."

Sexual savages

The place of male homosexuality in theories of cultural evolution is nevertheless unstable and the perception of male homosexuality amongst the subjected peoples of empire is mobilized both by groups seeking to stigmatize homosexuality further and by those wishing to depathologize and decriminalize[14] it. Sir Richard Francis Burton is decidedly clear that "homosexuality" is definitively unBritish, even though he was reputed to be sexually interested in men himself.[15] In the "Terminal Essay," he undertakes to explain same-sex passion to a presumably ignorant and potentially scandalized metropolitan audience; he makes it clear that it is his experiences in the colonies that have prepared him for such explications:

> The "excrebalis familia pathicorum" first came before me by chance of earlier life. In 1845, when Sir Charles Napier had conquered and annexed Sind, despite a fraction (mostly venal) which sought favour with the now defunct "Court of Directors to the Honourable East India Company," the veteran began to consider his conquest with a curious eye. It was reported to him that Karachi, a townlet of some two thousand souls and distant than not more than a mile from camp, supported no less than three lupanars or bordels, in which not women, but boys and eunuchs, the former demanding nearly a double price, lay for hire.
>
> *(Burton 1886, 205)*

Burton goes on to recount how he visited all these places and "obtained the fullest details which were duly dispatched to Government House" (Burton 1886, 206). Since these reports fall into the hands of his enemies within the colonial service he is threatened with dismissal. I refer to this incident because it indicates that an emergent colonial government was interested in the same-sex sexual practices of the people they were coming to rule, and because it reveals the endlessly displaceable national and racial origins of homosexuality.[16]

A series of incidents in East Africa in the mid-1880s also point to the fraught mobilization of same-sex "sexual" practices in the implementation of colonial rule. Many commentators have noted the opposition of the king of Buganda, Mwanga, to growing missionary influence, both Protestant and Roman Catholic, in his kingdom. While this opposition is clearly overdetermined, the refusal of pages at the royal court to engage in sexual relations with the king on account of their conversion to Christianity is widely acknowledged as a factor in the murder of over thirty young male Bugandans in 1886, and the subsequent expulsion of the missionaries from the kingdom.[17] The significance of the king's fondness of sodomy in a colonial representational field is fraught. Many of the missionaries claim that Mwanga learnt this "foul practice" from the Arab traders[18] who maintained a strong presence at the Bugandan court. On the one hand, "sodomy" can be invoked as an index of African savagery and depravity, and on the other the assertion that this was an alien and imported practice can be invoked as proof of African innocence and as an appeal to British paternalism.[19] The resistance of the pages to performing certain corporeal intimacies with the king and their subsequent execution prompts a civil war and, in September 1888, the Imperial British East Africa Company receives a royal charter from Lord Salisbury's government with instructions to preserve law and order in Buganda (Apter 1961, 71).

The presence of "homosexuality" amongst "the savage races" is engaged by ideologies of empire[20] and the imputed national/racial otherness of it can be hierarchized by the evolutionary narrative and will be speculatively posited by Freud as a precondition for civilization. The idea that "homosexual sex" is somehow more ritualized and primitive than its heterosexual counterpart in both mainstream and "subcultural" representations bears witness to the persistence of this figuration. Symonds in 1896 is already referring to sexual inverts as a tribe of sorts. Writing of stereotypes of inverts as feminized, he asserts "but it is a gross mistake to suppose that all the tribe betray these attributes" (Symonds 1896, 15). I can pick contemporary examples almost at random.[21] In late twentieth-century cultural stereotypes, promiscuity is one of the defining characteristics of gay male sexuality. In a nineteenth-century cultural imaginary, it was savages who were promiscuous, even though anthropologists such as Fison and Howitt had a difficult time locating such promiscuous behavior in the field.[22] In matters deemed sexual, primitive promiscuity was understood by nineteenth-century evolutionary anthropologists as the initial stage in human social organization:

> From an initial state of "promiscuous intercourse", there had arisen, in sequence, the "Communal Family" (founded on the intermarriage of brothers and sisters); the "Barbarian family"; … the "Patriarchal family" (founded on the marriage of one man to several wives); and the "Civilized Family" …
>
> *(Stocking 1995, 18–19; see also McLennan 1970)*

Promiscuity remains a defining attribute of those deemed primitive, whether primitive in the sphere of phylogeny—the savage, or primitive in his individual psychosexual development—the gay man. To speculate on a similar matter: the worship of the Phallus is another defining attribute of the category of the primitive in anthropological and derivative psychological literature from Richard Knight's 1786 *Discourse on the Worship of Priapus* to Freud's *Leonardo da Vinci: A Study in Psychosexuality* (1910) (cited in Abelove 1993), as well as a defining feature in psychoanalytic and popular cultural representations of gay male desire.[23]

Towards a normative homosexuality under the sign of evolution, or uses and abuses of Freudian psychoanalysis

The Freudian narration of sexuality and the relation of sexuality to subjectivity are extremely complex, and I do not have the space to do justice to them here. Over a large corpus in which many texts are multiply revised, the narration of a protagonist called "homosexuality" is often contradictory. I isolate one strand in Freud, the strand that regrettably gets taken up in ego-psychology and achieved pre-eminence over much of the twentieth century in medical discourse. While the Freudian text nuances, qualifies, and occasionally contradicts the figuring of homosexuality as arrested development, and other concepts—the unconscious, the death drives—threaten to render it meaningless, I would maintain that this figuration and a sustained tendency to buttress claims with phylogenetic arguments implicate psychoanalysis in the figure of its founder in the imperial discursive networks on race and sexuality that I am working to elucidate here. In *Three Essays on the Theory of Sexuality* (1982), Freud goes some way to denaturalizing questions of sexuality in that causation seems to operate almost accidentally. In the preface to the third edition, he writes: Throughout the entire work, the various factors are placed in a particular order of precedence: preference is given to the accidental factors, while disposition is left in the background, and more weight is attached to ontogenesis than to phylogenesis.[24] Nevertheless, his theorizing of male homosexuality can still be seen as a re-inscription of biological evolutionism into the sphere of the psychic. In a now famous 1935 letter to an American mother of a homosexual son, he writes:

Homosexuality is assuredly no advantage, but it is nothing to be ashamed of, no vice, no depredation, it cannot be classified as an illness, we consider it to be a variation of the sexual function produced by a certain arrest of sexual development... In a certain number of cases, we succeed in developing the blighted germs of heterosexual tendencies which are present in every homosexual.

(as cited in Abelove 1993, 381)

Freud moves from a figuration of homosexuality as a variant of the sexual function to an inscription of it as an "arrest" of sexual development. The cure involves the recuperation of the blighted heterosexual germs. In the idea of arrest and the metaphor of blight, equality, implicitly promised before, disappears through the back-door. While it would be agreeable to read "germs" as suggesting some notion of heterosexuality as disease, I think the term here is interchangeable with seeds. The letter is written in English, but the German word for illness bearing particles—*die Bazille*—is not used interchangeably with a thing that germinates— *der Keim*—which my German/English dictionary tells me means "germ, bud, spore, nucleus, embryo, origin."[25] I think it unlikely that Freud's "germs" here are little pathogens of heterosexuality though some ambiguity must remain. Earlier, Freud, in *Three Essays on the Theory of Sexuality*, writes in a language that denaturalizes homosexuality, but still produces it as truncated development: "What we have thrown together, for reasons of convenience, under the name homosexuality may derive from a diversity of processes of psychosocial *inhibition*" (Freud 1982, 146, italics mine).

This developmental theorizing of homosexual desire can still be figured developmentally even in ways that are not interchangeable with ideas of arrest or inhibition. In *Leonardo da Vinci: A Study in Psychosexuality* (1947), Leonardo's imputed "homosexuality" is explained in terms of a psychosexual precocity: "In the manner of all ungratified mothers she thus took her little son in place of her husband and robbed him of part of his virility by maturing too early his erotic life" (88).[26]

Most importantly, this insistence on figuring homosexuality in developmental terms always robs the homosexual of any claim to parity in the homo/hetero binary. It resists the issue of dispositional or constitutive difference in sexual desire as well as removing questions of individual agency in the choice of sexual-object and sexual aim.

Freud is, however, explicit in resisting the other evolutionary trope for understanding "homosexuality," namely "degeneracy." He views degeneracy in general as a term which is used too indiscriminately in explaining any symptom which is not immediately explicable by trauma or infection.

If we disregard the patients we come across in our medical practice, and cast our eyes round a wider horizon, we shall come in two directions upon facts which make it impossible to regard inversion as a sign of degeneracy:

(a) Account must be taken of the fact that inversion was a frequent phenomenon— one might almost say an institution charged with important functions—among the peoples of antiquity at the height of their civilization.

(b) it is remarkably widespread among many savage and primitive races, whereas the concept of degeneracy is usually restricted to states of high civilization (cf. Bloch); and, even amongst the civilized peoples of Europe, climate and race exercise the most powerful influence on the prevalence of inversion and upon the attitude adopted towards it

(Freud 1982, 139)

Although Freud has earlier in the essay claimed that the ontogenetic factors are more critical in his theory of sexuality, the use of the axis of civilized/primitive points to lurking phylogenetic questions. If "inversion" is to be found amongst the highest and lowest levels of human civilization, then it becomes difficult to explain in terms of the recapitulation of phylogeny by ontogeny. Ontogenetically, homosexuality is explicable by an arrest of the development of the sexual instinct in terms of both sexual object and sexual aim. Phylogenetically, it is difficult to explain at all, given the privileged place of reproductive heterosexuality as the evolutionary motor of species-life.

Freud's famous dictum in *Beyond the Pleasure Principle* that ontogenesis recapitulates phylogenesis imbricates the psychic and social in an evolutionary rhetoric (Freud 1989, 44). In this rhetoric, space is temporalized as contemporaneous non-European cultures are understood as the representatives of Europe's past. This move subsumes the possibility of cultural difference because the model insistently implies that "we," the "civilized," have already been the "primitive."

In his theorizing of the origin of the ego (and the libido that cathects it into being is always normatively heterosexual and male for Freud) in "On Narcissism," Freud refers back to his analysis of animism in *Totem and Taboo*, deeply imbricating the formation of the ego with the evolution of cultural organization, repeating the same subsuming of difference:

> The extension of the libido theory, in my opinion a legitimate one, receives reinforcement from a third quarter, namely from our observations and views on the mental life of children and primitive peoples. In the latter, we find characteristics which if they occurred singly, might be put down to megalomania: an over-estimation of the power of their wishes and mental acts, "the omnipotence of thoughts," a belief in the thaumaturgic force of words, and a technique for dealing with the external world—"magic"—which appears to be a logical application of these grandiose premises. In the children of today, whose development is much more obscure to us, we expect to find an exactly analogous attitude towards the external world. Thus, we form the idea of their being an original libidinal cathexis of the ego, from which some is later given off to objects, but which fundamentally persists and is related to object cathexes much as the body of an amoeba is related to the pseudopodia which it puts out.
>
> *(Freud 1950, 75)*

However, the subsuming of difference, be it along cultural, gender or sexual orientation lines, is never complete. Here, the hierarchizing of terms through a developmental narrative in the attempt to maintain norms that his theory threatens to destabilize is fascinating, and this destabilizing gives the opening for later "gay" psychoanalysts like Lewes paradoxically to renarrate the different as the normative within an evolutionist narrative (Lewes 1988). Nevertheless, the movement of the narrative is sustainedly evolutionist: the possible difference of the child, the primitive, and, implicitly, the homosexual is negated in its *a priori* incorporation into the body of the mature, the civilized and the heterosexual. In such a maneuver, there is a clear foreclosing of the possibility of alterity.

The subsumed position of the primitive in the virtual simultaneity of the Freudian psyche never allows him to speak except as the voice of arrest, repression, fixation, retardation. Not only is he not allowed to speak in any other register, he must continually be made to speak in this one. In terms of a parallel critique in the name of woman, Luce Irigaray's attack on the Lacanian model of the unconscious in "The Poverty of Psychoanalysis" can be made to bear on this narrative movement with some force. She addresses her polemic to "you"—the range of which is unspecified but includes "gentlemen psychoanalysts." This direct address to an *other* out there, infected with hostility as it is, already marks a different conception of the possibilities of dialogue. She is not speaking for or about a position that she has already incorporated. She asserts:

> You would constantly reduce the *yet-to be subjected to the already subjected*, the as-yet unspoken or unsaid of language [langage] to the already subjected to something that a language has already struck dumb or kept silent. And so—perhaps unwittingly?— aren't you the products and defendants of an existing order, the agents and servants of repression and censorship ensuring that this order subsists as though it were the only possible order, that there can be no imaginable speech, desire or language *other than those which have already taken place* no culture authorized by you other than the monocratism of patriarchal discourse?
>
> *(Irigaray 1991, 82, italics mine)*

I read Irigaray as pointing to the foreclosing of other possible desires, languages, cultures and positions in a critique of a set of evolutionary tropes. This becomes apparent if one inserts the language of the child, the primitive, the homosexual as the "yet-to be subjected" which has already been struck dumb by the relegation of their present to the past of the "you." To stay within Freud's revealing biological metaphor, the anaclitic pseudopodia have incorporated the narcissistic other into its body before the body has made the very pseudopodia. We need here to finesse the relation between an exoticizing, positing of *a priori* difference—"making the natives speak"—and creating a silence, so that something as yet unspoken can be heard.

Irigaray's challenge can be read as not only directed against Lacanian psychoanalysis, but more pervasively at the master narrative of evolution itself. An evolutionary narrative permits only one signifier: in classical evolutionism—civilized man; in Lacanian psychoanalysis—the phallus. Freud in a subsequent addition to the *Three Essays* remarks that "the assumption that all human beings have the same form of genitalia is the first of the many remarkable and momentous theories of children" (Freud, 1982, 195). Irigaray's positing of a feminine imaginary, predicated on the two lips in *This Sex which is Not One*, goes some way to undoing the tyranny of the single subsuming subject, which has always and already incorporated and transcended its others in evolutionary logics, though the feminine in psychoanalysis is not structurally related to the masculine in the same way that the homosexual and the primitive are connected to the heterosexual and the civilized, respectively. Men have never been women (though girls for Freud, in passing through a phallic stage have paradoxically been boys), whereas the civilized have necessarily passed through a primitive phase and the etiology of heterosexuality must include a homosexual stage.

Interestingly, there is a place for the retheorizing of homosexuality as normative within Freud's evolutionist paradigm, and the important work of reclaiming moments in Freud against the homophobic virulence of certain of his progeny has been undertaken by writers such as Henry Abelove, Dennis Altman and Kenneth Lewes.[27] Lewes in *The Psychoanalytic Theory of Male Homosexuality*, scrupulously outlines twelve possible structural resolutions of Oedipus, along the axes of instinctual aim, parental identification, Object, mode of object choice, sexual orientation and social stance, only two of which permit a heterosexual, masculine, active, anaclitic combination (Lewes 1988). The Oedipus complex, as a regulative mechanism for male heterosexual object-relatedness, is ineffective, as such, for it structurally permits other forms of deviant heterosexuality and normal homosexuality along the alternative normative axes of masculine/feminine identification and anaclitic/narcissistic object choice. Consequently, within this schema, predicated on the transforming moment of the boy's response to the mother as castrated (the impetus of Oedipus), Lewes outlines the possible normative positions of the homosexual within the regime of the transcendentally signifying phallus.

This attempt to renarrate homosexuality from within normative phallocentrism tends to characterize Irigaray as necessarily homophobic. In *Sexual Dissidence*, Dollimore claims:

> In some instances "sameness" comes to signify the tyranny of Western patriarchal metaphysics, and homosexuality its practice, or, more vaguely its metaphor. Luce Irigaray speaks of a dominant philosophic logos with a "power to reduce all others to the economy of the Same [and] eradicate the difference between the sexes," exalting the metaphor of homosexuality as a kind of anti-difference into nothing less than a far-reaching theory of patriarchal society.
>
> *(1991, 249–250)*

It seems to me that Dollimore is too quick to read homosexuality as the same, taking too literally the definitional term "homo." Arguably, Irigaray can just as easily be read as pointing to "heterosexuality" as the "same"—the "same" indicating an allegiance to normative "heterosexual" desire rather than denoting the lack of difference in the sex/gender of the participants. Sameness and difference split and complicate each other along lines of gender and sexuality. I am reading Irigaray as an advocate for "difference" along both gender and sexuality lines, and her attack on "sameness" as directed at the universal (white) male subject, who, if he participated in same-sex sex acts in much of Euro-America over the last century, ran the severe risk of being feminized, pathologized, arrested, in short, of losing his ability to stand in for the universal, becoming particular, rendered "different" rather than "same."

The attempt to figure the relation of sameness and difference is clearly related to Freud's problem in distinguishing anaclitic and narcissistic object cathexes in "On Narcissism," of understanding narcissism as both a pathological condition and "the libidinal complement to the egoism of the instinct of self preservation, which may be justifiably attributed to every living thing" (Freud 1957, 73–74). Narcissism as perversion is established as integral to the very normative development it later comes to pervert. Dollimore locates this pharmaconic figuration of perversion within a wider transgressive history going back to Augustine. For Dollimore,

> if perversion subverts, it is not as a unitary, pre-social libido, or an original plenitude, but as a transgressive agency inseparable from a dynamic intrinsic to social process … The displacements which constitute certain repressive discriminations are partly enabled by a proximity, which though disavowed, remains to enable a perverse return, an undoing, a transformation.
>
> *(Dollimore 1991, 33)*

He also maintains that dissidence within sexuality is not confined to sexuality and that psychosexual disorder effected by perversion is always more than sexual (Dollimore 1991, 33, 72). For the shattering effect of perversion arises from the fact that it is integral to just those things it threatens.

This reading of perversion, somewhat brutally summarized here, is acute in its sense of the contradictory moments in Freud's narrativizing of homosexuality, displaying a similar awareness to Lewes that the successful normative resolution of Oedipus that permits male, active, anaclitic heterosexuality, can be dependent on homosexual object cathexis onto the father, and narcissistic cathexis onto the boy's own penis to begin latency. Similar points can and have been made about male homosexual object choice arising from a refusal to give up the heterosexual object choice of the mother and so on. Always, the normative contains a subsumed form of the perverse. The relations within and between the binaries homosexuality/ heterosexuality, anaclitic/narcissistic remain slippery. The terms are always and already reversible and displaced within Freud, only hierarchized by a partially interrogated sequential narrative. The difference between the perverse and the normal can only be understood in terms of development. As Freud asserts in "On Narcissism": "Not until there is an object cathexis is it possible to discriminate a sexual energy—the libido—from an energy of the ego-instincts" (Freud 1957, 76). Only once the amoeba has grown its pseudopodia—literally, its fake legs—can it march to embrace the other, only then to incorporate it into its body, if one remembers why an amoeba grows pseudopodia.

Thus, a spatial rather than sequential take on the analysis of male same-sex object choice is quite capable of producing such an object choice as normative rather than pathological. Since the perverse (the homosexual) is already and always present even if only in a subsumed or transcended or perhaps even sublated form in the normal, its term of difference remains held under the signifying regime of the phallus. Consequently Dollimore's attack on Irigaray's pointing to the phallocentric nature of male homosexuality as necessarily homophobic over-privileges the transgressive social potential of this brand of perversion, and fascinatingly his historical bracketing of his discussion of sexual dissidence in the west to an originary point in Augustine allows for an elision of a consideration of classical Greek male "homosexual" desire, where male same-sex object choice can possibly be theorized as normative, and consequently Dollimore's claim that psychosexual disorder effected by perversion is always more than just sexual becomes much more difficult to sustain.

In Sedgwick's tantalizing phrasing: "Are bonds between men the social solvent or the social glue?" If we consider that the primal horde in *Totem and Taboo* were able to mobilize "homosexual feelings and acts" in the constitution of the first human society, we see how Freud's theorizing of the phylogenesis of homosexuality uses a developmental narrative to manage the separation of the homosocial and the homosexual (Freud 1950, 144). To institute the homosocial, the brothers need to have had and to have sublimated homosexual feelings. In a rhetorical pattern deeply typical of Freud, a potentially normative homosexuality is the repressed that continually threatens to return. By building homosexuality into the foundations of the social, Freud is literally and figuratively able to contain it.

This strategy of Freud's still can be brought to bear on contemporary figurations of "gay" identity and community. Sedgwick makes a useful distinction between universalizing and minoritizing models of "homosexuality," a distinction she hopes will come to supplant the essentialist/constructionist split. The ethical and political imperative behind these distinctions is to renarrate or reimagine the homo–hetero binary in terms that are not hierarchical—perhaps, an impossible task or to explode this constitutive binary of western modernity altogether. What is the difference of "the homosexual?" Freud uses the nineteenth-century master-narrative of evolution, transposing it from the phylogenetic sphere of racial "development" to the ontogenetic sphere of psychic development to render the difference of the "homosexual" internal and developmental. The primitive, never an embodied individuated subject for psychoanalysis, disappears. He remains as a category of development, an analog, a marker of subsumed normative deviance in the story of the evolution of the white heterosexual male subject, a position he shares with the white male homosexual, who can, however, be subjectified in the ontogeny/phylogeny recapitulation.

To return to an evolutionary paradigm and a set of debates preceding my Foundational ruse (Foucault's claim of the emergence of the homosexual as species circa 1870), I want to point to how the attempt to create difference is deeply problematic. Ideas that mankind (sic) is polygenetic[28] rather than monogenetic were historically more reactionary, and simply re-inscribed the evolutionary narrative, and so any translation of Irigaray's thoughts on sexual difference into the arena of global cultures must be viewed with considerable circumspection.

The insistence on the difference of the sexually and racially other can take the shape of exoticism or, to remain in a psychoanalytic register, begin to assume the character of the fetish. The transvaluation of the "primitive" from a figure of transcended abjection to a site of originary plenitude has a long history in European theories of racial difference going back, at least, as far as Rousseau. Evolution offers a particular inflection of the discourse of the primitive. I would argue that the temporalities of a teleological evolution—which to be fair to Darwin he fairly explicitly disavows—upset the lapsarian temporality of noble savage discourse. In terms of evolution, we have evolved out of and beyond the primitive. A return to primitivity can thus not be figured as a fallback to an Edenic state of grace or nature—but as degeneracy of varying degrees of seductive power. Nevertheless the primitive, whether he functions as a nostalgic ideal or projected nightmare or transcended origin, remains the definitional buttress to the term "civilized."

This is why Irigaray's attempt to contest the universality of the subject in the evolutionary narrative remains more useful for me than the attempt to give the primitives a voice or the insistence on the normative aspects of homosexuality within the psychoanalytic schema. Although I am sympathetic with this renarration, and recognize its political efficacy for certain gay struggles, its re-inscription of phallocentrism remains problematic, especially when the above extract from "On Narcissism" and Freud's chapter on animism in *Totem and Taboo*, reveal the explicitly colonizing thrust of such phallocentric narrativization. In rereading Freud, do we simply want to claim our "birthright"—the privileges of the phallus?[29]

Asserting *a priori* difference creates another set of problems to the assumption of sameness with difference understood as *developmental* within a unified field. Since the three critical systems in which "modern (homo)sexuality" is articulated, evolutionary sexology, psychoanalysis and gay rights, all make universalist assumptions and inhabit willy-nilly what I have defined as evolutionary or developmental narratives, I have attempted a critique of the assumption of sameness, rather than a critique of the claim of difference.

Developing homosexuality in the developing world

While, perhaps, it would be more comfortable for me to bracket evolutionary theorizings to the age of empire, they show up in a variety of different contexts today: in the contestation over the political status of gay men and lesbians as an ethnic minority in the US, in the use of tribal metaphors in much gay cultural self-representation, in the debates between the "social constructionists" and "biological essentialists" (on both sides of the debates), in the international politics of homosexual identity,[30] and most alarmingly in the cultural representations of AIDS as a distinctively African or Haitian and homosexual disease. I would further argue that these racialised tropes have taken on a new "inverted" life in the repeated claims of many sub-Saharan African politicians that homosexuality is "a decadent western import" and "a white man's disease."[31]

The failure to engage the sexual/cultural indifference and problematic universalism at the core of the evolutionary narrative also plays out in ostensibly liberatory histories and theories of gay community, particularly when they consider "sexual" practices outside of Euro-America. My remarks about the writings of a number of gay studies scholars that follow are not intended as an indictment. Rather, I read the places and manner in which these scholars turn their attention to issues of same-sex corporeal intimacies outside western contexts as symptomatic of deep cultural blind spots, as overdetermined consequences of often unconscious allegiances to predigested narratives and metaphors that are part of the legacy of colonialism, in which all of us who try to think about these matters are implicated. These deep rhetorical patterns and predigested narratives—what I term the rhetorics of evolutionary narratives, themselves part of axioms of imperialism—are often rendered visible only in small slips of language and may be at odds with explicit political positions. In terms of explicit political positions, many lesbian and gay organizations in the US, particularly during the 1970s were vociferously opposed to acts of American imperialism. The Gay Liberation Front took its name from the National Liberation Front in Vietnam (D'Emilio 1992, 242–246). While this act of naming is partly an appropriative gesture, it looks to an *other* of the west for a model of agency in ways that confound evolutionary axioms, and may suggest how neocolonialism allowed for different figurations of difference.

Historians of male homosexuality in the west, however careful they may be about drawing connections between the emergence of the modern homosexual and empire, can still figure difference as *developmental*. Jeffrey Weeks offers the following characterization:

> There were several drives against homosexuality in the 1780s, with the discovery of homosexual groupings in London and Exeter. This embryonic sub-culture was closely associated with transvestism and stereotyped effeminate behaviour, in a mode which still characterises the relatively undeveloped sub-cultures of areas outside the major cities of western Europe and North America.
>
> *(Weeks in Schmitte and Sofer 1992, ix)*

While there may be some empirical truth in noting the connection between gender roles and same-sex erotic practices in many parts of the world, an unacknowledged allegiance to the evolutionary axioms of colonial discourse can only distort the ways these gender roles, related erotic practices, not to mention these "subcultures of areas outside major cities of western Europe," can be understood. For, in this extract, the rest of the world is understood as equivalent to the past of the now dominant form of male homosexuality in the western metropolis: we were like them, but have developed, they are like we were and have yet to develop. Space is temporalized and difference hierarchized, with the modern male homosexual taking the place of the normative white male heterosexual in an uninterrogated replication of the old evolutionary narrative. It is also played out in the language of the body, with culture implicitly biologized in the metaphor of the embryo.

The gendered terms of this encapsulated empirical history of homosexuality also bear traces of the evolutionary script. The embryonic, the primitive, the undeveloped are equated with "stereotyped femininity and transvestism" in a manner of thinking not that far removed from Spencer's notion of the arrest of embryonic female evolution, except here culture is used to carry the meanings a more blatantly sexist and racist age could consign to biology. White masculinity (albeit white *homosexual* masculinity) is necessarily posited as the pinnacle and measure of all development in this story of homosexuality.

Arguably, what permits such characterizations is an allegiance to an empiricism which gestures towards the historicity and/or social construction of its objects, but fails to subject its analytic categories to the same procedures. In his preface, Weeks is scrupulous in pointing out that sexuality is always constructed, that it takes different forms in different places at different times, that it is not an innate human attribute:

> To put it bluntly, *homosexuality, like all forms of sexuality, has different meanings in different cultures*—so much that it becomes difficult to find any common essence which links the different ways it is lived, apart that is, from the *pure sexual activity itself.*[32]
>
> *(Weeks in Schmitt and Sofer 1992, xi; italics mine)*

Ironically, then, in the name of a historical materialism, the category "sexuality" floats through history and across the planet like one of Plato's forms, just making costume changes here and there. Critics/historians deploying "sexuality" retain an aporia in perceiving its own historical staging and deployment. Given that no "common essence" can be established, can the category "pure sexual activity itself" hold? May pure sexual activity itself not hold other meanings than "sexuality"?

In the foreword referred to above, Weeks concludes:

> This book, like a photographic image, captures the sexual culture of the Muslim societies at a crucial moment. Only time will tell whether that culture will approximate more and more to the secularized Western model, or come increasingly under the sway of a new religious militancy.
>
> *(Weeks 1977, 36)*

Here, the evolutionary topos immediately forecloses options of dialogue, scripting performances that are then heralded as empirical. Unpacking the comparison to a "snapshot": what appears to be an appeal to the incontrovertibility of the photographic image can be read as a refusal to interrogate the apparatus of the camera, the position of the photographer, the selection of the moment, the location where the image is processed, the sites of its consumption. Consequently, such an empirically true picture can only see the *other* as accommodating itself to the western present or, despite the word "new," being repressed by religion—the fate of male same-sex desire in the western past. We are left with only one possible progressive trajectory—the transformation of actors in same-sex genital activity into political subjects. Since Weeks's tale is one of historical rather than evolutionary development, and given the tendency of gay identity to follow capitalist encroachments, Weeks may very well be right, except that the effects of globalizing capital are spectacularly uneven and may make generalizing about "the sexual culture of Muslim societies"—itself an odd concatenation of a category—impossible.

A wealth of gay studies anthropology fails to consider what may be at stake in its related figuration of certain acts as homosexual.[33] In a cavalier moment, one could be tempted to retitle Gil Herdt's *Ritualized Homosexuality in Melanesia* as *Homosexualized Ritual in the Anthropological Gaze* for the way the various articles attribute sexual significance to what the participants may understand in many other ways.[34] David Greenberg's cataloging of the behavior of other cultures in the chapter entitled "Homosexuality in Kinship Societies" in his *The Construction of Homosexuality*, relentlessly adheres to an evolutionist narrative in discussing temple remains in the Ukraine:

> In many contemporary primitive cultures, men worship goddesses, and this could certainly have been true in Stone Age cultures as well. In any event, the sculptures

are not detailed enough to tell us whether some of these seemingly female figures
are actually male transvestites.

(Greenberg 1988, 64)

In a desire to locate the presence of transgender shamans in Paleolithic Europe, the past
of Europe is the present of elsewhere. The category of sexuality is inserted in such a way that
the evolutionist narrative is not destabilized at all, suggesting its flexibility in accommodating
apparently innovative categories of social analysis to produce the same empirical findings. I
think similar points can, must and have been made about transcendental and reifying uses
of race, class and gender across temporal and cultural borders. The chapter headings of
this encyclopedic book reveal a critical tension in evolutionary narratives of "homosexual"
difference. Part I is entitled "Before Homosexuality," yet the first three chapters are
entitled "Homosexual Relations in Kinship-Structured Societies," "Inequality and the
State: Homosexual Innovations in Archaic Civilizations," "Early Civilizations: Variations
on Homosexual Themes," respectively. What can the adjective "homosexual" mean when
we have "homosexual relations, innovations and themes" before we can have the noun
"homosexuality"? Retrospectively, the apparently innocent descriptor "homosexual" gives
form and meaning to a range of corporeal relations between members of the same-sex,
which may have been marked in radically different ways, if they were marked at all. The
subsequent concept produces all its prior evolutionary stages.

Michael Warner in *Fear of a Queer Planet*, attempts to invoke queerness as a tool for
undoing the heteronormativity of class and gender analysis, suggesting the ways in which
such categories are embedded in a history of sexuality. Discussing Andrew Parker's reading
of homophobia in Marx's *The Eighteenth Brumaire of Louis Bonaparte* in the context of the
collaboration of Marx and Engels, he claims:

> By calling our attention to the homosocial dynamics of that collaboration, Parker
> suggests that Marxist thought is embedded in a history of sexuality, reproductivism,
> and homosociality in a way that prevents it from grasping these problems as
> conditioning its own project … Core elements of the Marxist paradigm may
> have to be seen as properly ideological moments in the history of reproductive
> heterosexuality.

(Warner 1993, 14)

While Warner is clearly not deploying queerness in the same way that Greenberg, Herdt or
Weeks deploy sexuality, I suspect that Warner needs to follow through in trying to grasp the
problems in the historical and rhetorical conditioning of the project of queerness, as defined by
responses to morality discourses, bound up with evolutionary ideas about modernity. Charmed
as I am, by his use of Vidal's Myra Breckinridge as a messiah for global queerness, I cannot see
the metaphor of a queer planet as *only* a metaphor, unrelated to the site of queer subjectivity
in the US and innocent of its own colonizing fantasies.[35] In as much as queer theory points to
the underlying historical script of sexuality in the constitution of the terms of class and gender
analysis, it needs to be equally sensitive to the historical conditions of the production of the
category sexuality and to its contemporary global deployments and continual resignifications.[36]

I do not wish naively to assume a range of speaking subalterns, thereby subscribing to
another assumption about the fullness of the agency of the other in an anthropological gaze,
nor to pretend that the penetration of capital has left pure cultures, intact, untainted by the west.
Instead I wish to register the risks of certain dangerous, if necessary, interpretive impositions.

It is within this racialized history that contemporary representations of homosexuality as a form of western imperialism need to be understood. In using the terms, western and non-western, I am not claiming that either pole of the binary is monolithic in its reference. Specificities of place will always complicate, if not undo the binary. Nevertheless, since the discourses I discuss embraced and continue to embrace such a dichotomy, and the terms, western/non-western, refer to being on different ends of important global power differentials, I believe that the abstraction—confounded as it may be by its specificities—is still a useful one in this context. I agree with Weeks that a clear distinction between acts and identities needs to be made. Additionally, the very idea of "sexuality," or "pure sexual activity itself" as a registerable transcultural category needs to be questioned. While it is clear that acts that look homosexual to a contemporary western gaze are by and large universal, the emergence of a homosexual social identity—"gayness"—as we know it needs to be carefully historically and geographically bracketed.

Thus attacks on "gayness" in the "developing" world need to be situated in a complex discursive field. Well meaning cries of homophobia from the west are not adequate to this task. Given the hypersexualization of blackness in western cultural representations and the assignation of Africa and other parts of the non-western world as the site of the primitively polymorphously perverse in the ontogeny/phylogeny recapitulation,[37] anti-imperialist attacks on homosexuality can be seen as refusals to carry the imputation of primitiveness, and to counter-project the racist charge of retardation and/or degeneration onto its western source, by scapegoating the west's own sexual deviants or what these attacks perceive as their local proxies.

This is in addition to the often crassly material exploitation experienced through the growth of homosexual sex tourism over the last century, which often deserves the designation imperialism. I wish to make it clear here that I do not make a special case for sex-work, and that prostitution functions in many places as one of many possible sweat-shops where "Third World" labor is exploited. The shift in the last hundred years from the perception, attested to in writers from Edward Carpenter to William Burroughs, that "homosexual" practices were much less subject to censure in non-western societies to the contemporary situation in which the west is held up as the place in which homosexual acts are most free from persecution can only be accounted for by the particularly western, liberal capitalist articulation of the person of the homosexual.[38]

Current economic and human rights discourses of development inflect definitions and discussions of homosexuality as people outside of Euro-America are increasingly laying claim to homosexual identity. This creates a new set of developmental contradictions in figuring homosexuality as an identity that travels. I agree with John D'Emilio when he argues that gay identity follows capitalism, and that capitalism is profoundly double-edged for gay identity:

> On the one hand, capitalism continually weakens the material foundation of family life, making it possible for individuals to live outside the family, and for a lesbian and gay male identity to develop. On the other, it needs to push men and women into families, at least long enough to reproduce the next generation of workers. The elevation of the family to ideological preeminence guarantees that capitalist society will reproduce not just children, but heterosexism and homophobia.
>
> *(D'Emilio 1993, 474)*

The emergence of small yet vocal and visible gay rights movements predominantly among the urban classes in many Latin American, Asian and African countries testifies to the effect of capitalist penetration on the emergence of lesbian and gay identity, even though these identities are inflected by local "traditions" and gender and class variables.[39] Though considered globally, the assertion that capitalism makes it possible for individuals to live outside the family acquires a certain irony. Arguably, transnational capitalism's weakening of "the material foundations of family life" is making it harder for many people to live at all. If Sedgwick is right that the homo/hetero binary is central to all epistemologies of modernity, the presence of "homosexuals" in societies outside the west can be read as a mark of capitalist development, and in certain nationalist contexts is seen as a sign of overdevelopment or decadence. The understanding of "homosexuality" as the marker of western decadence *par excellence* may also suggest ways in which the person laying claim to homosexual identity in an era of global capitalism can be made to carry the anxieties surrounding the social ruptures produced by economic development.

The relationship between discourses of economic development and what I have characterized as evolutionary rhetorics is a critical one, but too vast for me to do any more than touch briefly upon it in this essay. As Marx and Engels argue in "The Communist Manifesto," bourgeois cultural forms and subjectivities will ineluctably follow the encroachment of capitalist forms of production across the globe:

> The bourgeoisie, by the rapid improvement of all instruments of production, by the immensely facilitated means of communication, draws all, even the most barbarian, nations into civilization. The cheap prices of its commodities are the heavy artillery with which it batters down all Chinese walls, with which it forces the barbarians' obstinate hatred of foreigners to capitulate. It compels all nations, on pain of extinction, to adopt the bourgeois mode of production; it compels them to introduce what it calls civilization into their midst, i.e. to become bourgeois themselves. In a word, it creates a world after its own image.
>
> *(Marx and Engels 1971, 93)*

John D'Emilio's thesis that gay identity follows capital may very well have global ramifications. The racial analogy I point to in the theorizing of homosexual identities is complicated by the class identities and trajectories of people laying claim to gay identity on the ground.[40]

Given the difficulties of establishing both the time and space of this entity called "homosexuality," the homophobia of anti-imperialist movements and regimes in such diverse contexts as Cuba, Iran and, more recently, Zimbabwe,[41] needs to be accounted for in more complex ways than simply privileging the putative freedom in the west. If I am trying to formulate the question of why anti-imperialism articulates homophobia, I wish to suggest that it is equally imperative to frame the question of the international homosexual rights movement's unwitting but fairly consistent invocation of anti-third world racism, in both its hostile and benevolent guises. The International Tribunal on Human Rights violations held in October 1995 in New York under the auspices of IGLHRC (International Gay and Lesbian Human Rights Commission) encapsulates many of these problems. The tribunal explicitly linked itself to the 50-year anniversary of the UN's Universal Declaration of Human Rights. The language of sexual orientation does not appear anywhere in that document. International legal recognition of discrimination against "homosexual" individuals as a human rights violation is contested, yet it is frequently articulated as the newest right in late liberalism. My first charge against such a tribunal is hypocrisy: in a country where roughly half the states have anti-sodomy laws on their statutes, with a single exception, the only violations investigated were those of third world and eastern European countries (International Tribunal on Human Rights Violations Against Sexual Minorities 1995). The second is obfuscation. While it would be very difficult not to support the work done by IGLHRC and other Human Rights organizations (Amnesty International, Human Rights Watch) on violations against sexual minorities, I maintain that they are highly interested sites for the production of knowledge about sexual practices and norms outside of western Europe and the US, and since much of their work centers around asylum cases, they have an interest in making conditions look as bad as possible in other countries.

If the white middle class heterosexual male is the universal subject of the earlier evolutionary narrative that I sketch and criticize, I suggest that the universalization of the homosexual as a transhistorical, trans-spatial subject as he/she is articulated in human rights discourse reproduces the same ethical violence. By attempting to transform participants in certain corporeal intimacies into homosexual persons, do we not do a great disservice to the vast majority of participants in same-sex acts in other places? To assert the universality of a specific historical agent can, and arguably is, closing down spaces for these participants without replicating the set of historical circumstances which allowed gayness to have historical agency in the west. This is especially so given the unevenness of capitalist development globally. The universalism that promises liberation ends up as oppression.

Ironically this piece of work, never mind my own identity, rests on the relatively successful evolution of the coming out project that typifies the emergence of the politicized or acculturated homosexual person in western culture. It is that which permits me some standing as an agent of knowledge in an emerging discipline, rather than as the subject of a set of pathologizing medical and legal codes. If I am biting the hand that feeds me, or hacking away at the ground under my feet, I do so in the attempt to mount a critique of the very conceptual tools that I cannot do without,[42] in order to try to begin to think a queer ethics that is not predicated on the violence implied in the process of othering that an evolutionary narrative necessarily entails.

Acknowledgements

This chapter was originally published as Neville Hoad (2000) "Arrested development or the queerness of savages: Resisting evolutionary narratives of difference," *Postcolonial Studies* Vol.3:2 pp.133–158 ©The Institute of Postcolonial Studies, reprinted by permission of Taylor & Francis Ltd, www.tandfonline.com on behalf of The Institute of Postcolonial Studies.

Notes

1 For the current state of pinkwashing, see https://electronicintifada.net/tags/pinkwashing
2 This essay has been a long time in the writing and many people have assisted it on its way. Gayatri Chakravorty Spivak and Henry Abelove encouraged me in this line of inquiry. Anne McClintock helped me focus many of the ideas and was patient with the involutions of my prose. Roger Lancaster gave it a tough but useful reading. Earlier drafts were presented at the First Southern African Colloquium on Gay and Lesbian Studies at the University of Cape Town in October, 1995, The Modern Languages Association Annual Convention in Washington, DC in December, 1996 and at the Sawyer Seminar Inaugural Symposium at the University of Chicago in October, 1997. I am appreciative of the comments and questions I received on these occasions. Fenella Macfarlane, Chandon Reddy and Martin Scherzinger read earlier versions and I am thankful for their comments and support. Special thanks to Joseph Massad for his sustained critical engagement with this essay.

3 These works are written in Europe or the United States but often take people from elsewhere in the world as their subjects. Bleys (1995) provides a wealth of documentation on travel writings about the sexual practices of the "natives" and how these inform European understandings of male same-sex desires back home. See particularly 206–272.

4 On the nineteenth-century configuration of this problematic, see Hall (1992, 11–40). For a consideration of how class, race and gender categories need to be understood in relation to each other, Anne McClintock (1995, 1–9) insists on the intersecting, mutually constituting and differentiating nature of race, gender and class as social and analytic categories. Stoler (1995, 7) attempts to deepen and glancingly contest Michel Foucault's *History of Sexuality* Vol. 1 by arguing that "Europe's eighteenth-century discourses on sexuality can—indeed must—be traced along a more circuitous imperial route that leads to nineteenth-century technologies of sex." Stoler pays scant attention to how colonial experiences and attendant racial discourses impact on metropolitan theories of homosexuality. Her discussion of homosexuality is framed in terms of how Dutch colonial officials justified inter-racial heterosexual sexual activity for colonial troops—"concubinage with native women was justified as preferable to homosexual contacts and intimacies outside the state's control" (180). Somerville (1994) offers a compelling tracing of how theories of scientific racism, themselves deeply enmeshed in evolutionary arguments, are used in the production of knowledge of the homosexual body. Since her focus on scientific racism draws mainly from American examples, she does not explicitly address the specificity of the British imperial context, and more concerned with the visual field—evident in her interest in explicating the legacy of comparative anatomy for sexuality studies—her concern is not directly with the set of developmental metaphors and assumptions that I maintain hold race, empire and sexuality together.

5 The paleonymy of the term "subject" is radically unsettling here. I am using the term more in an older grammatical sense, though overtones of "the individuated human psyche/body produced through language" are probably also at play.

6 I follow Foucault in the attempt to articulate the genealogy of the homosexual as "species." However, I wish to deepen the constitutive discourses of this emergent "species" beyond the medico-juridical apparatus to include their undergirdings of evolutionary theory and imperial practices. It must be noted that the French word *spèce* has a broader range of meaning than the English cognate "species." "Kind" or "type" could also be acceptable translations in this context.

7 According to Magnus Hirschfeld, many of the thousand or so works produced on the subject of homosexuals are directed at the legal profession. Symonds's *A Problem in Modern Ethics* is "addressed especially to medical psychologists and jurists," iii.

8 This idea may predate the era I am discussing. Greenblatt (1988, 77) has approached the issue of cross-dressed boy actors on the early modern stage via Renaissance theories that women are unfinished men and that thus "there are not two radically different sexual structures but only one—outward and visible in the man, inverted and hidden in the woman." Thanks to Fenella Macfarlane for finding this reference for me.

9 Richard Krafft-Ebing and Max Nordau are probably the two most prominent *fin de siècle* figures to theorize inversion/homosexuality in terms of a variety of degenerative processes. Krafft-Ebing's (1965, 360) discussion of "male antipathic sexual feeling" always attributes same sex desire to degeneration of mind, body and spirit: "By the side of the functional signs of degeneration attending antipathic sexual feeling are found other functional, and in many cases anatomical, evidences of degeneration." Nordau's attacks on aestheticism suggest a wider cultural climate of degeneration in which abnormal sexual behavior is implicated: "[H]e commits a serious error if, in the aesthetic schools of the last few years, he sees the heralds of a new era. They do not direct us towards the future, but point backwards towards the past … and what the ignorant hold to be outbursts of gushing youthful vigour and turbulent constructive impulses are nothing but the convulsions and spasms of exhaustion" (cited in Cohen 1993, 15–16).

10 Ornamentation feminizes "savage men" in Darwin's *Descent of Man* (1998, originally pubished in 1871), as it permits women to take over the male prerogative of sexual choice. Discussing the beard as a male ornament, Darwin remarks "in utterly barbarous times, women have more power in choosing, rejecting and tempting their lovers or of afterwards changing their husbands" (1998, 619–620). This lends the discourse of effeminacy an implicitly racialized dimension in late nineteenth-century Britain.

11 Interestingly in the Bugandan crisis (discussed in section II of this essay), the Anglican missionary, Alexander Murdoch Mackay, likens Mwanga, the "sodomizing" king, to Nero (Moorehead 1960, 296).

12 This idea is picked up by the sociobiologist, E.O. Wilson (1978).

13 I realize that I use these terms anachronistically. There was considerable slippage in late nineteenth-century definitions of race. Race could mean nation, as in "British race." It could also signify ancestry, as in "Anglo-Saxon race" as well as refer to the more familiar groups of people with varying skin tones and facial features. The modern understanding of homosexuality is emergent in this period, though homophobia is a much more recent coinage. I understand racism and homophobia as discourses which stigmatize any deviations from whiteness and heterosexuality, their respective norms, through a range of strategies, an important one being the evolutionary narrative of difference as developmental.

14 In an article which is useful in pointing to and complicating the mobilizations of anthropology that I am discussing, Jonathan Goldberg reads the English translation of Balboa's feeding of forty apparently transgender "sodomites" (some of whom were allegedly freely handed over to the Spaniards by the natives) to his dogs, following his defeat of the leaders of the Indians of Quarequa in present day Panama in 1511. Goldberg points to the multivalenced significance of this act, revealing how the account allows for Balboa to be staged as a proto-democratic hero, a fighter for native women, who must be degraded by the presence of these people in their midst, as well as crusader for Christ in the New World. In his analysis, the overdetermined nature of "homosexuality" in colonial encounters is suggested, with the elimination of "the preposterous vice" serving as some kind of justification for conquest, but never just that (Goldberg 1993).

15 For a discussion of Burton's varied sexual proclivities, see McLynn (1990, 15–16, 41–42, and 51–53).

16 For the French, it is the English vice. The English word "bugger" is derived from "Bulgarian." The word "berdache" is derived from a Turkish word and is then applied to cross-gendered Native Americans.

17 Père Lourdel, in charge of the Roman Catholic Mission in Buganda at the time of the massacres, writes: "The first cause is that the king, who does not himself want religion, cannot bear the thought that they whom he calls his slaves, know more about it than he does, and believes himself despised by the Christians the moment he does not follow their example. The second cause is the impossibility of satisfying his shameful passions" (cited in Thoonen 1941, 168). See also Oliver 1952, 103).

18 R.W. Beachey (1996, 193) claims of Mwanga, "He was capricious, lacking in courage and sapped by private vices reputedly acquired from the Arabs. He was soon in headlong collision with the missions, and there followed in the early summer of 1886 the cruel martyrdom of some 30 young Baganda youths." Marie de Kiewet Hemphill (1996, 400) agrees: "The immediate pretext, if not the whole cause, for the tragedy was the refusal of the young Christian pages at the court to yield to Mwanga's unnatural desires."

19 Sir Harry Johnstone, a figure instrumental in setting up the protectorates of Nyasaland and Northern Rhodesia, and the British representative in the Ugandan British Agreement of 1900, makes the following remarks about Mwanga: "Perhaps he might still have been king had not his vicious propensities taken a turn which disgusted even his negro people, and made them fear that his precept and example spreading widely among his imitative subjects might result in the disappearance in time of the Uganda race" (Johnstone 1902, 685). In *Light and Darkness in East Africa*, a writer for the World Dominion Survey Series, claims of Mwanga: "But he quickly revealed himself a dissolute profligate, and during the years 1885 and 1886 made a determined effort to swing the country back to heathenism. Neither the king nor his chiefs could brook the Christian requirement of monogamy, though it was being applied with charity and tact. A deeper cause however was Mwanga's resolve to make his court a center of unbridled heathen obscenity" (McLeish 1927, 26).

20 Relatedly, cannibalism and homosexuality are connected as the two "unspeakable acts" in a nineteenth-century Anglophone imaginary. See Crain (1994, 25–53).

21 The headline of a *Sunday Times* article describing the 1993 Gay Pride march in London read "The Colourful Tribes of the Gay Community"; and an article in the now defunct *Outlook* in 1990 laments the dearth of bathroom sex in the following terms: "Never will tribal rites be exercised so widely and so freely as in the recent past. Here and there intrepid tribesmen

continue to seek anonymous gratification, but with less and less success as caution conquers lust. Now that only a few fading Graffiti remain, the history of quick sex seekers has become as inaccessible as that of preliterate tribes. Just as the invading Catholic Spaniards destroyed the pagan Mayan codices in the New World, the tribal gay sex-seekers have destroyed their own literature and with it a key to a significant cultural history" (Waite 1990, 14). Interestingly, the metaphor of tribalism is invoked in a discussion of promiscuity.

22 See Fison and Howitt's 1878 *Kamilaroi and Kurnai* (Fison and Howitt 1991, 25–30) for an account of the difficulty of locating "primitive promiscuity" amongst people deemed to embody the early history of mankind.

23 How may the stereotype of the "size queen" be brought to bear on this? For contemporary gay male complicity with this discursive linking, see the decidedly juicy "anthropology" of Tobias Schneebaum, where the deeper into the jungle you go, the more things start to look like a sex club. His *Keep the River on your Right* (1969, 102–107 and 150) offers disturbingly sexualized descriptions of cannibalism.

24 Freud, 1982, 131. In German: "Überall wird ein gewisser Instanzenzug eingehalten, werden die akzidentellen Momente vorangestellt, die dispositionellen im Hintergrund gelassen und wird die ontogenetische Entwicklung vor der phylogenetische berü¨cksichtigt" (1982, Vol. 5, 29) The German captures the contingent nature of Freud's thought on sexuality more accurately. The set of structuring relational concepts—accidental, dispositional, ontogenetic and phylogenetic— can be maneuvered between foreground and background and are not necessarily always in the same relation to each other. Strachey's insertion of the ideas of "preference" and "more weight" gives Freud's prose more certainty and undermines the possibility of reversal present in the explicit spatial maneuvering in Freud's prose.

25 *Cassell's German Dictionary* (London: Cassell, 1971), 259. This cross-language attempt to ascertain the valence of germs results from being pushed on this point by Henry Abelove, whose essay cited above irrefutably establishes that Freud in his dealings with people identified as homosexuals cannot with any justice be called homophobic. It should be clear that I am not yet convinced that the ethics implied by the Freudian narration of homosexuality as arrested development can entirely avoid that charge as well as that of racism. I would not however make the strong claim that these historical "contaminations" render Freud only of historical interest, but am equally uncomfortable with attempts to ignore or summarily dismiss the presence of these received ideas of *fin de siècle* Europe in Freud's text.

26 This is the account of male homosexuality in Freud that gripped the twentieth-century popular imagination. Gay boys have too intense a relationship with the mothers, causing an identification with the mother and consequent desire for men. "My mother made me a homosexual. If I gave her the wool, would she make me one too."

27 As early as 1971, Dennis Altman suggests the utility of Freud for gay liberation projects. See also Abelove (1993, 381–386) for a useful account of how psychoanalytic thinking on sexuality refuses to separate homosexuals as a special group from the rest of humanity. In an historically nuanced reading, Abelove finds in Freud a critique of gay identity politics, producing Freud as a kind of queer theorist, long before the term queer had acquired its current critical valence.

28 See Gould (1996, 71–72 and 102–105) for a discussion of the debates between the monogenists who claimed that mankind was one species and the polygenists who claimed that many different species were contained under the label "man."

29 I am not quite sure who this "we" can be: "Anti-imperialist Fags for Psychoanalysis" perhaps?

30 The problem with transposing western, liberal capitalist versions of the practitioner of same-sex acts onto other social landscapes has become particularly acute in the area of HIV prevention campaigns. See Roberts (1995).

31 For a discussion of claims of the unAfrican nature of homosexuality, see Phillips (1997) and Hoad (1998).

32 Weeks, "Foreword" to Schmitt, Arno and Sofer, Jehoeda. *Sexuality and Eroticism among Males in Moslem Societies* (New York: Haworth Press, 1992), xi.

33 For an extensive discussion of many such studies, see Weston (1993). Weston claims that "lesbian/gay studies in anthropology has not been immune to the documentary impulse that brushes aside theory in the rush for 'facts.'" (340) For a trenchant and, at times, brilliant critique of the "gay, white missionary impulses" that underlie much gay studies anthropology, see Bustos-Aguilar (1995).

34 As Kath Weston notes, Herdt and other ethnographers of Melanesia have subsequently recast "ritualized homosexuality" as "semen transactions" or "boy inseminating rituals," and often employ local terms to discuss these practices. Discussing Unni Wikan's use of the indigenous term xanith, rather than transvestite or transsexual, Weston argues: "Yet the move to employ indigenous categories is no more neutral in its effects than the earlier less reflective application of 'homosexuality' to a multitude of occasions. Although intended as a corrective to ethnocentrism and overgeneralization, the use of foreign names constructs the subject of inquiry as always and already other. Now seemingly without parallel, the xanith becomes implicated in a renewed form of orientalism in which linguistic terms subtly reify differences and buttress ethnographic authority" (Weston 1998, 158–159).

35 The crisis engendered in both US gay and left-wing circles by the position of gay and lesbian Cubans under the revolution reveals the over-determination of gay and lesbian identity internationally—the term "queer," dependent on an understanding of being stigmatized by Western heteronormativity within the Anglophone West, is consequently subject to the same problems. Looking at the changing situation of émigré communities in the US, US anti-communism and the experiences of gay men and lesbians in Cuba, Rich and Arguelles are able to explain the remarkable achievement of an anti-Castro campaign, predicated on Cuba's repression of homosexual rights, within the virulent homophobia of the Cuban émigré enclaves and the US right-wing.

36 Warner has subsequently revised his position, acknowledging the American location of "queer:" "In the New World Order, we should be more than usually cautious about global utopianisms that require American slang" (1995, 361–371).

37 Bustos-Aguilar in "Mister Don't Touch the Banana" (1995) reads the "surplus of savage sexuality" as a constitutive trope in US representations of sex south of the border.

38 For a compelling analysis of category trouble in international gay and lesbian organizing in relation to Filipino "gay" men living in New York, but with much wider theoretical and political implications, see Manalansan (1996, 425–438).

39 For a lucid chronicling of this process of the globalizing aspects of gay identity, with particular focus on south-east Asia, see Altman (1997, 417–436).

40 I am grateful to Henry Abelove for raising these issues with me.

41 For a lucid discussion of the contemporary Southern African situation squarely within a Human Rights paradigm see Dunton and Palmberg (1996, 7–18).

42 Here I am adapting Gayatri Chakravorty Spivak's definition of deconstruction as "the critique of a structure you cannot wish not to inhabit" (Spivak 1996, 7).

References

Abelove, Henry. 1993. "Freud, Homosexuality and the Americans." In *The Lesbian and Gay Studies Reader*, edited by Henry Abelove, Michele Aina Barale, M. Halperin, pp. 381–396. New York: Routledge.

Altman, D. 1971. *Homosexual: Oppression and Liberation*. New York: Avon Books.

Altman, D. 1997. "Global Gaze/Global Gays." *GLQ* 3: 417–436.

Apter, David E. 1961. *The Political Kingdom in Uganda: A Study in Bureaucratic Nationalism*. Princeton, NJ: Princeton University Press.

Beachey, R.W. 1996. *A History of East Africa, 1592–1902*. New York: Tauris.

Bleys, Rudi. 1995. *The Geography of Perversion: Male-to-Male Sexual Behaviour outside the West and the Ethnographic Imagination, 1750–1918*. New York: New York University Press.

Burton, Richard Francis. 1886. *Arabian Nights*. London: Benares Edition.

Bustos-Aguilar, Pedro. 1995. "Mister Don't Touch the Banana: Notes on the Popularity of the Ethnosexed Body South of the Border." *Critique of Anthropology* 15, no. 2: 149–170.

Carpenter, Edward. 1921. *Intermediate Types among Primitive Folk*. New York, London: Mitchell Kennerly.

Chauncey, George. 1994. *Gay New York and the Making of the Gay Male World 1890–1940*. New York: Basic Books.

Cheney, Kristen. 2009. "Locating Neocolonialism: Tradition and Human Rights in Uganda's Gay Death Penalty." *African Studies Review* 55, no. 2: 31–66.

Cohen, Ed. 1993. *Talk on the Wilde Side*. New York: Routledge.

Conway, J. 1972. "Stereotypes of Femininity in a Theory of Sexual Evolution." In *Suffer and Be Still: Women in the Victorian Age*, edited by Martha Vicinus, pp. 140–154. Bloomington, IN: University of Indiana Press.

Crain, Caleb. 1994. "Lovers of Human Flesh: Cannibalism and Homosexuality in Melville." *American Literature*, Spring, 25–53.

D'Emilio, John. 1992. *Making Trouble: Essays on Gay History, Politics and the University*. New York: Routledge.

D'Emilio, John. 1993. "Capitalism and Gay Identity." In *The Lesbian and Gay Studies Reader*, edited by Henry Abelove, Michele Aina Barale, M. Halperin, pp. 467–478. New York: Routledge.

Darwin, Charles. 1998. *The Descent of Man*. New York: Promotheus Books.

de Kiewet Hemphill, Marie. 1996. "The British Sphere, 1884–1894." In *History of East Africa* edited by R. Oliver and G. Matthew. Oxford: Oxford University Press.

Dollimore, Jonathan. 1987. "Different Desires: Subjectivity and Transgression in Wilde and Gide." *Textual Practice* 1, no. 1: 48–67.

Dollimore, Jonathan. 1991. *Sexual Dissidence: Augustine to Wilde, Freud to Foucault*. Oxford: Oxford University Press.

Dunton, Chris and Palmberg, Mai. 1996. *Human Rights and Homosexuality in Southern Africa*. Uppsala, Sweden: Nordiska Afrikainstituet.

Fabian, Johannes. 1983. *Time and the Other: How Anthropology Makes its Object*. New York: Columbia University Press.

Ferguson, Roderick. 2003. *Aberrations in Black: Toward a Queer of Color Critique*. Minneapolis, MN: University of Minnesota Press.

Fison, L. and Howitt, A.W. 1991. *Kamilaroi and Kurnai*. Canberra: Aboriginal Studies Press.

Foucault, Michel. 1978. *History of Sexuality*. Vol. 1. New York: Pantheon Books.

Freud, Sigmund.1947. *Leonardo da Vinci: A Study in Psychosexuality*. Trans. A.A. Brill. New York: Random.

Freud, Sigmund. 1950. *Totem and Taboo*. New York: Norton.

Freud, Sigmund. 1957. "On narcissism: An introduction." In *The Standard Edition of the Complete Psychological Works of Sigmund Freud*, Vol. 14, edited and translated by J. Strachey, pp. 73–102. London: Hogarth Press.

Freud, Sigmund.1982. *Three Essays on the Theory of Sexuality*. New York: Basic Books.

Freud, Sigmund.1989. *Beyond the Pleasure Principle*. New York: Norton.

Fryer, Jonathan. 1998. *Andre & Oscar: The Literary Friendship of Andre Gide and Oscar Wilde*. London: St Martin's Press.

Geddes, Patrick and Thomson, J. Arthur. 1998. "The Evolution of Sex." In *Sexology Uncensored: The Documents of Sexual Science*, edited by Lucy Bland and Laura Doan, pp. 1–14. Chicago, IL: University of Chicago Press.

Goldberg, Jonathan. 1993. "Sodomy in the New World: Anthropologies Old and New." In *Fear of a Queer Planet*, edited by Michael Warner, pp. 3–18. Minneapolis, MN: University of Minnesota Press.

Gould, Stephen Jay. 1996. *The Mismeasure of Man*. New York: Norton.

Greenberg, David. 1988. *The Construction of Homosexuality*. Chicago, IL: The University of Chicago Press.

Greenblatt, Stephen. 1988. *Shakespearian Negotiations*. Berkeley, CA: University of California Press.

Hall, Catherine. 1992. *White, Male and Middle-Class: Explorations in Feminism and History*. New York: Routledge.

Hoad, Neville. 1998. "Tradition, Modernity and Human Rights: An Interrogation of Contemporary Lesbian and Gay Rights Claims in Southern African Nationalist Discourses." *Development Update* 2, no. 2: 32–43.

Hoad, Neville. 2016. "Queer Customs against the Law." *Research in African Literature* 47, no. 2: 1–19

Houlbrook, Matt. 2006. *Queer London: Perils and Pleasures in the Sexual Metropolis, 1918-1957*. Chicago, IL: University of Chicago Press.

Huxley, Thomas Henry. 1911. *Man's Place in Nature and Other Essays*. London: Dent.

International Tribunal on Human Rights Violations against Sexual Minorities. 1995. Press Packet. October 27. New York City.

Irigaray, Luce. 1991. "The Poverty of Psychoanalysis." In *The Irigaray Reader*, edited by Margaret Whitford, Oxford: Basil Blackwell.

Jackson, Peter. 2011. *Queer Bangkok: 21st Century Markets, Media, and Rights*. Hong Kong: Hong Kong University Press.

Johnstone, Harry H. 1902. *The Uganda Protectorate*, Vol. II. London: Hutchinson and Co.

Justice, Daniel Heath and Cox, James H. 2008. "Queering Native Literature, Indigenizing Queer Theory." *Studies in American Indian Literatures* 20, no.1: xiii–xiv.

Krafft-Ebing, Richard. 1965. *Psychopathia Sexualis*. New York: Putnam.

Lewes, K. 1988. *The Psychoanalytic Theory of Male Homosexuality*. New York: Simon & Schuster.

Manalansan, Martin. 1996. "In the Shadows of Stonewall: Examining Gay Transnational Politics and the Diasporic Dilemma." *GLQ* 2: 425–438.

Marx, Karl and Engels, Friedrich. 1971. "The Communist Manifesto." In *Birth of The Communist Manifesto*, edited by J. Struik, pp. 93. New York: International Publishers.

Massad, Joseph. 2002. "Re-Orienting Desire: The Gay International and the Arab World." *Public Culture* 14, no. 2: 361–385.

Massad, Joseph. 2007. *Desiring Arabs*. Chicago, IL: University of Chicago Press.

McClintock, Anne. 1995. *Imperial Leather: Race, Gender and Sexuality in the Colonial Conquest*. New York: Routledge.

McLeish, Alexander. 1927. *Light and Darkness in East Africa*. London: World Dominion Press.

McLennan, J.F. 1970. *Primitive Marriage: An inquiry into the origin of the form of capture in marriage ceremonies*. Chicago, IL: University of Chicago Press.

McLynn, Frank. 1990. *Burton: Snow upon the Desert*. London: John Murray.

Moorehead, Alan. 1960. *The White Nile*. New York: Harper.

Okoli, Al Chukwama and Halidn, Abdullali Snehn. 2014. "Betwixt Civil Liberty and National Sensibility: Implications of Nigeria's Anti-Gay Law." *International Affairs and Global Strategy* 19: 17–24.

Oliver, Roland. 1952. *The Missionary Factor in East Africa*. London: Longmans.

Phillips, Oliver. 1997. "Zimbabwean Law and the Production of a White Man's Disease," *Social and Legal Studies*, 6, no. 4: 471–491.

Puar, Jasbir K. 2007. *Terrorist Assemblages: Homonationalism in Queer Times*. Durham, NC: Duke University Press.

Rifkin, Mark. 2012. *The Erotics of Sovereignty: Queer Native Writing in the Era of Self-Determination*. Minneapolis, MN: University of Minnesota Press.

Roberts, Matthew. 1995. "Emergence of Gay Identity and Gay Social Movements in Developing Countries: The AIDS Crisis as Catalyst." *Alternatives* 20: 243–264.

Rubin, Gayle. 1975. "The Traffic in Women: Notes on the 'Political Economy' of Sex." In *Toward an Anthropology of Women*, edited by Rayna Reiter, pp. 157–210. New York: Monthly Review Press.

Said, Edward W. 1980. *Orientalism*. New York: Vintage.

Schneebaum, Tobias. 1969. *Keep the River on your Right*. New York: Grove Press.

Schulman, Sarah. 2012. *The Gentrification of the Mind*. Berkeley, CA: University of California Press.

Sedgwick, Eve Kosofsky. 1990. *Epistemology of the Closet*. Los Angeles, CA: University of California Press.

Sinfield, Alan. 1994. *The Wilde Century: Oscar Wilde, Effeminacy and the Queer Moment*. New York: Columbia University Press.

Schmitt, Arno and Sofer, Jehoeda. 1992. *Sexuality and Eroticism among Males in Moslem Societies*. New York: Haworth Press.

Somerville, Siobhan. 1994. "Scientific Racism and the Emergence of the Homosexual Body." *Journal of the History of Sexuality* 5, no. 2: 243–266.

Spivak, G.C. 1996. *The Spivak Reader* (eds. D. Landry and G. MacLean) New York: Routledge.

Stein, Marc. 2000. *City of Sisterly and Brotherly Loves: Lesbian and Gay Philadelphia, 1945–1972*. Chicago, IL: University of Chicago Press.

Stocking, George. 1987. *Victorian Anthropology*. New York: Free Press.

Stocking, George. 1995. *After Tylor: British Social Anthropology 1888–1951*. Madison, WI: University of Wisconsin Press.

Stoler, Anne Laura. 1995. *Race and the Education of Desire: Foucault's History of Sexuality and the Colonial Order of Things*. Durham, NC: Duke University Press.

Symonds, John Addington. 1896. *A Problem in Modern Ethics*. London: Privately Printed.

Tallie, T.J. 2012. "Racialised Masculinity and the Limits of Settlement: John Dunn and Natal, 1879-1883." *Journal of Natal and Zulu History* 30: 1–22.

Tallie, T.J. 2013. "Queering Natal: Settler Logics and the Disruptive Challenge of Zulu Polygamy." *GLQ: A Journal of Lesbian and Gay Studies* 19, no. 2: 167–189.

Thoonen, J.P. 1941. *Black Martyrs*. London: Sheed and Ward.

Tylor, Edward Burnett. 1874. *Primitive Culture Vol. 1*. Boston, MA: Estes and Lauriat.

Tylor, Edward Burnett. 1894. "On the Tasmanians as Representatives of Paleolithic Man." *Journal of the Anthropological Institute* 23: 141–152.

Waite, D.J. 1990. "Lost Tribal Rites: A Lament." *Outlook* No. 9, Summer.

Warner, Michael. 1993. *Fear of a Queer Planet*. Minneapolis, MN: University of Minnesota Press.

Warner, Michael. 1995. "Something Queer about the Nation-State." In *After Political Correctness*, edited by Christopher Newfield. Boulder, CO: Westview.

Weeks, Jeffrey. 1977. *Coming Out: Homosexual Politics in Britain from the Nineteenth Century to the Present*. London: Quartet Books.

Weston, Kath. 1993. "Lesbian/Gay Studies in the House of Anthropology." *Annual Review of Anthropology* 22: 339–367.

Weston, Kath. 1998. *Long Slow Burn*. New York: Routledge.

Wilson, E.O. 1978. *On Human Nature*. Cambridge, MA: Harvard University Press.

6

DANGEROUS LIAISONS?

(Homo)developmentalism, sexual modernization and LGBTIQ rights in Europe

Christine M. Klapeer

For queer politics, it is the best of times,
and it is the worst of times.

Nikita Dhawan

The rise of LGBTIQ-inclusive development frameworks

In the last decade several development institutions in the Global North have undergone major organizational, legal and discursive shifts regarding the visibility and acknowledgment of lesbian, gay, bisexual, transgender, intersex and queer people (LGBTIQ) as 'target groups', 'recipients' and 'beneficiaries' of development policies and development aid. Supported by the relative success of LGBTIQ movements in EUrope[1] in improving the (sexual) citizenship status of (some) sexual and gender dissidents in the European Union, and further promoted by major political changes concerning the recognition of LGBTIQ rights as human rights in the United Nations (UN) system,[2] questions of LGBTIQ rights have – at least on a discursive and political level – moved from being on the complete margin, or even absent, to the center of international development politics (Gosine 2015; Bergenfield and Miller 2014; Ncube 2014). In the late 1990s, the Dutch development non-governmental organization (NGO) Hivos[3] was among the first development organizations in EUrope to systematically include and address human rights for sexual and gender dissidents in their development work, initially mainly in the context of their HIV/AIDS[4] programs. The Swedish Development Agency (SIDA) followed in 2005/2006 by adopting for its work on sexual orientation and gender identity (SOGI) in international development cooperation an 'action plan' that considered LGBT(IQ) rights an important 'human rights issue' (SIDA 2006: 2). It is not only SIDA that frames LGBTIQ rights through the lens of human rights: the increased employment of the so-called 'human rights based approach' (HRBA) as a new development paradigm has provided '*the*' entry point for LGBTIQ concerns in development politics (Klapeer 2016).

Since 2009, when the so-called 'Anti-Homosexuality Bill' was introduced in the Ugandan parliament,[5] a 'discursive explosion' on the topic of LGBTIQ rights and development aid has become evident, propelling LGBTIQ rights to the center of international development politics and development discourse (Bergenfield and Miller 2014). Not only have major political actors such as US President Barack Obama,[6] former British Prime Minister David Cameron,[7] and Catherine Ashton,[8] High Representative of the EU for Foreign Affairs and Security Policy, made public statements in support of LGBTIQ rights as an important field for development intervention, but the question of how donor countries and donor organizations should use their 'authority' and normative and economic power as aid-givers on behalf of LGBTIQs in various countries has become a broadly, albeit very controversially, debated issue exceeding the narrow field of development and foreign politics. Since then, the promotion of LGBTIQ human rights and a climate of 'homo-tolerance' in development cooperation and development politics remains a very contentious topic, particularly when it comes to the question of aid conditionalities[9] (Laskar 2014; Bergenfield and Miller 2014; Gosine 2015; Abbas 2012; Pambazuka News 2011). Likewise, LGBTIQ rights and questions of (anti-)discrimination also remain a highly contested topic within EUrope and EUropean donor organizations, despite the fact that homo-tolerance has been inscribed into normative constructions of 'Europeaness' (Kulpa 2014; Mos 2013; Ayoub and Paternotte 2014).

Nevertheless, substantive institutional policy commitments have since then been made within Europe. In 2013, respect for LGBTIQ human rights entered EUropean foreign and diplomatic relations more prominently by becoming an integral part of EUropean foreign policy, including development cooperation. The Council 'upgraded' its 2010 LGBT human rights 'toolkit' on the human rights of LGBTI persons to 'guidelines', which are now part of EU foreign policy (Council of the European Union 2010 and 2013). Furthermore, an increasing number of national development agencies, such as those in Sweden, Denmark, Norway, the Netherlands, the UK and Germany, as well as development NGOs and international (private and semi-private) foundations[10] have begun to deal systematically with questions of SOGI, particularly by funding projects and initiatives that are engaged in the promotion of LGBTIQ rights on a bilateral[11] or small scale level. Even though the amount of money provided for projects in the Global South/East is still very low, it is slowly increasing (Funders for LGBT Issues 2011). In 2010 around US$35 million (around 31 million) was provided by European and US donors and grant givers for projects in the Global South/East[12] that explicitly addressed the human rights, experiences of violence or health issues of LGBTIQs or people engaged in same-sex/gender relationships or sexual activities (e.g. MSM) (ibid.). SIDA and the Dutch development NGO Hivos are not only the most important EUropean donors to LGBTIQ issues in the Global South/East, but also spend the most worldwide on the promotion of LGBTIQ (human) rights in the Global South/East (ibid.).[13] In order to stimulate awareness of questions of sexual orientation and gender identity within the development sector, several handbooks, manuals, guidelines and research reports on the marginalization of LGBTIQ human rights in development have been published, mainly by Scandinavian, Dutch and German development agencies and mainly in cooperation with national LGBTIQ or human rights organizations (Samelius et al. 2005; SIDA 2005; LGBT Denmark 2012; Deutsche Gesellschaft für Internationale Zusammenarbeit 2013; Kämpf 2015).

What is of particular importance with regard to this increased attention to LGBTIQ rights among EUropean development institutions is the strong role played by EUropean LGBTIQ organizations and queer identified development practitioners in trying to make development more inclusive for sexual and gender dissidents, thereby shaping the meaning and implications of a 'queering' of development (see also: Lind 2010b; Gosine 2015). Some of the leading, most influential (and well-funded) LGBTIQ organizations in EUrope, such as the COC[14] in the Netherlands, the RFSL[15] from Sweden, the German LSVD[16] and LGBT Danmark,[17] are therefore becoming increasingly involved in the configuration of development agendas and programs. They have established international branches that, in raising funds from national agencies, foreign and development ministries and other international donor organizations, actively participate in development networks and institutions. Sexual and gender dissidents and queer activists from the Global South/East have likewise started to engage strategically with the requirements and 'languages'[18] of development institutions, most literally by seeking aid for projects and initiatives, thereby also challenging (asymmetrical) logics of development and providing intersectional critiques of Western normativities from the start (Lind 2010b; Currier 2010; Pambazuka News 2011).

De/constructing frames of development: critical perspectives from postcolonial development studies and transnational queer research

All these institutional, legal and discursive transformations with regard to LGBTIQ rights and/in development, which I presented above, were paralleled, even authorized, by a multi-faceted and polyphonic process of knowledge production generating new frames and argumentative figures, logics and discourses on the role and relevance of LGBTIQ rights for and in development politics (this is also why I speak of a 'discursive explosion'). Thus, LGBTIQs have become intelligible 'objects' of development and 'LGBTIQ-inclusive development' has emerged as a legitimate and genuine, if contested, topic of knowledge production, thereby also challenging some elements of the 'straight' path of development (Jolly 2011). Each of the new frames generated within this process has come with a constellation of concepts, metaphors and values that provide the scaffolding for the inclusion of LGBTIQ rights in development and explain and legitimize how and why these changes are necessary and important. Growing attention to sexual and gender dissidents in the field of development politics and development cooperation therefore provokes critical questions about which knowledge and frames are being (re-)produced and what 'side effects' and risks may arise when LGBTIQ rights enter the field of development (Ferguson 1994). The effort to bring LGBTIQ rights into development therefore has necessarily to be seen, according to Amy Lind, as 'a paradoxical process from the start, one that is imbued with hegemonic as well as oppositional forms of knowledge, consciousness and experience' (Lind 2010b, 7).

Thus, questions regarding the 'liberatory' and 'transformative' potentials of LGBTIQ-inclusive development frameworks remain an important issue to be addressed, particularly when examined from a postcolonial or 'radical' development studies perspective. I am thus interested in the following questions: How do these new LGBTIQ-inclusive development frameworks become entangled with (established) developmental governmentalities, particularly with racialized processes of (sexual) othering? How do LGBTIQ-inclusive development strategies interact with (older) models of 'sexual modernization' and developmental frameworks, such as 'unilinearity', 'teleology', 'catching up', or 'Western exceptionalism'? How does growing attention to sexual and gender dissidents in the field of development become intertwined with the workings of (racialized) 'homo(trans) nationalisms' (Puar 2007; Bacchetta and Haritaworn 2011; Laskar 2014) and a new 'gay imperialism' (Haritaworn et al. 2008; Rao 2015)? By critically interlinking insights from radical development studies (Kothari 2006a; Kothari 2006b; Escobar 2012; Wilson 2012; Baaz 2005; Kapoor 2008) with queer and postcolonial research on transnational LGBTQ politics and movements (Puar 2007; Haritaworn et al. 2008; Rao 2015; Cruz-Malavé and Manalansan 2002; Weber 2016; Rahman 2014b; Dhawan 2013), as well as with criticisms articulated by (queer) activists, scholars and organizations directly engaged with development institutions (Theron et al. 2016; Abbas 2012; Ekine and Abbas 2013), this chapter aims to shed light on how and in which ways tropes of (sexual) modernization and (under-)development are reiterated in development frameworks that present themselves, and are mainly read, as 'progressive'.

In what follows, I primarily examine discursive representations of and debates on LGBTIQ rights in the field of development politics and development cooperation, thereby combining postcolonial methodologies, decolonial and post-development approaches with 'critical frame analysis' (Verloo 2005). The material analyzed can be characterized as policy documents in a very broad sense, including speeches, action plans, policy programs, manuals and instructions, as well as media articles and political debates. By asking critical questions about the ambivalent implications and problematic undercurrents of the discourses and (meta-)frames around LGBTIQ-inclusive development strategies I neither deny the importance and necessity of 'queering' development, nor do I want to negate or play down the massive violence and exclusion that is experienced by those sexual and gender dissidents in the Global South/East who are the targeted beneficiaries from such frameworks. Against the backdrop of my extensive research on how LGBTIQ rights are negotiated and re-articulated in the development arena, I am also highly aware that there are differences between EUropean development organizations and donor agencies and, moreover, that (queer) activists in so-called 'partner countries', as well as (some) development practitioners, have been engaged subversively and/or strategically with these frameworks and the development apparatus more generally, thereby using the arena of development as an important diplomatic forum for, or erotic site of, (trans-)national queer politics (see: Klapeer 2017; Lind 2010b; Wilson 2010). Most importantly, many organizations and projects in the Global South/East depend on external funding and thus rightly demand of development politics and cooperation a heightened awareness of sexual and gender dissidents and heteronormativity, along with complex approaches that do 'not reinforce the disproportionate power dynamics between donor countries and recipients'[19] (Pambazuka News 2011; see also: Lind 2010a). Thus, I am not calling for an end to development cooperation per se: my goal is rather to demonstrate how a more robust intersectional and power-sensitive framework, defined as a critique of how colonial/racialized genealogies and ideas of sexual development and modernization continue to influence the project of development, may open up possibilities for more radical and decolonial approaches to queer/ing development.

LGBTIQ rights as solution to a lack of modernity? Sexual development within unequal geographies of time

Responding to discussions on the Ugandan Parliament's Anti-Homosexuality Act and reacting to pressure from (some) British LGBTIQ groups to tackle LGBTIQ rights at the Commonwealth Heads of Government Meeting in late 2011, British premier David Cameron stated in a BBC interview that countries that 'do not adhere to proper human rights' for LGBT(IQ)s 'are in a *different place from us* on this issue' (Cameron 2011, emphasis added). He added that 'these countries are all *on a journey* and it's up to us to try and *help* them along on that journey' (ibid., emphasis added). I consider this statement an excellent illustration of the workings of a new 'sexual modernization frame' that implicitly shapes several politicians' and development workers' statements as well as policy papers and media articles, and is also (re-) produced by LGBTIQ and human rights organizations in the Global North and South. This new sexual modernization frame, as can be seen in the Cameron quote, is similar to older tropes and ideas of modernization and development based on a (colonial) conceptualization of geopolitical differences (and inequalities) as temporal differences, or what Uma Kothari describes as 'unequal geographies of time' (Kothari 2011; see also: Kothari 2006a). In many development contexts one observes that processes of development and processes of social change towards (more) sexual diversity and tolerance for LGBTIQs are framed as a 'journey through time'. People or societies that, in Cameron's words, 'do not adhere to proper human rights' are considered 'trapped' in another temporal stage. They are portrayed as some sort of 'living anachronism' (Nichols 2012, 54), frozen moments of EUrope's own past embodying a 'backward' (homophobic) culture not developed enough to perform and absorb homo-tolerance without 'external help'. Anne McClintock likewise highlights in her well known analysis of the discursive tropes and rationalities of British colonialism that

> time became a geography of social power, a map from which to read a global allegory of [...] social differences. [P]rogress [...] is figured as a journey backward in time to an anachronistic moment of prehistory. Geographical difference across space is figured as a historical difference across time.
>
> *(McClintock 1995, 37–40)*

Thus, (political) homo- and transphobia becomes not only spatialized and associated with certain geopolitical places (in the non-West) but is also temporalized and projected into an 'anachronistic space' (ibid.). A lack of homo-tolerance is regarded as a phenomenon that belongs to an earlier, 'pre-modern' stage of (European) development or denotes 'backward' societies in the present (see also: Rao 2014; Hoad 2000). The Global South and East, particularly sub-Saharan Africa, Muslim societies, and probably also Eastern Europe including Russia, are imagined as contemporary re-enactments of EUrope's past: '[W]e were like them, but have developed, they are like we were and have yet to develop' (Rao 2014, 174).

Despite the fact that many development organizations demonstrate an awareness of structural asymmetries within the aid business, thereby acknowledging the danger of reinstituting global inequalities through international interventions, I argue that improvements with regard to LGBTIQ rights are nevertheless mainly framed as manifestations of a process of 'modernization' and, furthermore, that LGBTIQ rights are presented as a 'solution' to a lack of modernity (Rahman 2014b: 95; Rahman 2014a). Although the term 'modernization' is not explicitly used, the frameworks and strategies presented can be read as modernizational, which becomes even more evident with regard to perceptions of queer organizing and identity formation. Queer movements, organizations and activists in the so-called partner countries are framed as mainly demanding 'things' and rights that have already been 'achieved' in EUrope. This does not take into account, first, the limited space for 'other' frameworks or strategies of queer organizing within an unequal donor–recipient relationship and with regard to the (predetermined) structures of the international system (see, for instance, the intense critique of 'managerialism' and the 'predominance of donor-driven agendas' in 'African queer/LGBTIA+ activism', published on Pambazuka News 2016); second, the specific translocal appropriations, re-articulations, re-framings and re-definitions of concepts and models developed in the West; and, third, the different (political) meanings and implications of concepts such as human rights or LGBTIQ rights due to different contexts and the effects of colonialism, capitalist exploitation and anti-colonial struggles (see also Dhawan 2013).

From this it follows that the project of development and the inclusion of LGBTIQs as a previously marginalized group are imagined as a 'conflict-free' endeavor. For instance, a policy paper published by the national German development agency GIZ (Gesellschaft für Internationale Zusammenarbeit 2013) suggests that LGBTIQ and human rights NGOs in 'partner countries [...] connect international donors and civil society', thus proposing that all actors involved are connected through an equal relationship and share the same goals and objectives. Scholars from the field of postcolonial and radical development studies have widely criticized this assumption of a 'harmonious' and 'uncomplicated' donor–recipient relationship and the idea that all actors share 'mutual goals and interests' (Baaz 2005, 73; Kothari 2006b). Moreover, political differences and socio-economic disparities between different LGBTIQ/ queer activists and organizations based on class, caste or other intersectional categories are also blurred by 'harmony approaches' (see also: Bergenfield and Miller 2014).

Notions of harmonious transnational cooperation furthermore produce an interesting new frame regarding the role of sexual and gender dissidents/LGBTIQs in the process of development (in 'developing countries'). In line with my previous arguments, I suggest that due to the fact that homosexuality and (gender/sexual) diversity are mainly read as 'signs' or 'achievements' related to 'modernity', LGBTIQs in 'developing countries' are – in contrast to women – interpreted as sexual subjects who already 'embody' (some) elements of modernity (see also Bracke 2012). As a consequence, they only have to be 'activated' or supported in order to be able to begin a process of queer identity formation that will transform them from 'naïve actors', secretly practicing same-sex genital activities or gender subversion, into 'self-aware' and 'out' political subjects and thus into important agents of modernization and development (Hoad 2000; Sabsay 2012; Cruz-Malavé and Manalansan 2002). While queers have long been seen as unproductive to development, LGBTIQs are now constructed within these new frameworks as 'temporal' and 'cultural brokers' who are able, due to their embodied modernity, to break willingly with their 'time' and 'culture'. They are read as cultural mediators, as 'integrable others', who, in contrast to 'non-integrable others', want to take part in the project of modernity (see also Nichols 2012). To be clear, my argument here is not, thereby also troubling the work of Massad (2007), that there *is* necessarily such a unilinear movement from 'behavior' to 'identity', or that all sexual and gender dissidents in aid-receiving countries are necessarily being transformed into LGBTIQs, or that such processes can solely be interpreted as 'imperial' or 'obtruded' effects from 'outside'. Such an interpretation would completely deny the agency of LGBTIQs and sexual/gender dissidents and their power to actively to appropriate, re-articulate, utilize and rework such appellations from the development apparatus (Rao 2015; Lind 2010b; Currier 2010). It is nevertheless important to realize that 'development policies, practices, and institutions work as instruments of governance' and, by doing so, are involved in constructing and legitimizing *only* certain identities, such as, for instance, those identifying as LGBTIs or those that can be read as proto-queer (Lind 2010b, 5; see also Bergenfield and Miller 2014).

Actualizing tropes of (sexual) modernization: homo-tolerance as new indicator for development

From the above discussions it follows that homo-tolerance and specific (homonormative) interpretations of LGBTI(Q) (human) rights and of (modern) sexual identities tend to be interpreted as new signifiers or indicators of a certain 'developmental stage', thereby actualizing earlier models of modernization and unilinear development, as proposed by, for instance, Walt Rostow (1960), Talcott Parsons (1964) or Alex Inkeles (1969). According to early modernization theorists, (all) societies must pass certain 'stages' and develop specific institutional, cultural and social patterns in order to overcome the 'traditional stage' and to reach 'modernity'. But while the US and (some) European countries have already, or at least nearly, reached 'modernity', so-called developing countries are, according to this logic, in need of incentives or external support (such as aid, technical assistance or other knowledge) to go through these stages. From this it follows that modernization frameworks, which still shape many development practices, require and produce a more or less clear 'categorization', 'classification' and 'identification' of the developmental stage of societies/nations, thereby disregarding their specific cultural contexts, historical/colonial genealogies and global entanglements in a capitalist world system. Thus, countries/societies are mapped and organized with regard to prescribed models of development, demarcating and creating an 'imaginative geography' of the world that relies, however, on colonial and oriental tropes of the 'underdeveloped other' (Escobar 2012, 9). Many post-development theorists, such as Arturo Escobar or James Ferguson, have demonstrated how development models systematically transform complex political issues into signs of '(under-)development', which than can be objectively 'measured', 'compared' and 'solved'. According to Arturo Escobar, development is a regime of truth production, 'a politics of knowledge' that allows experts 'to classify problems and formulate policies, to pass judgment on entire social groups and forecast their future – to produce, in short, a regime of truth and norms about them' (Escobar 2012, 45–46). The inclusion of LGBTIQ rights in development is likewise legitimized and made intelligible on the basis of an imaginative geography of sexual modernization, thereby 'locating' homophobia and homo-tolerance in certain spaces of the world (Rao 2014). Global cartographies and mappings of LGBTIQ rights are thus important points of reference for LGBTIQ-inclusive development frameworks. The most prominent 'location of homophobia' is the 'Lesbian, Gay and Bisexual Map of World Laws'[20] provided by the International Lesbian, Gay, Bisexual, Trans and Intersex Association (ILGA), which uses a traffic light system in order to depict the status of lesbian and gay rights in the world (Rao 2014). According to Rao (2014, 170) the way states are color-coded implies a 'ranking impulse' and produces 'a Western – more specifically, northern European – temporal narrative' of sexual modernization: A society/nation moves from 'decriminalization' to 'anti-discrimination' and finally to the institutionalization of 'partnership rights', preferably same-sex marriage (170). Putting aside the general difficulty of global mappings that do not consider wider transnational asymmetries, colonial entanglements and translocal dynamics, as well as the problematic universalization of identity and gender categories, what is striking about such cartographies is the selection of indicators itself. Western donor countries always appear as the 'prototype' of homo-tolerance with, for instance, a Western conceptualization of 'gay marriage' read as inherently progressive (see also Browne et al. 2015). Thus, only a certain type of 'rights', 'development' or 'liberation' is used to represent 'the West' or, according to my inquiry, 'EUrope'. All the 'others' are therefore not only 'lagging behind' but are necessarily seen as 'inferior' and/or 'less developed' due to their inability to reach an 'advanced' stage of sexual modernization (see also Rahman 2014b). In the words of Hakima Abbas:

> LGBTI issues have gained ground in the international arena as a barometer to determine who the 'good liberal' countries versus the 'bad backward' are. With racist undertones about the 'barbaric' and 'uncivilized', it has been written that the 'cultures' and 'traditions' of the Black and Brown peoples of the world have not yet been civilized enough to tolerate gay and lesbian people.
>
> *(Abbas 2012)*

What is furthermore important about these mappings is that they fit perfectly into a developmental framework because they enable donors to 'monitor' and 'measure' processes of (sexual) development as well as the 'impact' of their interventions 'objectively' on the basis of a clear 'cause–effect' framework. SIDA, for instance, states in its 'action plan' 'that in those countries where Sweden systematically includes an LGBT perspective in the development cooperation, the rights and poverty situation for LGBT persons is expected to improve' (SIDA 2006, 4). The 'development' or 'time journey' of others to a (predetermined) sexual modernity can therefore be watched (and what Gayatri Spivak would also call 'wronged') as an anachronistic 'spectacle' from a 'panoptical point of view' and an assumed 'evolutionary superiority' (McClintock 1995; Spivak 2004).

The culturalization of sexual (under-)development: homotransnationalisms and LGBTQ-inclusive development frameworks

Despite an increased awareness of the problematic effects of colonial legislation on the current lives of sexual and gender dissidents, a lack of homo-tolerance and/or sexual modernization, as well as the supposed inability to employ other sexual/intimate values perceived as 'modern' (such as for instance 'romantic love', sexual norms based on secular frameworks), tends to be attributed to 'local' or 'cultural' factors such as religion or tradition. For instance, within the EUropean foreign policy 'guidelines' (Council of the European Union 2013) 'cultural, traditional, or religious values' are considered the main obstacles that may hinder LGBTIQs enjoyment of the universality of human rights. It has been argued that organizations thus often have to '(over-)emphasize the local cultural, social and political obstacles' they face in order to meet donor requirements (Currier 2010, 155; see also Theron et al. 2016). I would even go so far as to argue that the fact that an increasing number of policy papers point to the necessity of taking account of 'local' circumstances, including 'local' sex/gender systems and 'local' organizing, risks re-enforcing a new culturalization of political homo- and transphobia as well as a concept of sexual/gender identity detached from historical and contemporary global entanglements. Many critical scholars from the field of transnational and postcolonial queer studies have demonstrated that, to use Nikita Dhawan's (2013) words, 'Western and non-Western sexual epistemologies are inextricably entangled' and there are no 'uncontaminated', 'local' sexual and gender identities, whether in the so-called West or in postcolonial states (Cruz-Malavé and Manalansan 2002).

Manifestations of violence and discrimination against sexual and gender dissidents are rarely contextualized within these complex historical and transnational 'triangulations' (see also Rahman 2014a; Rao 2014) and, moreover, international institutions such as development organizations are hardly understood as being involved[21] in producing violence and/or asymmetries (through, for instance, structural adjustment programs). Questions as to *why* some countries and regions have the financial, economic and/ or epistemic power to 'support' LGBTQ rights 'elsewhere' are thus not being tackled. Interestingly, the marginalization of global power dynamics and asymmetries also becomes apparent when examining the usage of the term 'local': whereas approaches, strategies and conditions (of queers) in aid-receiving countries are perceived as 'local', policies and practices rooted in donor countries are never described as 'local' (see, for instance, the handbook *LGBT in Development*, RFSL 2009). 'Local' seems to refer only to 'developing' societies whereas 'modern' societies produce 'universal' strategies that can, or should be, transnationalized.

However, the recent rise of racialized constructions of the 'homophobic (Muslim) migrant' or 'terrorist' who are perceived as anti-modern aberrations within otherwise modern, liberal and homo-tolerant EUropean societies, have furthermore promoted culturalized readings of violence and discrimination against sexual and gender dissidents from and in the 'non-West' (Haritaworn et al. 2008; Petzen 2012; Bracke 2012; Puar 2007). Whereas Western societies are (again) identified as self-determining inventors, arbiters and bearers of (homo-)tolerance, intolerant societies are rendered as static 'prisoners' of their cultures, not 'enlightened' enough to accept the 'fact' of human sexual and gender diversity (Brown 2006; Nichols 2012). Wendy Brown likewise indicates a new culturalization of tolerance, arguing that tolerance is understood as 'to be available only to certain cultures' (Brown 2006, 15): Thus, 'the liberal individual' is 'uniquely identified with the capacity for tolerance and tolerance itself is identified with civilization' (Brown 2006, 150, 166). As part of a new 'civilizational frame', cultural difference has emerged as the 'salient site for the practice of tolerance or intolerance' (ibid.). EUrope is then, as postcolonial scholars have already critically discussed, (again) constructed as a site of (homo-)tolerance and sexual modernization while all (internal or external) 'others' such as migrants, Muslims or fragile states are rendered as 'backward' and 'non-European', unable to develop tolerance (Nichols 2012; Haritaworn, Erdem and Tauqir 2008; Rahman 2014b; Petzen 2012; Rao 2015).

From this it follows that the inscription of LGBTIQ rights into development frameworks is intrinsically intertwined with the rise of a new (queer/ed) version of a European sexual exceptionalism. LGBTIQ rights and homo-tolerance are thus proffered as 'exceptional' achievements of Western, and more particularly, European societies. Momin Rahman even argues that 'sexual exceptionalism is conjured as *the* marker of *civilizational* exceptionalism', actualizing the idea of the superiority of (Western) modernity itself (Rahman 2014b, 121; emphasis added). This means that LGBTIQ rights are 'not simply located within the space of the West', or Europe, but rather positioned as *the* 'apex of Western exceptionalism' itself (Rahman 2014a, 279). Such a new (queered) version of a sexual/civilization exceptionalism is also related to and (co-)produced by the emergence of a specific European 'homotransnationalism' (Laskar 2014). EUropean versions of homotransnationalisms are based on the idea that 'accomplishments' (not only) with regard to LGBTIQ and/or human rights should be 'transnationalized', but that laws in less homo-tolerant countries (even member states) should be harmonized with EUropean law and that more 'developed' nations have a responsibility to intervene in 'homophobic' countries and regions in order to 'protect' queer minority groups (Laskar 2014). EUropean homotransnationalism is thus mutually intertwined with national varieties of homotransnationalism *and* homonationalism, particularly manifest in the Scandinavian and Dutch contexts (Bracke 2011). These countries are not only at the forefront of inscribing homo-tolerance and sexual diversity in their imagined national communities but, as I have already outlined in the introduction, occupy a leading role in promoting LGBTIQ-inclusive development frameworks often in mutual cooperation with national LGBTIQ organizations. Homotransnationalism is thus also presented as, to use Gayatri Spivak in this context, a necessary and humanist 'burden of the fittest': '[T]he fittest […] must shoulder the burden of righting the wrongs of the unfit' but thereby reinstitute an asymmetrical split 'between those who right wrongs and those who are wronged' (Spivak 2004 523, 563). Those countries that are the most (sexually) 'developed' must 'take the burden' and responsibility to transnationalize their achievements. This split also entails and reiterates, drawing on the critical thoughts of Rahul Rao (2014, 171), a divide between 'shamers and shamed' thereby authorizing the shamers to *help* the shamed to move in the direction of a (predetermined) path of (sexual) modernization.

This split became particular visible with regard to the EU enlargement processes in Central and Eastern Europe. Tolerance towards LGBTIQs was being established as a defining component, a prerequisite, of becoming 'European', not only by politicians but also by LGBTIQ activists themselves. LGBTIQ rights, or, rather, respect for the human rights of LGBTIQs, have thus been increasingly inscribed into ideas of 'Europeanness' and concepts of the (EUropean) nation (Kulpa 2014; Mos 2013; Ayoub and Paternotte 2014). Ayoub and Paternotte also speak of the emergence of a "special relationship' [...] between LGBT rights and a certain idea of Europe' that extends beyond strict institutional categories (Ayoub and Paternotte 2014, 2). Homophobic reactions or policies such as Uganda's 'Anti-Homosexuality Bill' or Russia's criminalization of 'gay propaganda' therefore often seem, by providing a counterpoint, to confirm the 'imagined Europeanness' of LGBTIQ rights.

The project of LGBTIQ-inclusive development hence obtains a 'special connection' with homotransnationalist tropes and a new version of a EUropean sexual exceptionalism, and is even made intelligible through these emerging discourses. It is also important to note, however, that homo(trans)nationalist frameworks are not only performed by state actors but are an ambivalent outcome of the various struggles of LGBTIQ and feminist movements against homo- and transphobic violence, as well as their longstanding fight for the acknowledgment and protection of LGBTIQ rights as an important obligation and responsibility of liberal democracies, the European community and international human rights institutions such as the UN.

New and old dichotomies: the charmed circle of sexual modernization

The idea that the way 'sexual activities' or 'gender' are performed indicates a certain 'civilizational stage' or 'phase of development' is definitely not new. Many postcolonial and race-critical authors have demonstrated how non-European 'others' have consistently been constructed as 'sexually deviant', as 'promiscuous animals' and as 'abnormal' with regard to their gender performance or family organization (McClintock 1995; Stoler 1989; Nyanzi 2011; Kapoor 2015). Anne McClintock coined the term 'porno-tropics' in order to describe how Europeans imagined the 'far-off lands' as highly sexualized places full of sexual aberrations and 'forbidden sexual desires' (McClintock 1995, 22). Critical development scholars have likewise shown how development programs have further contributed to the actualization of colonial constructions of a 'sexual backwardness' and/or racialized notions of 'sexual deviance' (Wilson 2012; Gosine 2005b and 2009). Andil Gosine (2009, 26) argues, for instance, that '[i]nternational development theory and practice have long been fixated upon [...] dissident sexual subjects' that provided 'a rationale and impetus for the pursuit of development', thereby ensuring 'that sexuality is one of its primary components'. Kalpana Wilson also draws attention to racialized constructions of an 'overly reproductive Third World woman' in many development programs concerned with health, reproduction, and sexual rights, as well as the 'Third World men' stigmatized as inherently sexually violent and promiscuous (Wilson 2012). A constant 'problematization' of Black/non-Western sexualities and sexual norms can thus be said to lie at the very heart of development itself. Ilan Kapoor also suggests, moreover, that '[t]he sexualisation of the Third World' and the projection of 'perversity' onto non-European others 'helped discursively to construct the Third World' itself (Kapoor 2015, 1615).

The emergence of homo-tolerance as a sign of sexual development has therefore to be contextualized within a broader developmental sexual value system, or what I systematize

Christine M. Klapeer

as the 'charmed circle of sexual modernization'. By drawing on Gayle Rubin's prominent systematization of sexual values in the US context (1999 [1984]) and following Stella Nyanzi's (2011) suggestion of using the charmed circle for a postcolonial and race-critical analysis, I re-construct the embeddedness of homo-tolerance as a new development goal and indicator of sexual modernization in a broader system of sex values in development that not only underlies much current 'progressive' development discourse on sexual and reproductive rights but is also intrinsically interwoven with colonial and orientalist frameworks. The inner circle shows those sexual activities or attitudes towards sexual activities that are perceived as 'modern' or 'developed', while the outer circle illustrates everything perceived as 'traditional' and therefore to be overcome (Figure 6.1).

The irony is, of course, that while 'proper' (white) heterosexuality was long been seen as an indicator of modernity, the exact opposite has become the case in the contemporary context. Yet the underlying dichotomy based on racialized constructions of sexual (under-) development remains the same (Kapoor 2015). Queer theorist Eve Kosofsky Sedgwick's critical insight (1990) is thus actualized when applied to current development politics: we cannot understand the functioning and logics of current aid policies, development rhetorics and strategies without examining the constitutive function of the dichotomy between hetero- and homosexuality, the 'normal' and the 'perverse', the 'sexually developed' and the 'sexually underdeveloped' (see also Weber 2014 and Weber 2016).

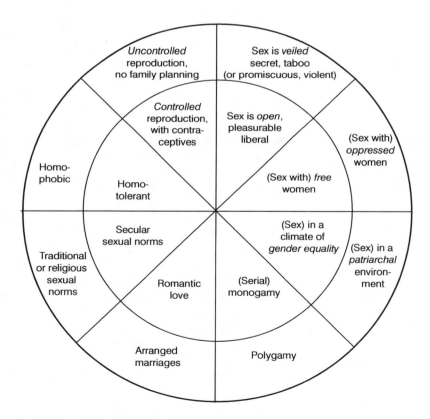

Figure 6.1 Charmed circle of sexual modernization

Conclusion: homo-developmentalism as a new development paradigm?

By focusing on discourses and strategies aimed at making development more inclusive for sexual and gender dissidents/LGBTIQs, I have demonstrated how a new queer/ed version of developmentalism has emerged within the field of development. To grasp the special relationship and complex entanglements between established development paradigms and the inclusion of LGBTIQ rights as a new indicator and goal of development and homo(trans)nationalist projects, I propose the concept of 'homo-developmentalism'. Homo-developmentalism describes the specific employment and translation of homotransnationalist patterns and ideas of sexual exceptionalism into 'development speak'. Homo-developmentalist frameworks are, however, based on an idea of 'catching up', implying that countries or societies move 'forward' in 'stages' with regard to LGBTIQ rights and that they should try to follow EUrope's trajectory on a linear axis of sexual modernization. Thus, a geopolitical progress narrative (of queer 'liberation'; of LGBTIQ identity formation) and a new spatialized temporalization of homo- and transphobia is (re-)produced. A homo-developmentalist framework thus not only leaves the unequal architecture of the international (development) system intact but also reinstates a new queered version of a spatial–temporal divide between a sexually 'developed' and 'homo-tolerant' EUrope and a 'barbaric' and 'homophobic rest'. I argue therefore that contemporary articulations and contestations of 'sexual development' and 'sexual modernization' cannot be fully understood without situating them along a hierarchical, structured, spatial-temporal axis. Because homo-tolerance is perceived as an 'exceptional' achievement of Western/EUropean societies, 'less developed' countries/societies are in need of external incentives, support or pressure (for instance, aid conditionalities) in order to 'modernize'. Due to a new culturalization of (homo-)tolerance *and* homo- and transphobia, current attempts to include LGBTIQ rights in development frameworks are therefore at risk of authorizing and actualizing the 'need' for homotransnationalist 'interventions' with new and 'progressive' arguments. It has hence become clear that conceptualizations of sexuality and gender, of what is perceived as (sexually) 'developed' or 'underdeveloped', play a key role in the configuration of international (development) politics and still function as an important signifier of cultural othering.

As a consequence, a critical analysis of the manifestations and problematic implications of homo-developmentalist practices and discourses neither means that one should not tackle violence against sexual and gender dissidents (not only) in aid-receiving countries, nor that one should not critically engage with the field of development. I do, however, call for a critical interrogation of the framing of the 'problems' and 'solutions' through a homo-developmentalist lens: that pointing to violence and discrimination against sexual and gender dissidents always collapses into a conflict of 'modern' versus 'traditional', 'tolerant' versus 'backward'. I am therefore convinced that only if we, as researchers, activists and practitioners, reach beyond such a dichotomy will we be able to interrogate, 'hear' and 'see' multiple forms, modulations and transnational entanglements of violence and political homo- and transphobias. I therefore end with the suggestion of grounding a queer/ing of development frameworks and politics on a more radical, anti-linear, anti-teleological, intersectional and probably also 'anti-modern sexual politics'[22] (Petzen 2012) that radically breaks with and dismantles (white) 'homonostalgia' (Bracke 2012; Haritaworn 2015), precisely because racialized and civilizational imaginaries of modernity and sexual modernization are constantly actualized when LGBTIQ rights are integrated into development frameworks. Thus, we have to ask whether 'queering development' is about 'adding' or 'including' LGBTIQs or rather about a radical rethinking and transformation of development itself (if this is possible at all). I thus propose that the task, rather than rejecting LGBTIQ-inclusive development frameworks, is, as Spivak put it, to 'engage in a persistent critique of what one cannot not want' (Spivak 1993, 284).

Acknowledgements

My special thanks go to Kasha Jacqueline Nabagesera for her critical statements and perspectives on 'LGBTI in Development Discourse' at the Center for Development Research in June 2016. I am very grateful to have had the opportunity to discuss my arguments and thoughts with Kasha on and after the panel.

Notes

1 I use the term 'EUropean' to indicate a predominant position of the European Union (EU) in defining the notion of Europe and what is being considered as 'European'.
2 Such as, for instance, the groundbreaking resolution 17/19 on 'Human Rights, Sexual Orientation and Gender Identity' adopted by the UN Human Rights Council in 2011.
3 *Humanistisch Instituut voor Ontwikkelingssamenwerking* (Humanist Institute for Development Cooperation).
4 During the AIDS crises non-heterosexual practices were 'officially' recognized and visible in development for the first time. These practices were mainly addressed, however, through the lens of regulation, 'containment' and control and focused on men who have sex with men (MSM) (Lind 2010b; Gosine 2005a).
5 The Anti-Homosexuality Act was passed by parliament in December 2013, signed by President Musaveni in February 2014, and annulled by Uganda's Constitutional Court in August 2014.
6 In December 2011 US President Barack Obama released a presidential memorandum directing all US agencies involved in foreign and development policy to ensure that their actions promote the human rights of LGBT people.
7 David Cameron declared in an interview with the BBC that the UK will probably withhold aid from governments that do not reform legislation banning homosexuality. His threats incited a massive international discussion about whether aid should be made conditional upon a country's track record on LGBTIQ rights.
8 Catherine Ashton publicly condemned the signing of the Anti-Homosexuality Act by President Museveni in February 2014.
9 Despite the fact that several queer groups, human rights and social justice activists from Uganda and other affected countries rejected aid conditionalities in a public statement, European countries including Sweden, the Netherlands and Denmark canceled or redirected their aid for Uganda after the Anti-Homosexuality Act was signed by President Museveni in February 2014. Even the World Bank postponed a loan for Uganda's health system after the Act was signed.
10 Some of the most prominent (private) foundations funding LGBTIQ projects in the Global South/East are based in the US, such as for instance the Astrea Lesbian Foundation for Justice. In EUrope funding for LGBTIQ rights, although distributed through development NGOs or other human rights organizations, is mainly provided by state donors.
11 The fact that development organizations are mainly funding LGBTIQ projects in the Global South/East on a bilateral level and are not engaged in 'queering' all their programs and aid distribution procedures has also drawn some critique (Bergenfield and Miller 2014).
12 The majority of the financial resources provided by European and US based institutions goes to projects and organizations in Africa (32 %), with a focus on Uganda, Kenya and South Africa, as well as to Latin America (16 %) (Funders for LGBT Issues 2011).
13 In 2010 SIDA provided around US$5 million for the promotion of LGBTIQ rights in the Global South/East; Hivos around US$3.5 million.
14 COC originally stood for *Cultuur en Ontspanningscentrum* (Center for Culture and Leisure) and was founded 1946 in Amsterdam. The COC is one of the oldest existing LGB(TIQ)

organizations in EUrope. The organization has also special consultative status with the United Nations.

15 The Swedish Federation for Lesbian, Gay, Bisexual, Transgender and Queer Rights (*Riksförbundet för homosexuellas, bisexuellas, transpersoners och queeras rättigheter*, formerly *Riksförbundet för sexuellt likaberättigande*) is the most prominent and oldest Swedish LGBTIQ organization. RFSL was founded in 1950 and also gained consultative status at the United Nations Economic and Social Council (ECOSOC) in 2007.

16 The Lesbian and Gay Federation in Germany (*Lesben- und Schwulenverband in Deutschland*) was originally founded as the Gay Men's Federation in Germany (SVD) in the East German city of Leipzig in 1990. In 1999 the organization expanded to become the LSVD, which aims to represent the issues facing lesbians as well as gay men. In 2007 the LSVD established the Hirschfeld-Eddy Foundation, which intends to fight and lobby for the human rights of LGBTIQ people globally. LSVD also holds consultative status at the ECOSOC.

17 LGBT Denmark, the Danish National Organization for Gay Men, Lesbians, Bisexuals and Transgender persons. LGBT Denmark, formerly known as *Kredsen af 1948* (Circle of 1948), *Forbundet af 1948* and *Landsforeningen for Bøsser og Lesbiske*, was founded in 1948 and is therefore also one of the oldest EUropean LGBTIQ organizations. LGBT Denmark holds consultative status at the ECOSOC.

18 Such, as for instance, the AIDS/HIV discourse, or the recent rise of human rights based approaches (Gosine 2005a; Lind 2010b; Theron, McAllister and Armisen 2016; Currier 2010).

19 In 2011, shortly after David Cameron was considering making aid conditional upon adherence to human rights for LGBTIs, several social justice, human rights and LGBTIQ organizations and activists released a statement opposing aid conditionalities and donor sanctions imposed in 'support' of LGBTIQs in the Global South: 'The imposition of donor sanctions [...] does not, in and of itself, result in the improved protection of the rights of LGBTI people. Donor sanctions are by their nature coercive and reinforce the disproportionate power dynamics between donor countries and recipients. They are often based on assumptions about African sexualities and the needs of African LGBTI people. They disregard the agency of African civil society movements and political leadership. [...] The history of colonialism and sexuality cannot be overlooked when seeking solutions to this issue. The colonial legacy of the British Empire in the form of laws that criminalize same-sex sex continues to serve as the legal foundation for the persecution of LGBTI people throughout the Commonwealth. In seeking solutions to the multi-faceted violations facing LGBTI people across Africa, old approaches and ways of engaging our continent have to be stopped' (Pambazuka News 2011).

20 For the ILGA world map, see: http://old.ilga.org/Statehomophobia/ILGA_WorldMap_2015_ENG.pdf

21 I am not saying here that *only* international institutions are involved in producing violence against sexual and gender dissidents. On the contrary, political homo- and transphobia is being enacted by postcolonial states and societies, albeit in complex and manifold ways (see Dhawan 2013).

22 Due to the increase of racialized constructions of 'sexual backwardness', particularly with regard to Muslim populations in Europe, queer theorist Jennifer Petzen calls for an 'anti-modern sexual politics' critiquing the fact that racialized notions of sexuality and gender are particularly reproduced and maintained through new discourses of being 'modern' and 'European' (Petzen 2012).

References

Abbas, H. 2012. 'Aid, resistance and queer power.' *Pambazuka News*, Apr 5. Accessed July 26, 2012. http://www.pambazuka.org/governance/aid-resistance-and-queer-power

Ayoub, P. M., and D. Paternotte. 2014. 'Introduction.' In *LGBT Activism and the Making of Europe: A Rainbow Europe?* edited by P.M. Ayoub and D. Paternotte, pp. 1–25. Basingstoke: Palgrave Macmillan.

Baaz, M. E. 2005. *The Paternalism of Partnership: A Postcolonial Reading of Identity in Development Aid.* London: Zed Books.

Bacchetta, P., and J. Haritaworn. 2011. 'There are many transatlantics. Homonationalism, homotransnationalism.' In *Transatlantic Conversations: Feminism as Travelling Theory*, edited by K. Davis and M. Evans, pp. 127–144. London: Routledge.

Bergenfield, R., and A. Miller. 2014. 'Queering international development? An examination of new 'LGBT rights' rhetoric, policy, and programming among international development agencies.' *Harvard Kennedy School LGBT Policy Journal*. Accessed May 31, 2015. http://www.hkslgbtq.com/wp-content/uploads/2014/11/Queering-International-Development_-An-Examination-of-New-_LGBT-Rights_-Rhetoric-Policy-and-Programming-among-International-Development-Agencies-1.pdf

Bracke, S. 2011. 'Subjects of debate: Secular and sexual exceptionalism, and Muslim women in the Netherlands.' *Feminist Review* no. 98: 28–46.

Bracke, S. 2012. 'From 'saving women' to 'saving gays': Rescue narratives and their dis/continuities.' *European Journal of Women's Studies* 19, no. 2: 237–252.

Brown, W. 2006. *Regulating Aversion. Tolerance in the Age of Identity and Empire*. Princeton, NJ: Princeton University Press.

Browne, K., N. Banerjea, L. Bakshi, and N. McGlynn. 2015. 'Intervention – 'gay-friendly or homophobic'? The absence and problems of global standards.' Antipode Foundation. Accessed Dec 3, 2015) http://antipodefoundation.org/2015/05/11/gay-friendly-or-homophobic/

Cameron, D. 2011. 'Interview with David Cameron on BBC', October 30. Accessed February 15, 2016. http://www.youtube.com/watch?v=IYhEkB0AOQs.

Council of the European Union. 2010. 'Toolkit to promote and protect the enjoyment of all human rights by lesbian, gay, bisexual and transgender (LGBT) people.' Brussels.

Council of the European Union. 2013. 'Guidelines to promote and protect the enjoyment of all human rights by lesbian, gay, bisexual, transgender and intersex (LGBTI) persons.' Luxembourg.

Cruz-Malavé, A., and M. F. Manalansan IV. 2002. *Queer Globalizations: Citizenship and the Afterlife of Colonialism*. New York: New York University Press.

Currier, A. 2010. 'Behind the mask: Developing LGBTI visibility in Africa.' In *Development, Sexual Rights and Global Governance*, edited by A. Lind, pp. 155–168. New York: Routledge.

Dhawan, N. 2013. 'The empire prays back: Religion, secularity, and queer critique.' *Boundary 2* 40, no. 1: 191–222.

Ekine, S., and H. Abbas, 2013. *Queer African Reader*. Oxford: Pamabazuka Presee/Fahamu.

Escobar, A. 2012. *Encountering Development: The Making and Unmaking of the Third World*. Princeton, NJ: Princeton University Press.

Ferguson, J. 1994. *The Anti-Politics Machine: Development, Depoliticization, and Bureaucratic Power in Lesotho*. Minneapolis, MN: University of Minnesota Press.

Funders for LGBT Issues. 2011. 'A global gaze: lesbian, gay, bisexual, transgender and intersex grantmaking in the Global South and East.' Accessed May 5, 2013. http://www.lgbtfunders.org/files/A_Global_Gaze_2010.pdf

GIZ – Deutsche Gesellschaft für Internationale Zusammenarbeit. 2013. *Sexual Orientation and Gender Identity as Human Rights Issue in Development Cooperation*. Bonn and Eschborn: GIZ.

Gosine, A. 2005a. 'Sex for pleasure, rights to participation, and alternatives to AIDS: Placing sexual minorities or dissidents in development.' IDS Working Paper 228. Accessed Nov 2, 2011. https://www.ids.ac.uk/ids/bookshop/wp/wp228.pdf

Gosine, A. 2005b. 'Stumbling into sexualities: International development encounters dissident desire.' *Canadian Woman Studies/Les Cahiers de la Femme* 24, no. 2/3: 59–63.

Gosine, A. 2009. 'Monster, womb, MSM: The work of sex in international development.' *Development* 52, no. 1: 25–33.

Gosine, A. 2015. 'Rescue, And Real Love: Same Sex Desire In International Development.' IDS Sexuality and Development Programme. Accessed May 31, 2015. http://opendocs.ids.ac.uk/opendocs/bitstream/handle/123456789/5891/Resue%20and%20Real%20Love.pdf?sequence=1

Haritaworn, J. 2015. *Queer Lovers and Hateful Others: Regenerating Violent Times and Places*. London: Pluto Press.

Haritaworn, J., E. Erdem, and T. Tauqir. 2008. 'Gay imperialism: The role of gender and sexuality discourses in the war on terror.' In *Out of Place, Queerness and Raciality*, edited by A. Kuntsman and E. Miyake, pp. 9–34. York: Raw Nerve Books.

Hoad, N. 2000. 'Arrested development or the queerness of savages: Resisting evolutionary narratives of difference.' *Postcolonial Studies* 3, no. 2: 133–158.

Inkeles, A. 1969. 'Making men modern: On the causes and consequences of individual change in six developing countries.' *American Journal of Sociology* 75, no. 2: 208–225.

Jolly, S. (2011). 'Why is development work so straight? Heteronormativity in the international development industry.' *Development in Practice* 21, no. 1: 18–28.

Kämpf, A. 2015. *'Just Head-Banging Won't Work': How State Donors Can Further Human Rights of LGBTI in Development Cooperation and What LGBTI Think About It.* Berlin: German Institute for Human Rights.

Kapoor, I. 2008.*The Postcolonial Politics of Development.* New York: Routledge.

Kapoor, I. 2015. 'The queer Third World.' *Third World Quarterly* 36, no. 9: 1611–1628.

Klapeer, C. 2016. 'LGBTIQ-Rechte als Indikatoren von 'Entwicklung'? Postkolonial-queere Perspektiven auf entwicklungspolitische Debatten um sexuelle Menschenrechte.' In *Feministische Kritiken und Menschenrechte. Reflexionen auf ein produktives Spannungsverhältnis*, edited by I. Leicht, N. Meisterhans, C. Löw, and K. Volk, pp. 95–112. Opladen: Barbara Budrich.

Klapeer, C. 2017. 'Queer mimicry on the international stage? Homo(trans)nationalist diplomacies, queer aid and the contingent trajectories of global LGBTIQ rights policies.' In *Routledge Handbook of Postcolonial Politics*, edited by R. Shilliam, and O. Rutazibwa. London: Routledge.

Kothari, U. 2006a. 'Spatial practices and imaginaries. Experiences of colonial officers and development professionals.' *Singapore Journal of Tropical Geography* 27, no. 3: 235–253.

Kothari, U. 2006b. 'An agenda for thinking about 'race' in development.' *Progress in Development Studies* 6, no. 1: 9–23.

Kothari, U. 2011. 'The unequal geographies of time: enduring poverty amidst rapid change,' Public Lecture, University of Toronto, October 21.

Kulpa, R. 2014. 'Western leveraged pedagogy of Central and Eastern Europe: Discourses of homophobia, tolerance, and nationhood.' *Gender, Place & Culture – A Journal of Feminist Geography* 21, no. 4: 431–448.

Laskar, P. 2014. 'The illiberal turn. Aid conditionality and the queering of sexual citizenship.' *Lambda Nordica*, no. 1: 87–100.

LGBT Denmark. 2012. *Sexual Orientation and Gender Identity in Development Cooperation.* Copenhagen: LGBT Denmark.

Lind, A. 2010a. *Development, Sexual Rights and Global Governance.* New York: Routledge.

Lind, A. 2010b. 'Introduction: Development, global governance, and sexual subjectivities.' In *Development, Sexual Rights and Global Governance* edited by A. Lind, pp. 1–19. New York: Routledge.

Massad, J. A. 2007. *Desiring Arabs.* Chicago, IL: University of Chicago Press.

McClintock, A. 1995. *Imperial Leather: Race, Gender and Sexuality in the Colonial Contest.* New York: Routledge.

Mos, M. 2013. 'Conflicted normative power Europe: The European Union and sexual minority rights.' *Journal of Contemporary European Research* 9, no. 1: 78–93.

Ncube, G. 2014. 'Hypocrisies and contradictions: Western aid and LGBT rights in Africa.' Accessed Mar 6, 2015. http://consultancyafrica.com/index.php?option=com_content&view=article&id=1673:hypocrisies-and-contradictions-western-aid-and-lgbt-rights-in-africa&catid=91:rights-in-focus&Itemid=296

Nichols, R. 2012. 'Empire and the Dispositif of Queerness.' *Foucault Studies*, no. 4: 41–60.

Nyanzi, S. 2011. 'Unpacking the [govern]mentality of African sexualities.' In *African Sexualities: A Reader*, edited by S. Tamale, pp. 477–501. Cape Town: Pambazuka Press.

Pambazuka News. 2011. 'Statement on British aid cut threats to African countries that violate LBGTI rights.' Oct 27. Accessed Feb 2, 2012. http://pambazuka.org/en/category/advocacy/77470

Pambazuka News. 2016. 'Where do we go from here? A call for critical reflection on queer/LGBTIA+ activism in Africa.' May 12. Accessed August 3, 2016. https://www.pambazuka.org/gender-minorities/where-do-we-go-here

Parsons, T. 1964. 'Evolutionary universals in society.' *American Sociological Review* 29, no. 3: 339–357.

Petzen, J. 2012. 'Contesting Europe: A call for an anti-modern sexual politics.' *European Journal of Women's Studies* 19, no. 1: 97–114.

Puar, J. 2007. *Terrorist Assemblages: Homonationalism in Queer Times.* Durham, NC: Duke University Press.

Rahman, M. 2014a. 'Queer rights and the triangulation of Western exceptionalism.' *Journal of Human Rights* 13, no. 3: 274–289.

Rahman, M. 2014b. *Homosexualities, Muslim Cultures and Modernity.* Basingstoke: Palgrave Macmillan.

Rao, R. 2014. 'The locations of homophobia.' *London Review of International Law* 2, no. 2: 169–199.

Rao, R. 2015. 'Echoes of imperialism in LGBT activism.' In *Echoes of Empire. Memory, Identity and Colonial Legacies*, edited by K. Nicolaïdis, B. Sèbe, and G. Maas, pp. 355–372. London: I.B. Tauris.

RFSL. 2009. *LGBT in Development: A Handbook on LGBT Perspectives in Development Cooperation.* Stockholm: RFSL.

Rostow, W. W. 1960. *The Stages of Economic Growth: A Non-Communist Manifesto*. Cambridge: Cambridge University Press.

Rubin, G. 1999 (1984). 'Thinking sex: Notes for a radical theory of the politics of sexuality.' In *Culture, Society and Sexuality: A Reader*, edited by R. Parker and P. Aggleton, pp. 143–178. London: UCL Press.

Sabsay, L. 2012. 'The emergence of the other sexual citizen: Orientalism and the modernisation of sexuality.' *Citizenship Studies* 16, no. 5/6: 605–623.

Samelius, L., E. Wagberg, and SIDA. 2005. *Sexual Orientation and Gender Identity: Issues in Development. A Study of Policy and Administration*. Stockholm: Swedish Ministry for Foreign Affairs.

Sedgwick, E. K. 1990. *Epistemology of the Closet*. Berkeley, CA: University of California Press.

SIDA. 2006. 'Action plan for Sida's work on sexual orientation and gender identity in international development cooperation 2007-2009.' Stockholm: Department for Democracy and Social Development.

Spivak, G. 1993. *Outside in the Teaching Machine*. London: Routledge.

Spivak, G. 2004. 'Righting wrongs.' *The South Atlantic Quarterly* 103, no 2/3: 523–581.

Stoler, A. L. 1989. 'Making empire respectable: The politics of race and sexual morality in the 20th century.' *American Ethnologist* 16, no. 4: 634–660.

Theron, L., J. McAllister, and M. Armisen. 2016. 'Where do we go from here? A call for a critical reflection on queer/LGBTIA+ activism in Africa.' Pambazuka News, May 12. Accessed June 1, 2016. http://www.pambazuka.org/gender-minorities/where-do-we-go-here

Verloo, M. 2005. 'Mainstreaming gender equality in Europe: A critical frame analysis approach.' *The Greek Review of Social Research* 117 (B): 11–34.

Weber, C. 2014. 'Queer international relations: From queer to queer IR.' *International Studies Review*, no. 16: 596–622.

Weber, C. 2016. *Queer International Relations: Sovereignty, Sexuality and the Will to Knowledge*. Oxford: Oxford University Press.

Wilson, A. 2010. 'NGOs as erotic sites.' In *Development, Sexual Rights and Global Governance*, edited by A. Lind, pp. 86–98. New York: Routledge.

Wilson, K. 2012. *Race, Racism and Development: Interrogating History, Discourse and Practice*. London: Zed Books.

7

DECOLONISING DEVELOPMENT WORK

A transfeminist perspective[1]

Chamindra Weerawardhana

At the Berlin office of a German international non-governmental organisation (INGO) specialised in peacebuilding and conflict management, I once heard the personal account of a talented young researcher from a South Asian country. He was cisgender male, a graduate of a university in Turtle Island with a specialised Master's degree, and was completing a doctorate. The most intriguing part of this account was also the most frustrating. He noted that, when working with several organisations in his native country (in the SAARC (South Asian Association for Regional Cooperation) region) at project officer level, his salary was less than that of a Caucasian person in the same position. Most importantly, whenever the necessity of 'expert advice' arose in relation to their specific area of specialisation, his junior colleagues (his fellow citizens) would automatically seek advice not from him, but from a Caucasian employee. In some cases, that much-solicited Caucasian employee happened to be an undergraduate on a summer internship. This anecdote sums up an aspect of development work that too many people from the global South with an interest and/or expertise in Development Studies could identify with. The rationale behind the inclination of non-Caucasian staff in development organisations to seek 'Caucasian' expertise has a long, tedious and oppressive history. It is couched in a racially stratified colonial perception of the (cis-heteronormative) white Western coloniser as the saviour carrying knowledge, skills, culture and, most importantly, funding. In terms of academic research, one can also notice a domination of scholarship produced by Caucasian academics from the global North, after an x or y number of months of fieldwork in a given country. Spending a few months in a location in the global South confers upon them, or so it is assumed, a level of high-profile expertise. Very often, it is this 'expertise' (of the near 98 per cent Caucasian, citizen of the global North, academic) that is accepted as the 'status quo' in supranational organisations. When influential Western governments formulate their foreign policy and international aid agendas, it is once again this body of work produced by Western academics that is largely considered as expert knowledge. In the summer of 2016, an academic sitting next to this writer at the dinner of a high-profile Canadian learned society (which specialises in politics and international affairs) claimed: 'it is true that the majority of work on places in the global South is done by Western academics – I don't see anything wrong in that, but…'. This writer, a Sri Lankan visiting from Western Europe, happened to be the only person from a visible minority at the conference dinner. Disparities in terms of representation, power imbalances, and the tremendous privileges between researchers from the 'North' and 'South' were of no interest to their discourse. Over ten years of teaching, postgraduate studies, PhD research and postdoctoral research, the list of identical encounters is long. In the large majority of cases, these opinions amount to an effort, consciously or otherwise, to 'whitesplain' the conduct of academic research, and to end up justifying the existing pattern.

The anecdotes mentioned above are not isolated one-off incidents. Many people, especially people of colour, and very especially cis and Trans women of colour, indigenous peoples, non-cisnormative and non-heteronormative peoples often share similar experiences in their work in academic, research and practitioner structures, especially when it pertains to international development, aid distribution and international politics. When carrying out development research in deeply divided societies, for example, issues of gender are systematically understood through a cis-heteronormative lens. In the minority of cases when researchers do identify the necessity of challenging this approach, the steps taken remain parsimonious. This involves, for example, creating focus areas on 'women and girls', and yet another area on lesbian, gay, bisexual, transgender, queer, intersex and asexual (LGBTQIA+) people, but somehow sidelining the necessity of acknowledging the interrelatedness of the systemic factors that cause gender-based marginalisation, discrimination and violence. This chapter is an effort to highlight the necessity of fundamentally challenging the conduct of development research and development praxis, by questioning its cis-heteronormativity and its excessive centring on the global North in terms of expertise and knowledge production. This inevitably involves a call for changes in approaches to research, and also a reformulation of research priorities. In so doing, I shall argue that the most insightful theoretical perspectives, epistemic and ontological inspiration comes from theoretical innovations in Transfeminist discourses.

The sector of international development is one that has its unapologetic racial hierarchies, financial dependencies and, in some cases, financial indiscipline. To a very large extent, it is also a field that is characterised by its cis-heteronormativity. Non-heteronormativity or a non-cisgender gender identity, it appears, are almost perceived as impediments to success in a career in international development, except perhaps in a small section of sexual health, LGBTQIA rights-related development work. This hostility towards non-cis-het people is especially evident in field missions in places of the global South where non-cis-het people are seldom represented. In this chapter, I emphasise the fact that the cis-heteronormativity in terms of personnel in development work is also reflected in the near totality of development praxis, policy formulation, funding allocation and in the identification of strategic priorities. This makes development work, and the interdisciplinary research area we know as 'Development Studies' ignore a large number of people who do not fall into the cis-heteronormative binary. This also results in development initiatives that are oblivious to non-cis-heteronormativity, when approaching gender politics-related issues.

In this chapter, I argue that an increased understanding of Transfeminist thought, especially Transfeminist-of-colour epistemologies are of tremendous relevance to the worldwide sphere of Development Studies, in theory as well as in practice. I will begin with a discussion of the terrain in question – the academic discipline of Development Studies and development praxis at international level – which share complex interlinkages with queer politics. Reflecting upon scholarly efforts at 'queering' development work (an aspect that is seldom acknowledged in the high corridors of development aid) provides a helpful terrain to contextualising the cisnormative nature of Development Studies and development praxis.

This will be followed by a discussion of the *grandes lignes* of Transfeminist theory. I will then move on to discuss how a Transfeminist focus can contribute as an effective analytical tool to constructively challenge many of the exclusionary practices of development work. This chapter concludes – continuing the reflection through a Transfeminist lens – with an emphasis on the necessity of making development work not only non-cis-heteronormative, but also profoundly inscribed in a logic of self-critique and empowerment.

Development research and queer politics: critical insights?

The discipline of Development Studies and development praxis tended to avoid, over a long period of time, discussions about sexuality (Jolly 2000 81). Over the years, international development agencies, United Nations (UN) bodies, donor governments and funding bodies have increasingly begun to pay attention to the intersections of 'gender and development'. The UN, for example, claims to systematically prioritise gender equality in its Sustainable Development Goals (SDG).[2] This has also strengthened the horizons of the academic discipline of Development Studies. Of specific interest to this chapter is a body of recent research that has identified close correlations between the terms 'queer' and 'third world', identifying important parallels. These include, especially, the fact that both 'queer' and 'third world' are all too often understood, conceptualised and interpreted through the prism of a form of norm entrepreneurship coming from the global North. In the preceding centuries, the West supplied the model for many places in the global South, through rigid colonial-era laws (especially in cultivating homophobia and transphobia, and a lasting inferiority complex among colonised peoples). Today, politics of queer liberalism, funded and maintained by the international LGBTQIA NGO lobby, often adopts a patronising tone that somewhat replicates this bitter precedent, calling upon governments in the global South to comply with queer liberal perspectives. These strategies of domination of yesteryear and of present times, albeit in contrasting forms yet united in the same zest for capital and setting norms for non-Western people to follow, have encouraged scholars to raise questions about the concept of 'queering' the 'third world' (Kapoor 2015).

In the mainstream discourse of international development, what is implied as 'third' world, comes off looking remarkably queer. This term refers to the way in which the West perceives economically under-developed places in the global South (which were also subjected to centuries-long occupation, exploitation and unauthorised control over the natural resources of these countries by the West) as places that need to be aided, as backward spaces full of chaos and problems. As Kapoor (2015 1612) further explains, the third world's economic development is depicted as abnormal, always needing to emulate the West, yet never living up to the mark – 'emerging', perhaps – but never quite arriving. Many governments of the global South loathe this attitude and often castigate the patronising nature of Western perspectives towards them, but are still intent upon seeing the West as *the* model, increasingly moving towards neoliberal capitalist economic policies. Any dialogue on development research or praxis is incomplete in the absence of an appraisal of the strong links between Western colonialism and the present-day politics of development aid and policy formulation. Across the global South, Western colonial domination was imposed by forcing colonised peoples to conform to strict cis-heteronormative lifestyles, thereby destroying local traditions of gender identity/ies, family structures and social cohesion, just as racism and sexism, homophobia and transphobia (if not gender plurality-phobia), were part and parcel of the Western colonial project, contributing to create what we know today as a global South hostile to non-cis-heteronormative peoples. Consequently, fundamental rights pertaining to sexual orientation, gender identity/expression and sex characteristics (SOGIESC) are severely restricted in many countries across the global South. Today, the same colonising governments, having taken a (neo)liberal turn, call for the replacement of homophobia and transphobia, which they themselves actively propagated in the past. This has resulted in the West once again emerging as the quintessential model, the template to be emulated by the non-West. In the same high-minded spirit of colonial times, the West today resorts to judging countries across the global South as either LGBTQIA-friendly or not, trying to 'discipline' them when they fail to comply, through methods such as withholding development aid (Kapoor 2015 1616). However, such policies are largely dependent upon geopolitical, diplomatic and strategic priorities. This results in some extremely homophobic and transphobic governments never receiving the West's wrath in any form. Whenever a state not favourable towards LGBTQIA rights practices an overall policy agenda that is perceived as detrimental to the West's interests, regime change operations are orchestrated in the name of gender justice and the rights of LGBTQIA people. The overall strategy is, once again, one of caricaturing and looking down upon governments in the global South, indicating to them that they have a long way to go in corresponding to the fine 'norms' and ideals that the West espouses. It is also a strategy of using LGBTQIA peoples as pawns in political and diplomatic manoeuvring. As Kapoor articulately notes,

> this new [queer liberal] Western stand is also a form of queering: the colonial manoeuvre may well have hinged on homophobia, which the West now conveniently condemns; but the current Western strategy nonetheless pivots on a manipulative homo-righteousness…both are equally orientalist technologies of power aimed at estranging the Third World, belittling it, putting it in its place.
>
> *(Kapoor 2015 1616–1617)*

We can thus conclude with certainty that international development agendas represent a present-day manifestation of setting a model, if not a standard to be achieved, to the global South. This may work in numerous instances, when governments are keen to amass development aid. However, on certain fronts, the high politics and international diplomacy of queer liberalism falls short of being effective. This was, for instance, the case of the UN's 2016 vote on the appointment of a Special Expert on SOGIESC issues. At the two votes in Geneva and New York, a large number of member states in the global South voted against the appointment of the Special Expert. In delivering a speech on behalf of her country the Permanent Representative of the USA attempted to make the point that this was not a case of 'the North trying to impose its values on the South'. Instead, she maintained, the necessity of appointing the Special Expert was an issue of respecting the human rights and dignity of all people, everywhere, also reiterating 'that is what we mean when we say that LGBTI [sic] rights are universal human rights' (quoted in Weerawardhana 2017a). This message is yet to be effectively transmitted to the global South, where SOGIESC-related fundamental rights are directly associated with Western queer liberalism and strategic agendas.

When reflecting upon development initiatives that incorporate LGBTQIA communities, the limitations of queer liberalism and homo-righteous imperatives come to light. A logic of development aid based on a neoliberal advocacy template results in strengthening what can be termed the NGO-industrial complex, creating dependencies and unhealthy hierarchies among activist lobbies (Raha 2015). Liberal LGBTQIA activism also reinforces LGBTQIA communities across the global South who are for the most part apolitical, and passive towards the international structures that exercise control upon them through funding cycles and dictates of best practice. Most often, international development and aid initiatives – especially pertaining to LGBTQIA rights – result in 'white saviour' complexes in the global South, with many activists perceiving Western funders and governments as indispensable for their activism and survival, and governments despising LGBTQIA rights activists, entire LGBTQIA communities among their citizenries, as well as global structures of LGBTQIA rights promotion. In sum, the sphere of development work has long had a problem with non-cisnormativity and non-heteronormativity. This is evident, for instance, in the tendency in much of the literature to refer to non-cisnormative and non-heteronormative gender identities, sexualities and lifestyles as 'dissident' (Klapeer 2015). Dialogues on queer politics often verge on the idea of dissidence, dissonance and challenging establishments. This is the rationale of academic thinking on queering the academy (Allen 2015).[3]

Queer politics of development aid: a brief recapitulation

The foremost form in which queer politics connect to development aid and praxis is in terms of donor-funded projects that focus on LGBTQIA communities, especially in the global South. Very often, development aid granted to LGBTQIA rights organisations is their only form of subsistence, as their existence as citizens and their work are categorically ignored by many governments in the global South. As mentioned above, donor-funded LGBTQIA work leads to lasting dependencies, in which LGBTQIA activists often find themselves with next to no alternative than that of expanding their funding mechanisms, satisfying the exigencies of their funders and orienting their projects and initiatives in line with the priorities of their funders. This NGO-industrial complex results in an LGBTQIA rights advocacy sector which finds it difficult to connect with local contexts, or to ground their activism locally (Raha 2015, Weerawardhana 2017b). Despite persistent problems, a cursory glance provides evidence that the international development sector continues to pay attention to making LGBTQIA-related development assistance more effective.[4] Discussions often centre on managing aid in such a way that makes LGBTQIA activism in the global South more effective (Godfrey 2014). In the early part of his prime ministerial mandate, Britain's David Cameron publicly stated a willingness to withhold international aid from governments that do not reform anti-LGBTQIA legislation (BBC News 2011). Research and activist evidence from the global South has shown the ineffectiveness of this method (see, for example, Kretz 2013). Despite advancements in thinking on LGBTQIA rights beyond binaries to more inclusive discourses,[5] the sector of international aid for LGBTQIA work is largely shaped by the priorities of Western governments and funding bodies (and not of adversely affected LGBTQIA communities in the global South); the scope of action of the NGO-industrial sector remains inherently limited. To a very large extent, an excessive focus on the gender binary continues to hinder global advocacy on LGBTQIA rights. To many international organisations, discussions on issues such as women's health and reproductive justice, for example, are topics that exclusively focus on cisgender women, with the LGBTQIA communities and gender pluralities being near-categorically ignored (Yamin 2013 248). Goal 5 of the UN's Agenda 2030 has recently included the sentence: 'Make sure that all programmes working on gender equality and violence against women and girls address the particular issues faced by lesbian, bi and trans women.'[6] However, the practical implementation of this clause across gender equality and justice mechanisms at supranational, regional and national is yet to be consolidated.

Beyond the realm of queer development, there has been an active current of thought in development research that is relevant to the present reflection – on the importance of decolonising development work. Langdon (2013) argues for decolonising approaches to teaching and research in Development Studies in university contexts, challenging Eurocentric conceptual frameworks, and also questioning and contesting persistent inequities in university programmes and campuses. Indeed, there is a clear necessity for teaching and research in Development Studies to take into account theoretical and epistemological forays into the politics of inequities of knowledge in higher education, researched through intersectional feminist, inherently anti-racist and anticolonial theorising.[7] This line of analysis is highly relevant to the broader realm of theorising in development research as a whole. As it will be outlined below, much of the knowledge in development work is generated in the global North, and the dominant perspective is almost always one of the global South having to learn from, or emulate examples in the global North. The perspective highlighted below, that of a Transfeminist approach to development work, is one that profoundly advocates for decolonising development research and praxis.

Transfeminism: a brief recapitulation

In mounting a workable and trenchant challenge, if not an alternative to liberal LGBTQIA activism, a different set of ideas focused on LGBTQIA liberation, if not Queer liberation, is essential. In filling this void, I contend that some of the most insightful perspectives come from Transfeminist thought. Prior to a discussion of how development work can be strengthened and made productive when conceptualised through a Transfeminist lens, it is essential to reflect upon what I mean by 'Transfeminism'. The term 'Transfeminism' basically implies a Trans-inclusive form of feminism, which recognises the existences, challenges and life experiences of Trans women, or women who are not assigned female at birth (Koyama 2001, 2003, Enke 2012 1–5, Stryker and Bettcher 2016 11–14). Transfeminist thought profoundly challenges currents of feminism that focus exclusively on cisgender women, and over the last few years, one can notice significant developments in Transfeminist thought. A cursory glance at the *Transgender Studies Quarterly* journal, for instance, would reveal the vibrancy of research on Transfeminism, in English-speaking Western universities as well as in non-Anglophone institutions, including Brazil (see, for instance, Silva and Ornat 2016).

My definition and understanding of the Transfeminism, and the perspective that is developed in this chapter, is imperatively inscribed in a Trans woman of colour and global South perspective. The scope of this Transfeminism-of-colour largely exceeds the epistemological innovations on Transfeminism achieved in the Western academy (especially in Turtle Island), where Trans scholarship has been, and continues to be, dominated by white settler Trans people, who command higher levels of privileges and positions of influence in the academy, especially in comparison with Trans people of colour.[8] Indeed, in carving out the theoretical foundations of Transfeminism, their work has been important and certainly deserves credit. The point made here, however, is that insights of crucial relevance to development praxis are best gleaned when examined from a Transfeminist-of-colour perspective. It is rooted in a rich legacy of Trans-inclusive feminist activism, especially developed by pioneering Trans women of colour in Turtle Island, such as the late Marsha P. Johnson and Silvia Rae Riviera. Their work on the ground, at a time when Transfemininity was far less welcome in movements for the rights of (mostly cis) women and non-heteronormative people, enabled the development of a strong movement, creating important precedents in making Transfeminist voices heard, and claiming space in activist circles. Pioneered by Black Trans women, and inspired and influenced by Black feminist thought, global South and transnational feminist perspectives and indigenous feminisms, Transfeminism-of-colour also forms the primary epistemic tool that enables my existence, as a Trans woman of colour navigating hostile academic contexts in the global North, engaging in political activity and carrying out activism in multiple places. Transfeminism-of-colour is therefore a way of life, as well as a source of survival in a world that continues to marginalise Trans women's identities and other gender pluralities, especially among people of colour and non-Western as well as indigenous peoples. This reading of Transfeminism, however, surpasses a mere focus on Trans and queer identities. Instead, its overall focus, inspired especially by Black and indigenous feminisms, is one of solidarity and movement building. Audre Lorde's claim 'I am not free while any other woman is unfree, even if her shackles are very different from my own' (Lorde 2007 125) strongly characterises Transfeminist activism, which espouses a strong sense of solidarity in all activist, advocacy, movement-building, political and policy formulation engagements. Transfeminist-of-colour epistemologies provide pride of place to transnational feminist solidarities, movement-building, and through an intersectional lens, focus primarily on the most marginalised. It is also an epistemological framework that embraces different traditions and structures of gender pluralities in non-Western societies.

In what follows, and unless otherwise specified, the term 'Transfeminism' imperatively refers to Transfeminism-of-colour. The terms 'woman' and 'women' imply both cis and Trans women. Given the existing gatekeeping hierarchies, the number of Trans women of colour in the academy being extremely low, some of the most important theoretical contributions to Transfeminism-of-colour takes place outside the ivory tower of the academy, in activist, movement-building and artistic circles.[9] This constant closeness to the challenges of day-to-day lives provides Transfeminist-of-colour perspectives with an activist and critical twist.

Transgender studies: acknowledgement comes slowly?

Despite inherent limitations, the discipline of Transgender Studies provides space for critical engagement. It is conducive to mounting challenges against the aforementioned practices of exclusion. The latest issue of the *TSQ: Transgender Studies Quarterly* journal at the time of writing (vol. 4 no. 2), for instance, is devoted to the theme of 'Blackness' and/ in Transgender Studies, bringing together a number of contributions that explore how the institutionalisation of transgender studies as a discipline functions as a scene of subjection of Blackness – for Black people and places (Ellison et al. 2017 162). As the editors of this volume rightly admit, they are a Black Trans masculine editorial team, and even the entire edited volume contains only two contributions by Black Trans women. This marginalisation of Transfeminist-of-colour voices and the disregard for the intellectual labour and socio-political, cultural, literary and economic contributions of Trans women of colour (especially Black Trans women) is, from a perspective of a Trans woman of colour navigating the ivory towers of the academies of multiple Western contexts, the defining feature of the present-day sphere of Transgender Studies.

Transfeminism-of-colour is also an acknowledgement of a crucial reality, that of the acute need for Trans women and gender-plural peoples to organise, and develop analytical tools, ontologies and epistemologies of our own – something that has been happening with vigorous energy for many years, getting next to no mention in the academy. These perspectives are present and disseminated in activist and artistic circles but not within the academy, given the academy's long-standing reluctance to host Trans people of colour, especially Trans women of colour, in positions that enhance their agency. To sum up, this women-of-colour perspective on what is generally understood as 'Transfeminism' in the Western academy is, most importantly, 'global' in scope. It follows Professor Chandra Mohanty's call for 'emancipatory knowledges' in developing feminist epistemologies (Mohanty 2003). It also follows and is inspired by the teachings of Black feminist pioneers, from Audre Lorde to Patricia Hill Collins and many others. This, however, does not imply an appropriation of Black feminist thought. Instead, the very birthplace of Transfeminist-of-colour perspectives is in the work of Black Trans and queer people such as Marsha Johnson. It is precisely in this sphere of fierce and cutting-edge activism that today's Black Trans people are tirelessly involved in gender, racial and social justice activism. Transfeminist perspectives are not limited to the realms of Queer Studies or Transgender Studies. Instead, it is an epistemological and ontological base that is of direct relevance to all aspects of local, national and international governance and policymaking.[10]

Transfeminism in action: Transfeminist perspectives and the politics of international development

The cis-normativities of development work through a Transfeminist lens

In delving into the relevance of Transfeminist epistemologies to development praxis, it is worth taking a look at the problems associated with the UN's 2030 SDGs. Responding to lacunae in the previous strategic plan of Millennium Development Goals (MDGs), the SDGs are generally seen as more advanced in terms of gender politics. The ongoing 2030 agenda of SDGs comprises seventeen goals and 169 targets with universal application. In terms of gender issues, the foremost problem with the 2030 SDGs lies in the formulators' understanding of the term 'gender'. The UN's grasp of gender, to go by the 2030 SDGs discourse, is exclusively based on the cisnormative gender binary. Indeed, when the very term 'gender equality' is mentioned in contexts of international development and the politics of aid, the term is often understood in such a way that it is seen as synonymous to a notion of equality strictly limited to the gender binary. In this literature, when the terms 'woman' or 'women' are referred to, they almost always imply cisgender women. This results in creating multiple categories of people, something that the neoliberal international system appears to assume as acceptable. Whereas gender equality is all about cisgender women, another emphasis is on LGBTQIA people. Even organisations that stand for the rights of non-cisgender and non-heteronormative people often steer clear of challenging the UN's cis-normativity. In a policy paper that specifically focuses on LGBTQIA peoples and the 2030 SDGs, Stonewall, for instance, comments on Goal 5 (achieving gender equality and empower women and girls), that '…while women in general are taken less seriously than men when reporting crimes to the authorities, they will be taken even less seriously if they are identified as lesbian or bi'.[11] The same goal also calls for Trans-inclusivity in gender equality initiatives, a call that does not appear to correspond to the functional dynamics of bodies such as UN Women, which practice a policy of categorically ignoring non-cisnormative women and gender plural peoples.

Addressing the Francophone Conference organised by Montréal Pride in mid-2017, I raised the issue of the near-total cis-normativity of people working in the international sector, from government bodies, the UN to any other supranational organisations (Weerawardhana 2017c). Most often, opportunities in government departments, civil service and diplomatic appointments are held exclusively by cisgender people. These spaces, where the most important decisions affecting global governance, defence and multilateralism, development aid and strategic priorities are made, appear to be exclusively confined to cisgender people with strong networks. Cis-ness therefore becomes an absolute prerequisite to excel in the majority of professions, especially in governmental, diplomatic and supranational services. Examining the international sector from a Transfeminist perspective, this becomes a fundamental challenge, a problem that requires effective solutions. A Transfeminist approach is one that calls for a de-centring of 'mainstream' in the international sector. This involves working proactively towards making the presence of non-cisgender and non-cis-heteronormative people in positions of agency in the international sector something mainstream and 'normal', and not the exception.

This preference for cis people is a cause for concern on several grounds: firstly, it results in normalising politics of exclusion, of assuming that a non-cisgender person has next to nothing to do with the corridors of power. At a much earlier stage in life, my own interactions with a UN body as a gratis personal[12] entailed a series of micro-aggressions, and a clear indication from many quarters that I was far from welcome in that context. This aversion of non-cisnormative people affects Trans and queer women, especially women of colour, whose very legitimacy is constantly questioned, their agency systematically curtailed. Second, it amounts to an exclusionary practice that enables the structures of power to remain cis, largely heteronormative and dominantly white across the supranational sphere. It is in this context that the increased emphasis on SOGIESC issues at the UN and at other supranational bodies, funding agencies, and INGOs is best contextualised. Although we have an emphasis on SOGIESC, the UN and its core gender programmes (in particular UN Women and all relevant programmes within the United Nations Development Programme) continue to be cis-heteronormative in their composition and power politics. There is a clear imbalance and inconsistency between the well-articulated objectives of promoting equality and inclusivity, and the reality presents itself as markedly different. The structural practices that facilitate exclusion and marginalisation are kept intact. If a Transfeminist approach is to be pursued, a key change is required, first and foremost, in spearheading equality and justice initiatives. When the UN appointed a Special Expert on SOGIESC issues, they chose a cisgender gay man. When an international fund for Trans issues was created, its first head inevitably had to be a white Trans man. Working to change the parameters of such hierarchies, and dismantle them, is at the heart of a Transfeminist approach to international politics and queer development and international advocacy work.

Development policy and Transfeminist politics: towards equity?

In terms of development policy, a Transfeminist approach is one that refutes and challenges many, if not all, of the problems and limitations of international development work mentioned earlier in this chapter. A Transfeminist approach would, first and foremost, strongly challenge the NGO-industrial complex of queer development work. Instead, as Trans women-of-colour activists have highlighted time and again, the focus should be on Trans and Queer liberation, through strategies and plans of action specifically adapted to local contexts. The objective here is on grounding Trans and Queer liberation locally, reviving local traditions of gender plurality, and in connecting Trans and Queer liberation with wider imperatives of gender justice that concern people of all other gender identities, especially cis women. An approach of this nature would involve a strong emphasis on empowerment of Trans/Queer people, movement-building at the grassroots, and forging solidarities with Transfeminist resistance movements between the global South and the global North. In terms of reproductive justice, for instance, a Transfeminist perspective is of tremendous relevance, as it centres around bodily autonomy and the right to access safe and legal services when an individual so requests and requires. A Transfeminist approach can therefore be of specific relevance to international development work that focuses on women's empowerment and reproductive rights, by strengthening existing campaigns along a logic of bodily autonomy, and also zooming in on the much-despised reproductive rights of LGBTQIA and all gender-plural peoples.

Most importantly, Transfeminist politics strongly challenge any inclination to consider Trans identities and gender pluralities as an exception, or as 'dissident' identities that are positioned against a cis-normative 'mainstream'. This, by and large, is the basic template around which international development as well as the entire field of world politics operates. This is at the heart of the preference for cis bodies not only in development work in general, but also, as highlighted above, in queer development and LGBTQIA empowerment initiatives (see Raha 2017). A Transfeminist approach involves actively promoting the leadership of women, especially Trans, gender-plural, and indigenous women, as well as women at the lower echelons of social class and in some contexts caste stratifications. In practice, a Transfeminist discourse of development includes an essentially intersectional focus on 'empowerment', as opposed to politics of dependency that queer development work, in its existing form, seeks to generate.

Conclusion: beyond cisnormativity?

This chapter focused on the cisnormativity that characterises development work, including what we know as queer development work, or development aid that focuses on LGBTQIA communities. A Transfeminist perspective involves challenging the reliance of international aid on the gender binary, and also going beyond the politics of LGBTQIA rights as perceived from a neoliberal, NGO-industrial angle, which involves providing material support to LGBTIQA communities in the absence of a concrete and locally grounded discourse on empowerment. A Transfeminist approach is one that seeks to address these problems through solid re-readings and re-articulations of priorities, functional dynamics and strategies on the empowerment of (cis and trans) women, and especially non-cisnormative and non-heteronormative peoples. In terms of development praxis, this implies challenging the inherent cisnormativity in development work in general, and dismantling the trappings of the NGO-industrial complex of global LGBTQIA advocacy. A Transfeminist perspective would be beneficial in challenging international aid through a logic of empowering the targeted communities, instead of creating dependencies on international aid. It is also a perspective that provides an opportunity to think, and rethink outside the box, beyond parameters that are specific to given geographical and geo-strategic contexts, and instead view the broader picture, connecting and learning from our collective struggles for gender justice, from Indigenous epistemologies and campaigns for Turtle Island to Aotearoa, to women's movement building initiatives worldwide.

Notes

1 Unless otherwise mentioned, all URLs in this chapter were accessed on 1 July 2017.
2 See, for example, Goal 5 of the UN's seventeen SDGs: http://www.un.org/ sustainabledevelopment/gender-equality/
3 The Higher Education Research & Development journal, for example, devoted its Vol. 34, issue 4, entirely to the theme of 'queering the academy'. The writing published in this issue, despite important contributions to reflections on queer politics in the academy, are considerably short of addressing one crucial issue – that of 'empowerment'. The discussion is most often on queer students, postgrads, PhD candidates and teaching – but never on the question of

challenging the cisnormativity and hetero-normativity in the academy, its recruitment patterns and its institutional structures.

4   Events that focus on this issue are often organised by international LGBTQIA advocacy organisations. A revealing example is an event entitled 'Can aid donors help support LGBT rights in developing countries?' organised by the Kaleidoscope Trust in London (https://www.odi.org/events/3968-can-aid-donors-help-support-lgbt-rights-developing-countries).

5   An example is the launch, at the 2016 World Conference of the International Lesbian, Gay, Bisexual, Transgender and Intersex Association (ILGA) in Bangkok, of the International Trans Fund (http://www.transfund.org – ITF). The documentation related to the Fund's launch took into account the multiplicity of gender identities, especially mentioning the importance of acknowledging and fighting against the erasure of indigenous gender identities. However, the ITF is a tightly controlled mechanism that also emulates cisnormative practices in development aid, often appropriating gender hierarchies in the international development sector. This is evident, for instance, in the tendency in the ITF as well as in the entire realm of global Trans advocacy to favour white (and often cis-passing) Trans men for positions of high-level responsibility, and to ensure that Trans activists in the global North wield controlling prerogatives of the Fund.

6   The sustainable development goals and LGBT inclusion. Stonewall International: https://www.stonewall.org.uk/sites/default/files/sdg-guide_2.pdf

7   For examples of existing work in this area that is highly relevant to the conduct of teaching and research in the field of Development Studies, see, for example, Wane et al. 2004, Langdon 2013). On developing pedagogies of solidarity committed to decolonising knowledge – yet another highly relevant theme for development research and praxis, see Gaztambide-Fernández 2012.

8   This tendency is clearly evident in universities across Turtle Island (the territories known as Canada and USA), and also in Europe. Despite being highly qualified, Trans people of colour are extremely rare in tenured positions. In most cases, the system downgrades their achievements and potential by relegating them to precarious contractual employment, driving many Trans-of-colour academics away from academia.

9   Insights into Transfeminist epistemologies can be especially gleaned in the work of Trans women of colour artists and writers such as Kama la Mackerel (https://lamackerel.net) and Nat Raha (https://sussex.academia.edu/NatRaha).

10 On a Transfeminist perspective on international relations, see Weerawardhana 2017d (forthcoming).

11 Sustainable development goals and LGBT inclusion, Stonewall International: https://www.stonewall.org.uk/sites/default/files/sdg-guide_2.pdf, p. 5.

12 The UN's main channel of gratis-personal, if not unpaid employment is in the form of internships in UN agencies worldwide. Despite repeated calls to acknowledge the work of unpaid interns through a remuneration package, the organisation resolutely continues its policy of entry level unpaid employment.

References

Allen, Louisa (2015). Queering the academy: new directions in LGBT research in higher education, *Higher Education Research & Development*. 34:4, 681–684.

BBC News. 2011. Cameron threat to dock some UK aid to anti-gay nations. 30 October: http://www.bbc.co.uk/news/uk-15511081

Ellison, T., Green, K.M., Richardson, M. and Riley Snorton, C. 2017. We have issues: toward a Black Trans/studies. *Transgender Studies Quarterly*, 4:2, 162–169.

Enke, A. (ed.) 2012. *Transfeminist Perspectives in and Beyond Transgender and Gender Studies*. Philadelphia, PA: Temple University Press.

Gaztambide-Fernández, Rubén A. 2012. Decolonization and the pedagogy of solidarity. *Decolonization: Indigeneity, Education & Society* 1:1, 41–67.

Godfrey, C. 2014. Is Britain's pro-gay foreign policy actually helping the global LGBTI community? *Vice*, 10 December: https://www.vice.com/en_uk/article/dpw94a/exporting-lgbti-rights-from-the-uk-abroad-327

Jolly, Susie (2000). 'Queering' development: exploring the links between same-sex sexualities, gender, and development. *Gender & Development*, 8:1, 78–88.

Kapoor, I. 2015. The queer third world. *Third World Quarterly*, 36:9, 1611–1628.

Klapeer, C.M. 2015. Queer/ing development?! Contesting the subversive potentials of LGBTIQ-inclusive development agendas from a post-/decolonial perspective. Paper, ECPG conference, Uppsala, 2015: https://ecpr.eu/Filestore/PaperProposal/01169085-4c3d-46e9-8dc0-42fe504fd4da.pdf

Koyama, Emi. 2001. The Transfeminist manifesto (and related contributions, regrouped into one PDF). http://eminism.org/readings/pdf-rdg/tfmanifesto.pdf (accessed 28 June 2016).

Koyama, Emi. 2003. Transfeminist Manifesto. In *Catching a Wave: Reclaiming Feminism for the Twenty-First Century*, ed. R. Dicker and A. Piepmeier, 1–15. Boston, MA: Northeastern University Press.

Kretz, A.J. 2013. Is aid conditionality an answer to antigay legislation? An analysis of British and American foreign aid policies designed to protect sexual minorities. *Vienna Journal of International Constitutional Law*, 7. https://papers.ssrn.com/sol3/papers.cfm?abstract_id=2183810

Langdon, J. 2013. Decolonising development studies: reflections on critical pedagogies in action. *Canadian Journal of Development Studies / Revue canadienne d'études du développement*, 34:3, 384–399.

Lorde, Audre. 2007. *Sister Outsider: Essays & Speeches by Audre Lorde.* Berkeley, CA: Crossing Press.

Mohanty, C.T. 2003. *Feminism without Borders: Decolonizing Theory, Practicing Solidarity.* Durham, NC: Duke University Press.

Raha, N. 2015. The limits of trans liberalism. Verso blog, 21 September: http://www.versobooks.com/blogs/2245-the-limits-of-trans-liberalism-by-nat-raha

Raha, Natalia. 2017. Transfeminine brokenness, radical Transfeminism. *South Atlantic Quarterly,* 116:3, 632–646.

Silva, J.M. and Ornat, M.J. 2016. Transfeminism and decolonial thought: the contribution of Brazilian travestis. *Transgender Studies Quarterly*, 3:1–2, 220–227.

Stryker, S. and Bettcher, T.M. 2016. Introduction: Trans/feminisms. *Transgender Studies Quarterly*, 3:1–2, 5–14.

Wane, Riyad Ahmed Shahjahan and Wagner, Anne (2004). Walking the talk: decolonizing the politics of equity of knowledge and charting the course for an inclusive curriculum in higher education. *Canadian Journal of Development Studies / Revue canadienne d'études du développement*, 25:3, 499–510.

Weerawardhana, C. 2017a. Needed: international support for culturally savvy LGBTQI leaders. 76 Crimes, 1 March: https://76crimes.com/2017/03/01/needed-international-support-for-culturally-savvy-lgbtqi-leaders/

Weerawardhana, C. 2017b. Beyond neoliberal LGBTQI politics: on duplicities, challenges & hope for change. *Colombo Telegraph*, 17 February: https://www.colombotelegraph.com/index.php/beyond-neoliberal-lgbtqi-politics-on-duplicities-challenges-hope-for-change/

Weerawardhana, C. 2017c. Décloniser l'activisme LGBTQI et Solidarités transnationales du/des « sud/s » : une réflexion Transféministe. Unpublished paper presented at the 2017 Fierté Montréal Francophone Conference, Montréal, 18 August.

Weerawardhana, C. 2017d Profoundly decolonizing? Reflections on a Transfeminist perspective of international relations. *Meridians Journal*, 16:1, 184–213

Yamin, A.E. 2013. Sexual and reproductive health, rights and MDG 5. In *The Millennium Development Goals and Human Rights: Past, Present and Future*, eds M. Langford and A.E. Yamin, 232–254. Cambridge: Cambridge University Press.

PART III

Global LGBTIQ rights

8

CRITIQUE OF 'SEXUAL ORIENTATION' AND 'GENDER IDENTITY' IN HUMAN RIGHTS DISCOURSE

Global queer politics beyond the Yogyakarta Principles

Matthew Waites

The categories 'sexual orientation' and 'gender identity' have emerged as pivotal in the contestation of human rights discourses and global governance by prevailing international lesbian, gay, bisexual and transgender (LGBT) and human rights non-governmental organizations (NGOs) and activist networks. They are central in the Yogyakarta Principles on the Application of International Human Rights Law in Relation to Sexual Orientation and Gender Identity (Corrêa and Muntarbhorn 2007), and also used in the Declaration of Montreal (International Conference on LGBT Human Rights 2006a; see Kollman and Waites 2009, and Swiebel 2009). These declarations have in turn influenced developments such as the groundbreaking 'Statement on Human Rights, Sexual Orientation and Gender Identity', read by Argentina on behalf of 66 states at the General Assembly of the United Nations on 18 December 2008 (Secrétariat d'État 2008, United Nations General Assembly 2008a). Furthermore, and in part consequently, 'sexual orientation' and 'gender identity' have become important concepts in contemporary global politics more broadly, including conflicts over cultural diversity, identities, religion and globalization, in which sexual politics is a crucial element.

This contribution presents a systematic analysis of the implications of the concepts 'sexual orientation' and 'gender identity' entering human rights discourses, drawing upon social constructionist, post-structuralist, feminist, transgender and queer theories. I argue that rather than viewing this emergence as signalling the eradication of the normative privileging of particular genders and sexualities, it can usefully be interpreted as a reconfiguration of what Judith Butler calls the 'heterosexual matrix': 'that grid of cultural intelligibility through which bodies, genders and desires are naturalized' (Butler 1990, 151). I argue that the emergent grid of intelligibility continues to be subject to dominant interpretations which privilege a binary model of gender, and sexual behaviours, identities and desires that are defined exclusively in relation to a single gender within this binary. Hence this new matrix needs to be contested.

As social research on gender and sexuality increasingly addresses global change and globalization (Adam et al. 1999, Altman 2001, Weeks et al. 2003, Binnie 2004), including socio-legal and politics literature (Stychin and Herman 2000, Buss and Herman 2003, Stychin 2003), and interdisciplinary work on sexuality, gender and human rights develops (Petchesky 2000, Gruskin et al. 2004, Graupner and Tahmindjis 2005, Corrêa et al. 2008) it is necessary to consider the relationship of marginalized sexual and gender minorities to human rights, global politics and governance, in light of related debates over global citizenship (Delanty 2000) and 'global civil society' (Kaldor 2003, Keane 2003). In this contribution I employ interdisciplinary gender and sexuality research and theory to illuminate contemporary processes through which human rights, particularly as defined by the United Nations, are contested in relation to sexuality and transgenderism by transnational social movements and international NGOs.

Using documentary sources, particularly key human rights conventions and legal statutes, I trace and critically analyse the historical emergence of the key concepts 'sexual orientation' and 'gender identity' in law and human rights discourses. Even the most impressive recent global scholarship on sexuality, gender and human rights, despite consistently deploying a critical social analysis, lacks a focus on 'sexual orientation' and 'gender identity' as crucial elements in the emerging conceptual architecture of global human rights discourses (Corrêa et al. 2008). Yet these concepts are central, and particularly important given that they translate quite directly into various languages used most commonly in international organizations where English does not dominate (for example in French, *l'orientation sexuelle et l'identité de genre*; in Spanish, *la orientación sexual y la identidad de género*: Secrétariat d'État 2008).

In the analysis that follows I contribute to answering all three of the questions posed in the introduction to the special issue on 'The Global Politics of LGBT Human Rights' in *Contemporary Politics* (2009). Question one asks: 'How can recent global developments related to LGBT human rights advocacy and organizing be explained by political and sociological theories?' In response I demonstrate how the recent ascendance of the concepts 'sexual orientation' and 'gender identity' in human rights organizing can be partly explained with reference to sociological theories including 'social constructionist' and post-structuralist theories concerning sexual and gender identities, which identify the concepts' specifically Western origins and hence explain their growing prominence in global governance and global civil society. Question two asks: 'What is at stake in focusing on "human rights" rather than concepts such as "equality", "justice", "liberation", "self-determination" or "queer politics"?' By identifying and analysing the specific categories being employed to attempt reformulations of human rights discourses, and by contrasting use of these particularly with the approach of 'queer politics', I illuminate key issues at stake in a focus on 'human rights'. Finally Question three asks: 'How do transnational human rights networks and global norms of LGBT rights affect domestic politics in both the global North and global South?' The analysis reveals ways in which international LGBT and human rights NGOs, and associated transnational sexuality and gender rights networks, are shaping global politics. It also illuminates some culturally specific implications of global human rights discourses in both 'global North' and 'global South' contexts. While relationships between global and local levels are complex, mediated and considerably indeterminate, it is suggested that the consolidation of the categories 'sexual orientation' and 'gender identity' as pivotal elements in emerging global human rights discourses signals the establishment of a new discursive framework, in tension with what can be called a simultaneously emergent 'global queer politics'. The concept 'queer politics', while Anglo-American in origin (Warner 1993, Seidman 1996), is legitimate to use in a global context where it has become adopted for its flexibility in some significant activist organizing in the global South – for example in India (Narrain and Bhan 2005), where *Aravani*, known by others as *hijras*, are a prominent 'third gender' (Herdt 1994, Patel 2006), and where sexuality and gender forms elude Western categories (Boyce 2007), problematizing the Western gender/sexuality distinction itself. In light of such politics (and works cited here), sexuality and gender must be conceptualized as intertwined in their relations to social structures, but without an assumption that they are distinguishable in subjectivity or identity; the distinction between sexual orientation and gender identity is to be approached as itself a product of a Western sexuality/gender distinction (Jackson 2007).

The discussion takes the following structure. The first section 'Gender, sexuality and human rights' offers a brief historical overview of the place of gender and sexuality in human rights discourses, moving to focus on how issues of 'sexual orientation' and 'gender identity' have been dealt with in international human rights law and at the United Nations. The next section 'Orienting human rights: the politics of "sexual orientation"' turns more specifically to the concept of sexual orientation. It notes critiques of gay identity politics and 'LGBT human rights', then examines the emergence of 'sexual orientation' in national and international laws, before discussing academic problematizations of this concept, from sociology, history, post-structuralism and queer theory. Existing applications of these perspectives in law and socio-legal studies are discussed. The following section 'Identifying human rights: the politics of "gender identity"' examines how issues of transgenderism and gender diversity relate to international human rights law and discourses. Some academic discussions of the concept 'gender identity' are reviewed and the concept's emergence in human rights discourses is considered in this light. The section 'Queer dis-orientations and dis-identifications' then examines how recent queer theory, including the work of Sara Ahmed in her book *Queer Phenomenology: Orientations, Objects, Others* (2006), has developed the most sustained critical account of the concept 'sexual orientation', also with implications for conceptualizing 'gender identity'. It is argued that the ascendance of 'sexual orientation' and 'gender identity' in human rights discourses can usefully be interpreted with reference to the work of Judith Butler (1990) as marking the installation of the 'heterosexual matrix' in human rights discourses in a particular new form, albeit subject to ongoing shifts and contestation. However, I argue against a queer strategy of refuting and abandoning concepts of 'sexual orientation' and 'gender identity'. Instead I argue for the necessity of utilizing but contesting such categories. I conclude by suggesting how LGBT, queer and allied NGOs, and related movements and networks might advance this process.

Gender, sexuality and human rights

To understand the relationship of 'sexual orientation' and 'gender identity' to human rights, it is useful to begin by outlining the historically shifting relationship of gender and sexuality to human rights, focusing on the United Nations human rights conventions. As discussed in the introduction (Kollman and Waites 2009), feminist commentators such as Ros Petchesky (2000) have demonstrated the ways in which gendered assumptions have permeated human rights conventions, and the related historical absence of 'sexuality' from these conventions. The Universal Declaration of Human Rights (United Nations 1948), like other major human rights conventions such as the European Convention on Human Rights signed in 1950 (Council of Europe 2003), was formulated with rights to 'privacy', 'family' and 'marriage', and the assumption of a binary model of sex and gender involving only 'men' and 'women', but without mention of sexuality, revealing a patriarchal inheritance:

Article 12.

No one shall be subjected to arbitrary interference with his privacy, family, home or correspondence, nor to attacks upon his honour and reputation.

Article 16.

(1) Men and women of full age, without any limitation due to race, nationality or religion, have the right to marry and to found a family. They are entitled to equal rights as to marriage, during marriage and at its dissolution.
(2) Marriage shall be entered into only with the free and full consent of the intending spouses.
(3) The family is the natural and fundamental group unit of society and is entitled to protection by society and the State.

Since the emergence of feminist movements from the 1960s, feminists have problematized key concepts used in the Declaration such as marriage and 'the family' – described by Millett (1971) as 'patriarchy's chief institution' – and have identified the public/private distinction as culturally specific and central to women's subordination in the domestic realm (Pateman 1988).

In light of feminist and queer theory it can be suggested that the Universal Declaration has been shaped by heterosexuality and 'heteronormativity', defined by queer theorists Lauren Berlant and Michael Warner as 'the institutions, structures of understanding and practical orientations that make heterosexuality seem not only coherent – that is organised as a sexuality – but also privileged' (Berlant and Warner 1998, 548). Yet it is also possible to recognize possibilities for redefinition: for example, the concepts 'family' and 'marriage' are not explicitly defined as involving male/female partnerships, so are potentially subject to imaginative reinterpretation. It is thus from a context of implicit assumptions about sex, gender and sexuality that feminist attempts to address women's rights, gender and sexuality as human rights issues have emerged, as in the United Nations (1979) Convention on the Elimination of All Forms of Discrimination Against Women (in force from 1981; Lockwood 2006).

'Sexual rights' has been described by Ros Petchesky as 'the newest kid on the block' in international debates about human rights (Petchesky 2000). The years since the early 1990s have seen a variety of strategies of legal and political engagement with, and reinterpretation of, existing human rights conventions in relation to sexuality. As Petchesky has documented, international feminist activism led to references to sexuality emerging first in relation to 'health' and 'reproduction', and then 'rights', in declarations from international conferences in Cairo (1994) and Beijing (1995) following struggles with Christian and Islamic state delegations and international organizations (Petchesky 2000, Girard 2007). These strategies have achieved considerable extensions of the scope of 'human rights' (Corrêa et al. 2008).

The most important development in the contestation of United Nations human rights conventions with respect to same-sex sexualities was the landmark ruling by the United Nations Human Rights Committee in *Toonen* v. *Australia* 1994 (Morgan 2000, 211). This found that non-discrimination provisions concerning 'sex' in Article 2(1) of the

International Covenant on Civil and Political Rights (United Nations 1966, in force 1976) could be interpreted as also prohibiting discrimination on grounds of 'sexual orientation', thus rendering discrimination against same-sex sexual behaviour illegal when considered in conjunction with Article 17's right to privacy (Wintemute and Andenaes 2001). The significance of this ruling is limited by the fact that the International Covenant on Civil and Political Rights is only legally enforceable in states which have signed the Covenant's Optional Protocol; nevertheless this was a hugely important development. However, subsequent cases such as *Juliet Joslin et al.* v. *New Zealand* (1999) which upheld exclusion from civil marriage, and *Young* v. *Australia* (2003), which successfully challenged pensions available only to married and unmarried heterosexual couples, but did not face opposing arguments, show the Human Rights Committee has not interpreted the Covenant as requiring non-discrimination with respect to marriage or partnership rights when 'protection of the family' may be at issue (Saiz 2004, 54; Wintemute 2005, 195–197).

As Ignacio Saiz has commented, 'sexuality remains a battleground within the UN human rights system' (Saiz 2004, 50). Human rights relating to sexual orientation continue to be opposed with reference to heteronormative understandings of cultural tradition, national identity and religious belief (Buss and Herman 2003, Rothschild et al. 2005, Corrêa et al. 2008). A resolution in the former UN Commission on Human Rights (CHR) on extrajudicial, summary or arbitrary executions (EJEs) in 2000 first mentioned 'sexual orientation', but UN World Conferences, including that in Beijing, have refused to address the issue (Girard 2007, 340, 342). Similarly, in the former CHR, a Brazilian resolution, 'Human Rights and Sexual Orientation', was refused in 2003 and 2004, and dropped in 2005, after fierce opposition from members of the Organization of Islamic Conference (OIC) and the Holy See representing the Vatican (Saiz 2004, 51, 57, Girard 2007, O'Flaherty and Fisher 2008, 229–230). Interestingly opponents criticized 'sexual orientation' as an 'undefined term' that, if defined as a human right, could prevent protection of children (Saiz 2004, 56–57, Girard 2007, 344–346; for relevant discussion, see Gamson 1997, Waites, 2005a).

Transgender issues have been even more starkly absent from United Nations human rights debates, despite the formulation of claims by transgender people into a suggested Bill of Gender Rights in the United States in 1991, revised several times by the International Conference of Transgender Law and Employment Policy into the International Bill of Gender Rights agreed in 1996 (Frye 2006; see also Graupner and Tahmindjis 2005, Stryker and Whittle 2006, Hines 2009). 'Gender mainstreaming' policies at the United Nations, which might have opened new possibilities, have understood 'gender' as a synonym for biological sex and hence have not prompted new policy initiatives on sexuality or 'gender identity' (Charlesworth 2005, Secretary General 2005). 'Gender identity' is a controversial and highly marginal category.

Since the Commission on Human Rights was abolished in June 2006, United Nations reforms have replaced it with a permanent standing Human Rights Council, which has yet to grasp the issues, despite Norway's groundbreaking statement to the council on 'sexual orientation' and 'gender identity' at the end of 2006 (see Kollman and Waites 2009). However, initiatives such as the Declaration of Montreal (International Conference on LGBT Human Rights 2006a), and particularly the launch at the Human Rights Council of the Yogyakarta Principles on the Application of International Human Rights Law in Relation to Sexual Orientation and Gender Identity (Corrêa and Muntarbhorn 2007, Corrêa et al. 2008, 29, O'Flaherty and Fisher 2008), have assisted in pushing 'sexual orientation' and 'gender identity' onto the international agenda. The Yogyakarta Principles have been invoked successfully in court cases in states such as Nepal (Roy 2007).

Most recently the issues have been raised, at last, in the United Nations General Assembly. The NGO International Day Against Homophobia (IDAHO) inspired an initiative by France and the Netherlands to develop a groundbreaking statement, read to the Assembly on 18 December 2008 by Argentina on behalf of 66 states (including 6 in Africa, but not the USA: Secrétariat d'État 2008; United Nations General Assembly 2008a). This was met by an opposing statement by 57 states, promoted by the Organisation for the Islamic Conference and read by Syria, which again argued against 'so-called notions' of 'sexual orientation' and 'gender identity', suggesting these notions 'have no legal foundation', and expressing concern that

> the notion of orientation spans a wide range of personal choices that expand way beyond the individual's sexual interest in copulatory behaviour with normal consenting adult human beings, thereby ushering in the social normalization, and possibly legitimization of many deplorable acts including paedophilia.
>
> *(United Nations General Assembly 2008b)*

This statement conflated paedophile subjectivity and behaviour (United Nations General Assembly 2008b). Similarly, the Holy See argued that 'the categories "sexual orientation" and "gender identity", used in the text, find no recognition or clear and agreed definition in international law' (Archbishop Celestino Migliore quoted in Spero News 2008). A press release jointly issued after the statements reveals a crucial international network of 10 NGOs working to advance human rights irrespective of 'sexual orientation' and 'gender identity': Amnesty International, ARC International, the Center for Women's Global Leadership, COC Netherlands, Global Rights, Human Rights Watch, International Lesbian and Gay Association (ILGA), Inter-LGBT France, the International Day Against Homophobia, and the International Gay and Lesbian Human Rights Commission (see International Gay and Lesbian Human Rights Commission 2008).

How can these developments be analysed with reference to social theories concerning gender and sexuality? A questioning of how sexual and gender identities are socially constituted is central to contemporary gender and sexuality theory, as social constructionist and queer theory gain influence (Foucault 1981, Plummer 1981, Butler 1990, 2004, Warner 1993, Seidman 1996), including research on the diverse organization of sexualities and genders in non-Western cultures, which has demonstrated the structuring of sexual relations along multiple axes, including biological sex, gender and age, as well as the existence of more than two genders in many cultures (Herdt 1994, 1997, Drucker 2000). Yet this is in tension with the emphasis on fixed adult sexual and gender identities (Waites 2005b, 2006), as apparent particularly in the impact of the globalization of 'lesbian' and 'gay' identities on international lesbian and gay politics (Drucker 1996, 2000, Adam et al. 1999, Phillips 2000, Altman 2001, Binnie 2004). The relationship between essentialist and/or fixed conceptions of sexual and gender identity and the political discourses and strategies employed by LGBT movements in global human rights struggles is therefore a vital topic of academic debate.

There has been growing academic debate over the appropriate relationship of human rights to 'sexual orientation' (e.g. Heinze 1995) and, more recently, to transgenderism (Currah et al. 2006). These issues have become a key focus of debate for feminist, lesbian, gay and queer theorists, including Judith Butler (2005). The discussion here surveys, synthesizes and engages with existing work on 'sexual orientation' and 'gender identity' from various activist and disciplinary perspectives to develop particular themes, first analysing the increasingly pervasive concept 'sexual orientation'.

Orienting human rights: the politics of 'sexual orientation'

There has been a strong focus on seeking inclusion of 'sexual orientation' in human rights discourses by LGBT international organizations and legal scholars since the 1990s (Heinze 1995, Wintemute 1995). This would parallel the inclusion of 'sexual orientation' in some state laws, such as in South Africa's constitution (Palmberg 1999). However, proposals by scholars like Heinze and Wintemute for protection against 'sexual orientation' discrimination to be a human right have been critiqued by Morgan (2000), who demonstrates that human rights law is shaped by 'heteronormativity' (Warner 1993, Berlant and Warner 1998). Morgan has convincingly argued that such claims by Heinze and Wintemute tend to assume essentialist understandings of sexual identity and 'the naturalness of the homo-hetero binary' (Morgan 2000, 215), and hence do not challenge many aspects of 'heteronormativity' in human rights law and discourse. Drawing upon broader critical and post-structuralist approaches, Morgan's work also challenges Heinze's legal positivism, whereby Heinze claims (methodologically and philosophically) to derive the principle of 'sexual orientation' as a human right from existing human rights. However, Morgan does not focus closely on the restrictive implications of 'sexual orientation' as a concept in itself. How should we critically evaluate this concept, as it is employed in attempts to redefine human rights?

Concerns have been expressed by many commentators over the years about employing the concepts 'homosexual', 'gay', 'LGBT rights' and 'LGBT human rights' rather than less culturally specific concepts such as 'sexual rights'. For example, Peter Drucker has discussed the problematic relationship of LGBT identities to the global South (Drucker 2000). Dennis Altman has commented that international LGBT organizations such as the International Gay and Lesbian Human Rights Commission (IGLHRC) and the International Gay and Lesbian Association (ILGA) 'promote a universal language of identity politics' (Altman 2001, 126). Ignacio Saiz has drawn attention to the problematic ways in which an exaggerated emphasis on 'LGBT rights' can unhelpfully detach some issues from other sexuality and gender rights issues (Saiz 2004). So the critical questioning of the concept of 'LGBT rights' is well-established in legal and human rights scholarship and activism – as suggested by this volume's title, 'The Global Politics of LGBT Human Rights' (see also Seckinelgin 2009).

However, the concept 'sexual orientation' – like 'gender identity', to be addressed later – has been subject to less critical scrutiny in relation to human rights. Typically, even commentators who problematize the relationships of identity labels such as 'lesbian' or 'gay' to anti-discrimination and human rights law regard 'sexual orientation' as entirely unproblematic. For example in a recent human rights text, Bamforth has commented on the problematic nature of 'the idea of LGBT rights'; he discusses the criticism that 'it is artificial to explain rights claims in terms of a person's lesbian or gay sexual orientation', but there is no critical comment on the inclusiveness of 'sexual orientation' as a category in itself (Bamforth 2005, 226–229; see also Graupner and Tahmindjis 2005).

An important example of this is the work of legal scholar Robert Wintemute, in which there is reflection on the distinction between symbolic and instrumental uses of law in relation to 'LGBT' categories, yet in which the category 'sexual orientation' is foregrounded as a foundational category without problematization (Wintemute 1995, 1997, 2005). Wintemute favours an expansive understanding of human rights, in which same-sex partnership rights are human rights (Wintemute and Andenas 2001, Wintemute 2005), and has argued that sex discrimination provisions in human rights law should be invoked to encompass sexual orientation discrimination (Wintemute 1997). Wintemute contributed to advancing the Declaration of Montreal from the International Conference on LGBT Human Rights

(2006a), of which he was co-president with Joke Swiebel when this was held in Canada in July 2006 (Swiebel 2009). The Declaration uses the categories 'sexual orientation' and 'gender identity' to formulate its proposals for worldwide government policies against discrimination, though it also uses 'LGBT' and the concept 'LGBT human rights' extensively. The concept 'homosexuality' is also used without clarification of whether this refers to identity or behaviour, therefore conflating these: for example, section 1, 'Essential Rights', states that 'Nine countries punish homosexuality with the Death Penalty' (International Conference on LGBT Human Rights 2006a, 1) (for a critique of such conflations of identity and behaviour via analysis of 'homosexual act' in the history of English law, see Moran 1996).

But while the implications of using 'homosexual' and 'LGBT' have been widely criticized, it is the concept 'sexual orientation' above all which is now being advanced for incorporation in global human rights law and discourse. It is therefore necessary to focus on this concept and critically evaluate the costs and benefits of its use. Just as Moran (1996) has investigated 'the homosexual(ity) of law', we need to investigate the 'sexual orientation' of human rights discourses. It has been argued since the emergence of gay liberation (Wittmann 1997, 381) that the concept implies undesirable restrictions upon forms of sexual subjectivity, identity and 'ways of being' (Bech 1997).

It is first useful to examine the history of 'sexual orientation' in national and international laws. The federal state of Quebec in Canada was the first government in the world (other than a city) to include 'sexual orientation' in its anti-discrimination legislation in 1977 (International Conference on LGBT Human Rights 2006b, 27). In Canada it has been ruled by the Supreme Court since the early 1990s that 'sexual orientation' discrimination is prohibited (Stychin 1995, 109). South Africa, however, was the first state to explicitly prohibit 'sexual orientation' discrimination, in 1994, in its constitution (Louw 1998, 141, Palmberg 1999).

In Europe, the European Court of Human Rights has come to rule all sexual orientation discrimination unacceptable (Council of Europe 2003; Graupner 2005, 117). The European Union's Treaty of Amsterdam (1997) included an anti-discrimination clause which included 'sexual orientation', Article 6a, following lobbying by the International Lesbian and Gay Association (Bell 1998, 65). Subsequent measures included European Council Directive 2000/78/EC, requiring all European Union states to prohibit 'sexual orientation' discrimination in public and private sector employment and vocational training (Wintemute 2005, 190). In the UK the concept 'sexual orientation' tended initially to emerge in law via rulings of the European Court (and former Commission) of Human Rights (e.g. Waites 2005a, 160) but later also via European Union law, and has now been written into the Equality Act 2006, which created a new Commission for Equality and Human Rights from 2007. The novelty of 'sexual orientation' acquiring this centrality in UK law and policy is apparent in its absence from the index of Moran's authoritative *The Homosexual(ity) of Law* (Moran 1996).

At the international level, 'sexual orientation' is the concept now mobilized in claims for reinterpretation and reform of human rights, as, for example, by Human Rights Watch (2005). In the Yogyakarta Principles 'sexual orientation' is utilized, defined as follows: 'Sexual Orientation is understood to refer to each person's capacity for profound emotional, affectional and sexual attraction to, and intimate and sexual relations with, individuals of a different gender or the same gender or more than one gender' (Corrêa and Muntarbhorn 2007, 6, footnote 1). Sexual orientation is thus defined by footnote to encompass both subjectivity ('attraction to') and behaviour/action ('relations with'), in a manner which could implicitly include bisexuality ('with individuals... of more than one gender'). But interestingly the Introduction to the Yogyakarta Principles states in its opening paragraph that

'Sexual orientation and gender identity are integral to every person's dignity and humanity' – a universalist claim which can be questioned, for example, in light of groups defining themselves as 'asexual' (Scherrer 2008). Interestingly, with respect to sexuality, 'identity' is now generally avoided in favour of 'orientation' in the human rights claims of key groups, whereas 'gender identity' has become standard in relation to transgenderism (Wintemute 1995, 188, Human Rights Watch 2005).

Having outlined the emergence of the concept 'sexual orientation', it is now useful to examine academic analyses of the concept in sociology and queer theory, and their influence on some critical scholarship in law. The concept has been debated in sexuality studies, including legal and political studies, and also within LGBT and queer social and political movements, but perhaps not as much as many scholars in sexuality studies might think. In general the concept is more used in biomedical and psychological literature (e.g. Herek 1998, Whitehead and Whitehead 2009) than in the social sciences. A review finds the concept of 'orientation' absent, for example, from the title of any article in the international journal *Sexualities* (which has a social focus), and also from a surprising number of core texts for the social study of sexuality, lesbian and gay studies and queer theory (e.g. Butler 1990, Beasley 2005), despite examples of greater attention to this 'fragile and tendentious construct', implicated in 'orientationalist accounts' (Wilton 2004, 21, 75).

The concept has become increasingly used in biomedical and psychological research and sexological texts since the 1980s. Wilson and Rahman (2005, 9) provide an overview of research on the 'psychobiology of sex orientation', including the 'gay gene', which exemplifies how this approach views 'sexual orientation' as 'a fundamental aspect of our underlying human nature'. As Wilton commented in a sociological review of such biomedical science approaches and 'discourses of orientation': 'They produce a strong construct of something called sexual orientation, a taxonomic tool by which human beings are subdivided' (Wilton 2004, 20). Related to the influence of the natural sciences, the concept has been emerging to increasing prominence in legal and policy literature and statutes, as previously described. Given that 'sexual orientation' was employed in anti-discrimination law from the late 1970s, the lack of earlier detailed critical attention to the concept in politics and law research is perhaps surprising.

However, the concept 'sexual orientation' was first problematized in the sociological literature. Ken Plummer's foundational social constructionist text *The Making of the Modern Homosexual* (1981) distinguished 'two broad ways of approaching the problem of building a homosexual identity: the *sexual orientation model* and the *identity construct model*'. Plummer stated that: 'the orientation model is found among geneticists, clinicians and behaviourists alike and suggests that a person's sexual orientation is firmly established by mid childhood' (Plummer 1981, 68). The alternative 'identity-construct view' in this account was that of symbolic interactionists. Plummer proposed a synthesis of these two approaches, but in general Plummer supported the interactionist critique (1981, 71).

The important point in the present context is that critical accounts such as Plummer's have associated the concept 'sexual orientation' with medical and psychological theories in which 'sexual orientation' is conceptualized as a fixed and given characteristic of an individual, at least after a given period of childhood. Existing research has shown how medical and psychological perspectives on sexuality inform and structure political debates: for example, in the UK, the concept 'sexual orientation' was foregrounded by the British Medical Association (BMA), and also (with explicit reference to the BMA) by the leading UK lesbian and gay organization Stonewall, in support for equalization of the age of consent for sex between men (British Medical Association 1994, Waites 2003, 2005a, 2005b). Such analysis, together with work demonstrating the international power of health and medicine discourses (Corrêa et al. 2008, 29–33) also influenced by the legacy of Foucault (1981), suggests the value of examining the extent to which biomedical and psychological expertise concerning 'sexual orientation' is implicated in global configurations of power.

Following social constructionist interventions from sociologists such as Plummer, the concept 'sexual orientation' became subject to critical interrogation during the 'social constructionist/essentialist debate' over the formation of sexual identities (Stein 1992). Increasingly the notion of sexual orientation as a universal characteristic defined by desire with respect to gender was questioned, ever more so with the emergence of what became known as 'queer theory', which challenged gay and lesbian identity politics. In *Epistemology of the Closet* (1990), widely cited as one of the founding texts of 'queer theory', Eve Kosofsky Sedgwick commented:

> It is a rather amazing fact that, of the very many dimensions along which the genital activity of one person can be differentiated from that of another ..., precisely one, the gender of object choice, emerged from the turn of the century, and has remained as the dimension denoted by the now ubiquitous category of 'sexual orientation'.
>
> *(Sedgwick 1990, 8)*

Here Sedgwick neatly identified a central issue, that 'orientation' is overwhelmingly interpreted as existing in relation to *gender*. This is clearly limiting from the point of view of a queer sexual politics concerned with validating forms of sexual desire and practice that do not have this focus (e.g. Warner 1993, Seidman 1996). On similar lines, the anthropologist Gilbert Herdt has tellingly commented: 'Sexual orientation and identity are not the keys to conceptualizing a third sex and gender across time and space' (Herdt 1994, 47).

A particular concern, which helps illuminate broader issues, is the incompatibility of 'sexual orientation' with 'bisexuality', in light of the bisexual politics that has identified a prevailing homosexual/heterosexual binary in Western societies as excluding bisexuality (Storr 1999, Hemmings 2002, Waites 2005b). As Sedgwick noted, 'sexual orientation' tends overwhelmingly to be understood in relation to a particular gender; and this occurs in a context where the existence of only two genders, men and women, is assumed. In the context of these dominant understandings of the categories 'man' and 'woman', in a dichotomous relationship of both difference and perhaps opposition, the dominant meaning of 'sexual orientation' is that it refers to an individual's desire towards one gender, or the other – man *or* woman. Within this framework of understandings, bisexuality is unthinkable and nonsensical as a singular 'sexual orientation', or as multiple simultaneous 'sexual orientations' (since the latter would conflict with dominant Western meanings of sexuality and 'sexual orientation' as a single core aspect of a singular self: Foucault 1981). In this context it is unsurprising to find that historically 'bisexuality' has generally not been described in these terms, as indicated by their almost complete absence from the index of Storr's edited collection *Bisexuality: A Critical Reader*, which encompasses historical and contemporary medical, psychological, psychoanalytic, sexological and critical social scientific literature (Storr 1999).

The social constructionist and queer theory approaches to 'sexual orientation' outlined here have not been critically focused by many sociologists into applied discussions of law, policy or human rights – although in her final book Tamsin Wilton commented on the concept's arrival in UK law: 'even the most liberalising legislation will – inevitably – continue to replicate the orientationalist discourses of sexuality which attempt to contain desire within restrictive parameters in the interests of reproducing heteronormativity' (Wilton 2004, 178).

Wilton also productively problematized how 'Human rights legislation emanating from the European Union [...assumed] an essentialist sexual *orientation*' (Wilton 2004, 183).

However, some earlier critical academic commentaries from the margins of the discipline of law have proposed a queer approach to 'sexual orientation'. Carl Stychin addressed the category in the concluding chapter of *Law's Desire*, where he proposes the development of a 'Queer Legal Theory' (Stychin 1995, 140–156). In the context of dilemmas posed about identity in debates over postmodernism and poststructuralism, Stychin commented (via quotation of Judith Butler):

> Thus, sexual orientation as a category underscores the problems of categorical thinking more generally. Claims that the category warrants legal protection from invidious discrimination demand that it be understood as coherent, possessing some degree of stability, and also that sexual orientation is a relatively central aspect of individual identity. In other words, it must be argued that the primary gender direction of sexual object choice creates a category that *matters* and that warrants legal protection. The category is important because it has been historically invested with a meaning which must be acknowledged and remedied. At the same time, the category must maintain a certain provisionality in its deployment, so that: 'as much as identity terms must be used, as much as "outness" is to be affirmed, these same notions must become subject to a critique of the exclusionary operations of their own production [Butler 1993, 227].'
>
> *(Quoted from Stychin 1995, 155)*

He continued:

> While the exclusionary forces of political movements should always be recognized, political life continues, and our efforts must be aimed, not simply at the exclusions performed around identities, but principally at the exclusions caused by the constitution of the dominant background norm itself.
>
> *(Stychin 1995, 155)*

Stychin thus called attention to the specificity of the label 'sexual orientation', and the need to analyse uses of this category. However, in its context, his final statement can be read as a defence of installing categories such as 'sexual orientation' in law, as a means to contest and challenge heteronormativity. Here Stychin shares the general emphasis of Michael Warner's queer theory on pervasive power of heteronormativity, and the political necessity of de-centring this (Warner 1993). Yet, there remains scope for further critical attention to how 'sexual orientation' is defined and the complex implications of its use in human rights law and discourses. Before pursuing this, the issue of 'gender identity' must be examined, prior to an integrated final discussion.

Identifying human rights: the politics of 'gender identity'

Transgender politics have established a political concern with the concept 'gender identity'. Transgenderism is here understood as a concept encompassing a variety of forms of identification and behaviour defying the dominant sex and gender binaries, as explored in the emerging interdisciplinary field of transgender studies. Contemporary transgender theorists, often influenced by post-structuralism and queer theory (Butler 1990, 1993, 2004), typically argue that Western societies are structured by a restrictive and dualistic two-gender system (Stryker and Whittle 2006, Currah et al. 2006, Hines 2007, 2009), and that the global South is misinterpreted in the West in this light (Patel 2006).

There is debate in progress over whether transgender people should aspire to 'simply human rights', rather than 'transgender rights', as suggested by Shannon Price Minter. In response to this Kendall Thomas has argued convincingly for a more critical approach to human rights, which could address the problematic formulation of existing human rights with respect to transgender people through a 'strategic transgender human politics' (see essays by Minter and Thomas in Currah et al. 2006). The approach of Thomas suggests the need to consider revising existing human rights discourses, perhaps by introducing new concepts, though he problematizes 'gender identity' as a restrictive concept.

'Gender identity' tends to privilege notions of a clear, coherent and unitary identity over conceptions of blurred identifications. In dominant medical and psychological understandings of transsexualism, an experience of 'gender identity' at odds with the biologically defined sexed body can lead to a diagnosis of 'gender dysmorphia', often as a prelude to medical treatment and surgery (Waites 2006). Yet in contemporary social and cultural theory notions of 'identity' as complete and straightforward are challenged. For example Stuart Hall, in his influential discussion of the concept argues for the benefits of a focus on processes of 'identification' rather than identity, in order to grasp the always incomplete process of relating subjectivity to social identity through the process he calls 'articulation' (Hall 1996). The dominant dualist model of gender identity in most societies is also at odds with social research documenting 'third genders', as, for example, in many societies (Herdt 1994).

In this light a dilemma has emerged for transgender politics focused on strategic efforts to win legal change, over whether to utilize the concept 'gender identity' or a more diffuse and encompassing concept such as 'gender expression', which is used by some radical trans activists to 'dis-establish gender' (discussed in essays by Currah and Thomas in Currah et al. 2006). This choice particularly faced the two openly transgender-identified individuals – Professor Stephen Whittle of Manchester Metropolitan University, UK (Stryker and Whittle 2006) and Mauro Cabral of the National University of Córdoba, Argentina (Cabral and Viturro 2006) – who participated in the meeting of 29 human rights experts which produced the Yogyakarta Principles in 2006 (according to Cabral at the launch of the principles in South America, at a plenary on 28 June of the International Association for the Study of Sexuality, Culture and Society Conference 'Disorganised Pleasures: Changing Bodies, Rights and Cultures', in Lima, Peru, 27–29 June 2007). While 'sexual orientation' was necessarily the legal category to use with respect to sexuality, given its existing presence in international human rights law through the case of *Toonen* (discussed above), existing international case law did not provide a similarly clear existing category to address transgender issues, although Sweden had included 'gender identity' in a CHR resolution on extrajudicial executions from 2005 (Girard 2007, 351). According to Cabral, his decision with Whittle to adopt 'gender identity', despite misgivings, was influenced by considerations of political strategy in engaging with other human rights experts present at the conference (some of whom might have preferred the Principles to focus only on sexual orientation), as well as with broader contexts. However, Whittle and Cabral successfully argued for inclusion of the broad notion of 'expressions of gender' in the principles' footnoted definition of 'gender identity':

> Gender identity is understood to refer to each person's deeply felt internal and individual experience of gender, which may or may not correspond with the sex assigned at birth, including the personal sense of the body (which may involve, if

freely chosen, modification of bodily appearance or function by medical, surgical or other means) and other expressions of gender, including dress, speech and mannerisms.

(Corrêa and Muntarbhorn 2007, 6, footnote 2)

It can be noted that 'expressions of gender' is not entirely open or unproblematic from the perspective of radical queer and transgender theory seeking destabilization of gender identities, since the phrase might tend to be interpreted as implying an inner, essential, pre-existing psychological 'gender' which is 'expressed'. However, the most significant aspects of the Yogyakarta Principles to note with respect to transgender politics are that on the one hand the prominent concept 'gender identity' privileges identity above gender blurring, but on the other hand the definition of this concept opens possibilities for future contestation of meanings.

This discussion of the persistence of dualisms in conceptions of gender interpreted via 'gender identity' clearly re-contextualizes what can be understood by a 'sexual orientation', to which the following section now returns to commence an integrated analysis.

Queer dis-orientations and dis-identifications

Having reviewed past problematizations of 'orientation', it is useful to initiate a move towards a deeper reconceptualization of the concept by considering evidence of its dominant cultural meanings. The *New Shorter Oxford English Dictionary* (Brown 1993) defines 'orientation' as a noun apparently deriving from the verb 'orient' in the mid-nineteenth century, in a variety of ways:

1 The placing or arranging of something to face the east; (*specifically*) the construction of a church with the longer axis running due east and west; b) The action of turning to the east, especially in an act of worship.
2 Position or arrangement of a building, natural object, etc, relative to the points of the compass or other defined data.
3 The action or process of ascertaining one's bearings or relative position, or of taking up a known bearing or position; the faculty of doing this, sense of relative position. b) (*Chemistry*) The orienting effect of a substituent in a ring; the process of ascertaining the relative positions of the substituents in a ring.
4 (figuratively) A person's (especially political or psychological) attitude or adjustment in relation to circumstances, ideas, etc; determination of one's mental or emotional position. b) An introductory talk, course etc., given especially to newcomers to a university, organization etc.

These definitions are followed by illustrative quotations, which for the fourth includes: 'J. GATHORNE-HARDY An adult's sexual orientation is determined between the ages of one and five.' It is apparent that this quotation associates 'sexual orientation' with the first part of the fourth, figurative, definition.

The dictionary thus offers an interesting set of supposedly authoritative definitions of 'orientation'. It can be noted that they all share an emphasis upon conceptualizing orientation as being relative to given, and sometimes *specific*, characteristics of a real external world: 'to face the east' (1); 'relative to the points of the compass or other defined data' (2); 'sense of relative position' (3); 'in relation to circumstances, ideas etc' (4). In some, such as definitions

2 and 4, there is the sense that orientation is relative to a *particular* aspect of reality ('relative to… defined data'; 'relation to circumstances'). It can be suggested that these definitions resonate with wider cultural meanings, whereby orientation is understood to be relative to specific objects. For sexual orientation, these objects are specific forms of *sexed* and *gendered* individuals, which we can conceptualize as constituted through the ascription of sex through gender discourses (cf. Butler 1990, 1993, 2004).

In conjunction with the earlier critical discussion of the dominance of biomedical and psychological conceptions of sexual orientation as a fixed characteristic, this suggests that the dominant meaning of 'sexual orientation' tends to be as a characteristic, is defined relative to gendered individuals understood as men and women. A problem with this dominant understanding of sexual orientation, from the queer perspective suggested by Sedgwick above, is the tendency for it to be associated with the privileging of a traditional gender dichotomy in defining sexual desire.

In response to such limiting conceptions, the question 'what does it mean to be orientated?' is of growing concern in queer studies, having recently also been posed by Sara Ahmed in her book *Queer Phenomenology: Orientations, Objects, Others* (Ahmed 2006). A view of sexuality as part of an experience of being which is constituted in relation to social context is advanced. Ahmed usefully foregrounds phenomenology as a resource for reconceptualizing subjectivity, and particularly 'sexual orientation'.

According to Harvie Ferguson, phenomenology in the twentieth century from its origin in the work of Edmund Husserl 'seizes experience as the essential subject matter of philosophy', and seeks to overcome dualisms separating individuals from the objects of their perception (Ferguson 2006, 37–38):

> Perception does not consist in staring blankly at something lodged in consciousness, inserted there by some strange wonder as if something were first there and then consciousness would somehow embrace it… it is an accomplishment that must be new for every novel object.
> *(Husserl 1982, Ideas Pertaining to a Pure Phenomenology and to a Phenomenological Philosophy: First Book, quoted in Ferguson 2006, 37)*

Phenomenology focuses on the power of things to generate 'wonder' and 'astonishment'; the 'initiatory power of phenomena themselves' (Ferguson 2006, 17). A 'phenomenon is, first of all, phenomenal; something astonishing' (ibid., 17). This focus refutes an emphasis on the detachment of subjects from the objective world, in favour of understanding states of subjectivity as being inseparable from experience of the external world, including people in the social world. At the heart of phenomenology is an insistence on the absence of absolute distinctions between subjects, conceived with an emphasis on the embodiment of lived experience, and the objects of their perceptions; also central is an emphasis upon the power of objects to inspire emergent and novel subjective states in those who perceive or encounter them (see also Moran 2000).

Much sociological literature on the social construction of sexualities has tended to refer to psychoanalysis to allow for the social formation of desires in the unconscious, albeit while rejecting most psychoanalytic thinking for its assumptions about how sex and gender binaries shape the unconscious (e.g. Weeks 1985). Desire and consciousness tend to be presented as distinct. A great benefit of phenomenology, by contrast, is that it permits conceptualization of a spectrum of forms and aspects of subjectivity, some of which might be like dominant conceptions of unconscious 'desire', while others, importantly, can be thought of as at least partially aspects of 'consciousness'. Ahmed comments that 'consciousness is intentional – it is directed towards something' (Ahmed 2006, 27). In this light, 'sexual orientation' and 'gender identity' can be reconceptualized as aspects of subjectivity which are at least to a degree part of consciousness, not entirely beyond the scope of individual will.

However, crucially, a phenomenological approach also emphasizes that for a subject to become orientated it must be 'lining itself up with the direction of the space it inhabits'; 'orientation involves aligning body and space' (Ahmed 2006, 13, 14). Ahmed quotes Husserl's view that interpretation of an object involves a 'twofold directednesss' (Husserl 1969, quoted in Ahmed 2006, 28). As expressed by Ahmed 'First, I am directed toward an object (I face it) and then I take a direction toward it (for instance I might or might not admire it)' (Ahmed 2006, 28). This captures Husserl's idea that 'orientation' and 'admiration' are not entirely involuntary, but simultaneously that we need a sense of orientation in order to make sense of and negotiate our world. From this, Ahmed develops a valuable queer critique of orientation as directionality, arguing that in certain political contexts we should resist the directions that are given to us by our context, and adopt a different sense of direction.

Phenomenology thus suggests that 'sexual orientation' and 'gender identity' are not features of subjectivity entirely beyond consciousness and intentionality. Hence it can be invoked in defiance of notions of 'sexual orientation' and 'gender identity' as definitive natural psychological conditions, or as socially constituted but 'fixed' (Waites 2005b, 2006). Yet simultaneously, and highly productively, phenomenology provides a conceptual vocabulary for understanding how our experience of consciousness is structured; how the external world presents itself to our consciousness in regular ways; and how we develop dispositions towards these (Ahmed 2006). It appears to provide a way of conceptualizing agency and structure within consciousness.

'Sexual orientation', it was established earlier, is a concept historically aligned with a presumed heterosexual/homosexual binary, which has marginalized forms of sexual identification such as bisexuality and queerness. But the important question in evaluating the concept's entry into human rights discourses is whether it is open to reinterpretation via the assignation of new meanings, and contestation of the discourses in which it is contextualized. In light of queer post-structuralist theorizations of sexual subjectivity, and particularly Ahmed's (2006) queer phenomenology, it can be suggested that – particularly if reconceptualized in light of multiple forms of 'gender identity' and 'gender expression' (Stryker and Whittle 2006) – 'sexual orientation' is potentially a flexible enough concept to be redefined and expanded in meaning, to be applicable to an individual's subjectivity understood as changeable rather than as a continuous state.

However, such a notion of 'sexual orientation' is profoundly in tension with the essentialist understandings existing in mainstream scientific and public discourses. Stretching the concept 'sexual orientation' to contest and displace the latter would involve a process leading to uncertainties about meaning, ambiguity and incoherence.

For example, as suggested earlier, naming bisexuality as a singular 'sexual orientation' alongside notions of a 'gay', 'lesbian' or 'heterosexual' orientation generates certain degrees of inconsistency. Nevertheless, in recent decades bisexuality has occasionally, and increasingly, been understood as a 'sexual orientation', including by some states. This is the case in the UK's Equality Act 2006, which created a new Commission for Equality and Human Rights (from October 2007), and redefined the UK legal and policy framework relating to equality and diversity. Fascinatingly in section 35 of this legislation, 'sexual orientation' is defined as follows:

35. General

In this Part-

...

'sexual orientation' means an individual's sexual orientation towards -

(a) persons of the same sex as him or her,

(b) persons of the opposite sex, or

(c) both

Hence by the single, little word 'both', the law attempts to encompass bisexuality within 'sexual orientation'.

Minimizing the language used, 'both' appears to be a conscious or unconscious move by legislators to avoid drawing attention to or confronting this new and distinctive aspect of the law, or any incoherence of meaning it might generate. Yet here, in any case, is evidence that legislators can and do institutionalize explicit definitions of the concept 'sexual orientation' in law which move beyond the notion of attraction to a single sex or gender. But the preceding discussion tends to suggest that 'sexual orientation' cannot entirely perform this conceptual and legal work. The concept cannot be coherent if the *singular* concept orientation is understood as a core aspect of the self and is said to be conceivable towards persons of a single sex *and* persons of *both* sexes, if an orientation is imagined in the context of gender difference (particularly if in a context presented as gender dichotomy or 'opposite' sexes, as in the UK law quoted).

As noted earlier, international human rights conventions also use a binary model of the sexes, involving only men and women; and hence similar incoherences will arise if 'sexual orientation' is invoked in human rights discourses as encompassing bisexuals, without grasping issues raised in bisexual politics and related critiques of 'sexual orientation' (cf. Hemmings 2007, Ahmed 2006). Bisexuality tends not to make sense as a 'sexual orientation' in the terms of the gender dualism in existing human rights conventions and dominant international discourses; but more significantly this serves to illustrate the wider point that installing 'sexual orientation' in human rights discourses entails some exclusionary effects for a huge range of people worldwide who do not only relate sexually to a single gender.

Attempts to broaden conceptions of 'sexual orientation' in international human rights discourse to encompass attraction to multiple genders, as in the Yogyakarta Principles definition cited earlier, will not necessarily fail – since law and culture are full of contradictions. However, such attempts are likely to produce or reveal certain kinds of incoherence, slippages and disjunctures between signifiers and their intended signifieds, with potential to be destabilizing. Attempts to use 'sexual orientation' as a universal category in human rights law may nevertheless be sustainable, but it seems appropriate to expect and look for incoherence, and perhaps use this to contest and redefine 'sexual orientation', sexuality and gender.

In light of the mutability of 'sexual orientation' (and implicitly 'gender identity') suggested by Ahmed (2006), it is not necessary to argue for the abandonment of these concepts in human rights struggles. However, it is necessary to develop political analysis in the context of recognition of their dominant meanings. Politics and human rights literature, NGOs and activists allied to a radical sexual politics should in certain contexts start noting explicitly the exclusionary effects of using the concepts 'sexual orientation' and 'gender identity' within currently dominant discursive frames, in order to transform their dominant meanings.

Conclusion: global queer politics beyond the Yogyakarta Principles

We are witnessing a significant degree of mainstreaming of the concepts 'sexual orientation' and 'gender identity' in international human rights discourse. But, as in critical discussions of gender mainstreaming, it is apparent that while such processes may introduce new conceptual vocabularies, more radical understandings of gender, sexuality and power relations, and associated interpretations of concepts, risk being lost (see Charlesworth 2005, Squires 2007).

There are major problems with using these concepts in the context of their dominant mainstream meanings. Activist Hossam Bahgat has commented, based on his experience in the Middle East:

> There is a problem with sexual orientation as a concept, with identity frameworks.
> ... In my country [Egypt], people don't get arrested for who they are but for what
> they do; conduct is the issue. Of course identity politics are still useful for activism
> but we need to look at other frameworks.
>
> *(Quoted in Girard 2007, 350)*

This illuminates how use of 'sexual orientation', and implicitly 'gender identity', focuses attention on subjectivity before behaviour. However, the discussion of queer phenomenology here has suggested ways to conceptualize 'sexual orientation' and 'gender identity' as aspects of subjectivity which are not fixed and profoundly embedded in the self, but can be complex and fluid, and change.

As demonstrated in this analysis, dominant understandings of 'sexual orientation' tend to assume that it refers to a fixed characteristic of individuals, existing independently of their current socio-cultural reality, and that this characteristic involves a desire towards individuals of a single sex. However, it has been argued that 'sexual orientation' is not inherently incompatible with sexual diversity with respect to bisexuality, or queer sexualities which de-centre gender as the focus of sexual 'object-choice', 'desire' and/or behaviour. Rather, 'sexual orientation', and also 'gender identity', hold a range of potential meanings that are subject to ongoing contestation. The concepts bring forms of visibility which should be evaluated with an appreciation that there are both costs and benefits in any form of language used – placing 'sexual orientation' and 'gender identity' in human rights conventions and discourse brings visibility for certain groups in ways that simply addressing 'sexuality' and 'gender' cannot (cf. Saiz 2004).

It is already apparent in some existing human rights case law that 'sexual orientation' has been interpreted with detailed reference to biomedical and psychological knowledge-claims. For example, in the important case of *Sutherland* v. *the United Kingdom*, which led to a ruling in favour of an equal age of consent for sex between men, the European Convention's implications were decided by the European Commission of Human Rights with explicit reference to the evidence of the BMA and other medical authorities concerning the age at which 'sexual orientation' is established (European Commission of Human Rights 1997, paras 56–66, British Medical Association 1994; for critique of this evidence see: Waites 2005a, 175–182, 2005b). There has been limited research on the role of biomedical and psychological expertise in human rights case law and discourses concerning 'sexual orientation' and 'gender identity' at the global level, but leading commentators emphasize the power of biomedical and health 'science' discourses in international governance (Corrêa et al. 2008, 29–33). In this context, as the concepts arrive in global human rights discourse, one powerful interpretation of these concepts mediating between religious moralism and queer radicalism will be that of secular sexology and psychobiology (Wilson and Rahman 2005).

Foucault argued that: 'the movements for "sexual liberation" ought to be understood as movements of affirmation starting with sexuality. Which means two things: they are movements that start with sexuality, with the apparatus of sexuality in the midst of which we're caught, and which make it function to the limit; but at the same time, they are in motion relative to it, disengaging themselves and surmounting it (Foucault 1988, 114–115). Both tendencies can be seen in the employment of 'sexual orientation' and 'gender identity' in the Yogyakarta Principles – the terms are adopted from biomedical and psychological understandings, yet the broad definitions offered open possibilities for transcending these. But the crucial analytic issue to grasp is that, irrespective of authorial intent, when introduced into mainstream human rights discourse these concepts become subject to interpretation in the context of broader gender and sexuality discourses operating in global governance and a fragile, emergent global civil society. This is the context in which it is necessary to develop a strategy for engaging with these concepts, appraising costs and benefits for political movements.

Those allied to a broadly conceived 'global queer politics', including many individuals in pro-LGBT, pro-queer and human rights NGOs, legal practitioners and political activists, need more vigorously to conceptualize, define and situate the concepts – and contest their meanings.

This is not to deny that there will certainly be times and contexts when the best strategy is to avoid definitions and challenges. The repeated suggestions of opponents that 'sexual orientation' encompasses paedophile desires, for which LGBT activists have often been ill prepared, are evidence that sometimes at the forefront of debate it is best to avoid rather than engage in definitional debates (Girard 2007; see also Gamson 1997, Waites 2005a). Nevertheless in many contexts – public debates, the media, and school education – NGOs and activists need to switch from unproblematized, undefined uses of 'sexual orientation' and 'gender identity', to taking the opportunities that arise to offer careful, explicit definitions of the concepts that are compatible with the diversity of sexual and gender subjectivities discussed in this chapter. This might generally include use of the definitions in the Yogyakarta Principles, but perhaps with additional notes or commentary. What is needed is a practical strategy which can be operationalized at multiple levels, not only in official documents, but in public speech in a wide variety of settings. It is most definitely not a sufficient political strategy or focus, but it should be recognized that the process of contestation has the potential to facilitate valuable dialogue over sexual and gender diversity.

In relation to global governance this analysis demands reappraisal of developments at the United Nations. Even as 'sexual orientation' and 'gender identity' become at least partially incorporated in the global human rights framework, this does not signal the unqualified dissipation of inequalities in human rights relating to sexuality and gender. Rather it implies the installation of a particular new Western form of Butler's heterosexual matrix in human rights law and discourse, a reconfigured 'grid of intelligibility' in which 'sexual orientation' and 'gender identity' are key nodal points at the intersections of sexuality and gender (Butler 1990, 151). To contest this emergent matrix, not only in law and politics, but also via education and inventive public engagements throughout culture and society, is a vital task for global queer politics.

Acknowledgements

This chapter was originally published by Taylor & Francis Ltd as Matthew Waites (2009) "Critique of 'sexual orientation' and 'gender identity' in human rights discourse: global queer politics beyond the Yogyakarta Principles", *Contemporary Politics*, 15 (1), pp. 137–156 and is reproduced here by permission of the publisher.

References

Adam, B.D., Duyvendak, J.W. and Krouwel, A. 1999. *The global emergence of gay and lesbian politics: national imprints of a worldwide movement*. Philadelphia, PA: Temple University Press.

Ahmed, S. 2006. *Queer phenomenology: orientations, objects, others*. London: Duke University Press.

Altman, D. 2001. *Global sex*. Chicago, IL: Chicago University Press.

Bamforth, N. 2005. "Lesbian and gay rights." In *The essentials of human rights*, edited by Smith, R.K.M. and van den Anker, C., pp. 226–229. London: Hodder Arnold.

Beasley, C. 2005. *Gender and sexuality: critical theories, critical thinkers*. London: Sage.

Bech, H. 1997. *When men meet: homosexuality and modernity*. Cambridge: Polity Press.

Bell, M. 1998. "Sexual orientation and anti-discrimination policy: the European Community." In *Politics of sexuality: identity, gender, citizenship*, edited by Carver, T. and Mottier, V., pp. 58–67. London: Routledge.

Berlant, L. and Warner, M. 1998. "Sex in public." *Critical Inquiry* 24, no. 2: 547–566.

Binnie, J., 2004. *The globalization of sexuality*. London: Sage.

Boyce, P. 2007. "'Conceiving kothis': men who have sex with men in India and the cultural subject of HIV prevention." *Medical Anthropology* 26, no. 2: 175–203.

British Medical Association. 1994. *Age of consent for homosexual men: a scientific and medical perspective*. London: Board of Science and Education, British Medical Association.

Brown, L. 1993. *The new shorter oxford English dictionary*. Oxford: Clarendon Press.

Buss, D. and Herman, D. 2003. *Globalizing family values: the Christian Right in international politics*. Minneapolis, MN: University of Minnesota Press.

Butler, J. 1990. *Gender trouble: feminism and the subversion of identity*. London: Routledge.

Butler, J. 1993. *Bodies that matter: on the discursive limits of "sex"*. London: Routledge.

Butler, J. 2004. *Undoing gender*. London: Routledge.

Butler, J. 2005. "On being beside oneself: on the limits of sexual autonomy." In *Sex rights: the Oxford Amnesty lectures*, edited by Bamforth, N., pp. 48–78. Oxford: Oxford University Press.

Cabral, M. (A.I. Grinspan) and Viturro, P. 2006. "(Trans)sexual citizenship in contemporary Argentina." In *Transgender rights*, edited by Currah, P., Juang, R.M. and Minter, S.P., pp. 262–273. Minneapolis, MN: University of Minnesota Press.

Charlesworth, H. 2005. "Not waving but drowning: gender mainstreaming and human rights." *Harvard Human Rights Journal* 18: 1–18.

Corrêa, S. and Muntarbhorn, V. 2007. "The Yogyakarta Principles: principles on the application of international human rights law in relation to sexual orientation and gender identity." Retrieved from http://www.yogyakartaprinciples.org/principles_en.htm on 1 November 2007.

Corrêa, S., Petchesky, R. and Parker, R. 2008. *Sexuality, health and human rights*. New York: Routledge.

Council of Europe, 2003. "Convention for the protection of human rights and fundamental freedoms as amended by Protocol No.11with Protocol Nos.1, 4, 6, 7, 12 and 13." Retrieved from http://www.echr.coe.int/NR/rdonlyres/D5CC24A7-DC13-4318-B457-5C9014916D7A/0/EnglishAnglais.pdf on 21 December 2008.

Currah, P., Juang, R.M. and Minter, S.P. 2006. *Transgender rights*. Minneapolis, MN: University of Minnesota Press.

Delanty, G. 2000. *Citizenship in a global age: society, culture, politics*. Milton Keynes: Open University Press.

Drucker, P. 1996 "In the tropics there is no sin: sexuality and gay-lesbian movements in the third world." *New Left Review I*, 218: 75–101.

Drucker, P. 2000. *Different rainbows*. London: Gay Men's Press.

European Commission of Human Rights. 1997. *Application No. 25186/94, Euan Sutherland against the United Kingdom: Report of the Commission*, adopted 1 July 1997.

Ferguson, H. 2006. *Phenomenological sociology: experience and insight in modern society*. London: Sage.

Foucault, M. 1981. *The history of sexuality, volume one: an introduction*. London: Penguin.

Foucault, M. 1988. "Power and sex." In *Michel Foucault: politics philosophy culture: interviews and other writings 1977–1984,* edited by Kritzman, L.D., pp. 110–124. London: Routledge.

Frye, P.R. 2006. "Appendix: the International Bill of Gender Rights." In *Transgender rights*, edited by Currah, P., Juang, R.M. and Minter, S.P., pp. 327–331. Minneapolis, MN: University of Minnesota Press.

Gamson, J. 1997. "Messages of exclusion: gender, movements and symbolic boundaries." *Gender and Society*, 11, no. 2: 178–199.

Girard, F. 2007. "Negotiating sexual rights and sexual orientation at the UN." In *SexPolitics: reports from the frontlines*, edited by Parker, R., Petchesky, R. and Sember, R., pp. 311–358. Sexuality Policy Watch. Retrieved from http://www.sxpolitics.org/frontlines/home/index.php on 21 December 2008.

Graupner, H. 2005. "Sexuality and human rights in Europe." In *Sexuality and human rights: a global overview*, edited by Graupne, H. and Tahmindjis, P., pp. 107–139. New York: Harrington Park Press.

Graupner, H. and Tahmindjis, P. 2005. *Sexuality and human rights: a global overview*. New York: Harrington Park Press.

Gruskin, S., Miller, A.M. and Vance, C.S. 2004. *Health and Human Rights Special Issue – Special Focus: Sexuality, Health and Human Rights* 7, no. 2.

Hall, S. 1996. "Introduction: who needs 'identity'?" In *Questions of cultural identity*, edited by Hall, S. and Du Gay, P. pp. 1–17. London: Sage.

Heinze, E. 1995. *Sexual orientation: a human right*. Dordrecht: Martinus Nijhoff.

Hemmings, C. 2002. *Bisexual spaces: a geography of sexuality and gender*. London: Routledge.

Hemmings, C. 2007. "What's in a name? Bisexuality, transnational sexuality studies and Western colonial legacies." *International Journal of Human Rights* 11, no. 1–2: 13–32.

Herdt, G. 1994. *Third sex, third gender*. New York: Zone Books.

Herdt, G. 1997. *Same sex, different cultures: exploring gay and lesbian lives*. Oxford: Westview.

Herek, G. M. 1998. *Stigma and sexual orientation: understanding prejudice against lesbians, gay men and bisexuals*. London: Sage.

Hines, S. 2007. *Transforming gender*. Bristol: The Policy Press.

Hines, S. 2009. "A pathway to diversity?: human rights, citizenship and the politics of transgender." *Contemporary Politics* 15, no. 1: 87–102.

Human Rights Watch. 2005. "Sexual orientation and gender identity: Human Rights Watch concerns for the 61st Session of the U.N. Commission on Human Rights, Statement 10 March 2005." Retrieved from http://hrw.org/english/docs/2005/03/10/global10303_text.htm on 3 August 2005.

Husserl, E. 1969. *Ideas: general introduction to pure phenomenology*. London: George Allen and Unwin.

Husserl, E. 1982. *Ideas Pertaining to a pure phenomenology and to a phenomenological philosophy: first book*, trans. Kersten, F. Dordrecht: Kluwer.

International Conference on LGBT Human Rights. 2006a. "Declaration of Montreal." Retrieved from http://www.declarationofmontreal.org/declaration/ on 1 November 2007.

International Conference on LGBT Human Rights. 2006b. *Preliminary Programme*. Montreal: 1st World Outgames Montreal 2006.

International Gay and Lesbian Human Rights Commission. 2008. "66 states condemn violations based on sexual orientation and gender identity," Retrieved from http://www.iglhrc.org/site/iglhrc/section.php?id=5&detail=911 on 20 December 2008.

Jackson, P. 2007. "An explosion of Thai identities: global queering and re-imagining queer theory." In *Culture, society and sexuality: a reader*, edited by Parker, R. and Aggleton, P., pp. 341–357. London: Routledge.

Kaldor, M. 2003. *Global civil society: an answer to war*. Cambridge: Polity Press.

Keane, J. 2003. *Global civil society?* Cambridge: Cambridge University Press.

Kollman, K. and Waites, M. 2009. "The global politics of lesbian, gay, bisexual and transgender human rights: an introduction." *Contemporary Politics* 15, no.1: 1–17.

Lockwood, B. 2006. *Women's rights: a human rights quarterly reader*. Baltimore, MD: The Johns Hopkins University Press.

Louw, R. 1998. "Gay and lesbian sexualities in South Africa: from outlawed to constitutionally protected." In *Legal queeries: lesbian, gay and transgendered legal studies*, edited by Moran, L.J., Monk, D. and Beresford, S., pp. 139–154. London: Cassell.

Millett, K. 1971. *Sexual politics*. London: Rupert Hart-Davis Ltd.

Moran, D. 2000. *Introduction to phenomenology*. Abingdon: Routledge.

Moran, L.J. 1996. *The homosexual(ity) of law*. London: Routledge.

Morgan, W. 2000. "Queering international human rights law." In *Sexuality in the legal arena*, edited by Stychin, C. and Herman, D., pp. 208–225. London: Athlone Press.

Narrain, A. and Bhan, G. 2005. *Because I have a voice: queer politics in India*. New Delhi: Yoda Press.

O'Flaherty, M. and Fisher, J. 2008. "Sexual orientation, gender identity and international human rights law: contextualising the Yogyakarta Principles." *Human Rights Law Review* 8, no. 2: 207–248.

Palmberg, M. 1999. "Emerging visibility of gays and lesbians in southern Africa: contrasting contexts." In *The global emergence of gay and lesbian politics: national imprints of a worldwide movement*, edited by

Adam, B.D., Duyvendak, J.W., and Krouwel, A., pp. 266–292. Philadelphia, PA: Temple University Press.

Patel, G. 2006. "Risky subjects: insurance, sexuality and capital." *Social Text* 24, no. 4: 25–65.

Pateman, C. 1988. *The sexual contract*. Stanford, CA: Stanford University Press.

Petchesky, R. 2000. "Sexual rights: inventing a concept. Mapping an international practice." In *Framing the sexual subject: the politics of gender, sexuality and power*, edited by Parker, R., Barbosa, R.M. and Aggleton, P., pp. 81–103. Berkeley, CA: University of California Press.

Phillips, O. 2000. "Constituting the global gay: issues of individual subjectivity and sexuality in southern Africa." In *Sexuality in the legal arena,* edited by Herman, D and Stychin, C., pp. 17–34. London: The Athlone Press.

Plummer, K. 1981. *The making of the modern homosexual*. London: Hutchinson.

Rothschild, C., Long, S. and Fried, S.T. 2005. *Written out: how sexuality is used to attack women's organizing*. New York: International Gay and Lesbian Human Rights Commission/Center for Women's Global Leadership.

Roy, A. 2007. "Nepal Supreme court directs govt to safeguard gay rights." *Hindustan Times*, Retrieved from http://www.hindustantimes.com/StoryPage/StoryPage.aspx?id=25142e5f-789f-41b9-ba79-1441857b40e6&&Headline=SC+directs+Govt+to+safeguard+gay+rights on 6 June 2008.

Saiz, I. 2004. "Bracketing sexuality: human rights and sexual orientation: a decade of development and denial at the UN." *Health and Human Rights* 7, no. 2: 48–81.

Scherrer, K.S. 2008. "Coming to an asexual identity: negotiating identity, negotiating desires." *Sexualities* 11, no. 5: 621–641.

Seckinelgin, H. 2009. "Global activism and sexualities in the time of HIV/AIDS." *Contemporary Politics* 15, no. 1: 103–118.

Secrétariat d'État chargé des affaires étrangères et des droits de l'homme. 2008. Déclaration relative aux droits de l'homme et à l'orientation sexuelle, et l'identité de genre, présentée en marge de l'Assemblée générale des Nations unies/Statement on human rights, sexual orientation and gender identity, presented in the sidelines of the United Nations General Assembly, 18 December 2008. Paris: Ministère des Affaires Étrangères et Européennes. Retrieved from http://www.droitslgbt2008.fr/documents/?mode=download&id=2 on 20 December 2008.

Secretary General. 2005. Integrating the human rights of women throughout the United Nations system: Report of the Secretary General, E/CN.4/2005/68, 10 January 2005. United Nations Commission on Human Rights. Retrieved from http://daccessdds.un.org/doc/UNDOC/GEN/G05/102/56/PDF/G0510256.pdf?OpenElement on 18 December 2008.

Sedgwick, E. 1990. *Epistemology of the closet*. London: Penguin.

Seidman, S. 1996. *Queer theory/sociology*. Oxford: Blackwell.

Spero News. 2008. Vatican opines on UN sexuality initiative. Spero News, 20 Retrieved from http://www.speroforum.com/site/article.asp?idCategory=33&idsub=128&id=17321 on 20 January 2008.

Squires, J. 2007. *The new politics of gender equality*. Basingstoke: Palgrave Macmillan.

Stein, E. 1992. *Forms of desire: sexual orientation and the social constructionist controversy*. London: Routledge.

Storr, M. 1999. *Bisexuality: a critical reader*. London: Routledge.

Stryker, S. and Whittle, S. 2006. *The transgender studies reader*. London: Routledge.

Stychin, C. 1995. *Law's desire: sexuality and the limits of justice*. London: Routledge.

Stychin, C. 2003. *Governing sexuality: the changing politics of citizenship and law reform*. Oxford: Hart.

Stychin, C. and Herman, D. 2000. *Sexuality in the legal arena*. London: Athlone.

Swiebel, J. 2009. "Lesbian, gay, bisexual and transgender human rights: the search for an international strategy." *Contemporary Politics* 15, no. 1: 19–35.

United Nations. 1948. "Universal Declaration of Human Rights." Retrieved from http://www.un.org/Overview/rights.html on 20 December 2008.

United Nations. 1966. "International Covenant on Civil and Political Rights." Retrieved from http://www.unhchr.ch/html/menu3/b/a_ccpr.htm on 21 December 2008.

United Nations. 1979. "Convention on the Elimination of All Forms of Discrimination Against Women." Retrieved from http://www.un.org/womenwatch/daw/cedaw/cedaw.htm on 21 December 2008.

United Nations General Assembly. 2008a. Letter dated 18 December 2008 from the Permanent Representatives of Argentina, Brazil, Croatia, France, Gabon, Japan, the Netherlands and Norway to the United Nations. Retrieved from http://downloads.aibai.cn/N0866799.pdf on 21 January 2009.

United Nations General Assembly. 2008b. Note verbale dated 19 December 2008 from the Permanent Mission of the Syrian Arab Republic to the United Nations addressed to the Secretary-General. A/63/663 United Nations. Retrieved from http://daccessdds.un.org/doc/UNDOC/GEN/N08/669/79/PDF/N0866979.pdf?OpenElement on 21 January 2008.

Waites, M. 2003. "Equality at last? Homosexuality, heterosexuality and the age of consent in the United Kingdom." *Sociology* 37, no. 4: 637–656.

Waites, M. 2005a. *The age of consent: young people, sexuality and citizenship*. Palgrave Macmillan: Basingstoke.

Waites, M. 2005b. "The fixity of sexual identities in the public sphere: biomedical knowledge, liberalism and the heterosexual/homosexual binary in late modernity." *Sexualities* 8, no. 5: 539–569.

Waites, M. 2006. "Sexual politics." In *The Blackwell encyclopedia of sociology*, edited by Ritzer, G., pp. 4244–4247. Oxford: Blackwell Publishing Ltd.

Warner, M. 1993. *Fear of a queer planet*. Minneapolis, MN: Minnesota University Press.

Weeks, J. 1985. *Sexuality and its discontents*. Minneapolis, MN: Routledge.

Weeks, J., Holland, J. and Waites, M. 2003. *Sexualities and society: a reader*. Cambridge: Polity Press.

Whitehead, N. and Whitehead, B. 2009. *My genes made me do it! A scientific look at sexual orientation*. Retrieved from: http://www.mygenes.co.nz/download.htm on 21 January 2009.

Wilson, G. and Rahman, Q. 2005. *Born gay: the psychobiology of sex orientation*. London: Peter Owen

Wilton, T. 2004. *Sexual (dis)orientation: gender, sex, desire and self-fashioning*. Basingstoke: Palgrave Macmillan.

Wintemute, R. 1995. *Sexual orientation and human rights: the United States Constitution, the European Convention and the Canadian Charter*. Oxford: Clarendon Press.

Wintemute, R. 1997. "Recognising new kinds of direct sex discrimination: transsexualism, sexual orientation and dress codes." *Modern Law Review*, 60, no. 3: 334–359.

Wintemute, R. 2005. "From 'sex rights' to 'love rights': partnership rights as human rights." In *Sex rights: Oxford Amnesty lectures*, edited by Bamforth, N., pp. 186–224. Oxford: Oxford University Press.

Wintemute, R. and Andenaes, M. 2001. *Legal recognition of same-sex partnerships: a study of national, European and international law*. Oxford: Hart Publishing.

Wittman, C. 1997. "A gay manifesto (1969–70)." In *We are everywhere: a historical sourcebook of gay and lesbian politics*, edited by Blasius, M. and Phelan, S., pp. 380–388. New York: Routledge.

9

LGBTIQ (IN)VISIBILITY

A human security approach to SOGIESC

Ariel G. Mekler

In 2015, the United Nations Development Programme (UNDP), after consulting numerous lesbian, gay, bisexual, transgender, intersex, and queer (LGBTIQ) civil society actors, created a Lesbian, Gay, Bisexual, Transgender, and Intersex (LGBTI) Inclusion Index in an effort to strengthen the 'leave no one behind' specification articulated within United Nations Sustainable Development Goals.[1] Although by no means exhaustive, the index identified five significant priority measures of inclusion: Health, Economic Well-Being, Personal Security and Violence, Education, and Political and Civic Participation (Badgett and Crehan 2016, 10). But, what does true LGBTIQ inclusion look like and how can we safely ensure that the voices of the most marginalized are included within inclusion efforts? LGBTIQ considerations have long been addressed through human rights frameworks opposed to international development procedures. Legacies of colonialism, access to resources, and unique threats to one's human security are but a few of the realities impacting the lived experiences of LGBTIQ persons throughout the world. These histories and lived experiences shape how international development is experienced, received, and viewed by those it currently seeks to include. Since international intervention has the capacity to frame issues in certain respects, it must be cognizant of the needs, desires, and wants of those for whom it advocates and to be consciously reflective of 'who speaks for whom' when it come to LGBTIQ inclusion.

If we are to truly include LGBTIQ considerations within international development, we must examine the intersectionality of LGBTIQ considerations as they concurrently intersect among the interlinkages between international development, human rights, and security praxis. These global affairs do not function in silos and must be examined comprehensively when looking at LGBTIQ inclusion. LGBTIQ individuals experience international development, human rights, and security differently on account of their sexual orientation, gender identity/expression, and sex characteristics (SOGIESC) status within heteronormative and cisnormative contexts, thus novel perspectives need to be considered when international institutions, like UNDP, attempt to mainstream LGBTIQ inclusion. Drawing on a queer perspective, this chapter seeks to apply a human security approach as originally outlined by UNDP as a means to examine the structural oppressions and systemic marginalizations hindering the progression of LGBTIQ/SOGIESC inclusion. For the purpose of this analysis, a queer perspective is one that examines the lived realities of LGBTIQ persons as they exist within, and among, systems of power and privilege that are deeply entrenched within heteronormative and cisnormative contexts. Such a perspective concurrently challenges said systems by examining nonmonolitic notions of gender, sex, sexuality, and sexual orientation. Specifically, this chapter aims to reconceptualize each individual human security measure in order to highlight how the numerous vulnerabilities impacting the lived realities of LGBTIQ persons are situated amidst international development, human rights, and security praxis. Furthermore, it hopes that such an analysis can help advance the promotion and protection of LGBTIQ inclusion within sustainable international development practices.

Brief note on terminology

Before moving forward, it is important to note the terminology used within this chapter. Designated gender and sexuality identifiers, whether presumed or self-proclaimed, have ebbed and flowed over the years. LGBTI(Q), as an understood Western signifier, is often used by various international sectors to describe people existing outside of traditional heteronormative/cisnormative status quos. Heteronormativity, in this context, legitimizes heterosexuality, and in turn all aspects of traditional sex/gender dichotomies, as natural and normal. The SOGIESC acronym has evolved within international institutions, such as the United Nations, the World Health Organization, and the World Bank, as an additional way to describe components attributed to gender and sexuality. This chapter uses the acronym SOGIESC and LGBTIQ because they are regularly used identifiers. The acronyms are not an absolute marker of how someone who exists outside of heteronormative and cisnormative contexts would necessarily identify. Although not prevalent within international institutions, and still carrying negative connotations in certain contexts, the Q is included, within the LGBTI acronym, to pay homage to a queer history and perspective that is equally deserving of respect, dignity, and recognition.

The word queer has many dimensions. For decades, the term was used in a derogatory way against someone who was perceived to be in the LGBTIQ community. Over the years the word has been reclaimed by many within the LGBTIQ community and is often used as a gender identity/expression indicator, an anti-assimilation marker, a non-binary declaration, and an analysis tool. These definitions of queer are by no means exhaustive, and it is important to note that the use of queer as a disparaging epithet is still widely practiced against those who are presumed to be in the LGBTIQ community. Queerness itself is relative and one's experience of queerness differs depending on their context. However, regardless of context, many queers experience systemic discrimination, oppression, and marginalization. Using a queer perspective enables us to comprehensively address these discriminations, oppressions, and marginalizations within heteronormative structures that are equally influenced by various other institutional discriminations such as race, class, poverty, and so on (Gunkel 2010, 15; Cohen 1997, 441). It further allows us to critically examine multi-faceted praxis, and their intersecting points, amid power dynamics constructed within hegemonic hierarchies and how these intersecting points effect LGBTIQ inclusion.

Contextual background

Human security concepts developed in the early 1990s as a response to traditional macro security agendas that favored state security through political and military means. It sought a new understanding of human vulnerabilities that exist beyond state borders. In 1994, the UNDP introduced the concept of human security within their Human Development Report defining human security as comprehensive, multi-sectorial, context-specific, prevention-oriented, and, above all else, people-centered. The report highlighted seven individualized areas most vulnerable to threats. These include: economic security, environmental security, food security, personal security, health security, political security, and community security. It also emphasized two major components of human security, freedom from want and freedom from fear, with a third component the freedom to live with dignity, emerging from the work of the Commission on Human Security in 2001. This triangulated concept is now referred to as the human security paradigm (United Nations Commission on Human Security 2003, 21). In 2004, a Human Security Unit was established within the United Nations with the objective of streamlining human security throughout all United Nations practices.

In 2012, the United Nations General Assembly agreed upon a common human security definition enabling the approach to be used across all bodies of the United Nations. The definition established how human security acknowledges the interlinkages between development, rights, and peace while emphasizing that vulnerable populations are equally entitled to develop their potential (United Nations General Assembly 2012).

Queering human security

As Cynthia Weber explains, the LGBTIQ subject is often conflated into a singular figuration of either/or logic:e ither the 'perverse homosexual' or the 'normal homosexual' (Weber 2016, 42). These figurations end up dividing sovereign states into either a 'normal state,' that promotes and protects the LGBTIQ subject, or a 'pathological state,' that refuses to recognize the LGBTIQ subject (Weber 2016, 105). Much like the singular LGBTIQ figuration, singular sovereign state figurations, and their respective international protocols, create a sexualized international order (Weber 2016, 105). However, Weber's appeal for an integrated 'and/or' logic, in addition to the traditional 'either/or' logic, emphasizes the inherent plurality of queer subjects, one in which the homosexual is both the 'perverse homosexual' and/or the 'normal homosexual' (Weber 2016, 45). This queer plurality, in turn, reorders international politics and the perception of singular sovereignties (Weber 2016, 196). Although highlighting aspects of the sovereign nation state, Weber's 'and/or' framework is a valuable method when examining international institutions working on LGBTIQ inclusion because of its emphasis on the plurality of the LGBTIQ subject as well as the plurality of international political orders. Using a human security approach enables us to apply an 'and/or' logic by examining how LGBTIQ security, development and/or rights are allocated differently on account of one's SOGIESC. It enables us to distinguish how security, development and/or rights become situated for individuals whose identities, presumed, self-proclaimed and/or inherently plural, differ from the dominant heteronormative/cisnormative status quo. If we assume that the social world is organized into hegemonic heteronormative/cisnormative hierarchies, than anything existing outside of this structure is situated to exist in relationship to it by way of its oppression. The social world becomes organized into power structures that assume hetero/cisnormativity, and its various systems of oppression, as normal and anything outside of it as deviant, transgressive, unnatural, sinful, and ultimately queer. The queer subject does not receive the security of being human because the queer is deemed deviant, cursed, abnormal, and immoral. Queer subjects,[2] as Weber explains, living within sexualized international orders regulated by Western/global North ideology are securitized to ensure that Western/global North hetero/cis/homonormative structures remain secure from the queer subjects that pose a potential threat to Western/global North security (Weber 2016, 79). As such, the

LGBTIQ or queer experience has its own understanding of inclusion and what it means to live free from want, free from fear, and with dignity.

Analysis into the how, when, and why LGBTIQ individuals identity themselves is crucial when examining anti-homophobic methods (Hames-Garcia 2006, 79). Identification by others, whether true or false, has the potential to perpetuate homophobic practices. Humans have identities, whether assumed, ascribed, self-proclaimed, essentialist, or constructed. Identity informs how the human is placed within societal structures and how one sees oneself in relation to others and societal norms. LGBTIQ security, and in turn LGBTIQ development and/or LGBTIQ rights, become compromised in relation to normalized assumptions of needs based on conventions enshrined within hetero/cisnormative systems of oppression including racism, classism, and gender discrimination. Human security has the capacity to analyze the relationship between the marginalized and the power dynamics that fuel oppressions within the system, whether the international development system, human rights system, or peace and security system. Doing so can further advance LGBTIQ inclusion within said systems by looking at the actual needs of LGBTIQ persons within their respective contexts.

Freedom from fear

The first human security paradigm component, 'living free from fear' largely encompasses the safety of people and their right to basic subsistence and personal freedom. Living free from fear embodies the right to live free from violence in all forms, direct, cultural, and structural, and the right to live free from armed conflict. For LGBTIQ individuals, the concept of living free from fear is far too often overshadowed by the threat of physical violence. LGBTIQ individuals and communities experience multidimensional vulnerabilities associated with the threat of violence on account of their SOGIESC. These threats of violence in turn perpetuate unique impacts further challenging LGBTIQ inclusion at the international institutional level. This section explores the threat of gender-based violence and medical violence experienced by LGBTIQ individuals and how these threats impact LGBTIQ inclusion at international levels.

Personal security

Security from physical violence is considered to be one of the most pressing human security concerns (United Nations Development Programme 1994, 30). Threats like torture, war, child abuse, domestic violence, rape, and gender-based violence violate one's personal security. Gender-based violence, or the direct, cultural, and structural violence directed at populations because of their sex or how they express their gender or sexuality, is one of the greatest threats to personal security affecting countless people around the world. For LGBTIQ persons, especially gender non-conforming (GNC) and transgender individuals, gender-based violence is nothing less than an exacerbated form of direct violence disabling one's personal security and the right to live free from fear. Gender-based violence can also include sexuality-based violence. Black South African lesbians, for example, who express masculine traits, dress, or behavior are viewed as pushing the boundaries of, or being defiant against, traditional gender norms. This perception has created a violent backlash amongst black South African communities who commit direct forms of gender-based violence through sexuality-based violence like corrective rape. The phenomenon of corrective rape, whereby a man rapes a lesbian in an attempt to cure her of her orientation (Human Rights

Watch 2011, 2), has become a fearful reality of gender-based and sexuality-based violence. For transgender individuals, particularly transgender women, gender-based violence becomes compacted by an accumulation of various other vulnerabilities, including systematic discrimination attached to the gender category of woman.

Understanding gender as a category of analysis, as opposed to the frequently conflated belief that gender equals woman, reveals a greater marginalization of transgender and GNC individuals. Their personal security becomes undermined on account of non-conformity in relation to gender roles and expectation. Other susceptibilities impairing the personal security of transwomen exist at the institutional level through the state's unwillingness to recognize the legal identity of trans-people. Not having a properly recognized identity leaves transwomen more vulnerable to direct forms of violence and transphobia. Additionally, the absence of a state-recognized identity disables the persecution of those who commit gender-based violence against transwomen on account of the state not defending transwomen as women. The fear of secondary victimization by the police, the courts, and greater society at large further exacerbates the under-reporting of crimes committed against transgender people (Yeung 2016).

An even greater threat to the personal security of transgender individuals is the threat of murder and/or arbitrary execution. In November of 2012, the United Nations General Assembly passed a historic resolution adding gender identity to the list of categories at risk of extrajudicial and arbitrary executions. Although non-binding, the resolution brings to the forefront SOGIESC considerations in the context of arbitrary executions and those vulnerable to murder. According to the Trans Murder Monitoring project, there have been 2,343 documented reported killings of transgender in 69 countries worldwide (TransRespect verses Transphobia 2017). Capturing accurate data on murdered transgender people is very challenging because of the amount of unreported cases.

For LGBTIQ persons, the threat to one's personal security by means of direct, structural, and cultural violence is a reality experienced by far too many individuals throughout the world. SOGIESC must be taken into account at all institutional levels to ensure the protection and personal security of all human beings. The threat of direct violence, arbitrary execution, and gender-based violence through structural and cultural systems disables the protection of LGBTIQ communities at the local level, including but not limited to local law enforcement, civil society organizations, and local health care facilities, all the way throughout institutional systems. As a result, violations to personal security can create domino effects leading to threats against health security, economic security, food security, and community security. The above section is by no means an exhaustive account of personal security threats experienced by LGBTIQ communities; however, once we begin to examine the interwoven connections as they apply to SOGIESC considerations, international development efforts can truly begin to incorporate LGBTIQ inclusion practices that are reflective of the populations' needs.

Health security

Health security concepts have evolved since the 1994 Human Development Report approached the topic from the perspective of developing and industrial countries. Many of the same targets from the report including disease and maternal mortality continue to be the main focus of international development efforts along with the growing attention paid to mental health and substance uses/abuse. For decades LGBTIQ health security has been regularly addressed through avenues related to HIV/AIDS including education, prevention, and care. Frequently left out of the conversation is the involuntary or coerced medical violence experienced by people born with sex characteristic variations.

Intersex is a signifier used to describe people whose variations of sex characteristics fall beyond the traditionally understood male/female binary (Darlington Statement 2017, 1; Amnesty International 2017). Not everyone born with variations of sex characteristics identify as intersex. Medical communities commonly refer to sex characteristic variations as a disorder of sex development (DSD). This type of terminology is problematic in numerous ways. For one, it pathologizes variations of sex characteristics as something that is broken and in need of being fixed (Johnson 2017; Darlington Statement 2017, 2). Labeling a natural occurring variation as a disorder perpetuates stigma and medicalization efforts seeking to 'normalize' the intersex body.

Practices to rid the world of people born with sex characteristic variations occur in all regions through various different means including infanticide, sterilization, *in utero* drug administration, and surgical intervention (Darlington Statement 2017, 3; Amnesty International 2017; Third International Intersex Forum 2013; Greenberg 2012, 23–24). Infants displaying sex characteristic variations are often subjected to medically irreversible surgery as a way to 'normalize' the infant into either a boy or a girl. This type of medical intervention creates lifelong physical and mental health complications creating health (in)security for those subjected to surgical interventions as an infant. Children of these practices grow up to face long-term physical health and psychological implications, especially if the child decides later in life that the 'educated guess,' and in turn their rearing of assigned sex, does not reflect their self-determined sex or gender identity (Darlington Statement 2017, 3). Physicians, and any form of medical violence perpetrated against the child, are circuitously released of any accountability or responsibility.

Transgender individuals also experience medical violence when forced to undergo sterilization procedures in order to receive proper identification documents that reflect their gender identity/expression. Twenty countries in Europe require transgender individuals to undergo sterilization procedures before any legal gender change is made to identification documents (Transgender Europe 2017). Forcing transgender individuals to undergo surgery as the only means by which to obtain identity documentations reflective of their gender identity/expression creates structural violence by way of medical violence. It also sets in motion a domino effect of consequence, both physical and mental, that can impact future securities including personal, economic, environmental, and food. By not having a proper identification document reflective of one's true gender identity/expression, transgender individuals face higher levels of discrimination and stigma, and are systematically denied access to adequate medical care for issues related to either male or female aspects of living.

As international development efforts attempt to advance LGBTIQ inclusion, they must incorporate the health threats intersex and transgender individuals experience when not given the right to their own bodily integrity, physical autonomy, and self-determination. Health security threats perpetuate further marginalization while also enabling the continuation of medical violence practices. Advancing self-determination, bodily integrity, and physical autonomy efforts within international development practices would ultimately benefit the entire well-being of any LGBTIQ individual impacted by the myriad of consequences brought on through health insecurity.

Freedom from want

Freedom from want expands human security concepts into the realm of international development and humanitarian assistance. Vulnerabilities associated with this component are frequently attributed to inequality and a lack of social justice (Hampson et al. 2002, 18).

For LGBTIQ persons, these inequalities subsist on account of one's SOGIESC. Threats to socio-economic security, environmental security, and food security become heightened on account of LGBTIQ persons' already marginalized position within society, in turn decreasing one's access to international development and humanitarian assistance.

Economic security

For LGBTIQ individuals, reclaiming economic security spans numerous different methods. For some, staying invisible within the public sphere, particularly in relation to formal employment, is the only viable option. For others, avenues like sex work offer a means of economic security. Although a highly contentious industry, those advocating on behalf of sex worker rights call for sex work to be decriminalized and recognized as a legitimate form of labor.

Punitive laws in many regions around the world criminalize sex work. Such laws push sex workers into dangerous and isolated areas to avoid persecution and harassment from the police. Condom criminalization, for example, puts LGBTIQ sex workers, who are already labeled as high risk, in greater jeopardy of contracting HIV, sexually transmitted infections (STIs) and hepatitis. This in turn influences future economic (in)securities related to heath care. Not given proper gender identification documentation further impacts transgender sex workers (in)security. State-sponsored homo/transphobia further marginalize LGBTIQ sex workers, forcing them underground and away from services (Global Network of Sex Work Projects 2011, 13).

Stigma associated with sex work gets compacted onto the stigma associated with homophobia/transphobia, further marginalizing the individual, in turn marginalizing their economic opportunities. Having limited economic opportunities, and low social status, leaves sexual minorities, particularly transgender individuals and men who have sex with men (MSM), in positions where sex work becomes a viable and accessible form of employment and income. However, the informality of their work removes elements of economic security, such as proper bank accounts, insurance, and employment security (Bhattacharjya 2008). Attempts to save or deposit money become even further compromised causing a vicious cycle of festering economic insecurity compacted by the marginalization and discrimination associated with SOGIESC considerations.

Decriminalization efforts surrounding LGBTIQ sex work should become a priority for international development efforts at local and regional levels, in order to decrease the economic insecurity of LGBTIQ sex workers. Decriminalization would further enable economic security by enabling access and protection under labor laws while at the same time combating the institutionalized discrimination inherent within the sex work industry. The needs of LGBTIQ sex workers and their rights to autonomy and economic security should be factored into international development operations as they seek to increase LGBTIQ inclusion.

Environmental security

Environmental security is defined in terms of a combination of threats including the destruction of local and global ecosystems (United Nations Development Programme 1994, 28). Population increases, water scarcity, and pollution upsurges are linked to the rising number of natural disasters occurring worldwide. Growing evidence on the increased marginalization of LGBTIQ people during times of natural and environmental disasters have surfaced over the last few years. Transgender individuals on hormone therapy, for example, reported losing access to medical treatment after the 2011 earthquake in Japan, while MSM and gay men reported not being able to access HIV/AIDS medication (Yamshita et al. 2017). In India, transwomen were denied access to shelters because of their gender identity/ expression after the 2005 tsunami (Knight 2016). Concurrently, SOGIESC considerations are rarely reflected in disaster risk reduction (DRR) policies leaving LGBTIQ populations on the fringe of relief and rehabilitations efforts; however, non-governmental organizations (NGOs), like the Blue Diamond Society, have partnered with the United States Agency for International Development (USAID) in recent years in an effort to strengthen LGBTIQ inclusion within disaster relief efforts (Global Equality 2012).

Marginalized populations, like LGBTIQ persons, often have local organizations providing services for their specific population during pre-disaster times. This creates a complicated interaction when international entities arise specifically to provide emergency aid or assistance after natural disasters. The marginalized often turn to their own groups for assistance rather than large mainstream organizations (Eads 2002). When disasters occur in already scarcely resourced areas the probability of local civil society organizations being equally affected by the natural disaster is high. This further impacts local civil society organizations' capacity to support local LGBTIQ persons' needs. Additionally, when international organizations intervene it can often involve forced relocation to 'safer' sites. Such tactics leave LGBTIQ people without access to LGBTIQ sensitive services, including sexual health and HIV treatment. Simultaneously, closeted LGBTIQ people have incentive to stay away from public service providers, relief providers, and police to avoid public recognition, stigma, and discrimination (Colvin 2010).

Additional environmental security threats affecting LGBTIQ populations can be found at social and institutional levels. International NGOs may be internally discriminatory through their own human resource practices, paving the way for bias and discrimination against LGBTIQ individuals during service provisions. Transgender populations are some of the most outwardly affected populations of this discrimination. Since affected groups in DRR are usually categorized into either male or female populations, transgender individuals are not documented as an affected group and are therefore denied relief services including temporary housing, health access and even basic sanitation services. After the 2005 tsunami in India, Aravanis, India's gender variant people, experienced systematic discrimination when it came to health care, housing, and sanitation (Knight and Sollom 2012). In Pakistan, transgender people were denied access to internally displaced person (IDP) camps after disaster flooding because they had no proper identification cards (Knight and Sollom 2012).

Environmental security threats are linked to food and food security post-disaster. Mainstream relief organizations often define family for purposes of aid distribution, including distribution of food, and often do so in ways that exclude LGBTIQ people. When family is solely defined in nuclear terms, that is, man, woman, and child, those whose families exist on the periphery of traditional norms get denied access to the same relief efforts that are granted to others. This negatively affects LGBTIQ eligibility criteria, in turn denying access to relief efforts. Such blatant discrimination further marginalizes LGBTIQ populations through compromised environmental security relief efforts. During the 2008 earthquake in Haiti, MSM were systematically denied food because rations were directed at women. MSM had no registered women in their home and were thus not eligible to receive rations (Knight and Sollom 2012). This led to the coercion of LGBTIQ individuals in Haiti IDP camps to engage in sexual relations in exchange for food and services provided by relief workers (International Gay and Lesbian Human Rights Commission 2011, 4).

SOGIESC considerations are slowly being added to DRR efforts. For many LGBTIQ individuals, the fear of further marginalization leaves them in the shadows of disaster relief efforts, far too often remaining invisible during very vulnerable times. The need to continuously qualify one's place of being, further impacts LGBTIQ individuals during times of environmental crisis. In order to secure a sense of personal security during times of environmental insecurity, SOGIESC considerations must be incorporated at every international development level to provide comprehensive, safe, and accessible services during times of crisis and disaster.

Food security

Food security is informed upon three pillars: food availability, food access, and food use. For LGBTIQ individuals already facing health challenges such a HIV/AIDS, hepatitis, and/or tuberculosis, proper nutrition becomes an essential necessity to maintain a healthy and balanced life. LGBTIQ individuals marginalized due to stigma sequentially become hindered from food access and availability. This in turn generates malnutrition. The links between malnutrition and the development of disease are extensively studied and proven to be mutually reinforcing (Semba and Tang 1999, 182). Intermesh malnutrition on top of high-risk exposure to disease from homelessness, marginalization, and/or sexual violence, and we once again see LGBTIQ individuals' relationship to food security compromised on account of their SOGIESC.

In developing regions, food security remains largely contingent on agricultural sectors. Food security challenges facing LGBTIQ individuals in these regions comprise undermined access to land, land rights, and land inheritance. Land is frequently passed down to male heads of the household, which are regularly defined as heterosexual, nuclear, or traditional. When distribution of land based upon heteronormative household ideals becomes the norm, LGBTIQ individuals face further marginalization from food security through diminished access to resources and/or decision-making. Simultaneously, gender divisions of labor, such as males being responsible for clearing and females being responsible for weeding and post-harvest work, draws attention to the difficulties facing single gender (i.e. all female or all male) households. According to the Food and Agricultural Organization of the United Nations, food security for single gender households is jeopardized through imbalances such as: access to resources, access to land, access to credit, access to agricultural inputs, access to education and training, and, finally, access to decision-making (Food and Agriculture Organization 2012). Although analyzed from a heteronormative context, the challenges single gender households face regarding food security can also apply to LGBTIQ households.

For LGBTIQ agricultural households in countries promoting state-sponsored homophobia/transphobia, all above listed challenges are compacted upon the fear that one might be outted within their community. Stigma encountered if outted could disable the selling of one's agricultural goods at a marketplace because the risk of violence to the individual could be too great. Simultaneously, stigma associated with homosexuality as being a curse or disease could ultimately stop buyers from purchasing, in turn destroying the livelihood of the seller. Another issue impacting LGBTIQ food (in)security is water collection. Water collection, usually allocated to women, could be perceived as suspicious if handled by a man or transgender individual. This suspicion could in turn dismantle one's access to obtaining water while simultaneously putting their personal security at risk.

Food insecurity is a disturbing reality for many LGBTIQ individuals. Repercussions of this insecurity set in motion numerous consequences, many of which have negative impacts upon the health, economic, and personal livelihoods of LGBTIQ persons. In order to transform these vulnerabilities, international development sectors must take an intersectional approach to capacity building that is SOGIESC cognizant and capable of bridging LGBTIQ access, availability, and food use.

Freedom to live with dignity

The freedom to live with dignity presumes all humans and communities have the right to exist with worth, value, and merit in lieu of difference, discrepancy, or disparity. As a human security component, the freedom to live with dignity advocates for the respect of all people through every sector of international affairs, regardless of background, culture, or identity. At an international level, the right to live with dignity ensures that individuals have worth, be treated with worth, and are deserving of such worthiness no matter their difference.

For LGBTIQ persons, the very notion of being treated with worth and dignity lies in the simple acknowledgement that one is not sick, diseased, or unnatural, and deserving of protection, support, and visibility regardless of their SOGIESC. The study of homosexual behavior from the nineteenth century on paved the way for a gay identity to progress and in turn speak for itself (Foucault 1990, 101). For many, claiming a gay identity reinforces one's own dignity and worth. This empowerment creates a sense of belonging and legitimacy that one is not sick, diseased, or perverse but authentic and true. In contemporary international contexts, a gay identity is often associated with Western discourses and labeled as a foreign import. The freedom to live with dignity guarantees the preservation of individual worth regardless of how one identifies, how international institutions classify, or how one behaves in a same-sex sexual relationship.

Political security

Political security seeks to ensure that individuals have the right to enjoy their civil and political rights, in addition to living free from political oppression. LGBTIQ individuals, especially those living in countries where state-sponsored homophobia and transphobia seeks to recriminalize SOGIESC considerations, directly violates one's freedom to live with dignity and worth.

Countries like Ukraine, Russia, Hungary, Lithuania, Moldova, and Latvia, have deliberated on bills over the last few years, in an attempt to criminalize 'homosexual propaganda' (International Commission of Jurists and ILGA-Europe 2012). Both Ukraine and Russia have voted in favor of such bans at the national level. In October 2012, the Ukrainian parliament passed a draft law that modified current laws to impose sanctions on imports or the distribution of product that promotes homosexuality (2012). On January 25, 2013, the Russian parliament voted in favor (388 out of 390) of an anti-homosexual propaganda bill that prohibits spreading homosexual propaganda to children through criminal law provisions. Russian Legislator Vitaly Milonov, author of the anti-propaganda bill, framed the criminalization effort as a public health concern against sodomy while also stressing that LGBTIQ people are not socially valuable (Davidoff 2013). Member of Parliament, Yelena Mizulina, additionally framed the criminalization effort as a necessity to safeguard the health and moral development of children (Ponomareva 2013). Ultimately, the anti-homosexual propaganda bills in Ukraine and Russia disable the societies' freedom of expression, right to public assembly, and right to access information.

By establishing SOGIESC considerations as a threat worthy of being punished by criminalization efforts, these countries are attempting to eradicate LGBTIQ issues, and in turn LGBTIQ people. Such an environment further impedes upon the greater society at large by creating an air of societal oppressions within all sectors. From media personal, fearful to report on the issues, to health care providers, fearful of addressing sexual health concerns, the anti-homosexual propaganda bills promote the exclusion of LGBTIQ individuals while concurrently undermining the security of the entire population. Yet, despite these possibilities, suppressing LGBTIQ persons' political security within countries attempting to ban homosexual propaganda has multilayered consequences. Access to appropriate sexual health education would be limited, in turn creating greater public health risks for all individuals. Fear of being outed by family or friends would leave one susceptible to being terminated from employment and/or denied resources and services.

In reality, the continuum of rights, development, and security for LGBTIQ individuals would be hindered at all levels on account of the nation state attempting to erase LGBTIQ existence. All civil liberties and political freedoms are overshadowed by the political oppression embedded within the anti-homosexual propaganda bills, making LGBTIQ inclusion efforts within international development efforts in these countries unfeasible. Criminalization efforts are but a few of the political (in)securities impacting LGBTIQ people. Exported politicized homophobia and state-sponsored punitive arrests/detention, like those sanctioned in the spring of 2017 by Chechnya, dismantle LGBTIQ inclusion efforts in the regions that need it the most. International development efforts would do well to incorporate conflict assessment methods and conflict transformation techniques within these environments to ensure that inclusion practices are reflective of the population's political security needs.

Community security

Community security invokes a reassuring set of values providing a cultural identity through membership within a group, family, organization, ethnicity, and so forth (United Nations Development Programme 1994, 31). It cultivates relationships among members and generates camaraderie, safety, understanding and security. The concept of community enables a kinship among members, in turn generating a network of connections between people of varying degrees. The previous sections analyzed the multidimensional oppression impacting LGBTIQ human security. This last section seeks to conceptualize community security as it already exists within LGBTIQ communities as a way to further advance SOGIESC communities of practice.

Communities of practice are a process of collective learning that has three crucial characteristics (Wenger-Trayner and Wenger-Trayner 2015, 2–3). The first is the domain, or shared point of interest. The second is the community, or space where members of the domain participate in joint activities and discussions, with the purpose of learning and building from each other, and the third is the practice, or area in which community members become practitioners. If the advancement of LGBTIQ rights, development, and security is defined as a community of practice, where the advancement of equality, freedoms, and dignity are the domain, then we begin to recognize the numerous communities, like human rights defenders, already practicing within this domain.

From the human right defender, to the law student, to the ally facilitating a coalition building event, LGBTIQ communities of practice exist within every institution and have the capacity to share and receive best practices from within and beyond their own community. Many LGBTIQ organizations working on civil and political rights typically do so with a small staff and limited resources (Global Gaze 2005, 7). Yet, despite these limited reserves, the dedication to the cause, and the desire to share best practices, propels many LGBTIQ organizations forward to work in collaboration.

In places where SOGIESC considerations are criminalized, many LGBTIQ communities of practice work in coalition with various other organizations, such as human rights groups, HIV/AID health organizations, and women's organizations. Such advances recognize the necessity for communities of practice around SOGIESC to be included within other knowledge-sharing endeavors. Notwithstanding these advances, a reflective process should always be questioning what voices are not being represented in the community of practice and in what ways they can be included. This is especially important at the international institution level and within development programs like UNDP as they continue to mainstream SOGIESC considerations and advance efforts with programmatic initiatives like the recent Being LGBT in Asia.[3]

Concluding thoughts

As the mainstreaming of SOGIESC considerations continue to evolve within international development efforts, so must the way international development organizations address the realities of sustainable models of inclusion. LGBTIQ people are not a homogenous population and their needs are many. Sadly, one can have rights and still experience systematic forms of insecurity, oppression, and violence. Such intersectional insecurities require strategic intersectional solutions. This chapter sought to reconceptualize how a human security approach could help develop a comprehensive model of inclusion by shedding light on the multidimensional oppressions LGBTIQ individuals face. Human security allows us to examine the root causes of conflict, oppression, and marginalization in a manner reflective of needs and a set of fundamental freedoms, that is, freedom from fear, freedom from want, and the freedom to live with dignity. It also allows us to critically explore how those needs intersect amid the interlinkages between security, development, and human rights. It is through these interdependencies where the voices of the most marginalized can begin to surface within SOGIESC mainstreaming.

As international institutions continue to advance SOGIESC mainstreaming they must continuously ask whose voice is at the table? Whose voice is left out? Why are those voices left out and how can they safely and effectively be brought into a dialogue about inclusion within their own context? Recognizing and appreciating the histories, both indigenous and those reminiscent of colonialism, is crucial when mainstreaming SOGIESC considerations within international development practices. Lived histories and lived experiences shape how LGBTIQ individuals experience the world. These histories must be respected when seeking to include a population that is, and so often has been, excluded from the freedoms associated with living free from fear, free from want, and with dignity.

Notes

1 The reasons why international institutions fail to include the Q within the LGBTI acronym is still unclear. Whether because of its anti-assimilationist origins or its non-binary fluidity, queer as an identifier has yet to be included at the international level within institutions like UNDP. As mentioned in the Brief Note on Terminology section, I include the Q within the LGBTIQ acronym because, despite the relative nature of queerness, the lived experiences of those whose gender, sex, and/or sexuality exist beyond a monolithic understanding, are worthy of being included within dialogues that attempt to further analyze the impact of LGBTIQ oppression, marginalization, and discrimination.

2 Weber's analysis of the 'perverse homosexual' examines figurations associated with the Victorian 'underdeveloped' and 'underdevelopable' and contemporary 'unwanted im/migrant' and 'terrorist.' Her analysis highlights the inherent plurality of these queer figurations in relation to modern sovereignty as explained through Richard Ashley's 'statecraft as mancraft' argument.
3 Beginning in 2014, UNDP, in partnership with USAID, embarked on a regional program program called LGBT in Asia. The program addresses LGBTI(Q) marginalization, oppression, and exclusion within the region, while simultaneously encouraging a deeper understanding and cooperation among key regional stakeholders. The initiative has produced eight country reports to date and is scheduled to conclude in 2017.

References

Amnesty International. 2017. "First, Do No Harm: Ensuring the Rights of Children Born Intersex." Available from: https://oii.org.au/darlington-statement/ (accessed May 25, 2017).

Ashley, R. 1989. "Living on the Borderlines: Man Poststructuralism and War" In *International/ Intertextual Relations*, edited by J.D. Derian and M. J. Shapiro, pp. 259–321. Lexington: Lexington Books.

Badgett, M.V. Lee and Crehan, P. 2016. "Investing in a Research Revolution for LGBTI Inclusion." United Nations Development Programme and the World Bank. http://www.worldbank.org/en/events/2016/11/16/investing-in-research-for-lgbti-inclusion (accessed September 26, 2017).

Bhattacharjya, M. 2008. "Sex Workers as Economic Agents." Info change agenda. http://infochangeindia.org/agenda/social-exclusion/sex-workers-as-economic-agents.html (accessed April 4, 2013).

Cohen, C.J. 1997. "Punks, Bulldaggers, and Welfare Queens: The Radical Potential of Queer Politics?" *GLQ: A Journal of Lesbian and Gay Studies*, 3, no. 4: 437–465.

Colvin, R. 2010. "Critical Incidents, Invisible Populations, and Public Policy: A Case of the LGBT Community." *The Journal of the Academy for Critical Incident Analysis* 1 no. 1. http://jcia.aciajj.org/volume-1-no-1/critical-incidents-invisible-populations-and-public-policy-a-case-of-the-lgbt-community/ (accessed April 22, 2017).

Darlington Statement. 2017. "Joint Consensus Statement from the Intersex Community Retreat in Darlington." https://oii.org.au/darlington-statement/ (accessed May 25, 2017).

Davidoff, V. 2013. "Russia's Fertile Grounds for Homophobia." *The Moscow Times.* https://themoscowtimes.com/articles/russias-fertile-grounds-for-homophobia-22391 (accessed April 4, 2017).

Eads, M. 2002. *Marginalized Groups in Times of Crisis: Identity, Needs, and Response.* Quick Response Research Report #152. Boulder, CO: Natural Hazards Research and Applications Information Center, University of Colorado.

Food and Agriculture Organization. 2012. *Women and Sustainable Food Security.* http://www.fao.org/docrep/x0171e/x0171e02.htm (accessed May 3, 2017).

Foucault, M. 1990. *History of Sexuality: An Introduction Vol. 1.* New York: Random House.

Global Equality. 2012. "U.S. Embassy and Blue Diamond Society Partner to Make Disaster Risk Reduction LGBTI-Inclusive." https://globalequality.wordpress.com/2012/04/27/u-s-embassy-and-blue-diamond-society-partner-to-make-disaster-risk-reduction-lgbti-inclusive/ (accessed June 21, 2017).

Global Gaze. 2005. "Lesbian, Gay, Bisexual, Transgender and Intersex Grantmaking in the Global South and East." http://www.opensocietyfoundations.org/sites/default/files/global_20070820_0.pdf (accessed February 2, 2013).

Global Network of Sex Work Projects (2011) "Female, Male, and Transgender Sex Workers' Perspectives on HIV & STI Prevention and Treatment Services: A Global Sex Worker Consultation." http://www.nswp.org/sites/nswp.org/files/NSWP-WHO%20Community%20Consultation%20Report%20archived.pdf (accessed September 26, 2017).

Gunkel, H. 2010. *The Cultural Politics of Female Sexuality of South Africa.* New York: Routledge.

Greenberg, J. 2012. *Intersexuality and the Law: Why Sex Matters.* New York: New York University Press.

Hames-Garcia, M. 2006. "What's at Stake in 'Gay' Identities?" In *Identity Politics Reconsidered*, edited by S. Mohanty, P. Moya, M.H. Garcia, and S. Mohanty, pp. 78–96. New York: Palgrave Macmillan.

Hampson, F.O., Daudelin, J., Hay, J.B., Marin, T., and Reid, H. 2002. *Madness in the Multitude: Human Security and World Disorder.* Toronto: Oxford University Press.

Human Rights Watch. 2011. *"We'll Show You You're a Woman": Violence and Discrimination against Black Lesbians and Transgender Men in South Africa.* Report. https://www.hrw.org/report/2011/12/05/well-show-you-youre-woman/violence-and-discrimination-against-black-lesbians-and

International Commission of Jurists and ILGA-Europe. 2012 *"Homosexual Propaganda" Bans: Analysis and Recommendations*. Advocacy: Analysis Briefs. https://www.icj.org/homosexual-propaganda-bans-analysis-and-recommendations/ (accessed April 8, 2013).

International Gay and Lesbian Human Rights Commission. 2011. "The Impact of the Earthquake, and Relief and Recovery Programs on Haitian LGBT People." Briefing Paper. https://www.outrightinternational.org/content/impact-earthquake-and-relief-and-recovery-programs-haitian-lgbt-people (accessed May 13, 2017).

Johnson, E.K. 2017. "Term 'Disorders of Sex Development' May have Negative Impact." News Wise. http://newswise.com/articles/term-disorders-of-sex-development-may-have-negative-impact (accessed May 25, 2017).

Knight, K. 2016. "LGBT People in Emergencies – Risks and Service Gaps." Human Rights Watch. https://www.hrw.org/news/2016/05/20/lgbt-people-emergencies-risks-and-service-gaps (accessed June 15, 2017).

Knight, K. and Sollom, R. 2012. "Making Disaster Risk Reduction and Relief Programmes LGBTI Inclusive: Examples from Nepal." *Humanitarian Exchange Magazine*, 55. http://odihpn.org/magazine/making-disaster-risk-reduction-and-relief-programmes-lgbti-inclusive-examples-from-nepal/ (accessed May 10, 2017).

Ponomareva, Y. 2013. "'Gay Propaganda' Ban Stirs High Emotion. Russia beyond the Headlines." https://romanovs-mystery.rbth.com/amp/492243 (accessed April 24, 2017).

Semba, R.D. and Tang, A.M. 1999. "Micronutrients and the Pathogenesis of Human Immunodeficiency Virus Infection." *British Journal of Nutrition*, 81, no. 3: 181–189.

Third International Intersex Forum. 2013. "Public Statement by the Third International Intersex Forum." http://ilga-europe.org/what-we-do/our-advocacy-work/trans-and-intersex/intersex/events/3rd-international-intersex-forum (accessed May 23, 2017).

Transgender Europe. 2017. "The Momentum is Now! Forced Sterilization on Its Way Out, But Trans Pathologisation Remains." http://tgeu.org/idahot_forum_map-launch/ (accessed May 17, 2017).

TransRespect verses Transphobia. 2017. "Trans Day of Visibility 2017" Press Release. http://transrespect.org/en/tdov-2017-tmm-update/ (accessed May 15, 2017).

United Nations Commission on Human Security. 2003. *Human Security Now*. Report. New York: UNCHS. http://www.un.org/humansecurity/sites/www.un.org.humansecurity/files/chs_final_report_-_english.pdf (accessed June 21, 2017).

United Nations Development Programme. 1994. *Human Development Report 1994*. New York: Oxford University Press. http://hdr.undp.org/sites/default/files/reports/255/hdr_1994_en_complete_nostats.pdf (accessed February 2, 2017).

United Nations General Assembly 66th session. 2012. "Resolution adopted by the General Assembly on 10 September 2012". (A/RES/66/290).

Weber, C. 2016. *Queer International Relations: Sovereignty, Sexuality, and the Will to Knowledge*. New York: Oxford University Press.

Wenger-Trayner, E. and Wenger-Trayner, B. 2015. "Communities of Practice: A Brief Introduction." http://wenger-trayner.com/wp-content/uploads/2015/04/07-Brief-introduction-to-communities-of-practice.pdf (accessed May 10, 2017).

Yamshita, A., Gomex, C. and Dombroski, K. 2017. "Segregation, Exclusion and LGBT People in Disaster Impacted Areas: Experiences from the Higashinihon DaiShinsai (Great East-Japan Disaster)." *Gender, Place & Culture*, 24, no. 1: 64–71.

Yeung, P. 2016. "Transphobic hate crimes in 'sickening' 170% rise as low prosecution rates create 'lack of trust' in police." *Independent*. http://www.independent.co.uk/news/uk/home-news/transphobic-hate-crime-statistics-violence-transgender-uk-police-a7159026.html (accessed October 15, 2017).

10

LIVEABLE LIVES

A transnational queer-feminist reflection on sexuality, development and governance

Niharika Banerjea and Kath Browne

Heteronationalist frame of governance

The global development industry – including multilateral institutions, aid agencies, state agencies, non-governmental organizations (NGOs) – is imbricated with anxieties about sex and sexuality (Gosine 2009; Lind 2009). In this industry, mechanisms of governance – that define "how communities or nations are planned" and "how individuals are 'targeted' as citizens, workers and recipients of aid" (Lind 2009, 35) – work to define and regulate the sexual lives of people. On the one hand, while women as mothers are made hypervisible in development frameworks, those who are outside such roles are invisibilized. Such development efforts serve to heteronationalize nation states (Gosine 2009). Read either only as a health issue[1] or slighted as a luxury, sexuality hardly enters development debates outside these parameters (Cornwall and Jolly 2006). Women's empowerment and poverty reduction programs – emerging within political economies of funding – privilege a heteronormative and moral[2] pairing between a man and a woman because little or no attention is paid to the health and livelihood concerns of sex workers, single-headed households and lesbian, gay, bisexual, transgender, queer (LGBTQ) persons. Programs around HIV/AIDS have brought non-normative sexualities and non-procreative sex to the forefront, but its representations have been quite normative (Gosine 2005). Intervention around HIV/AIDS in places in the global south has been modeled on idealized moral representations of sexuality, rather than on lived realities, perpetuating myths and completely missing the mark. Persons engaged in same-sex and same-gender relations and sex workers were identified by states as new threats as they crossed normative boundaries, which were thought to result in disease and death, and ultimately the downfall of the nation (Gosine 2009; Shah 2012; 2014). Sexuality is thus understood more as a social problem requiring a certain kind of state intervention, rather than a complex part of experience integral to human livelihoods.

As this reader demonstrates, there is a well-established literature that has brought to light sexuality's "neglect" and "silence" (Cornwall and Jolly 2006, 1) within development and its connection to states of governance. This is hinged on a particular (hetero)normative and (cis)gendered subject. While there are differences in specific development agendas, the universalizing nature of heteronormativity is common – and is an abiding concern for feminist politics in general and queer-feminist politics in particular. In the context of India, for example, an able-bodied, male, heteronormative middle-class Hindu as the ideal citizen subject undergirds state-sponsored policies and programs, excluding and making abject those who deviate from the ideal citizen-subject. As Devika (2009) in her interrogation of the development discourse in Kerala argues, the abjects – who are the constitutive outside development discourses – are the impossible, "abnormal", "deviant" subjects relegated to the spheres of life that are not liveable. Such abjection and simultaneous disciplining of subjects is intimately tied to a necessary mechanism of governance that keeps the state "relevant" in the larger neoliberal context (Puri 2016). Therefore, there are continuing demands on theorists and practitioners to critically engage with sexual norms and morals that underpin the ideal subject of development. This chapter develops a queer-feminist and transnational (see Browne et al. 2017) interrogation of an underlying binary of progress/backwardness that often informs development agenda's engagement with LGBTQ issues.

Although studies of sexualities are not confined to queer frames and conversely queer thinking can exceed its starting point in sexualities, we deploy queer here in terms of the questioning of normativities, including sexual and racial hegemonies. Here we are particularly questioning the taken for granted and causal linkage between the presence or absence of juridico-political reforms and liveabilities of LGBTQ persons. Such linkages are often used by nation states to create normative and comparative hierarchies between nations. Drawing on Kulpa and Mizielinska (2011), we address the discursive placing of certain nations as "backwards" within spatio-temporal hierarchies that see others as "progressing" because of the operationalization and representations of their juridico-political reforms leading to sexual and gendered liberations. In this discourse, nations in the global north are typically seen as an ideal place for LGBTQ persons and other sexual and gender dissidents in comparison to the global south. Moving beyond this position, this chapter will argue for centering the question of liveability[3] within the situated and "lived experiences" of LGBTQ persons, thereby de-linking its connection to solely the presence or absence of juridico-political reforms. By taking this position, we are not reifying sexuality and sexual lives as something that can be only captured within some authentic and autonomous situated contexts; the discursive construction of sexuality has a complex history (Foucault 1980). Neither do we want to pose lived experience as an unproblematic, authentic and evidentiary site of understanding liveability in opposition to the number and volume of juridico-political reforms. Experience is contingent, mediated, historically variable, and "discursive productions of knowledge of the self" (Scott 1992, 35–36). Instead, we deploy lived experiences – as a composite through which subjects are formed and respond to – in order to complicate the causal linkages between juridico-political reforms, sexual and gendered liberations and liveability. The aim of this chapter is not to arrive at a final solution for this causal linkage, but to generate some possibilities out of this problematic. This problematic is not merely a conceptual dilemma, but has material effects, because linking liveability to solely legal reform – as we alluded to earlier – has the potential to further enhance neoliberal governmentality.[4] We also work with the premise that this causal connection is not a monolith but is operationalized through place specific historicities. In other words, we are making a call to link sexualities, gender identities and expressions and sexual lives to liveabilities – as they are produced, navigated and transformed in situated practices and discursive contexts.

For the purposes of this chapter, we draw our critique from our larger project, "Making Liveable Lives: Rethinking Social Exclusion",[5] a transnational academic-activist and queer-feminist research study between University of Brighton, Ambedkar University, Delhi and Sappho for Equality.[6] One of the stated goals of this work is to interrupt the naturalized consolidation of LGBTQ liveabilities around the juridico-political question. Overall, we contend that a transnational queer-feminist critique, which seeks to understand sexual lives through a lens of liveability based on the complex of lived experiences, may help address the problematic causal linkage between juridico-political reforms, national development and progress. This lens has the potential to create a counter-narrative to the "sexual other" that can resignify our politics to address heteronationalist frames in neoliberal development agendas.

Backwards/progress: sexualities and nations

By focusing our research on those who transgress the boundaries of normative (hetero) sexualities, it became clear that development discourses are formed relationally, for example where the "other" is noted but the center remains an absent presence. (Hetero)sexualities, whilst potentially nativized and claimed as "natural" to a nation, with homosexualities read as "foreign contagion", are part of colonial, post-colonial and development framings. Increasingly, international development discourses label some nations as backward and some as forward-thinking/progressive on the basis of laws and legislation that offer rights and protections to LGBTQ people, as we will elaborate on in the following pages. The absence or presence of LGBTQ rights in a country is then connected to economic growth as a development indicator and this can be used to denote the "progress" or "backwardness" of nations.

We are not arguing against legislative rights, as the presence of such rights is indeed a welcome reprieve for many marginalized groups. Work such as Badgett's (2014) discussion of the economic losses to India because of homophobia, can strategically augment activist work and pressure the state to push through legal reforms that can support LGBTQ people.[7] Conversely, the international outcry against legislation such as the reinstatement of Section 377 of the Indian Penal Code in India,[8] support those within specific Indian contexts to push back against exclusionary legislation. At the same time, it is important to note that legal reforms are also driven by nations such as South Africa, and are not the preserve of the global north, and should not be seen as originating there and spreading to/diffusing to the global south.

Here, we are arguing that the presence of LGBTQ rights can be viewed as an indicator of progressive change in ways that address global homophobia (Browne et al. 2015). Presumptions regarding the origins of sexual and gender acceptances, and the location of gender and sexual liberations within a supposedly global identity of LGBTQ, recreates specific dichotomies that create geo-temporal hierarchies. Such presumptions are based on a rights-bearing universal citizen subject, which further helps to consolidate the paradoxes of violence in a neoliberal state. This, in turn, creates the superiority of the global north in relation to sexual rights and others as lagging behind a Western European and USA norm.[9] The presence of LGBTQ rights then are invoked as a rationale not only for moral superiority but at times leading to military intervention (Browne et al. 2015). Monetary aid disbursement has also been linked to the creation and/or continuation of homophobic legislation. For instance, Norway and Denmark cut aid support to Uganda when President Yoweri Museveni signed the Anti-Homosexuality Bill (Plaut 2014). The linking of development aid to LGBTQ legislations and rights is a seductive stance by neoliberal regimes that has discursive as well as material implications. Mainstreaming of LGBTQ rights is also on the development agenda of the World Bank (Tyson 2014). As indicated earlier, an economic assessment report for homophobia in India is already out (Badgett 2014) and the European Parliament has also voted to include lesbian, gay, black, transgender, intersex and queer (LGBTIQ) rights in its development policies (European Parliament Intergroup on LGBT Rights 2014). This is reminiscent of the "add women and stir approach" that feminists concerned about gender mainstreaming have critiqued since the 1990s (see for example Milward, Mukhopadhyay, and Wong 2015; Moser 2005). Sexuality rights therefore often function as a relational category to help solidify the linkage between national development and progress.

The question of liveability – if placed within the seductive relation between sexuality rights and national development and progress – can be increasingly used as a measure to create oppositions between forward (those that have legal rights) and backward (those that do not have legal rights) states, between living (as only resonating with happiness, stability) and surviving (as only resonating with turbulence, chaos). Hegemonic states typically use the discourse of human rights to measure the level of democracy of other states (Grewal 2005). Deploying the frame of "good governance", neoliberal states are less interested in deepening democracy and more in championing a certain kind of human rights within their development agendas. This is linked to legitimizing the otherwise exclusionary actions of the state, ultimately leading to homonationalist positionalities (Puar 2007). The dominant understanding of liveability around sexual lives within the imaginaries and practices of development therefore needs to be critically interrogated. If not, sexual lives in both places in the global north and south can become "the problem that one creates" (Ahmed 2010); those with legal rights, presumably "happy", will be expected to simply ask for perfecting existing legislation and/or ask for more legal recognition if "unhappy", and those without legal recognition, presumably "unhappy", will be expected to only ask for legal reforms to be "happy". This then explains – at a discursive level – how populations perceive the other; wherein the trope of culture is deployed to make comparisons between those who have legal recognition and those who do not, ultimately leading to what Narayan calls "death by culture" (1997).[10] Materially, as we have already argued earlier, this has consequences for the disbursement of development aid.

Measuring liveable lives

In our academic-activist research project, "Making Liveable Lives: Rethinking Social Exclusion", we first sought to examine the hierarchization of countries within these progress/ backward narratives. In particular, we explored how "LGBT friendliness" was measured on global scales. We chose to do this to locate the terms through which liveabilities are globally assigned. Surprisingly, a number of our assumptions were unmined. First, we anticipated that globally standardized measures might exist, given the way in which nation states are linking LGBTQ rights with development agendas. Second, in addition to measures broadly based on rights, equality, and friendliness, we expected to find more measures/indices. Third, we expected more geographically based measures. These paucities might be related to the recent introduction of legislations, a formalized understanding of human rights issues and the recent interest in measurements in this area where some cities/countries are seen to be progressive and thus can be ranked against other countries. The non-academic groups and organizations producing these measures are LGBT rights organizations (including national and international organizations such as the Human Rights Association (HRA) and the International Lesbian, Gay, Bisexual, Trans and Intersex Association (ILGA)), some of who are paid by companies to rank their LGBT friendliness (such as Stonewall in the UK).[11] We can conclude then that there is a lack of systematic agreement or indeed publicly accessible measures from major supra-national organizations. Out of the 39 measures that we identified through the Internet and academic searches in 2015, 27 were classified as specific measures and 13 as opinion pieces (see Browne et al. 2015 for further details; Table 10.1). The lack of robust triangulated studies on which to base decisions regarding foreign aid was striking, yet

Table 10.1 What is measured?

Measuring what?	Measures	Opinion based	Where?
Human/gay/LGBT rights/laws	10	1	US city/worldwide by country / World Cup competitors/Europe (6 ILGA)/UN countries
Workplaces/corporate	3		US/Australia/UK
Campus life	2		US/UK
Views of homosexuality based on morality/societal acceptance; gay tolerance	2	1	Global
Gay friendly tourist destinations	1	2	World cities/worldwide by countries
Healthcare	1		USA
Views on a 'good place to live' for gay and lesbian people/best place to be 'gay' or LGBT (for 20-somethings)/'surprising' places/more gay friendly than America	1	5	Worldwide, ranked by country; cities outside San Francisco/New York (LGBT 20-somethings); outside the USA
LGBT in the military	1		Worldwide, ranked by country
Social inclusion index	1		Americas
Trans rights	1		Europe
Gay cities'/cities by density of gay friendly/gay owned business	1	2	World cities
Blood donations	1		All countries listed
Relationships and penalties	1		
Decriminalization	1		
Homophobic countries	2		

these measures can be used to inform more generally development agendas, aid decisions, and corporate action globally (Browne et al. 2015).

One striking, if unsurprising, element of our findings, as is exemplified in Table 10.1, is the focus on laws/human rights and secondly, the ways in which corporations/businesses feature in the rankings, particularly in the primarily English speaking global north. It is also of course notable that the focus is on Europe, America and Australia. The definitions of LGBTQ friendliness/homophobia are also instructive. Table 10.2 outlines those approaches that used measures (rather than opinions of the authors). It emphasizes a very particular understanding of progress that is framed in legal protections, marriage and decriminalization. While there can be little doubt that state support of sexual and gender minority rights and the removal of discriminatory methods is desirable, we must also be critical of the assumptions underpinning these indices, that is, that the achievement of these goals will make liveable the lives of all of those who are subject to exclusion, violence and discriminations because of their gender identities, expression and/or sexual practices, relationships and desires.

It is clear from our research that juridico-political understandings of freedom and human rights and the role of nation states and professional organizations within them are accorded primacy. As a consequence, countries/cities are hierarchized as developed or not based on these juridico-political indices. We consider this frame flawed and needing reconsideration, both in terms of how countries are seen as "developing" and their place in various indices of LGBTQ inclusion/homophobia, and also because these measures fall short of understanding the complexities and contextual understanding of sexual and gender

Table 10.2 Code for categories used to make judgments – measure-based approaches

Category used	Number
Legal/policy-based protections for LGBT people	16
Same-sex marriage, civil partnerships etc.	16
De/criminalization of same-sex sexual activity	12
Employment	10
Free assembly of LGBT people, including events	8
Group or organization pro-/anti-LGBT friendliness	8
External promotion of LGBT friendliness etc.	8
Adoption, parenting and fertilization	7
Health and hospitals	6
Individual in authority pro-/anti-LGBT friendliness	6
LGBT-specific/-targeted services	6
Hate speech/crime legislation	5
Training/development on LGBT friendliness	5
Education and schools	4
Monitoring numbers of LGBT people	4
Strategy or policy to improve LGBT friendliness	4
Gender recognition	4
Societal acceptance/tolerance	3
Religion	3
Housing/accommodation	3
Supporting LGBT groups, organizations, charities or communities	3
LGBT people in the military	2
LGBT-owned/-friendly businesses or organizations	2
Non-LGBT people working for LGBT friendliness	2
HIV	2
Asylum	2
Conversion therapy	1

non-normative and/or non-recognized lives. An engagement with these complexities and contexts require us to understand that liveability may not automatically follow juridico-political reforms, but is deeply embedded in individual and collective navigations of everyday realities that may or may not be tied to the absence or presence of formal legal rights. Further, marginalizations continue to exist in places with legal protections (see Browne and Bakshi 2013) or are perpetuated in new forms of marginalization and exclusion through what we know as "homonormativity" (see for example Bryant 2008; Duggan 2002; Richardson 2004; 2005).

We are therefore not seeking the development of standardized measures, as such measures tend to do the following: (a) assume that sexual and gender identities and practices and related discriminations can be captured in the term "lesbian, gay, bisexual and trans/gender" that are globally applicable; (b) assume LGBTQ persons to be a uniform mass who are recipients of aid and share a single point agenda (Browne et al. 2015). This can be at the expense of multifarious lived experiences around the everyday politics of living to frame issues around sexuality politics.[12] Cartographic representations and reports by organizations such the ILGA[13] and Pew Research Center on "homophobia" and "global divide on homosexuality"[14] construct place-based imaginaries about freedom and rights for LGBTQ people, implicitly rank ordering nations as "backward" and "forward". The maps and reports may not explicitly espouse hierarchizing places on the basis of the presence or absence of legal provisions and social attitudes. But as Rao (2014) argues, they mobilize shame to "motivate states to improve their laws … by applauding those who move in the direction of progress and shaming those who do not" (170). Reminiscent of colonial tropes between the civilized and the savage, these artifacts are thus neo-Orientalist in nature (ibid.). Apart from the obvious problematic assumptions surrounding "backwardness" and "progress" that undergird these artifacts, we also argue that they render unintelligible the ways in which sexuality rights activists deploy "freedom" and "rights" to complicate relations with the state and social institutions. For instance, while "freedom" and "rights" involve an understanding of progress based on state-based recognition, they are also used to generate strategic critiques about marriage, kinship and family.

Liveabilities

Instead of standardized measures and global rankings that solely focus on legislation and its suggested causal relation to liveability, here we make a call to use a lens of liveability – unhinged from a causal frame – to engage with the lived experiences around the everyday politics and practices of living that goes beyond juridico-political understandings of LGBTQ freedom and human rights and associated development of nation states. This seeks to highlight the presence of resources other than juridico-political ones that will enable a more constructive navigation of everyday places in both state-sponsored "homophobic" and "non-homophobic" contexts (Browne et al. 2015).

Drawing from Judith Butler's work, we argue that a liveability lens could be a significant step toward moving beyond the hierarchies in development discourses, by addressing two questions. What makes life bearable, worth living? And, what makes certain lives bearable, what standards make or ought to make life worth living for some "abject" lives? Asking the question, what makes life liveable, is asking what norms and conditions need to be fulfilled for life to become life or life that is worth living. Talking of norms and conventions that can both facilitate and restrict lives, Butler writes, "What is most important is to cease legislating for all lives what is livable only for some, and similarly, to refrain from proscribing for all lives what is unlivable for some" (2004, 8). Butler argues that liveability is intimately linked to stability of recognition through identity categories but she also writes that inflexibility of such naming categories impose constraints on life itself and make it unliveable. The criteria that are used to grant the status of human to one individual may deprive another individual of that same status. Butler (2009) contends that not all lives are considered "a life"; before we can consider what it is to achieve a good life, one must first be recognized as having a life.

In other words, Butler's notion of livable life deals with figuring out ways to survive and persist, what she describes as "to become possible" (2009, 31). The "good life" then is what is available and/or granted only to people whose lives are already possible, recognizable and necessarily exclusive of those whose lives do not count (2009, 205). For a life to become a life, Butler asks us to consider "what humans require in order to maintain and reproduce the conditions of their own livability" (2004, 39). What humans require can be understood in two senses: one that indicates the bare minimum condition of biological and physiological processes of breathing and living, and another that indicates the optimal conditions required by humans to maintain and reproduce life favorably. We are interested in the latter. In our research study, we use the lens of liveability to understand the conditions and resources through which LGBTQ persons are making liveable lives across state-sponsored homophobic and non-homophobic contexts. We use this as one way of addressing the forward/backward binary in international development discourses.

In exploring what makes life liveable for LGBTQ persons we identified plural shades within the narratives around liveable lives in our larger research project on this topic. Liveable lives are not something that can be measured. There were multiple liveabilities – that were difficult to articulate and not necessarily shared by other people. It is beyond the scope of this chapter to discuss the plural, non-standardized understanding of liveability that runs through and connects the narratives in the research study. Instead, the presence of legal recognition is currently central to definitions of sexual justice within development agendas, and we need to move beyond legislation as a means of hierarchizing nations in order to address the violence of the hierarchizing discourses and practices of development related to sexuality in general and the lives of LGBTQ persons in particular.

Along with/moving beyond legislative securities, activists and academics are calling for the need to create and consolidate individual and collective social systems that will enable and facilitate queer loves and life-worlds. Yet, it is important to note that there is a danger in underplaying the place of the law and legislation in what is desired. Throughout the research in India, legislative change arose as something that was desired, necessary and advocated for. Legislation cannot be equated with liveability, but nor can it be ignored; it may make life survivable for some. Thus, the complex interplays of legislation and liveabilities need further exploration in ways that continue to question the homonormativities and hierarchies that are attributed to legislative change and its links to development and national progress.

Conclusion: place-based understanding of liveability

A certain kind of global queer subject is in the making, within a world that is already underscored by the global circulation of human rights through "powerful technologies of knowledge production" (Grewal 2005, 122). We continue to inhabit a world where neoliberal states keep on problematically including and mainstreaming gender in development work. We know by now that this has depoliticized much of the achievements in women's rights and feminist mobilizations. In a similar way, queer rights and mobilizations can also be depoliticized as they become part of homonationalist frames that range from linking development aid to existence of legal rights to LGBTQ organizations either supporting or failing to critique actions of right-wing states. We argue that one way to address this conundrum is to work through place-based realities and understandings of liveability – that has the potential to connect development narratives to lived experiences and ideas on the ground.

A place-based understanding of liveability can help us to connect across geopolitical borders and confront the consolidation of hierarchizing development discourses around LGBTQ rights. The multiple nuances around liveabilities across our geographical and cultural contexts can help us to dislocate the forward/backward binaries of sexuality rights within homonationalist and heteronationalist frames of governance that are in turn tied to development agendas. Plural understandings of liveability can be deployed to interrupt and/or destabilize the opposition between progress/backwardness. We thus refuse to see some places as uniformly "backwards" and others as "progressive" (see Kulpa and Mizielinska 2011; Long 2016) based on the presence or absence of legal rights. Rather, our take on liveability/ies has the potential to crack open narrow class, gender, race, caste and national standards that inform development discourses, by drawing attention to transnational concerns and processes that define the lives of LGBTQ people. There are counter-discourses to the totalizing and cultural narratives around progress and backwardness of nation states and LGBTQ persons that need further examinations and development. We do not use liveability as a universal lens; rather we are using it to avoid universalizing narratives.

We hope that this will allow us to create a more critical view of "necessary development" on the ground in ways that are sensitive to the desire for legal recognition, but are not wedded or indebted to it. Scholarship and activisms around queer politics are serving to depathologize sexuality and gender, pushing us to think beyond procreation toward normative reform and its strategic implications. Resignifying heteronationalisms in the international development industry cannot be thought of in terms of a revolutionary process but as a constant effort to chip away naturalizing discourses which attempt to regulate and discipline subjects that stray from normative scripts. Simply adding LGBTQ persons will not shift the existing configurations of power, as that too can provide a new rationale to both hetero and homonationalisms. Sexuality works to serve normative development efforts and governmentality and hence a more critical engagement around normativity, pleasure, desire and rights of LGBTQ persons are needed. Lastly, it is important to recognize that the development industry is not a monolith, and we need to recognize and bring into discourse work and activisms that are already challenging normative assumptions within development work and reclaiming development practices differently.

Acknowledgements

We wish to acknowledge Leela Bakshi, Sumita, Ranjita Biswas, Nick McGlynn, Rukmini Banerjee and all our participants in the UK and in India, including members of Sappho for Equality, for the intellectual and emotional possibilities that this transnational collaboration has opened up.

Notes

1 The development industry treats sexuality solely as a matter for the health sector, incorporating it around programs such as fertility control, and sex education that works to lower risks of pregnancy and prevent disease (see for example, Correa 2002; Klugman 2000; Adams and Pigg 2005).

2 For more on the moral underpinnings of development and sexuality see Adam and Pigg (2005).
3 We deploy Butler's concept of livability (2004; 2009) to frame our analysis. In our larger research project, "Making Liveable Lives: Rethinking Social Exclusion" (https://liveablelives.org), we use Butler's concept to think about the varied and complex conditions through which LGBTQ persons make their liveable lives across state-sponsored homophobic and non-homophobic contexts.
4 We use "neoliberal governmentality" to underscore the various ways in which states and state agencies govern the self and others in contemporary neoliberalisms, of which legal reform is a part. For further reading on governmentality see for example, Foucault (1991).
5 https://liveablelives.org, supported by the ESRC grant number ES/M000931/1.
6 http://www.sapphokolkata.in
7 As anthropologies of states have demonstrated, the state is complex, moving between care and violence (see for example, Sharma and Gupta 2006). Hence activists and queer feminists have always had a contradictory relationship with the state, critiquing it for its exclusions, while at the same time, approaching it as an arbitrator of justice.
8 In India, Section 377 of the Indian Penal Code (IPC 377) criminalizes "carnal intercourse against the order of nature". IPC 377 has its origins in an 1860 British colonial law. The Delhi High Court read down the code in the *Naz Foundation* v. *Government of NCT of Delhi* case on 2 July 2009 – thereby decriminalizing same-sex sexual acts, but the Supreme Court reinstated it in December 2013. One of the most perceivable shifts since 11 December 2013 has been the inclusion of transgender persons within the larger discourse of democracy. On 14 April 2014 the Supreme Court of India passed a verdict, more popularly known as the National Legal Services Authority (NALSA) verdict, that sought to recognize transgender people as socially backward and marginalized thereby requiring special protective measures and anti-discriminatory policies to ensure their well-being. The judgment also acknowledged the right of any person to self-identify as any gender of one's choice.
9 See Kulpa and Mizielińska (2011) for a discussion of West/East Europe in relation to these geo-temporalities.
10 While Narayan (1997) uses this in the context of trying to do a transnational feminist analysis of dowry deaths in India and domestic violence in the United States, we can extend this concept to understand how those in places with legislation understand sexual lives in places without legislation.
11 Stonewall, a UK-based LGBT charity, ranks companies and organizations on the basis of their LGB (and more recently T) friendliness. Companies pay to enter this index, complete a form and are then ranked according to set criteria. Paying for Stonewall/LGBT training is one way of improving the company's ranking. There are events associated with these ranking and global companies often top the rankings. Public sector services and universities also enter the Stonewall Index and tend to compare themselves with similar institutions, although all are ranked on the same table by Stonewall. Being in the top 100 is seen as prestigious.
12 A focus on lived experiences will also reveal the presence of resources other than juridico-political ones to constructively navigate everyday places in both state-sponsored homophobic and non-homophobic contexts.
13 See http://old.ilga.org/Statehomophobia/ILGA_SSHR_2014_Eng.pdf for ILGA's report on state sponsored homophobia.
14 See http://www.pewglobal.org/2013/06/04/the-global-divide-on-homosexuality/ for the global divide on homosexuality.

References

Adams, V. and Pigg, S. L. 2005. *Sex in development: Science, sexuality, and morality in global perspective*. Durham, NC: Duke University Press.
Ahmed, S. 2010. *The promise of happiness*. Durham, NC: Duke University Press.
Badgett, M. V. 2014. *The economic cost of stigma and the exclusion of LGBT people: A case study of India*. Washington DC: The World Bank.
Browne, K. and Bakshi, L. 2013. *Ordinary in Brighton? LGBT, activisms and the city*. Aldershot: Ashgate.
Browne, K., Banerjea, N., Bakshi, L. and McGlynn, N. 2015. "Intervention – 'Gay-Friendly or Homophobic? The Absence and Problems of Global Standards.'" Antipode. https://antipodefoundation.org/2015/05/11/gay-friendly-or-homophobic/

Browne, K., Banerjea, N., McGlynn, N., Banerjee, R., Sumita, Biswas, R. and Bakshi, L. 2017. "Toward transnational feminist queer methodologies." *Gender, Place and Culture.* http://www. tandfonline.com/doi/full/10.1080/0966369X.2017.1372374

Bryant, K. 2008. "In defense of gay children? 'Progay' homophobia and the production of homonormativity." *Sexualities* 11, no. 4: 455–475.

Butler, J. 2004. *Undoing gender.* New York and London: Routledge.

Butler, J. 2009 *Frames of war: When is life grievable?* London and New York: Verso.

Correa, S. 2002. "Sexual rights: Much has been said, much remains to be resolved." Sexuality, Health and Gender Seminar, Department of Social Sciences, Public Health School, Columbia University. http://docs.bridge.ids.ac.uk/vfile/upload/1/document/0708/DOC19699.pdf

Cornwall, A. and Jolly, S. 2006. "Introduction: Sexuality matters." *IDS Bulletin* 37, no. 5: 1–11.

Devika, J. 2009. "Bodies gone awry: The abjection of sexuality in development discourse in contemporary Kerala." *Indian Journal of Gender Studies* 16, no. 1: 21–46.

Duggan, L. 2002. "The new homonormativity: The sexual politics of neoliberalism." In *Materializing democracy: toward a revitalized cultural politics,* edited by R. Castronovo and D. Nelson, pp. 175–194. Durham, NC: Duke University Press.

European Parliament Intergroup on LGBT Rights. 2014. "European Parliament votes for UN development strategy to include LGBTI rights." http://www.lgbt-ep.eu/press- releases/european-parliament-votes-for-development-strategy-to-include-lgbti-rights/

Foucault, M. 1980. *The history of sexuality, volume one: An introduction.* New York: Vintage Books.

Foucault, M. 1991. "Governmentality." In *The Foucault effect: Studies in governmentality,* edited by G. Burchell, C. Gordon and P. Miller, pp. 87–104. Hemel Hempstead: Harvester Wheatsheaf.

Gosine, A. 2005. *Sex for pleasure, rights to participation, and alternatives to AIDS: Placing sexual minorities and/or dissidents in development.* IDS working paper 228. https://www.ids.ac.uk/files/Wp228.pdf

Gosine, A. 2009. "Monster, womb, MSM: The work of sex in international development." *Development* 52, no. 1: 25–33.

Grewal, I. 2005. *Transnational America: Feminisms, diasporas, neoliberalisms.* Durham, NC: Duke University Press.

Klugman, B. 2000. "Sexual rights in Southern Africa: A Beijing discourse or a strategic necessity?" *Health and Human Rights* 4, no. 2: 132–159.

Kulpa, R. and Mizielińska, J. 2011. "'Contemporary peripheries': Queer studies, circulation of knowledge and East/West divide." In *De-centering Western sexualities: Central and Eastern European perspectives,* edited by R. Kulpa and J. Mizielinska, pp. 11–26. London: Routledge.

Lind, A. 2009. "Governing intimacy, struggling for sexual rights: Challenging heteronormativity in the global development industry." *Development* 52, no. 1: 34–42.

Long, S. 2016. "Selling out: The gays and governmentality." A paper bird blog. https://paper-bird. net/2016/11/02/selling-out-the-gays-and-governmentality/

Milward, K., Mukhopadhyay, M. and Wong, F. F. 2015. "Gender mainstreaming critiques: Signposts or dead ends?" *IDS Bulletin* 46: 75–81.

Moser, C. 2005 "Has gender mainstreaming failed? A comment on international development agency experiences in the South." *International Feminist Journal of Politics* 7, no. 4: 576–590.

Narayan, U. 1997. *Dislocating cultures: Identities, traditions, and third world feminism.* London and New York: Routledge.

Plaut, M. 2014. "Uganda donors cut aid after president passes anti-gay law." *The Guardian.* 25 Februarty.http://www.theguardian.com/global-development/2014/feb/25/uganda-donors-cut-aid-anti-gay-law

Puar, J. 2007. *Terrorist assemblages: Homonationalism in queer times.* Durham, NC: Duke University Press.

Puri, J. 2016. *Sexual states: Governance and the struggle over the antisodomy law in India.* Durham, NC: Duke University Press.

Richardson, D. 2004. "Locating sexualities: From here to normality." *Sexualities* 7, no. 4: 391–411.

Richardson, D. 2005. "Desiring sameness? The rise of a neoliberal politics of normalisation." *Antipode* 37, no. 3: 515–535.

Rao, R. 2014. "The locations of homophobia." *London Review of International Law* 2, no. 2: 169–199.

Sappho for Equality. (n.d.) "Sappho for equality" http://www.sapphokolkata.in

Scott, J. W. 1992. "Experience." In *Feminists Theorize the Political,* edited by J. Butler and J. Scott, pp. 22–40. London and New York: Routledge.

Shah, S. 2012. "Sex workers' rights and women's movements in India: A very brief genealogy." In *New South Asian Feminisms*, edited by S. Roy, pp. 27–43. London and New York: Zed Books.

Shah, S. 2014. *Street corner secrets: Sex, work, and migration in the city of Mumbai*. New Delhi: Orient Longman.

Sharma, A. and Gupta, A. (eds) 2006. *The anthropology of the state: A reader*. Malden, MA: Blackwell.

Tyson, J. 2014. "The World Bank's uneasy relationship with LGBTI rights." devex.com https://www.devex.com/news/the-world-bank-s-uneasy-relationship-with-lgbti-rights-84896

11

THE GROWING CHASM

International polarization
around queer rights

Dennis Altman and Jonathan Symons

As we were finalising this chapter in June 2017, Germany became the twentieth country to legalize same-sex marriage. Only a few months earlier shocking images appeared across global media of the persecution of homosexual men in Chechnya. Beatings, electroshock torture, mass arrests and some murders were widely reported. A spokesperson for the Chechnyan leader explained "If such people existed in Chechnya, law enforcement would not have to worry about them, as their own relatives would have sent them to where they could never return" (Kramer 2017). Although Chechnya is part of Russia, promises of an inquiry by the Russian government have had little impact (Gessen 2017, 22–28).

Reports from Chechnya followed widespread reporting of horrific images of a Soweto lesbian, Lerato Tambai Moloi, who was beaten to death in what appears to have been an incidence of 'corrective rape.' The following month saw pictures of two men publicly flogged in Aceh, Indonesia, for homosexual relations. These images underline the reality that expansion of sexual freedom in some places is mirrored by increasing repression in others. Social, legal and intellectual changes with their roots in the 1960s have led some judicial bodies, and later some governments, to argue that discrimination based on 'sexual orientation and gender identity' (SOGI) is a violation of universal human rights. The most influential statement of this position is the 2006 'Yogyakarta Principles on the Application of International Human Rights Law in relation to Sexual Orientation and Gender Identity' (Alston et al. 2007). Conversely, states opposed to any recognition of queer rights argue that human rights are only valid if they are grounded in the universal 'traditional values of humankind' – from the perspective of traditional morality, homosexuality is a social vice and sin which may be legitimately criminalized.

Whereas several decades ago sexuality went unmentioned in global institutions, today sexual rights are the subject of heated international debate. The reports from Chechnya led to calls for an 'end to the persecution of people perceived to be gay or bisexual in the Chechen Republic who are living in a climate of fear fueled by homophobic speeches by local authorities' by United Nations (UN) Human Rights Council appointed Independent Experts (OHCHR 2017). Chancellor Angela Merkel and President Emmanuel Macron raised the issue in discussions with President Putin.

In June 2017, Vitit Muntarbhorn, the Human Rights Council's Independent Expert on "protection against violence and discrimination based on sexual orientation and gender identity," presented his initial report (Human Rights Council 2017), which found that: "Violations are pervasive in numerous settings. Killings, rape, mutilation, torture, cruel, inhuman and degrading treatment, lashings, abductions, arbitrary detention, harassment, physical and mental assaults, bullying from a young age, pressures leading to suicide." (Muntarbhorn was a co-chair of the meeting that drafted the Yogyakarta Principles.) To date there has been little response to this report.

The position of Independent Expert was created in 2016 as the culmination of a long and contested process in the Human Rights Council. Even after the position had been created, some countries fought a rearguard action for the UN General Assembly's Third Committee to permanently defer its creation, a vote which lost by seven votes. The narrowness of the vote illustrates the current global polarization around sexual rights among states, which we address in *Queer Wars* (Altman and Symons 2016), though we recognize the limits of the concept of polarization to describe the full complexity of transnational politics surrounding sexual orientation and gender identity (e.g. Snyder 2014).

Just as governments' international posturing doesn't always reflect their domestic practices, there is often a gap between the polarized debates in human rights bodies, and the practical work of some UN agencies. Likewise, while laws governing homosexuality are important, in many cases they do not reflect the reality of gay experience. Today, homosexual acts are lawful in Russia, but illegal in Singapore, yet Singapore is home to a flourishing gay scene and political movement that – unlike in Russia – is largely free from official or unofficial harassment. Yet while international human rights debates and legal trends do not determine the dynamics of persecution and acceptance that affect the lives of ordinary people, neither are they wholly disconnected. Discussions and resolutions in international bodies have repercussions for sexual freedoms on the ground, even if the interconnections between national politics and global trends are often complex.

Rival norms

Some international relations scholars have explained previous changes in international attitudes and values by depicting the 'life-cycle' of international norms as a product of social dynamics within international politics (Finnemore and Sikkink 1998). Countries use norms to establish hierarchies and to signal group membership (as liberal democracies, Slavic etc.). Governments' desire to maintain their esteem and legitimacy in international society means that their norms will tend to shift in patterns that resemble fashions sweeping through a schoolyard. A trend such as women's voting was at first adopted by only a few countries in the late nineteenth century, but once a group of influential countries accepted female enfranchisement, a 'tipping point' was reached, after which the norm cascaded through international society with increasingly less resistance. Today, there are only a very few nations (such as Saudi Arabia) that have not accepted the norm of female enfranchisement.

Unfortunately, knowledge that some norms 'cascade' internationally doesn't guarantee that human rights protection for SOGI will eventually be accepted everywhere. It is equally possible that sexuality may be an issue that continues to divide the international community for many decades into the future. Indeed, international polarization over whaling may be a closer analogy than female enfranchisement. When the International Whaling Commission imposed a 'moratorium' on commercial whaling in 1986 it seemed that a new norm of whale 'preservation' would cascade through the international community. However, the backlash against this US-sponsored norm has proved long-lasting. Japan and Norway, among others, have come to demand that scientific resource-management, not preservation, must govern whaling and have stacked the International Whaling Commission with allies to ensure that 'scientific whaling' can continue. For some Japanese, whaling has taken on a symbolic significance as an expression of Japanese national identity and resistance to Western domination. In many parts of the world repression of homosexuals may be acquiring a similar symbolism as an expression of national identity and defiance (see Symons and Altman 2015).

In an earlier paper, we described 'international norm polarization' as a 'process wherein a candidate norm is accepted by some states but is resisted by others leading to a period of international disputation between two groups in each of which socializing pressures pull states toward compliance with rival norms' (Symons and Altman 2015). Whereas some countries continue to assert a 'traditional' norm that views homosexuality as undesirable and a legitimate target of criminal or social sanctions, others have embraced a newer norm suggesting *that sexual orientation and gender identity should be subjects of human rights protection*. This new norm primarily prohibits criminalization of homosexuality; however, it is associated with a variety of other legal protections (non-discrimination, legal recognition of same-sex partnerships and marriage) that are less widely accepted and thus are not subjects of international polarization. We argue that two opposing, but overlapping, networks of states and civil society actors have coalesced around these rival norms and that they are creating opposing socializing pressures. The complex transnational politics involved are illustrated by states, like the US, where the two coalitions contend within domestic politics, and by states that have adjusted their domestic laws in ways that reflect both world and society trends. For example, while homosexual sex continues to be punishable with up to seven years jail in Botswana, in 2010 the national parliament adopted laws that prohibited discrimination in employment.

Recognizing how state regulation of sexuality is influenced by international trends might help to explain emerging patterns in domestic politics. There appears to be a widespread international adoption of what Tom Boellstorff, writing of Indonesia in the early 2000s, defined as 'political homophobia': 'an emergent cultural logic linking emotion, sexuality and political violence … making enraged violence against *gay* men [his italics] intelligible and socially efficacious' (Boellstorff 2007, 165). The stress on *political* or collective homophobia is important, as the term itself was coined to describe an individual fear of homosexuality, which is not necessarily involved in all cases of persecution (Weinberg 1972).

Regional politics

There are clear patterns in the formal responses of governments to questions of sexuality that align with international, regional and religious groupings. The majority of countries that retain criminal sanctions against homosexual behavior are either [or both] members of the Commonwealth or the Organization of Islamic Cooperation (OIC). While the Commonwealth is a loose organization of some fifty-five countries, almost all of them former British colonies, it has no means of enforcing norms other than through control of its membership, a move which began with the expulsion of South Africa in 1961 for its apartheid policies, and more recent expulsions of several countries for their lack of democracy.

The Commonwealth Charter claims that its members are united in support of democracy, human rights and the rule of law, and in recent years there have been demands for recognizing sexuality as included within the human rights penumbra. An Eminent Persons Group, established in 2011, recommended that existing criminal sanctions against homosexuality should be removed, in part because of their impact on effective HIV prevention. But while a meeting of Commonwealth foreign ministers adopted the recommendation for a human rights charter in 2012, Commonwealth member countries have been amongst those most active in increasing legal penalties against homosexuality in the past few years. It seems very unlikely that the Commonwealth will be a major avenue for pursuing sexual rights in the foreseeable future.

Another regional approach has responded to international debates about human rights and gender identity in a more distinctive way. In 2009 Pakistan's highest court recognized the status of a third gender, commonly referred to as 'hijra' or by the umbrella term *khawajasiras*. This traditional accommodation of gender non-conformity may be viewed as an indirect response to international legal debates over 'sexual orientation and gender identity' – the court accepted protection of gender identity that reflected local traditions, but has not accepted the case for decriminalization of homosexual acts (Dickson and Sanders 2014). In 2014 the Indian Supreme Court reached a similar decision when it extended legal recognition to transgender people, and referred to a raft of international precedents – including the Yogyakarta Principles and the Pakistani case – in reaching this decision. A distinct regional norm seems to have emerged in South Asia, with legal recognition of a 'third gender' category in Pakistan, Nepal, Bangladesh and India.

Meanwhile, most of 'Confucian' Asia has remained largely uninvolved in the international dispute over gay rights. While some governments, such as China, typically vote in opposition to sexuality rights internationally, there has been no obvious move toward increased domestic repression of sexual minorities or efforts to exploit the issue for political gain. Other states, such as Vietnam, have indicated partial acceptance of same-sex identities, but have not promoted this norm internationally, which is consistent with their opposition to any interference in the 'internal affairs' of other countries.

Over the past few years Russia under President Putin has emerged as a powerful leader in anti-homosexual rhetoric, both domestically and internationally. While homophobic public rhetoric is common and has been used to solidify links between Putin's regime and the Russian Orthodox Church, homosexual sex has been decriminalized since 1993. However, a more recent agreement between Putin and the Russian Orthodox Church gives the Church a particular role in reviewing possible legislation, and the Church has played an official role in promoting social conservatism.

Russia's homophobic rhetoric is part of a sophisticated international public diplomacy campaign, which seeks to narrow the validity of human rights to those that are consistent with 'universal traditional values.' Through this explicit rejection of sexuality rights, Putin has sought to form international alliances with those who critique secular human rights from religious or collectivist traditions and to encourage allies to use the issue of sexual rights to distinguish themselves from the West. In a 2013 speech Putin argued:

> Today, many nations are revising their moral values and ethical norms, eroding ethnic traditions and differences between peoples and cultures. Society is now required not only to recognise everyone's right to the freedom of consciousness, political views and privacy, but also to accept without question the equality of good and evil ... We know that there are more and more people in the world who support our position on defending traditional values that have made up the spiritual and moral foundation of civilization in every nation for thousands of years: the values of traditional families, real human life, including religious life, not just material existence but also spirituality, the values of humanism and global diversity.
>
> *(Putin 2013)*

Putin's allies have used a 'civilizational critique' of human rights to marginalize domestic liberal opponents, to consolidate the Orthodox Church's support for the Kremlin, to blunt the domestic impact of Western critiques of Putin's human rights record, and as an instrument of Russian soft power internationally (Horvath 2016). Allying with both Islamic and Christian opponents of gay rights adds to Russia's credibility in many parts of the world, and helps to define it as representing an alternative to Western values. Meanwhile, pro-Russian forces within Ukraine frequently link the European Union to the promotion of gay rights, claiming accession to the Union would require recognizing same-sex marriage.

Polarization in international human rights bodies

When new norms are proposed internationally, some states will typically defend the status quo by clarifying and formalizing their opposition. When the international community began to condemn apartheid in 1946, the South African government asserted the principle of non-interference in internal affairs and adopted laws that codified racial discrimination (Klotz 1999, 41–44). While battles over apartheid continued for several decades, the new norm of racial equality ultimately won widespread international acceptance. Female enfranchisement and prohibition of slavery are other examples of norms that have been adopted globally after initial resistance, even if they continue to be violated in practice – as in the tolerance for slavery in Mauritania. Despite these hopeful precedents, global acceptance of gay rights is not similarly inevitable – ongoing polarization is also a possible outcome. Discussion of sexuality is complicated by claims that national identity and traditions are being compromised by cultural imperialism.

Once some countries and human rights bodies accepted that human rights protect sexual minorities, it was inevitable that other countries would disagree, but it was not inevitable that the debate should become as polarized as it now appears. The dispute over whether human rights protection should cover "sexual orientation and gender identity" has become so fractious that it has created an opportunity for Russia and the OIC to undermine the wider concept of secular human rights and has begun to frustrate the work of some UN bodies. In 2010 the UN General Assembly rejected an otherwise innocuous report from the Special Rapporteur on Education because it supported access to 'comprehensive sexual education' – conservative governments worried such education might normalize sexual diversity. When the United Nations Postal Authority issued a series of stamps promoting the UN's "Free and Equal" campaign at the end of 2016, the African Group protested to the Secretary-General that this "contravened the United Nations' principles, as well as the culture, norms and beliefs of many Member States" (Deen 2017).

International disputation over homosexuality dates back several decades. In 1993 the International Lesbian and Gay Association (ILGA) was granted official consultative status with the United Nations Economic and Social Council (ECOSOC) (Sanders 1996). However, conservative US Senator Jesse Helms protested, claiming historical links between several of ILGA's member organizations and pedophile groups (while ILGA refused to admit pedophile groups, it was unable to guarantee that no member organization had continuing links). Helms persuaded the US Senate to make withdrawing ILGA's recognition a precondition for payment of the US's $118 million debt to the UN and its consultative status was suspended for several years. Nevertheless, lesbian, gay, bisexual and transgender (LGBT) organizations were officially accredited at both the 1993 World Conference on Human Rights and the 1995 Fourth World Conference on Women in Beijing and, in time, such representation has become commonplace.

In 1999, Asma Jahangir, the UN Special Rapporteur on extrajudicial executions submitted a report to the United Nations Commission on Human Rights (UNCHR) which argued that imposition of the death penalty for sexuality related offences breached the Covenant on Civil and Political Rights' guarantee of a "right to life." Jahangir called for universal decriminalization and drew attention to extrajudicial killings of homosexuals in Brazil, Colombia and Mexico (UNCHR 1999). The first response of the international community was to add specific reference to killings on the basis of "sexual orientation" to a regular resolution condemning extrajudicial killings. However, over the following decade while resolutions mentioning sexual orientation continued to pass, each vote was fiercely contested and the anti-gay camp gained strength. Finally, in November 2010, a motion sponsored by Benin deleted any reference to 'sexual orientation' from the resolution (International Service for Human Rights 2010).

In 2003, Brazil had introduced a broad draft resolution titled 'Human Rights and Sexual Orientation' to the UN Commission on Human Rights (the Commission was abolished and replaced by UN Human Rights Council in 2006). Strong resistance delayed an initial vote and Brazil eventually requested a permanent postponement. Discussion of the Brazilian resolution exposed deep divisions among governments and opposition from members of the OIC was particularly strong (Long 2005). Since the Bush Administration was also opposed (it planned to abstain rather than vote against), the Brazilian proposal was clearly untenable (Lau 2004). As long as the US sided with the conservatives, international debate over sexuality rights was contained. Despite significant international disagreement, there would be no serious challenge to the status quo while a tacit alliance existed between the world's only superpower and a network of conservative developing states.

Election of the Obama Administration shifted this balance. After the defeat of the resolution condemning extrajudicial killings on the basis of 'sexual orientation,' United States Ambassador Susan Rice sponsored an alternative resolution and the General Assembly reversed the earlier decision (93 to 55, 27 abstentions). The UN African Group and OIC are usually staunch opponents of sexual rights; however, in response to US pressure, the unity of the African Group was broken, and South Africa, Angola, Cape Verde and Rwanda were among the countries persuaded to vote for the resolution (International Service for Human Rights 2011).

Under Obama the US took an increasingly activist position on international gay rights, responding to growing interest and pressure from domestic organizations which make up a significant constituency for the Democratic Party. In 2015, the US appointed a "Special Envoy for the Human Rights of LGBT Persons," and disagreement with President Kenyatta over gay rights was a prominent theme in Obama's visit to Kenya in July 2015. US resourcing of SOGI-linked civil society groups has also been controversial – when the American Embassy in Pakistan hosted an event honoring 'gays and lesbians' in 2011 the Lahore High Court Association condemned this as a 'drone attack on culture and social life of the region' (Pakistan Voice 2011). This highlights the larger dilemma for activists and governments, who have to make hard choices about the consequences of drawing international attention to gross breaches of human rights which risk fostering a backlash against the very people they seek to defend.

In 2011, the US was instrumental in a resolution of the UN Human Rights Council commissioning the High Commissioner for Human Rights to prepare a report on 'discriminatory laws and practices … against individuals based on their sexual orientation and gender identity, and how international human rights law' could provide redress (UNHRC 2011, Resolution 17/19). Whereas the earlier Brazilian resolution suffered from a lack of coordination among supportive states and non-governmental organizations (NGOs), this new resolution was carefully planned. Voting (23 in favor, 19 against, 3 abstentions) again saw strong opposition from the OIC and African Group. However, in order to avoid the impression of Western neo-colonialism, South Africa was chosen to present the final text.

The newly energized State Department founded a US$3 million Global Equality Fund "to support programs that advance the human rights of lesbian, gay, bisexual and transgender (LGBT) persons around the world" (US State Department 2011) and backed a "LGBT Core Group" at the United Nations. The LGBT Core Group was a coalition of countries "committed to eliminating violence and discrimination against individuals based on their sexual orientation and gender identity" and to recognizing that LGBT individuals should enjoy human rights protection.

Over the past few years supportive governments have increasingly raised the profile of sexual rights. Thus, a ministerial declaration from France, Italy and Belgium in 2013 deliberately linked these rights to the idea of a European identity: "We want to live in a European space in which individual freedoms are effectively protected, regardless of one's sexual orientation or gender identity" (Ayoub and Paternotte 2014); and groups like ILGA-Europe have consciously linked themselves to the European project. When Malta voted to accept same-sex civil unions and adoptions in 2014 it boasted that this made them 'more liberal and more European.' UN Secretary-General Ban Ki Moon began to assert the need for universal recognition of sexual rights and, in 2013, the UN Human Rights Office launched a "Free & Equal" campaign. Gay rights are simultaneously being promoted in unprecedented ways and being assimilated into the legitimating narratives of global power structures.

The election of Donald Trump aroused widespread concern that the US would reverse its support for SOGI rights. The record to date is ambiguous. While the Trump Administration has consistently de-emphasized human rights as central to its foreign policy objectives, it has not specifically retreated from support for LGBT rights. Trump reappointed the US's Special Envoy, and the US representative at the Human Rights Council endorsed the work of the Independent Expert, Vitit Muntarbhorn. However, the huge cuts in international development funding, and the 'gag rule' withholding funding from any organization that can be seen as "promoting abortion" will affect programs supported by the US.

International development assistance

Beginning with tentative steps by Sweden and the Netherlands, donor governments over the past decade have sought to find ways to encourage groups working around sexual and gender diversity, often through programs for HIV prevention. (The Australian government funded a few such groups in the late 1980s, and helped to contribute to the emergence of gay networks in Southeast Asia.) The first few years of this century saw a strong emphasis on international efforts to combat the spread of HIV and AIDS, and to roll out effective treatments. AIDS was specifically named, along with malaria and tuberculosis, as a focus of the Millennium Development Goals, and while services directed at marginalized groups such as trans and men who have sex with men remain under-resourced, the emphasis on HIV and AIDS created new opportunities for both activists and sympathetic donors to increase attention on issues of sexuality.

While much of the focus of gay advocacy has been on resolutions by the Human Rights Council and other parts of the UN system, there has been increasing programmatic activity by some of the UN agencies around sexual rights. The creation of the United Nations Programme on HIV/AIDS (UNAIDS) in 1996 to coordinate the work of all UN agencies around HIV emphasized the link between health and human rights, and gave many LGBT groups access to decision making. At the same time, various parts of the UN system have taken up issues of sexual orientation and gender identity, with the support of the Secretary-General. Regional offices of the United Nations Educational, Scientific and Cultural Organization (UNESCO) have conducted workshops on homophobia, and the United Nations International Children's Emergency Fund (UNICEF) has committed itself to "Eliminating discrimination against children and parents based on sexual orientation and/ or gender identity" (UNICEF 2015), a position that was strongly condemned by some religious groups. At country level, often under pressure from determined staffers, many of the UN agencies have been able to provide resources and support to emerging queer groups, which in turn creates a constituency to continue this work. Perhaps most significantly the World Bank has pressured loan recipients to halt discrimination against people based on their sexuality and gender identity.

As donor governments pledged considerable funds to combatting HIV, assistance came with conditions not always acceptable to recipient countries. The clearest case was George W. Bush's very ambitious President's Emergency Plan for AIDS Relief (PEPFAR) which funded both treatment and prevention programs. However, the funding was conditional on accepting certain principles, especially a refusal to support groups working with sex workers, which led Brazil to refuse PEPFAR funding. The Bush Administration also lined up with conservative governments in refusing to name 'men who have sex with men' as particularly vulnerable to HIV infection in various UN resolutions.

The Global Fund to Fight AIDS, Tuberculosis and Malaria was founded in 2002 as a partnership between governments, civil society, the private sector and people affected by the diseases, and has sought to link funding to governments demonstrating that they are willing to work effectively with marginalized populations most vulnerable to HIV, usually identified as men who have sex with men, injecting drug users and sex workers.

Donor nations, particularly the Western Europeans and US, have increasingly raised sexual rights generally, and LGBT issues specifically, as part of their general approach to international development (Bergenfield and Miller 2014). In 2010 the renegotiation of the Cotonou Agreement, which covers trade and political relations between the European Union and seventy-nine African, Caribbean and Pacific nations, became acrimonious when the European Parliament demanded that 'actions conducted under the terms of the various partnerships be pursued without any discrimination on grounds of gender … sexual orientation or against people living with HIV/AIDS' (European Parliament 2010). The African, Caribbean and Pacific Group of States unanimously rejected this threat and wrote a statement which demanded that the European Union 'refrain from any attempts to impose its values' concerning the 'phenomenon of homosexuality' (African, Caribbean and Pacific Group of States 2010). The next controversy erupted when UK Prime Minister David Cameron raised the possibility of withdrawing bilateral aid if African countries increased criminal penalties for homosexuality. Again, targeted governments were furious and the threat appeared to backfire; Malawian politicians at one point blamed LGBT activists for British aid cuts that were wholly unrelated to gay rights. Moreover, critics pointed out that Cameron's announcement was not followed by specific policy descriptions – suggesting that it might have been motivated by domestic political concerns (Kretz 2013, 488–489).

A group of African social justice activists responded: "An effective response to the violations of the rights of LBGTI people has to be more nuanced than the mere imposition of donor sanctions. The history of colonialism and sexuality cannot be overlooked when seeking solutions to this issue." Sanctions "sustain the divide between the LGBTI and the broader civil society movement," "disregard the agency of African civil society" and "are by their nature coercive and reinforce the disproportionate power dynamics between donor countries and recipients." The activists went on to call on the UK to abandon aid conditionality, to support "national and regional human rights mechanisms" and expand support for community based and led LGBTI programs (African Social Justice Activists 2011).

Since the Obama Administration became a powerful advocate, countries that support 'gay rights' have been able to pass resolutions in international fora, and have had some successes in using the various mechanisms of the UN system to pressure governments to remove some forms of legal discrimination. Whether this will remain the case with a new American Administration is yet uncertain. But even if there are rhetorical gains, the realities of global division persist. Opponents of SOGI rights continue to make similar claims – that liberal treatment of sexuality violates religious traditions, national values and will lead to family and social breakdown. Sexual minorities continue to be targets of violence and political scapegoating across much of the world. In many cases efforts to promote or impose 'gay rights' have seemed to play into the hands of oppressive governments. The reality of international polarization and the sensitivities about Western imperialism in those countries that have only recently escaped colonial domination raise real questions for activists – how best to promote human rights and liberation within a divided world.

Acknowledgements

This chapter is updated and adapted from Chapter 5, Altman, D. and Symons, J. (2016) *Queer Wars: The New Global Polarization over Gay Rights*. Cambridge: Polity.

References

African, Caribbean and Pacific Group of States. 2010. "Declaration of the 21st Session of the ACP Parliamentary Assembly on the Peaceful Co-Existence of Religions and the Importance given to the Phenomenon of Homosexuality in the ACP-EU Partnership." African, Caribbean and Pacific Group of States. October 20. http://www. lgbt-ep.eu/wp-content/uploads/2010/11/20100928-ACP-unilateraldeclaration-on-interreligious-peace-and-homosexuality.pdf.

African Social Justice Activists. 2011. "Statement of African Social Justice on the Threats of the British Government to 'Cut Aid' to African Countries That Violate the Rights of LGBTI People in Africa." https://globalequality.files.wordpress.com/2011/11/statement-of-african-social-justice-activists.pdf

Alston, P., Anmeghichean, M. and Cabral, M. 2007. "Yogyakarta Principles on the Application of International Human Rights Law in Relation to Sexual Orientation and Gender Identity." International Panel of Experts in International Human Rights Law and on Sexual Orientation and Gender Identity. http://www.yogyakartaprinciples.org/

Altman, D. and Symons, J. 2016. *Queer Wars: The New Global Polarization over Gay Rights*. Cambridge: Polity.

Ayoub, P. and Paternotte, D. 2014. "Introduction." In *LGBT Activism and the Making of Europe: A Rainbow Europe?*, edited by Ayoub, P. and Paternotte, D., pp. 1–25. Basingstoke, UK: Palgrave Macmillan.

Bergenfield, R. and Miller, A. 2014. *Queering International Development? An Examination of New "LGBT Rights" Rhetoric, Policy, and Programming among International Development Agencies*. New Haven CT: Jackson Institute for Global Affairs.

Boellstorff, T. 2007. *A Coincidence of Desires: Anthropology, Queer Studies, Indonesia*. Durham, NC: Duke University Press.

Deen, T. 2017. "African Nations & Russia Protest UN Stamps on Gay, Lesbian Rights." IPS. July 3. http://www.ipsnews.net/2016/03/african-nations-russia-protest-un-stamps-on-gay-lesbian-rights/

Dickson, S. and Sanders, S. 2014. "India, Nepal, and Pakistan: A Unique South Asian Constitutional Discourse on Sexual Orientation and Gender Identity." In *Social Difference and Constitutionalism in Pan-Asia*, edited by Williams, S.H., pp. 316–348. Cambridge: Cambridge University Press.

European Parliament. 2010. "Resolution RC-B7-0693/2010." December 15. http://www.europarl.europa.eu/sides/getDoc.do?pubRef=-//EP//TEXT+TA+P7-TA-2010-0482+0+DOC+XML+V0//EN

Finnemore, M. and Sikkink, K. 1998. "International norm dynamics and political change." *International Organization*, 52, no. 4: 887–917.

Gessen, M 2007 "Forbidden Lives." *New Yorker* July 3, pp. 22–28.

Horvath, R. 2016. "The Reinvention of 'Traditional Values': Nataliya Narochnitskaya and Russia's Assault on Universal Human Rights." *Europe-Asia Studies* 68, no. 5: 862–892.

Human Rights Council. 2017. "Report of the Independent Expert on protection against violence and discrimination based on sexual orientation and gender identity." A/HRC/35/36. https://documents-dds-ny.un.org/doc/UNDOC/GEN/G17/095/53/PDF/G1709553.pdf?OpenElement

International Service for Human Rights. 2010. "GA Third Committee Deletes 'Sexual Orientation' from Resolution on Extrajudicial Executions." http://archive.today/4wUv

International Service for Human Rights. 2011. "GA Restores Sexual Orientation into EJEs Resolution, Adopts Key Texts on Death Penalty, Iran, DPRK." March 23. http://www.ishr.ch/general-assembly/983-gahttp://www.ishr.ch/general-assembly/983-ga-reintroduces-sexual-orientation-reference-into-ejes-resolution-adopts-key-texts-on-death-penaltyreintroduces-sexual-orientation-reference-into-ejes-resolution-adopts-key-texts-on-death-penalty

Klotz, A. 1999. *Norms in International Relations: The Struggle against Apartheid*. New York: Cornell University Press.

Kramer, A. 2017. "Chechen Authorities Arresting and Killing Gay Men, Russian Paper Says." *New York Times* April 1.

Kretz, A.J. 2013. "Aid Conditionality as (Partial) Answer to Antigay Legislation: An Analysis of British and American Foreign Aid Policies Designed to Protect Sexual Minorities." *Vienna Journal on International Constitutional Law* 7: 476–500.

Lau, H. 2004. "Sexual Orientation: Testing the Universality of International Human Rights Law." *University Chicago Law Review* 71, no. 4: 1689–1720.

Long, S. 2005. *Anatomy of a Backlash: Sexuality and the 'Cultural' War on Human Rights*. World Report. New York: Human Rights Watch, 15. http://hrw.org/wr2k5/anatomy/anatomy.pdf

OHCHR. 2017. "End Abuse and Detention of Gay Men in Chechnya, UN Human Rights Experts Tell Russia." Press Release, April 13. http://www.ohchr.org/EN/NewsEvents/Pages/DisplayNews.aspx?NewsID=21501

Pakistan Voice. 2011. "Controversy over US Support for LGBT in Pakistan Deepens." asiancorrespondent.com. July 15.

Putin, V. 2013. "Presidential Address to the Federal Assembly." http://eng.kremlin.ru/news/6402

Sanders, D. 1996. "Getting Lesbian and Gay Issues on the International Human Rights Agenda." *Human Rights Quarterly* 18, no. 1: 67–106.

Snyder, T. 2014. "Fascism, Russia and Ukraine." *New York Review of Books*, March 20.

Symons, J. and Altman, D. 2015. "International Norm Polarization: Sexuality as a Subject of Human Rights Protection." *International Theory* 7, no. 1: 61–95.

UNICEF, 2015. "Eliminating Discrimination against Children and Parent Based on Sexual Orientation and/or Gender Identity." https://www.unicef.org/videoaudio/PDFs/Current_Issues_Paper-_Sexual_Identification_Gender_Identity.pdf

United Nations Commission on Human Rights. 1999. "Extrajudicial, Summary or Arbitrary Executions, Report of the Special Rapporteur, Ms. Asma Jahangir." E/CN.4/1999/39CIVIL January 6.

US State Department. 2011. *Global Equality Fund*. http://archive.li/GcG6r

Weinberg, G. 1972. *Society and the Healthy Homosexual*. New York: St Martin's Press.

PART IV

Aiding queer mobilizations?

12

RESCUE, AND REAL LOVE

Same-sex desire in international development

Andil Gosine

Fifteen years ago, I found little room in international development to talk about sexual desire or diversity. In all of the undergraduate classes I attended at my Liberal Arts college in Canada, and in all the graduate courses I attended at the Institute of Development Studies (IDS) in the UK, and at all the talks and seminars I went to in other places up to that point, never did anyone stray from the characterization of Third World peoples as universally heterosexual. Never did any teacher or policymaker that I encountered seem aware that among development's "poor" might be some people not fully committed to heterosexual procreation. Instead, we were encouraged to think of the world's poor as masses of men and women whose reproductive choices were governed not by anyone's individual desires, but entirely a consequence of social, economic and cultural factors. Ten years ago, my supervisor at the World Bank, Agricultural Economist Hans Binswanger, did what many others in the field were doing at the time—seizing upon openings made available by fears about HIV and AIDS to incite broader conversations about sexual violence and sexual rights, particularly for people not uniquely engaged in heterosexual relationships. When Binswanger and I spoke at a forum on "Sexuality and Development" in 2006—a first inside the Bank—there was a great deal of concern about how many and who would come, and what kind of backlash might ensue (Gosine 2009). But when another such forum was staged this year, no such worries circulated. High-ranking officials from across all areas came, and the World Bank President himself was expected to join. It was rumored that Jim Yong Kim eventually cancelled his planned appearance due to some tensions within the Bank hierarchy about his decision to put a $90 million loan on hold to Uganda because of that country's parliament's recent passage of more punitive laws criminalizing homosexuality. Making his case in *The Washington Post*, Kim noted, "Institutionalized discrimination is bad for people and for societies. Widespread discrimination is also bad for economies. There is clear evidence that when societies enact laws that prevent productive people from fully participating in the workforce, economies suffer."

In fifteen years, we have moved from almost complete disavowal of homosexuality in international development[1] to the advocacy of sexual minority protection rights by the industry's[2] most powerful multilateral institution and champion of neoliberal capitalism. There is now a considerable body of work that documents and which itself has contributed to the growing attention to and normalization of same-sex desire in development [Adams and Pigg (2005), Bedford (2009), Cornwall, Correa and Jolly (2008), Cornwall and Jolly (2009), Gosine (2004, 2010a, 2010b), Lind (2010), Murray (2009), Oswin (2007)]. These studies reveal how anxieties about HIV and AIDS, as well as major sexual rights' victories in Western European and North American metropolises, challenged heteronormativity in development. For example, many development workers began to identify and organize themselves as queer subjects, with lesbian, gay, bisexual and transgender (LGBT) staff associations being established first at the World Bank, in 1993, and later at the International Monetary Fund and the United Nations (Gosine 2010a). Donors like the Swedish International Development Agency (Sida) also formally identified "sexuality" as a development funding priority, and in 2011 then Secretary of State Hillary Clinton established the Global Equality Fund to support programs that advance the human rights of LGBT persons around the world. Organizations like Human Rights Watch, Hivos and Amnesty International focused new attention on sexual rights' abuses in developing countries and new groups also emerged, like the Canada-based not-for-profit ARC International. The recent expressions of interest in the well-being of gays and lesbians by even representatives of the industry's more conservative players, like Kim, are also undoubtedly linked to victories by same-sex rights advocates, especially in the United States, and rising global awareness and reach of "gay" identity and culture.

The matter of recognition and rights for people engaged in same-sex relationships is far from settled. The journey of legal struggles over challenges to India's anti-sodomy legislation is telling of this volatile dynamic. A New Delhi High Court ruled the laws "unconstitutional" in July 2009, but in December 2013, India's Supreme Court overturned their ruling, leaving it to parliament to craft a new law; the 2014 victory of an unsympathetic, right-wing national government leaves human rights activists with little hope for such a change, but they are appealing the ruling through India's courts. The election of a socially conservative majority in Brazil's Congress in 2014 similarly threatens recently legislated protections afforded to sexual minorities and rights to same-sex marriage. In many other countries, severe discriminatory laws against people expressive of same-sex desire continue to exist, and many are punitively deployed. But it is also clear that within the development industry, there has been a dramatic turn in the last fifteen years, and over the last decade especially. How do we make sense of and what do we make of this massive shift? Should we view Kim's intervention, among others, as indication of on-going "progress" on sexuality rights? Do we celebrate the greater interest in the lives and well-being of people engaged in same-sex relationships by development organizations like Sida, the formation of sexuality-focused organizations like ARC International, and transnational interest by LGBT groups based in the North, in supporting rights of LGBT people in the South? In this paper, I suggest a more cautious and critical reading of the new-found enthusiasm to "rescue" LGBT people in Global South countries, and call for greater recognition of and respect for the complexly lived sexualities of "the World's poor." I lay out the fuller contexts in which imperatives to "rescue" LBGT people must be considered, and discuss some of their limitations and consequences. I also propose and explain my preference to speak about what I call "real love" rather than sex, in an attempt to both broaden and deepen comprehension of "desire" in development, and to restore and underline the humanity of development's primary subjects, the ones called "the poor."

Rescue

There is now considerable interest in and resources extended toward the rescue of non-heterosexual people from homophobia in Global South countries. State initiatives include

Sida's sexuality-themed program and the US Global Equality Fund, while support from multilateral institutions has come not just in the form of newspaper editorials, but also motions against violence based on sexual orientation, by the United Nations' General Assembly in 2011 and 2014, and the hiring of economist Lee Badgett by the World Bank to "cost" the impact of homophobia in India. International non-governmental organizations (NGOs) like Human Rights Watch, Hivos and Amnesty International pursue the cause of LGBT rights in many countries around the world, including Egypt, Kenya, Uganda, Indonesia, Gambia, Malaysia, South Africa and Brazil. As well, national LGBT organizations have become engaged in international development programs in the past decade, such as Sweden's RFSL (Riksförbundet för homosexuellas, bisexuellas och transpersoners rättigheter / Federation for Lesbian, Gay, Bisexual and Transgender Rights) and the Netherlands' COC (Cultuur en Ontspanningscentrum / "Center for Culture and Leisure"). What underlies the imperative of these groups to rescue, and what are the consequences of enacting "rescue" of LGBT people?

Surveys have recorded gradual shifts in public opinion over attitudes toward homosexual rights and gay marriage in many different parts of the world.[3] This shift has usually been attributed to the victorious efforts of LGBT advocates in winning support for their cause, and more often to the general progress of modernity. However, Jasbir Puar and Joseph Massad offer alternate and more complicated explanations for shifting views on particular sets' sexual rights. Puar (2007) is best known for her coining of the term "homonationalism" to characterize the process whereby some "queer" bodies are folded into the nation–state and achieve citizen-consumer membership through consumerism, economic mobility, and the securing of individual rights, such as gay marriage, at the expense of others, and of structural change that challenges institutional heteronormativity. Puar's framework pushes us to think about the gains and losses incurred in the identification and pursuit of certain kinds of sexual rights, especially same-sex marriage, and the context in which they occur. In *Terrorist Assemblages* (2007), she links rising support for same-sex marriage in the United States with its military response to 9/11 attacks at the World Trade Center and wars in Iraq and Afghanistan, and argues that queer bodies are being used to incite and support racialized violence. Massad makes a similar kind of claim in his critique of what he terms the "Gay International." He views the work of LGBT organizations engaged in North–South transnational advocacy an attempt to fulfill Western imperialism's unfinished tasks. In the Middle East, this Gay International lobby, Massad says, proposes that Arabic societies become educated to "catch up" to metropolitan Euro-American norms: "they must take on sexual identities, name themselves 'gay' and 'lesbian' (as conferred, for instance, by the 'Gay and Lesbian Arabic Society'), mimicking the more enlightened and civilized Occident" (2007, 173).

However well intentioned development efforts to support LGBT rights in the Global South may appear to be, and however welcome they are by some LGBT-identified people in host countries, they must be weighed against Puar's and Massad's critiques. For instance, while development interventions by North-based organizations are usually pitched as helping hands to the South, it is important to recognize that these interventions have tended to first serve the "helpers" themselves. LGBT activists from the Global North have made beautiful, and probably sincere, claims about their investments in rescue of same-sex desiring kin in the Global South. But this mission is hardly selfless. Consider the work of RFSL and COC, the two longest-existing LGBT organizations in the world. In a section entitled "Fighting for Acceptance All over the World," COC explains that:

Together, we fight for human rights for LGBT's [*sic*] all over the world and we counter those who oppose LGBT rights, groups that have become stronger and more organized over the last years. Although LGBT's [*sic*] in many countries suffer from discrimination and lack of equal rights, the situation in some parts of the world is extremely serious: pride manifestations are prohibited or violently attacked without police protection, prosecution, rape, murder, death penalties and other violations of basic human rights.

(COC 2014)

RFSL's 2008–2010 International Development Strategy similarly noted:

LGBT persons are daily subjected to persecution and discrimination all over the world. Homosexuality is criminal in 85 countries and punishable by death in seven. Discrimination, insulting treatment, harassment, assault, "conversion" rapes, forced marriages, dismissal from work, outing in the media, and murder are examples of what the persecution of LGBT persons can lead to. In many countries, not even the most basic human rights are respected, and LGBT persons are forced to deny themselves and their lives in order to survive. Furthermore, the negative attitudes of their surroundings force LGBT persons to commit suicide or work in the sex industry against their wills.

(RFSL 2008)

These characterizations lead to a bold claim: "this is something that RFSL can never accept." As a testament of their work, both groups are based in countries usually held up as exemplary champions of the sexual rights of gays and lesbians. Sweden was one of the first countries to recognize legal "partnership" rights for gay couples, in 1995, and to extend adoption rights to same-sex couples, in 2002. In 2009, full marriage rights were also approved by the Swedish parliament. The Dutch parliament granted same-sex couples domestic partnership benefits in 1998, and in 2001 the Netherlands became the first country in the world to legally recognize same-sex marriage. Faced with this sense of fait accompli, looking beyond their national boundaries has therefore served as one powerful justification for their continued existence to members and funders. Their adoption of international platforms opened up new sources of revenue; it has also offered justification for their continued existence. RFSL and COC access supporting funds from their national governments, the European Union and other donor agencies to carry out development projects in the Global South. COC Netherlands was first, its interest in international work spurred by cuts to institutional civil society funding by the Dutch government in 1989. As COC Director of Programs Pieter Boone explained in an interview with me held at their Amsterdam office in 2009, "Our organization had to transform into a project organization." After a short period during which time COC "didn't do a lot," Boone says, "Eventually, the movement realized we could actually formulate a project proposal, get money and use that money to subsidize our political activities. That is when we started to realize there was also funding for international work." There was "no thought behind it, [no] 'let's do international work because we have a responsibility there,'" he acknowledges, "It was really to pay for our national representation activities." During this "third phase," Boone says, "we were making money out of national projects and international projects. Those projects were really small scale and not managed very well, and the international activities did not really fit the profile of us as an organization." In 2009, he believed they were in phase four, where we realize that project-funded work is really the core of our activities, and international work is a core of our activities. We see we have responsibility there, and we know how to access the funds for that and we see we have added value there.

RFSL has similarly accessed development funds from Sida since 1999, including full funding for its cornerstone sexuality rights training program.

This characterization of self-interest as aid is not unique to LGBT organizations, of course. In *The Postcolonial Politics of Development*, Ilan Kapoor demonstrates how, on the one hand, "the discourse of aid is constructed as a non-reciprocated gift," but, on the other, "the discursive practice of aid is also tied to conditionalities, be they economic (tied aid), ideological (neoliberalism), or political (foreign policy objectives)" (2008, 78). What does it mean to view the "gift" of RFSL's and COC's expertise, knowledge and ability to access resources as a reciprocal act? Foreign aid discourse, Kapoor points out, constructs the donor–recipient relationship such that the donor country—Western, of course—is rich and enlightened. "Its privileged status makes it incumbent upon it to act with kindness and generosity," he explains, "while its superior wealth and knowhow somehow situates it as an exclusive agent of development" (79). "There is more than a tinge of Christianized paternalism here," he adds, "foreign aid sometimes being associated with good conscience, charity, benefaction, salvation." The recipient country or community, on the other hand, "is a victim of unfortunate circumstances (of its own making). And it is haplessly dependent on the benevolence and altruism of the Western donor (to which gratitude is owed)" (79). Barbara Heron also points out that there are also many important personal benefits that individuals involved as development workers earn other than financial ones. "For [white] women like myself," she says, "the development context can be a space where we actualize a fullness of subjectivity that we take to be who we truly are, for this is the self we are produced to want to be" (2007, 156). Consequently, "our desire for development, while a manifestation of the helping imperative, can be more accurately understood as a profound desire for the self" (156).

The "rescue" of LGBT people in the Global South, whether by RFSL, COC or the World Bank, also neatly maps into longstanding and powerful teleological narratives, which set the backward and barbaric South against the progressive and civilized North. As Maja Horn has observed:

> The progressiveness (or backwardness) of Latin American countries when it comes to LGBTQ issues and communities tends to be gauged through the presence (or absence) of LGBTQ social movements, political activism and organizing around sexual minority rights, and public expressions of gay and lesbian identities.
>
> *(Horn 2010, 169)*

Sexuality was as powerful a trope for gauging civility as it was in the colonial era, and so it now remains—except that the evaluation schematic has flipped. Evidence of homosexual sex in African, Asian and Latin American societies was used as evidence of their backwardness and waywardness in colonial times, because colonizing European nations were deeply anxious about, and punitively disciplined, sexual desires that challenged hegemonic heterosexuality. Britain and other European powers criminalized sodomy and other sexual acts in their colonies, and their laws were incorporated into postcolonial nation-building projects. Following the fall and/or retreat of colonial powers in the 1950s and 1960s, emergent states tasked with "development" by the newly formed Bretton Woods institutions, became obliged to work towards the kinds of advanced societies of their former colonizers. Not surprisingly, reforms mirrored those of the colonial era. Postcolonial states did not usurp old and imposed colonial measures of civility, like anti-sodomy, but aspired to meet them. Taking charge after winning independence required proof of fitness to lead. Disciplined sexuality was a key component of civility; as M. Jacqui Alexander argues:

> Erotic autonomy signals danger to the heterosexual family and to the nation. And because loyalty to the nation as citizen is perennially colonized within reproduction and heterosexuality, erotic autonomy brings with it the potential of undoing the nation entirely, a possible charge of irresponsible citizenship, or no responsibility at all.
>
> *(Alexander, 2005, 22–23)*

Writing about the Bahamian State as an example of this process, Alexander (2005) and Bedford (2009) show how it engaged in a program of "heteropatriarchal recolonization" in which the State's peoples were subsequently "sexualized and ranked into class of good, loyal, reproducing, heterosexual citizens, and a subordinated, marginalized class of noncitizens who, by virtue of choice and perversion, choose not to do so" (Alexander 2005, 46). This ambition of creating "loyal, reproducing heterosexual citizens" was folded into the development projects that promoted heteronormativity through education, health and economic programs. As Toni Morrison concluded, "respectability might well function as debt payment for rescue from incivility and from savagery" (Morrison 1992, vii–xxx, cited in Alexander 2005, 14).

The terms of this rescue have now changed. More than 500 years after the "first encounter" between native and colonizer, the latter's particular and purposeful racialized anxieties about sex still hang over the existence, and inhabits the psyches, of natives' descendants. Recently, however, a new consensus emerged. As more European and North American states have revised sexual regulation laws to legitimize particular forms of homosexual expression and unions (primarily ones that mimic dominant heterosexual forms, such as marriage), it is now other countries' expressed discomfort with that particular form of sexual expression that makes them uncivilized. Massad observes, "While the pre-modern West attacked the world of Islam's alleged sexual licentiousness, the modern West attacks its alleged *repression* of sexual freedoms" (2007, 37). In *Desiring Arabs*, he shows this transition in Orientalist writing and political work, from a "homosexual paradise" (2007, 176) to the worst place on earth for homosexuals. Supporters of what he terms the "Gay International's missionary tasks"[4] have produced two kinds of literature on the Muslim world to this end:

> an academic literature produced mostly by white male European or American gay scholars "describing" and "explaining" what they call "homosexuality" in Arab and Muslim history to the present; and journalistic accounts of the lives of so-called "gays" and (much less so) "lesbians" in the contemporary Arab and Muslim worlds.
>
> *(Massad 2007, 162)*

"The former is intended to unravel the mystery of Islam to a Western audience," he says, "while the latter has the unenviable task of informing white gay sex tourists about the region and to help 'liberate' Arab and Muslim 'gays and lesbians' from the oppression under which they allegedly live" (162). Not just tourists, but now development agents see themselves as having responsibility to take on this burden.

The recent pressure being exercised by Global North governments and organizations to advance sexual rights in the Global South must be understood in relation to this history. Given the great effort extended through the institutionalization of heteronormativity to demonstrate civility worthy of national sovereignty, it is not surprising, then, that challenges to heteronormativity would be met with aggressive apprehension. Although anti-sodomy laws might have been enacted by colonial powers, and although the pursuit of institutionalized heteronormativity across the Global South has always been linked to colonial history, many political and religious leaders from Global South countries are able to claim them as nationalist projects operating against the sexually liberalizing forces of the Global North. That is not to say pre-colonial cultures were not heteronormative, but rather that contemporary iterations of heteronormativity are specifically tied through law to both colonial rule and contemporary formations of geopolitical power. Those religious and political leaders who express homophobic nationalism of course are doing so through piecemeal and careless evaluation—few of them seem to be as concerned about neoliberal market policies, for instance, as Western impositions—but it's important to understand the fuller historical context of their operation. To do so resists characterization of opposition to LGBT rights in Global South countries as "cultural" homophobia. For example, India has been subject to the kind of oscillating representations of its sexual politics that Massad makes of the Middle East. Centuries-old depictions of its cultures represent India as a hotbed for same-sex eroticism, but contemporary representations characterize it as a homophobic culture; a much-circulated "Global Homophobia" map produced by *The Atlantic* revealed that worldwide, most people think it's among the worst places for a homosexual to live.[5] A historical review of the Indian Penal Code (IPC) provides more context to the latter characterization, however. The IPC was the first comprehensive codified law produced anywhere in the British Empire. Lord Macaulay spearheaded this project, following his appointment as the first Law Member of the Supreme Council of India in 1834. Macaulay reframed old and existing English laws on vagrancy, sex work and buggery to incorporate emergent fears about interracial mixing, homosexuality and bestiality, and presented a draft of the Penal Code in 1837. Prohibitions against sodomy appeared an act "against the order of nature" in Section 377 of the Penal Code, under the title "Unnatural offences." The final adoption of the IPC in 1860 resulted in revision of British law itself. In 1861, the "Offences against the Person Act" dropped the death penalty for the "abominable crime of buggery," imposing instead the sentence of ten years named in the IPC (Gupta and Long 2008, 20). The IPC also became the model for British colonies' legal systems, including in the Caribbean.[6] Further, as historically had been the case in Britain, anti-sodomy laws and prohibitions on sex work were packaged with vagrancy laws, revealing the real matter at hand: to mark non-white bodies as impure and dirty, and to emphasize the threat posed by their dirtiness to the superior and morally pure bodies of the imagined English heterosexual.

Rather than accept the racist characterization of Global South cultures as homophobic— *and indeed, which cultures anywhere in the world have never demonstrated social anxieties about same-sex desire?*—we must also ask: What are the underlying beliefs about 'race', culture, gender, difference, sexuality and civilization that drive Global North Queers' imperative to rescue? Similar to Gayatri Spivak's characterization of much gender and development work in India as "white men saving brown women from brown men," a great deal of work on sex rights in the South is configured as "white queers saving brown queers from brown homophobes" (1988, 296–297). In more sophisticated programs, acknowledgement is made of the colonial roots of anti-sodomy laws in the Global South, most often in the case of former British colonies. Looking at some of the demands made in offers of their "help" begins to provide some answers. As Massad so powerfully demonstrates is the case with the Gay Internationals' interventions in the Arab world, the "help" offered/insisted upon toward "liberation" requires both the evisceration of local histories and experiences and the valorization of particular, dominant metropolitan, Euro-American expressions of sexual cultures, including sexual identity. When RFSL sets up an international school to train LGBT activists from the South, organizers might be genuinely invested in sharing skills they've learned from their own experiences in Sweden, but how can any skills transfer operate in an ahistorical neutral space? Because of the particular and powerful ways in which sexual regulation and sexual practices are always historically and geographically configured and produced, how could any universalizing initiative support meaningful and considerate social change?

Because they are often so bereft of a historical consideration of power, "rescue" initiatives of LGBT people in the Global South have tended to reassure rather than challenge views of Global South cultures as barbaric and under-civilized. Kim's action to halt the loan to Uganda, for example, was premised in a notion of global community that allies "civilized people" of the Global North with gays and lesbians in the Global South. This alignment of LGBT people of the Global South with a Global North benevolence and civility that might sometimes prove helpful to some who become "rescued," does little to generate dialogue between people in the Global South. Explaining its decision to privilege dialogues between heterosexual and homosexual communities over and above alliances and work with Gay International groups, the Trinidad and Tobago LGBT organization CAISO notes, "What has distinguished local engagement with issues of sexual citizenship and faith community from the kinds of advocacy for 'gay rights' that take place in many other settings is that ours has been a fundamentally *nation-building* approach" (CAISO 2010). At a Sexual Rights forum held in Trinidad and Tobago in 2010, CAISO co-founder Colin Robinson (2010) further elaborated,

> Our nation of Trinidad and Tobago... was forged in the fires of overcoming several forms of domination and repression: *Colonialism* that says your land and decision making do not belong to you. *Imperialism* that says your resources do not belong to you and you do not think for yourself. *Indentureship* that says your labour does not belong to you. And *slavery* that says your *body* does not belong to you. And, as we know well from the history of miscegenation during slavery, when your body does not belong to you, neither do your sexuality nor your reproduction – they belong to the master. We cannot replace massa [Masters] with husbands; or political leaders; or the state; or laws and policies that say: yes *you* are free, but we will still tell you what you may do with your free *body*, with your sexuality, with your reproduction.

Both Robinson's references to the specific historical experiences that shaped contemporary Trinidad and Tobago, and CAISO's stated privileging of engagement between local people provide an alternate framing. It is no longer a matter of "rescue" from outside; rather than underlining and aggravating divisions between LGBT and heterosexual people in the same place, which serve and reiterate narratives of the backwardness and barbarism of Global South cultures and peoples, the appeal is toward self-reflective community interrogation and engagement. CAISO's approach does not resolve every difficult tension faced in negotiating sexuality rights in postcolonial states (Gosine, 2015) but it is a conscious, and productive, departure from the homonationalist and anti-historical inclinations of many international efforts. Its reframing of sexual regulation as a consequence of historical power interrupts dominant narratives of teleological progress and, I believe, most importantly, reshapes potential constituencies of allies in their struggles. For CAISO, the battle for rights is not between the civilized world (including LGBT peoples of the South) versus the backward, straight homophobes of the North, as so many development efforts suggest, but of a confrontation with the trauma of Oppression that has produced social anxiety about homosexuality.

Real love

While "rescue" missions of LGBT people in the Global South serve homonationalist ends, I would agree that acknowledgment that not all of the "world's poor" are heterosexual poses a significant challenge to dominant thinking and practice in international development. Heteronormativity persists throughout development programs, but over the last decade especially it has been troubled, and there are more opportunities to recognize familial and social relationships that are not fully invested in a closed, heterosexual model of procreation and affinity. Fifteen years ago, all development texts or policies implicitly or explicitly demanded and promoted heterosexuality; today, some do not. Still, representations of the sexual desires and lived sexual experiences of people from Global South countries have far to go in capturing and considering their complexity. When I first became interested in research on sexuality issues in development, it was not actually same-sex desire that concerned me but the development industry's representation of heterosexual, reproductive sex between "Third World peoples." I was upset about the ways in which people like my parents and the people with whom I grew up in rural Trinidad were understood, like all Third World people, to lack a complex subjectivity. In talks, texts and policies about family planning and control, "Third World peoples" were described as behaving the same way. The collective poor had reproduced for socioeconomic reasons; no individual had his/her/their own desire. As a child of parents who were always publicly expressive about their love—forty years on, they're still endlessly affectionate—as a nephew who witnessed his aunts risk security and safety in pursuit of their sexual desires, as someone whose own desires seemed to belong just to me—I found it outrageous that desire was written out of poor people's sexualities. As much as the discursive landscape has changed, and despite the proliferation of work about sex and sexuality, I still find myself looking for those expressions of "real love," complicated and experienced by people with individually wired desires. By "real love," I mean to suggest a notion of sexuality that recognizes the complexity of desire, one that cannot be explained entirely by identity markers or socioeconomic analysis, one that recognizes that its myriad conscious, subconscious and unconscious formations and iterations.

As I have said above, for some in the development industry, the "world's poor" now also includes homosexuals. Due to the greater economic power, travel and visibility of middle and elite classes of the Global South, especially as stagnant Euro-American economies become more dependent on incursions of capital by investors and expertise from the Global South, there appears to be more recognition that the sexual desires lives of *all* people are complex. Reviewing two important circulating fictionalized representations of the sexuality of people from the South, I demonstrate the political dynamics and limits of greater representation of sexual diversity in development, and identify the enormous challenges that remain in recognizing the complexity, and thus, sheer humanity, of "the poor."

The evolution of the character Rajesh ("Raj") Koothrapali in the American sitcom *The Big Bang Theory*—the most watched scripted comedy program worldwide[7]—provides a telling example of the move toward greater recognition of the complexity of the sexual lives of people from the Global South. *Big Bang* is focused on the trials and tribulations of a group of four young scientists whom are socially awkward and fascinated by comic books, other kinds of "geek" culture and an actress who lives across the hall from two of them. Raj plays the role of a former foreign student from India and current scientist. Between 2007 and 2013, through the first six seasons of the show, Raj was constituted though dominant racializing and sexual tropes that harken back to the colonial era. Echoing colonial renderings of Indian men that were emasculating (Sinha 1995, 1999; Reddy 2003), Raj was constructed as the most feminine character of the men who was not even capable of speaking to girls. Unlike his friends, he read *Archie* comics and enjoyed "chick flicks" like *Bridget Jones's Diary* and *Twilight*. Unlike the other men on the show, Raj enjoys preparing decadent gourmet meals and interior design, and a very close relationship to his small Yorkshire terrier, "Cinnamon." Because of these "feminine" interests, a recurring joke on the show concerns Raj's sexuality, as many characters speculate that he is in fact gay. However, Raj's heterosexuality is usually recuperated; he is straight, just the most feminine and most gay of the men. At the end of season six, Raj finally becomes capable of speaking to girls without the aid of alcohol. By this time, viewers of the show have glimpsed enough of Raj's life to know that he is from a very wealthy and well-educated family. By the beginning of season eight, long after every other character on the show has established a serious relationship, Raj finally has one. Raj's evolution over the eight years parallels what has happened to representations of Global South people's sexualities over the last decade. There are more representations of individuated desires in circulation, whether through independent cinema, YouTube, Bollywood or Hollywood productions. As on *The Big Bang Theory*, however, most of these representations appear to link human complexity to capital worth; Raj becomes a more complex and humane sexual subject after it is established that he and his family possess great material wealth.

A similar process is evident in one of the development industry's more visible and emboldened cultural representations of homosexuality. A video issued by the United Nations in 2014 in support of gay rights perhaps most vividly demonstrates how mainstream, identity-centered politics of LGBT groups in the North are framing sex rights campaigns directed at the Global South. *The Welcome* is a Bollywood-style two and a half minute pop video and marks the first UN Free & Equal campaign in India. The clip, which in its first five months of availability amassed over 2 million views, tells the story of a young man who brings his boyfriend home to meet his family for the first time. The family in the video is clearly positioned as upper/middle class. The first scene consists of a male decorator hanging lanterns for some kind of party. "Today, Sir is coming with a special friend," he says to a telephone. The camera then pans to a wide shot of a decadently styled party area, filled with flowers and silks. Even the dog is wearing a silk shirt. Bollywood actress Celina Jaitley, dressed as she might be for one of her Bollywood roles, is in a bejeweled sari top and gold jewelry. We then see "Sir," first through his clothes. We see his lush, gold-buttoned, velvet blazer, then his argyle socks and leather shoes, which he's seen brushing. "Sir" is then seen in his car and by the time he steps out of it, with his also beautiful, well-dressed male partner, there's little doubt about the social location of this family. They could be Raj's. When the family reacts with surprise, Jaitley reassures them with a phrase right out of a fashion advertisement: "It's a new look, it's a new attitude," she sings. "You might wonder where the old way of living has gone," she Jaitley continues, "but who is worried about who likes what, as long as in the world of love, two people want to be with each other." Everyone eventually dances cheerfully in an elaborately decorated room. Closing credits beckon, "To Stand for Human Rights with the United Nations, Share This Message."

The Welcome is a vivid demonstration of John D'Emilio's position that gay identities are shaped through capitalism. Drawing on D'Emilio, Rahul Rao argues that capitalism "enables the expression of sexuality as an aspect of individual personhood by promoting the individuation of wage labour, thereby disrupting traditional family and kinship arrangements," while at the same time asserting "an allegiance to heteronormativity in order to reproduce the next generation of workers." This process is evident in the way capital permits accessibility to personhood for Raj in *The Big Bang Theory* and "Sir" in *The Welcome*. Their acceptability as sexual beings is framed through the situation of both of them as "wealthy." Despite his apparent transgressions of gender, Raj remains fully committed to a heterosexual identity, and of course becomes attached to a female partner. The arrival of "Sir" and his partner mimics that of a bride and groom, and the closing scene of everyone dancing together seems to reassure viewers that their relationship will pose no threat to existing family structures. Notably, neither "Sir" nor his partner speak or sing in the video. "Far from contesting dominant heteronormative forms," Rao reminds us, "a new neoliberal sexual culture seeks inclusion within the protective embrace of the nation precisely by making its peace with state and market." Because 'LGBT' identities have journeyed along the circuits of transnational capital, through global media, HIV/AIDS funding, human rights discourses and diasporic travellers, he adds, they may be even more ensconced in the imperatives of capitalism. "Although these identities take their place within enormously complex and variegated landscapes populated by older indigenous gender matrices," Rao explains, "their disproportionate power and leadership role in those landscapes might render the movements that they lead less antithetical to capitalism than Western queer Marxist utopian texts had hoped" (2014). We may now see images of homosexuality in development texts like *The Welcome*, but any notion of complex desire—what I call "real love"—is afforded only to those whom are folded into the aspirations of neoliberal capitalism.

While capitalism has been resourceful for the advance of LGBT rights around the world (Sinfield 2000), the reinvention of people not engaged in exclusively heterosexual acts as "gay consumers," and so on, has important limits. For example, economist Lee Badgett's World Bank-financed costing out of homophobia may offer an effective tool for LBGT advocates inside the World Bank and in the broader development industry, but it does make the well-being and rights of people not exclusively engaged in heterosexual sex conditional to their market worth. Rao asks:

> What does such an argument do to those not judged to be "productive" within its terms—the disabled, the illiterate, the unemployed, the elderly, the development-induced displaced, and others who are constitutively unable and/or unwilling to function as good capitalist citizens?
>
> *(Rao 2014).*

One need not hypothesize about this conditionality, as it is already evident. Development resources on sexuality rights have explicitly demanded adherence to frameworks and terms of sexual identity that are hegemonic in Western Europe and North America. One *must* adapt the actual names "gay," "lesbian," "bisexual," "trans" to claim access to funds like the US Global Equality Fund, and be willing to understand sexuality as an identity that one claims. For example, RFSL's main development activity is a training school for sexual rights activists in the South. First held in 1999 and fully funded by Sida, RFSL's "Advanced International Training Programme on LGBT and Human Rights" brings together people from the developing world to complete a set of two training sessions. The first part takes place during three weeks in Sweden and focuses on theoretical and practical components within the field of LGBT and human rights. Participants are expected to work with their own projects in their home countries following completion of this first session, and to attend a "follow-up" week in their region six months later. As explained in introductory notes, "The programme is designed for participants working in organisations or sectors giving them an influence on issues concerning LGBT and human rights." The workshops are organized such that scholars and activists from the Global North are positioned as the expert-trainers and LGBT self-identified activists and workers as participants or informants. For example, in their 2007–2008 Asia-focused session, various British, Canadian and Swedish academics led sessions on such topics as "Basic perspectives on sexuality, gender identity and sexual identity," "Violations of LGBT human rights," and "Human rights, international law and founding principles. Protection of LGBT persons," at both the Stockholm leg of the training as well as the "Asia" leg held in Bali, and partnered with Indonesian LGBT organization Arus Pelangi. Where the training sessions led by Euro-Americans were instructive about theorizing sexuality, the few led by Arus Pelangi were geared as information sessions for visitors, describing their activities and challenges. Similarly, Ashley Currier's study (2010) of the work of African LGBT group, Behind the Mask, which has received funds from several development agencies for some of its work, including the World Bank, revealed donors' emphasis on "visibility" to accede support (see Currier's chapter with Julie Moreau in this volume).

Conditionality has serious consequences. Massad, who laments that the rise of a sexual identity discourse has produced "homosexuals, as well as gays and lesbians, where they do not exist, and represses same-sex desires and practices that refuse to be assimilated into its sexual epistemology," reveals how the imposition of these identities has created serious consequences for those most vulnerable to state and social violence (2007, 163).[8] On May 11, 2001, police raided a boat cruise on Egypt's Nile River, and arrested fifty-five people, thirty-four of whom were on the boat at the time of the arrests.[9] The arrests garnered global attention and became the central focus of international advocacy campaigns and a much-circulated documentary, "Coming Out in the Developing World." Massad points out that: "It is not same-sex sexual practices that are being repressed by the Egyptian police but rather the sociopolitical identification of these practices with the Western identity of gayness and the publicness that these gay-identified men seek" (2007, 183).

International gay activists ignored this distinction, Massad says, resulting in advocacy campaigns that ultimately served two constituencies: themselves and social conservatives in Egypt who called for new disciplinary measures against sexual freedom in response. Massad puts blame for the Egyptian government's repressive campaign on gay rights activists. "Despite the overwhelming evidence that gayness, as a choice, is proving to bring about more oppression, not 'liberation,' and less sexual freedom rather than more for Arab men practicing same-sex contact," he concluded, "the Gay International is undeterred in its missionary campaign" (2007, 184). Rebuking an American Arab gay activist's characterization of the Queen Boat raid as "our own Stonewall," Massad (2007) pointed out:

> The reaction of the drag Queens at the Stonewall bar was indeed significantly different from the reaction of the men at the Queen Boat discotheque; the latter … denied being 'homosexual' or 'gay'… Also, not only did these men not seek publicity for their alleged homosexuality, they resisted the very publicity of the events by the media by covering their faces in order to hide from the cameras and hysterical public scrutiny.
>
> *(Massad 2007, 184–185)*

"These," he concludes, "are hardly manifestations of gay pride or gay liberation" (2007, 184–185). More importantly, the intervention of the Gay International lobby resulted in a worse situation for men who have sex with men in Egypt. Massad notes that "harassment increased following the Queen Boat case, with police stepping up its surveillance and arrests of people suspected of 'debauchery'" and a report by Human Rights Watch claimed that Egyptian law enforcement officials took it as "an incentive to increasing rigor, or even a route to career advancement."

Deployment of an uncritical sexual identity-politics has also produced other dubious results that are not always helpful to intended subjects of aid. For example, India's gender bending *hijra* population has become increasingly visible in the past decade through HIV/AIDS discourses and intervention programs. This recognition has brought new resources directed at the population. But as Jyoti Puri (2010) points out, it has also meant heightened surveillance and scrutiny of Hijras, especially by NGOs with ties to the state as well as international donors and agencies. Along with non-transgendered women, sex workers and men truck drivers, Hijras are becoming the most maligned groups in the HIV/AIDS discourse in India, Puri says. Hijras have also been framed as "Transgender" in international discourses of sexuality, but such a reading might not actually reflect the way Hijras see themselves. Many humans rights organizations hailed the April 14, 2014 ruling by the Indian Supreme Court to recognize a third gender. The case was mounted largely on the basis of the longstanding history of Hijra in India. "Recognition of transgenders as a third gender is not a social or medical issue but a human rights issue," said Justice KS Radhakrishnan, who headed the two-judge Supreme Court bench. "Transgenders are also citizens of India" and they must be "provided equal opportunity to grow. The spirit of the Constitution is to provide equal opportunity to every citizen to grow and attain their potential, irrespective of caste, religion or gender" (BBC News 2014). However, within a few days, new challenges to the application of this notion of identity were made. A number of transgender women viewed the adoption of a third category would increase discrimination against them. "When I was 14, I chose to become a woman from a man. I am still fighting to be accepted as a woman. I want to build a respectable livelihood as one. I don't want to be a "other" gender person," said Pavithra, now thirty-two (Avani 2014), who is listed as Female on her Voter's ID and doesn't want to change it to 'Others'. She says, "It takes away my identity." Claiming sexual identity provides a recognizable and familiar basis for action; in the Supreme Court case on transgender rights, the judges asked the government to treat them in line with other minorities officially categorized as "socially and economically backward," to enable them to get quotas in jobs and education. However, as Pavithra's objection makes clear, it may not reflect the desires or interests of those on whose behalf actions are made.

A call for complexity

I believe that the most critical demand one can make of development actors engaged in pursuit of sexual rights at this juncture is for more complexity. That demand would include a deeper historical analysis, including of homophobia in the Global South, and a more cautious consideration of normalization strategies that incorporate same-sex desire into heteronormative institutions. Interestingly, attention to same-sex desire has forced recognition that desire exists among the poor outside of socioeconomic interests and hegemonic cultural demands. But in many ways, the challenge remains the same: recognition of the complex subjectivity and dignity of development's imagined subject of "the poor." The misleading but determined adherence to an unproven framework of stable heterosexual and homosexual identities is an affront to this complexity as are the endless representations of peoples of the Global South as essentially homophobic.

All sexual desires are complex, unwieldy, messy. Neither innocent nor controllable by our conscious, each person's sexual desires are formed through her/his/their life experience. They also shift, though rarely in ways we can consciously identify, much less entirely control.[10] While the arrival of homosexual/queer/LGBT subjects in international development has offered up more categories of sexual identity, it has not begun to grapple with the messiness of desire itself. Unlike most of my peers in the field, I prefer talking about "love" and "desire" over sex, not due to some kind of naïve allegiance to a notion of sexual morality, but rather because its very abstractness, its varied interpretations and its broader potential to include a range of physical, emotional, material and psychic matters make it a more honest characterization of what's at hand and what's at stake in negotiating erotic autonomy at this moment. The primary task, for me, is less about finding the most "effective" strategy or refining terms of identity or exchange, but in challenging ourselves to really see my parents, the people I grew up with, and all of those "simple," nameless, functional "poor" subjects of development as fully, complexly human, with social environments and histories and individual experiences and feelings, which demand more ethical and respectful engagement.

Acknowledgements

This chapter was originally published by the Institute of Development Studies (IDS) as Gosine, A. (2015) "Rescue, and Real Love: Same-sex Desire in International Development." Brighton: IDS, and is reproduced here by permission of IDS and the Swedish International Development Cooperation Agency (Sida).

Notes

1 By "development" I mean the discursive and institutional practices articulated and enacted through multilateral, government, private, community and other organizations engaged in projects that structure North–South economic, social and political relationships.

2 The "development industry" is an unstable amalgam of many different actors often working in support of, sometimes against, each other's interests: governments, international agencies like the World Bank and International Monetary Fund, non-governmental organizations of feminists, environmentalists, human rights activists or religious fundamentalists, health institutions, social service workers, economists, doctors, lawyers, educators and more.

3 See: http://www.pewglobal.org/2013/06/04/the-global-divide-on-homosexuality/

4 Citing the IGLHRC's mission statement to "protect and advance the human rights of all people and communities subject to discrimination or abuse on the basis of sexual orientation, gender identity, or HIV status," Massad characterizes "these missionary tasks, the discourse that produced them, and the organizations that represent them" as constitutive of the 'Gay International' (2007, 161).

5 http://www.citylab.com/politics/2014/02/global-map-homophobia/8309/ (accessed October 21, 2014).

6 The Straits Settlement Law of in 1871, covering territory that today encompasses Singapore, Malaysia and Brunei, effectively duplicated the IPC. Between 1897 and 1902 administrators applied the Indian Penal Code in Britain's African colonies, including Kenya and Uganda. By the time criminal codes were established in Trinidad and Tobago, Guyana, Jamaica and Barbados, they had also incorporated clarifications set in English law about the meaning of "natural offences," such as a 1885 revision that punished "Any male person who in public or private commits or is a party to the commission of or procures or attempts to procure the commission by any male person of any act of gross indecency with another male person" (20).

"Gross indecency" was a broad offence designed to include virtually all kinds of non-penetrative sexual acts between two men (21).

7   According to data compiled by Eurodata TV Worldwide; see also http://uproxx.com/tv/2014/01/big-bang-theory-officially-popular-sitcom-world/

8   In *Desiring Arabs*, Massad demonstrates how non-Western forms of sexuality are simultaneously erased and reconfigured through dominant Euro-American identity practices in the Middle East. Disputing a claim by one Western scholar that "Arabic synonyms for 'to fuck' have no form of reciprocity," Massad notes, "*both* classical *and* modern Arabic have the very 'tanayaka,' which does indicate reciprocity as when two people 'yatanayakan' meaning that they are 'fucking each other'" (170). This confusion over reading and representing the unstable sexual landscape of Arab societies dates back to colonization, he says, with the subsequent invention of Arabic words to fit European frameworks: "The word 'jins,' for example, meaning 'sex,' emerged in Arabic sometime in the earlier part of the twentieth century carrying with it not only its new meanings of a 'biological sex' and 'national origin,' but also its old meanings of 'type,' 'kind' and 'ethnolinguistic origin,' among others. The word in the sense of 'type' and 'kind' has existed since time immemorial and is derived from the Greek 'genos.' As late as 1870, its connotation of 'sex' had not yet taken place" (171). Similarly, "jinsiyyah" was coined by translators of Freud to mean sexuality, as were "mithliyyah" invented to mean homosexuality and "ghayriyyah," heterosexuality (172).

9   Women and European and American men were released immediately, as were three Egyptian men "found to be the sons of 'prominent' people" (181). The official charges brought against the men were of "offending religion" (182).

10 For more on desire in development, see Kapoor 2005 and 2014.

References

Adams, Vincanne and Pigg, Stacy Leigh. 2005. *Sex in Development*. Durham NC: Duke University Press.

Alexander, M. Jacqui. 2005. *Pedagogies of Crossing: Meditations on Feminism, Sexual Politics, Memory, and the Sacred*. Durham NC: Duke University Press.

Avani, Tanya. 2014. "Transgender Allowed to Vote as a 'Third' Sex, 'But I am a Woman not an 'Other'," video, www.loksabhaindia.org/en/photographers/avani-tanya/transgender-al-voto-cometerzo-sessoma-sono-una-donna-non-un-altro.html (accessed October 12, 2014).

BBC News India (2014) "India Court Recognises Transgender People as Third Gender," 15 April, www.bbc.co.uk/news/world-asia-india-27031180 (accessed February 11, 2015).

Bedford, Kate (2009) *Developing Partnerships: Gender, Sexuality, and the Reformed World Bank*. Minneapolis MN: University of Minnesota Press.

CAISO. 2010. "We Take a Pride in our Liberty," Gspottt, blog, 17 October, http://gspottt.wordpress.com/2010/10/17/we-take-a-pride-in-our-liberty/ (accessed October 20, 2014).

COC (n.d.) "Fighting for Acceptance All over the World," COC, www.coc.nl/engels (accessed October 18, 2014).

Cornwall, Andrea and Jolly, Susie. 2009. "Sexuality and the Development Industry." *Development* 52, no. 1: 5–12

Cornwall, Andrea, Correa, Sonia and Jolly, Susie. 2008. *Development with a Body: Sexuality, Human Rights and Development*. London: Zed Books.

Currier, Ashley. 2010. "Behind the Mask: Developing LGBTI Visibility in Africa." In *Development, Sexual Rights, and Global Governance*, edited by Amy Lind, pp. 155–168, New York: Routledge.

Gosine, Andil. 2004. *Sex for Pleasure, Rights to Participation and Alternatives to HIV/AIDS: Placing Sexual Minorities in Development*. IDS Working Paper 228, Brighton: IDS.

Gosine, Andil. 2010a. "Non-white Reproduction and Same-sex Eroticism: Queer Acts against Nature." In *Queer Ecology*, edited by C. Sandilands and B. Erickson, pp. 149–172. Bloomington IN: Indiana University Press.

Gosine, Andil. 2010b. "The World Bank's GLOBE: Queers In/Queering Development." In *Development, Sexual Rights and Global Governance*, edited by Amy Lind, pp. 67–85. New York: Routledge.

Gosine, Andil. 2015. "CAISO, CAISO: Negotiating Sexualities and Nationalisms in Trinidad and Tobago." *Sexualities* 18, no. 7: 859–884.

Gupta, Alok and Long, Scott. 2008. *This Alien Legacy: The Origins of "Sodomy" Laws in British Colonialism*. New York: Human Rights Watch.

Heron, Barbara. 2007. *Desire for Development: Whiteness, Gender, and the Helping Imperative*. Waterloo ON: Wilfrid Laurier University Press.

Horn, Maja. 2010. "Queer Dominican Moves: In the Interstices of Colonial Legacies and Global Impulses." *Development, Sexual Rights and Global Governance*, edited by Amy Lind, pp. 169–181. New York: Routledge.

Kapoor, Ilan. 2005. "Participatory Development, Complicity and Desire." *Third World Quarterly* 26, no.8: 1203–1220.

Kapoor, Ilan. 2008. *The Postcolonial Politics of Development*. London: Routledge

Kapoor, Ilan. 2014. "Psychoanalysis and Development: An Introduction." *Third World Quarterly* 35, no. 7: 1117–1119.

Kennedy, Helen. 2014. Presentation at the Toronto International Film Festival screening, 1 June, Toronto.

Kim, Jim Yong. 2014. "Jim Yong Kim: The High Costs of Institutional Discrimination." *Washington Post*, Opinions, 27 February, www.washingtonpost.com/opinions/jim-yong-kim-the-high-costs-ofinstitutional-discrimination/2014/02/27/8cd37ad0-9fc5-11e3-b8d8-94577ff66b28_story.html (accessed February 11, 2015).

Lind, Amy. 2010. *Development, Sexual Rights and Global Governance*. London: Routledge.

Massad, Joseph A. 2007. *Desiring Arabs*. Chicago, IL: University of Chicago Press.

Murray, David A.B. 2009. "Homo Hauntings." In *Homophobias: Lust and Loathing across Time and Space*, edited by David A.B. Murray, pp. 146–161. Durham NC: Duke University Press.

Nair, Yasmin. 2014. "The Same Sex Marriage Trap." In These Times. 3 February, http://inthesetimes.com/article/16132/the_same_sex_marriage_trap (accessed October 12, 2014).

Oosterhoff, Pauline, Waldman, Linda and Olerenshaw, Dee. 2014. *Literature Review on Sexuality and Poverty*. Brief Supporting Evidence Report 55. Brighton: IDS.

Oswin, Natalie. 2007. "Producing Homonormativity in Neoliberal South Africa: Recognition, Redistribution, and the Equality Project." *Signs* 32, no. 3: 649–669.

Puar, Jasbir. 2007. *Terrorist Assemblages: Homonationalism in Queer Times*. Durham NC: Duke University Press.

Puri, Jyoti. 2010. "Transgendering Development." In *Development, Sexual Rights and Global Governance*, edited by Amy Lind, pp. 39–53. New York: Routledge.

Rao, Rahul. 2014. "Staying Positivist in the Fight against Homophobia." Sexuality Policy Watch, 14 July, www.sxpolitics.org/?p=9411 (accessed October 13, 2014).

Reddy, Gayatri .2003. "'Men' Who Would be Kings: Celibacy, Emasculation, and the Re-production of Hijras in Contemporary Indian Politics." *Social Research: An International Quarterly* 70, no. 1: 163–200.

RFSL Sweden. 2008. *International Development Strategy 2008–2010*. Stockholm: RFSL Sweden.

Robinson, C. 2010. "Respecting the Right to Freedom of Thought, Opinion, and Expression of One's Sexuality." Gspottt, 22 March, http://gspottt.files.wordpress.com/2010/03/caiso_ippfsexualrights.pdf (accessed October 21, 2014).

Sida. 2011. LGBT and Human Rights: Advanced International Training Program. Part 1, Stockholm Sweden, October 17–November 4 2001; Part 2, Africa Region May 21–25, 2012. RFSU, Stockholm: Sweden. http://www.rfsu.se/Bildbank/Dokument/itp-kurser/268_Africa_LGBT%20and%20Human%20Rights%202011_Web.pdf

Sinfield, Alan. 2000. *Gay and After*. London: Serpent's Tail.

Sinha, Mrinalini. 1995. *Colonial Masculinity: The "Manly Englishman" and the "Effeminate Bengali" in the Late Nineteenth Century*. Vol. 1. Manchester: Manchester University Press

Sinha, Mrinalini. 1999. "Giving Masculinity a History: Some Contributions from the Historiography of Colonial India." *Gender & History* 11, no. 3: 445–460.

Spivak, Gayatri Chakravorty. 1988. "Can the Subaltern Speak?" In *Marxism and the Interpretation of Culture*, edited by Cary Nelson and Lawrence Grossberg, pp. 271–313. Champaign IL: University of Illinois Press.

13

QUEER PARADISE

Development and recognition in the Isthmus of Tehuantepec

Marcus McGee

A short film produced by the Inter-American Development Bank (IDB) in 2016 (GobApp 2014) opens with a montage of domestic scenes: early morning light illuminating the haze of a working class home in Southern Mexico, a hardened but meticulously manicured hand lighting a candle next to a pair of colorful statuettes of Jesus. A pair of pink shimmery eyelids appears on screen and the same hand comes up to apply mascara and eyeliner. Then, an off-screen hand runs a tube of dark red lipstick over a pair of isolated lips. A recording of the Mexican folk song, *La Llorona*, sung by popular Oaxacan-born singer Lila Downs, plays in the background.

The camera never reveals the whole face of the subject; instead it shifts between sequences of painted body parts and images of gold coin earrings, dark hair braided with silk ribbons, and a black satin huipil, embroidered with brightly colored carnations, roses and orchids. To the middle class Mexican eye these are all telltale markers of the *traje tehuana*, the folk-costume-cum-post-revolutionary symbol of national origins, conventionally worn by the Zapotec women of the Isthmus of Tehuantepec, Oaxaca—along with mestiza women at protests in Mexico City, tourists playing dress-up in Oaxaca de Juárez, Frida Kahlo (most famously), and the occasional politician (Howell 2006, 9). At the end of the montage sequence, the disembodied subject—until this moment presented as a collection of aestheticized objects—speaks over subtitles of her Isthmus Zapotec: "Cadi nacá ti gunaá. Cadi nacá ti nguiiu. Ná muxhe. [I am not a woman. I am not a man. I am muxe]" (GobApp 2014).

Since the mid-1990s, the small city of Juchitán de Zaragoza, located in the Isthmus of Tehuantepec, Oaxaca, has garnered increasing attention from national and international documentary film projects, news media, and scholars as a "queer paradise" (Fusion 2015; *Juchitán, Queer Paradise* 2002). In fact, a Google search of the words "queer paradise" at the time of writing this unearthed over ten pages of consistent material on Juchitán. This is because of Juchitán's famed population of muxe people, a group of (mostly) Zapotec-speaking people, designated male at birth, who identify as a third gender and ostensibly spend their everyday lives dressed not just as "women," but as *tehuana* women, and who are known for working in traditionally feminine lines of work, for example, as seamstresses and hairdressers. As the narrative goes, muxe people are a third gender that has existed in Zapotec culture since before the colonial encounter, and who experience an unprecedented level of tolerance and visibility in a country typically characterized both internally and externally for its unbridled levels of *machismo* and high rate of murders of women (BBC 2016; El Universal 2016; Wright 2011; Driver 2015).

"Tolerance," however, does not adequately describe what is unique here: in many scholarly and journalistic milieux, muxe people are represented (and often represent themselves) not just as a "tolerated," essentially foreign gender identity, but as a folkloric, characteristically regional charm—the product of ancient traditions and pre-colonial systems of gender identification, deeply associated with the indigenist aesthetics of the *traje tehuana* (see National Geographic 2017). Midway through the film produced by the IDB, a *Juchiteca* sociologist, Marina Meneses, tells us as much:

> In Juchitán there is a sexual division of labor in which the role of commercial exchange corresponds to women, and the role of muxe is in the preservation of our culture, in the transmission of knowledge and abilities. This is very important because it revives the economy and keeps it active.
>
> *(GobApp 2014)*[1]

Meneses' declaration about the muxe community's role in the maintenance of Zapotec cultural patrimony plays over a montage of (what are supposed to be) quotidian images. When she talks about the "sexual division of labor," *Juchiteca* women appear on screen, counting peso coins next to bins of fish in a local market. When Meneses mentions the "preservation of our culture," the torso of a nameless muxe person is shown, her back turned to the camera, wearing one of those famous *tehuana* huipils. The camera then turns its dithering eye to a muxe foot, working the peddle of a sewing machine, and a muxe hand, guiding an unfinished copy of that famed Zapoteca uniform under the machine's needle. Meneses' quote, combined with the accompanying procession of images, makes discernible through the discursive and visual fields an uncanny constellation: "muxe people are agents of progress and tolerance. Muxe people are ancient and authentic. These things are intrinsic qualities of their bodies, or at least assemblages of their body parts. The role of muxe bodies is to reproduce this authenticity. This reproduction is an engine of the economy."

At the end of the thirteen-minute film, the screen goes black and a final note appears in text that alerts the viewer to the interest a multibillion-dollar development bank might take in in the muxes of Juchitán. The text reads in Spanish:

> The fascinating history of the muxhes reminds us of three key elements for the development of our communities: [1] Institutions should be inclusive. [2] The improvement of living conditions empowers our communities. [3] The appreciation of every one of our voices enriches us as a society. These elements constitute the heart [corazón] and goal [reto] of the actions of the Department of Institutions for Development [IFD, a department within the IDB].
>
> *(Gobapp 2014)*

Muxe participation in local economies is apparently an apt representation for the IFD's values of inclusivity and representation, which constitute the "*corazón y reto*" of the IFD's actions.

So, how does the IFD promote inclusivity and representation? The feel-good corporate metaphysics in the note at the end of the film, and a jargon-heavy explanation of the IFD's function on the IDB website—"decentralization, ... the development of capital markets and financial institutions, [increasing] competitiveness" (BID 2017)— leave things somewhat ambiguous, but one can infer that the IFD is more or less the administrative overseer of creatively worded privatization campaigns originating from the IDB.[2] Of course, this creative wording is more than wording, generative of *something* (sentiments, bodies, identities) in excess of the "development of capital markets" and the like.

The IDB's main interest in the Isthmus of Tehuantepec is a series of wind farm projects that it has attempted to finance over the past five years (*The New York Times* 2016; La Jornada 2012). The Assembly of Indigenous Communities of the Isthmus of Tehuantepec in Defense of Soil and Territory (APITDTT) has denounced the projects as the "face of dispossession in the Isthmus," accusing the multinational companies with which the IDB has partnered of manipulating communal plot owners into leasing out their land for pennies on the dollar for irrevocable thirty-year periods (Sinembargo 2015). APITDTT and a number of journalists have also accused wind farm investors of hiring armed paramilitary groups to attack protestors and critics of the project (Sinembargo 2015; La Jornada 2012).

This is a familiar story: a major development bank in Latin America funds large private and mixed capital projects; these projects exacerbate the poverty of the people they claim to "empower"; Kafkaesque levels of violent intrigue (see Excelsior 2016a; Sinembargo 2015; La Jornada 2012) seem to follow the projects wherever they are implemented. But then there are the muxe (or at least representations of them): in the midst of violence, dispossession, and economic exodus they are dancing gaily and drinking mescal on screen, sewing away at their huipils, applying mascara, embodying the authentically new and the ever-unchanged in the limelight of international mass-mediated visibility.

Following James Ferguson's incisive question—"What do aid programmes do besides fail to help poor people?" (Ferguson 1994, 180)—this chapter conveys how in the midst (and in excess) of the general failure of neoliberal development projects in the Isthmus of Tehuantepec, a completely distinct politics and *aesthetics* of progress, gender and sexuality, and indigeneity has cropped up, interpellating a small group of gender divergent indigenous people into a peculiar kind of embodied difference. I observe that this embodied difference, in its discursive rendition, symbolically sutures together the latent contradictions of the neoliberal project in Latin America: the chimera of cultural authenticity with the equally chimerical commodity form, sexual modernity with the simultaneously restrictive and atavistic sexuality of the Other, and the rigid edges of racialized otherness with the smooth, encompassing surface of national progress.

Sexual citizenship and its complications in the Isthmus

This chapter is based on ethnographic fieldwork that I conducted in the summer of 2014 in Juchitán and the state capital, Oaxaca de Juárez. In my time there, I conducted interviews with members of the three largest muxe-led advocacy organizations in Juchitán: Biini Laanu, Guñaxhii Guendanabani, and Las Intrépidas Contra el SIDA, as well as with employees of the Office of Sexual Diversity in the Juchitán municipal government. I also visited the state headquarters of the two most powerful political parties in Oaxaca, the Institutional Revolutionary Party (PRI) and the Party of the Democratic Revolution (PRD), and conducted interviews with party officials that had varying degrees of financial and political connections to the muxe-led groups.

Through my fieldwork, and through interpretations of media like the short film described above, it becomes clear that muxe politics of advocacy and representation in the Isthmus have a complex affinity with global, "liberal diasporic" (Povinelli 2002) trends towards what scholars have called "sexual citizenship" (Laskar 2014) or a struggle for "sexual rights" (Howe 2013). Sexual citizenship, in short, is a framework for conceptualizing sexual difference wherein LGBT people have emerged in both global developmentalist and national political imaginaries as *rights-bearing* subjects. This subject, the sexual citizen, is first and foremost a private individual, ideally endowed with a series of negative rights that guarantee his or her autonomy and freedom from potential discrimination or abuse at the hands of the state. The sexual citizen is also endowed with a set of positive rights: the freedom to enter into legal contracts like marriage and adoption, and in that same vein, to assemble and communicate with other rights-bearing individuals and in doing so constitute a civil society.

The sexual citizen, in other words, ideally exists in the public sphere as a subject equal under the law to other citizen-subjects, and thus has access to a kind of universality *via* the particularity of a legally recognized identity. Here an aporia lurks, of course. The rights of the sexual citizen, indeed, his or her very citizen-ness, is contingent on an act of recognition, and therefore on a process of *becoming recognizable*, intelligible, and visible. Put differently, the center of gravity of the most inalienable, innate quality of the sexual citizen—his or her possession of rights—is an inscribed surface, an exterior.

Cymene Howe (2013) in her ethnography of lesbian activism in post-revolutionary Nicaragua provides an account of one way in which the international trend towards sexual rights translates into a struggle for recognition and intelligibility in the global South, that is, into an elaborate game of interiors and exteriors, inscriptions and forces. In Howe's account of what she called the "intimate pedagogies" of the Nicaraguan lesbian movement, the first step to being a rights-bearing subject is being a legible subject, and expressing a desire that is legible through an international human rights framework as "lesbian." In the activist workshops Howe observed, becoming legible as a lesbian often involved engaging in a combination of what seemed at times like group therapy, and at others like participation in a Sandinista consciousness-raising group. Women who had up until recently understood their sexuality and gender role as based on the gender presentation of their partner, were encouraged to take a more "enlightened" approach to their sexuality. Through the elaboration of a system of sexual subjectivity based on object preference rather than gendered sexual roles—one that Howe and her interview subjects insist has its origins in an earnestly egalitarian impulse—lesbian activists created both new sexual subjectivities and a new *sexual commons*, wherein "women," who previously had very little in common, in time found themselves in solidarity and community with members of their object-preference group.

Howe describes how some postcolonial sexual rights activists undertake the task of not only demanding equal protections under the law, but of creating new legal subjects—publics—by mediating sexual desire through taxonomies of sex and gender borrowed (and often permuted) from the global developmentalist discourse on sexual rights. In Nicaragua and other periphery contexts where sexualities outside of the "hetero-homo binarism" (Laskar 2014, 92) exist, where one's sexual object preference is not always the basis of identity-based taxonomies or a liberal democratic commons, becoming a sexual citizen most fundamentally means developing new engagements with the object of sexual desire. This curious mediating space between sexual subject and object is most precisely—at least in a Kantian sense—understood as the realm of *aesthetics*, and it this realm to which I refer in the introductory vignette while describing the sphere of development aesthetics in the Isthmus of Tehuantepec.

As many scholars of postcolonialism and queerness note (Laskar 2014; Waites 2009; Puar 2007), the process of becoming legible as a cosmopolitan sexual subject is deeply imbricated with the colonial notion of becoming "civilized." The modern(ist) object configurations of sexual desire, in addition to having a valence towards a certain kind of commons, also have a valence towards notions of "progress," the "modern" and the "civilized." In some sense this is one and the same valence: the universality to which the sexual citizen gains access is discursively tangential to the very same universality of the European Enlightenment, which in all cases is constituted through its generative relation to barbarism, particularity, tradition, and "oriental despotism."

This is the "sexual modernization" (Bosia and Weiss 2013, 11–14) component of the hegemonic international discourse on sexual rights, which represents sexual tolerance as an "all but inevitable stage of development," and a "harbinger and facilitator" (Bosia and Weiss 2013, 12) of both liberal democracy and economic vitality (a point on which the IDB would undoubtedly agree). The sexual modernization discourse imagines homophobia as the private disposition (and failure) of intolerant, maladapted individuals that exist not only in "other" (read: southern, eastern) hemispheres, but, as Bosia and Weiss write in reference to the International Lesbian and Gay Association's 2007 global report on homophobia, in other *times* as "artifacts" (Bosia and Weiss 2013, 13) of a traditionalist, pre-modern *gemeinschaft* (see Tönnies 1988; Weber 2015). The monolithic modernism of this paradigm is an easy target for criticism; not only does it erase the origins of the extant, obviously "homophobic" anti-sodomy laws written and administered under British and French colonial rule across the world, but it is emblematic of the manifold ways in which the ghost of the colonial "white man's burden" (Kipling 1899) haunts liberal cosmopolitan discourses on human rights (generally), and sexual citizenship (particularly).

Elaborating this discursive and affective architecture of global sexual citizenship brings the puzzle of muxe politics of representation into better focus. One way to think about this puzzle is that the muxe community does and *does not* seem to fit into a larger framework of sexual citizenship. Muxes and Juchitán are seemingly at the *cutting edge* of a cosmopolitan politics of tolerance as the inheritors of an apparent "queer paradise," yet this is based on allusions to a fantasy of folkloric purity and "ancient" traditions. In some ways, muxes best fit in the role of "homophobe" or "closet case" in the generic developmentalist narrative on sexual modernity; representations of the muxe community in development literature focus on the maintenance of tradition, and they themselves seem to remain unassimilated to an object preference-based mode of identification. Yet, at the same time, Juchitán has become the liberal multicultural darling of many in the international development community; public relations (PR) people at institutions like the IDB clearly want to see Juchitán as having achieved levels of visibility and normalization for sexual minorities that do not exist to the same extent in the most progressive corners of the global North.

Turning focus to what muxes say about their own solidarities further complicates the picture. Muxe advocacy groups and political organizations actively participate in larger national and international movements for sexual rights, and have done so since the inception of such movements in Mexico in the early 1980s (Miano Borruso 2010; De la Dehesa 2010). Take, for instance, the case of the *Las Intrépidas* (The Intrepid Women),[3] the oldest exclusively Muxe-run advocacy organization in the Isthmus. When I spoke with Maria Santiago,[4] a founding member of *Las Intrépidas* and godmother figure to a younger generation of muxes in Juchitán, she[5] explained that *Las Intrépidas* have collaborated with national LGBT organizations in nearly all of the major civil rights gains made by the Mexican LGBT community in the past two decades. *Intrépidas* marched in Mexico City in support of the first federal LGBT antidiscrimination bill, which became law in 1999. They marched again in 2006 in support of the passage of the *Ley de Sociedad de Convivencia* in Mexico City, which provided for legal recognition of civil unions between same sex couples. They did the same in 2010 in support of the legalization of same sex marriage in Mexico City, and yet again in support of a similar bill that was passed in the northern state of Coahuila in 2014.

As I spoke with Maria about national sexual rights movements in the hair salon that she owns in downtown Juchitán, another *Intrépidas* member chimed in, referring to the gay and lesbian beneficiaries of the same sex marriage law in Mexico City as "our brothers and sisters [*nuestros hermanos y hermanas*]." The past and present of muxe political engagement, including the way they talk about these political engagements, suggests participation in a national and international sexual commons, and a solidarity based on a shared aspiration to legal recognition and protection.

Yet muxe people ostensibly do not share a similarly legible gender-sex constellation with their partners, or with their "brothers and sisters" in the capital. As Alfredo Mirandé, one of the few other ethnographers of the muxe community, explains:

> One thing that distinguishes muxes from gays is that they do not date or have sex with one another and that their sexual partners are hombres, or straight men. … Almost all of the muxes I interviewed also said they assumed the *pasivo* (passive/insertee) rather than the *activo* (active/inserter) role in both oral and anal sex, and they all indicated that they preferred hombres as sexual partners.
>
> *(Mirandé 2016: 395)*[6]

One of the core implications here is that muxe people do not generally conform to an object-preference structure of sexual identification. As one muxe informant told me over drinks at a bar in Juchitán, for a man to perform the active role in sex with a muxe is a decidedly normative act, one that makes the active sexual participant "even more *macho*." A muxe partner is merely another notch in his belt.

In my interview with Maria, she concurred, explicitly defining muxe sexuality in contradistinction to an object-preference mode of identification that she sees as more common in non-*juchiteco* Mexican culture:

> When a muxe has sex with a man, this is a heterosexual relation. It goes through the heads of men [from other cultures] that "if I have sex with a muxe, I'm also a muxe, I'm also gay." This doesn't happen in the heads of the men from here. Having sex with muxes is just another option for having sex, whether or not it is a man or a woman. It doesn't affect his masculinity [*machismo*], his manhood [*hombría*]. On the contrary, a man that has sex with women and with muxes feels even more masculine because he can have sex with anyone, with him and with her alike. In another culture, whether [the passive partner] is trans or whatever, ultimately, the passive partner is a man, biologically—like in Oaxaca [the state capital], which isn't too far away … couples are two gays, or two muxe. This is normal.

It is clear from Maria's explanation that the men who have sex with muxe people are heterosexual men within the *juchiteco* cultural context—but what does this mean for muxe sexual identity? According to Maria, muxe people routinely, exclusively in most cases, engage in "heterosexual relations," although other interviewees and even Maria (at other parts in the interview) describe muxe identity as having a distinct "homoerotic" dimension. This only adds to the urgency (it almost sounds hysterical) of the question: Are muxe people heterosexual? When I asked Maria this later in the interview, Maria responded ambivalently: "No, not exactly," and finally, "I don't know."

This ambivalence is due, on one hand, to a hesitation to maintain a rhetorical or real distinction between sexuality and gender in a social context in which sexual role preference is one of the key ways in which gender is performed and embodied. Indeed, in a social context in which sexuality and gender have not been unbound and declared distinct dimensions of one's personality (as sexual modernization would have it), asking whether or not muxe sexuality in itself is "heterosexual" has no answer, but can only serve to illustrate the illegibility of muxe sexuality in the register of sexual modernization. Maria herself struggles to find words to explain the contradiction that is raised when one tries to apply a heuristic of sexual modernity to muxe desire. This would not be so cunning a problem if not for the fact that Maria herself evoked heterosexuality. Perhaps her use of the word was simply a discrepancy in translating between two distinct logics of sex and gender identification. That could very well be, but then it is readily apparent that muxe sexuality *needs translating*. We run into the same problem either way: the register of sexual modernity—translated or not—is precisely the register in which muxe political organizations must articulate their claim on a sexual commons.

Felicitous claims, nevertheless, and indigenism

Muxe sexuality may be difficult to read in the register of sexual citizenship, but this clearly does not preclude felicitous symbolic and practical claims to a national sexual commons and broader civil society. Muxe groups like *Las Intrépidas* have deep relationships with many national political parties, local and federal governments, and a number of transnational development organizations. On the non-governmental organization (NGO) front, *Las Intrépidas Contra el SIDA* works with the Washington-based Pan American Health Organization (PAHO) on a number of projects, and was founded in 1996 following a $35,000 (MXN) PAHO grant to put on a musical theater production in Spanish and Zapotec to raise awareness about HIV. Amaranta Gómez Regalado, the director of Biini Laanu, received a McArthur Grant in 1998. Subsequently in 2003, Gómez Regalado even ran for a seat in the lower house of the Mexican Congress on the ticket of a short-lived social democratic party, *México Posible*—a party presided over by another McArthur grant recipient, Patricia Mercado (Miano Borruso 2010, 5).

On the local level, 2017 marks the seventh consecutive year that there has been a muxe person in a managerial position in the municipal government of Juchitán. Maria was the first to receive such a position as Director of the Office of Sexual Diversity from 2010 to 2013 under the PRI municipal government. When a candidate from an *istmeño* coalition of activists and unionists won the 2013 municipal presidency with the financial backing of the PRD, Fernanda Ortega, who makes an extended appearance in the IDB film, became director of a similar department dubbed the Office of Public Policy on Sexual Diversity. Several members of Biini Laanu, one of whom I interviewed in 2014, were also brought on to work under Fernanda in the year of the interview, and continue their work in the municipal government following the successful bid of a PRD–PAN (National Action Party) coalition candidate in 2016.

These municipal positions are the result of a web of clientelistic relationships between muxe-led organizations, individuals, political candidates, and political parties. Maria and another *Intrépida* member happily told me that the PRI and an assortment of associated political candidates have for decades provided a large part of the funding for the most widely publicized event in Juchitán (Excelsior 2016b; Vice 2013; NPR 2012), *La Vela de las Intrépidas Buscadoras del Peligro*, a three-day carnival-like street festival complete with beauty pageants, feasts, and musical acts organized by *Las Intrépidas*. Maria summarized that the PRI is like "a *padrino* to me," that is, a godfather-like benefactor that provides funding for her projects in return for information, electoral support, and party loyalty, among other favors.

The late Juan Ramirez, a locally famous activist, scholar and educator from Juchitán, and founding member of the Isthmus anti-AIDS organization *Gunaxhii Guendanabani*, commented to me with tongue-in-cheek bitterness in a 2014 interview that "most of these illiterate bitches [*putas*] like Maria don't have a particular political vision; they get these positions because they make a deal with their *padrinos* in the political parties." Juan's biting tone underlines that the muxe community in Juchitán is not monolithic. There is intense competition for resources among muxe organizations, and resultantly there is ample internecine conflict. Maria had similar words for Fernanda, whom she accused of misrepresenting herself in her pact with the PRD to take a position in the administration's renovated Office of Sexual Diversity. Maria argued that Fernanda courted the PRD by creating a shell civil society organization that she used to convince party officials that she spoke for a broader group within muxe community than she really did in order to receive a government salary. Another *Intrépida* commented that "a lot of times these organizations exist just to traffic in favors." Most interestingly in relation to a politics of representation, Maria asserted that, "as far as the PRD was concerned, there was some big meeting that every Muxe in Juchitán … attended that made Fernanda our representative."

By all accounts, even a few muxe people with the right smoke, mirrors, floral prints and tax designation, seem to be able to make a felicitous claim to represent *something* that parties like the PAN, PRD, and PRI find worthy of investment. It is hard to believe that muxe organizations command so significant a portion of the vote that political candidates from virtually every locally active party would at some point engage one muxe organization or another to make a pact and offer significant resources—yet, according to my interviews with the key players in Juchitán and the state capital, this is precisely what candidates do.

What makes the muxe community legible to political parties as a discrete group of rights-bearing citizens, and an attractive electoral demographic? A high-ranking party official in the department of Civil-Society Collaboration at the state headquarters of the PRI described the muxe community and an *istmeño* sexual commons in the following way:

> In the Isthmus men are more given to not being closed off [literally, "covering up" *tapar*]—how can I say this—that is, men—*istmeños* call them muxes— are more open in saying "I like other men"—it's apparent as a way of being, a way of dressing, they grow their hair out, they are easy to identify in public, they dress *a la tehuana*. In the Isthmus, they say that there are women, men, and muxes, and, when a muxe is born, they say that the mom thinks of it as a sign of good luck, a blessing, because the muxe will stay and take care of her in old age … [Compared to the capital city region] in the Isthmus, they're more folklore [*más folklore*], more culture, more of the *tehuana*, and Zapotec tradition. There's also the climate—because of the heat, people tend to be more sexually open and happier, they drink more beer and they party more.

In this party official's description, we again find a deep ambiguity when it comes muxe sexual identity. Muxe people are semi-legible under the rubric of sexual modernity as gay men, yet they simultaneously constitute a category distinct from women and men. Much like their depiction in the IDB film, the party official describes muxe people as part of a larger assemblage of vague concepts: "folklore," "culture," "*la tehuana,*" "Zapotec tradition" and (implicitly), muxe. The official hedges her descriptions with "they say [*se dice*]," connoting an aspect of hearsay or regional legend. And the hearsay is that muxe people are a regional superstition, a good luck charm and the product of irreducibly particular cultural idiosyncrasies—indeed, the story about muxe people coming into the world as good luck charms or blessings is a common refrain, particularly outside of Juchitán and in English language publications (Buzzfeed 2013; *The Guardian* 2010). Moreover, in the party official's description, the sexual milieu of the Isthmus is a function of nature and a proximity to nature—heat literally translates to openness, promiscuity, drinking, revelry, and (implicitly), muxe sexuality. One might say that while the sexual modernization discourse requires a naturalization of sexual desire to make a felicitous claim to sexual citizenship (i.e. the "born this way" narrative), recognition of muxe people as sexual citizens has come to involve literally recognizing them *as nature* (*qua* indigenous alterity).

Muxe identity reads ambiguously in the script of sexual modernization, but this ambiguity—this lack of a concrete object of desire on which to base a taxonomy—is deferred as indigenized objects like culture, good luck, nature, tropical heat and, of course, the image of the *tehuana* function as ready stand-ins. This is appropriate to the milieu: Mexican civil society has a great deal of experience in developing (anxious, nostalgic, ecstatic) attachments to such objects, and politicians have a great deal of experience in deploying allusions to such object-worlds. In other words, the templates for an aesthetics of sexual citizenship and an aesthetics of indigenous citizenship are entwined in the case of muxe politics, and entwined in such a way that the excess—the extra term that eludes legibility in the dialectic of sexual rights—is folded into a different, older national system for imagining and engaging alerity: indigenism.

The *traje tehuana* in particular is an immensely generative and historically deep reference, and one of the best examples of such a dynamic. As Francie Chassen-López (2014) observed in her analysis of the emergence of Zapotec femininity in the post-revolutionary national imaginary,

> in the 1920s, just as Mexicans were forging this more inclusive national identity, the exoticism and primitivism popular among intellectuals and artists in Europe reached Mexico. *Tehuanas*—sensual and romanticized matriarchs in luxurious Zapotec dress—now emerged as representative of the primitive, set in exuberant nature.
>
> *(Chassen-López 2014, 285–286)*

Indigenism here can be formulated as a kind of nationalist ideology that seeks to establish a mythos of origins through which the collective body of the nation is naturalized as transhistorical. In this formulation, the image of the indigenous person is a vehicle through which the white or mestizo Mexican subject can see her own likeness *qua* a nation in the mists of natural history, but which is inevitably vexed by the continued existence of indigenous bodies as unassimilable alterity, and by the systematic violence, dispossession, and neglect that reproduces the material conditions of indigeneity as such. "Indigenism," then, is both the positing of the racialized nature from which the second nature of the nation emerged to begin its march through history, and simultaneously the framing of this march as a civilizing project of incorporating the excess material of its origin—that is, disturbingly, existing indigenous bodies.

The sensual, luxurious matriarchs of the Isthmus, *las tehuanas* have long served as the term in the formula of Mexican indigenism that represents likeness, national continuity with nature, and noble origins. *Tehuana* femininity has a long history of aesthetic associations with, as classical Mexican Anthropologist Miguel Covarrubias put it, "jungles that seem lifted from a Rousseau canvas; the oriental color of markets ... classic elegance ... stately grace ... gold-coin necklaces worth hundreds of dollars ..." (Covarrubias 1946, xxii as cited in Chassen-López 2014). Both Chassen-López in a historical study and Howell (2006) in a contemporary ethnographic account argue that much of the national fascination with *tehuana* femininity comes from its association with grace and wealth, making possible an attachment to a racially pure indigenous object held in contradistinction to the impoverished, neglected condition of indigenous life in many parts of the country.

In Mexico and abroad, there is a voracious appetite for likenesses of the *tehuana*; she is a recurring subject in the famous murals of Diego Rivera, where she figures as a "national body ... that would give birth, both literally and symbolically to a new mestizo nation" (Coffey 2012: 62). Her image is *literally money* (indigenism has a perverse fondness for the literal), gracing the front of the 1937 Mexican ten-peso bill that remained in circulation for forty years (Chassen-López 2014, 289). During debates in the early 1990s on the ratification of the North American Free Trade Agreement (NAFTA), middle class women in Mexico City dressed in the *tehuana*'s likeness as a sign of cultural authenticity and a statement "in opposition to the government's attempt to "polyesterize" the population" (Schaefer 1992, 26 as cited in Howell 2006) illustrating Elizabeth Povinelli's observation that, under a framework of liberal multiculturalism, "'indigenousness' [begins] to function as an interpretant to be experienced as an aura, naturalizing any struggle or commodity desire to which it [is] attached" (Povinelli 2002, 24).

The *traje tejuana*, however, is not a pre-colonial custom; virtually every aspect of the garment is the material product of transnational encounters and a global imperialist economy, including the availability of the textiles that are required for its authentic reproduction (i.e. linen, lace, velvet) (Chassen-López 2014, 307). Likewise, muxe use of the *traje* is not an eternal phenomenon. While ubiquitous in contemporary representations of muxe people, Maria and Juan, both over fifty at the time of interview, recalled a time in their lives when muxe people did not commonly wear the *traje*. Amaranta Gómez stated in an interview with a Mexican journalist that "It [adopting feminine dress] is relatively new, actually. Speaking with people over 50, they told me that in their era nobody did it because it was too dangerous" (Agencia Presentes 2016).

Needless to say, representations of muxe people in the *traje* are also relatively new. In our interview, Maria told me that requests for interviews, appearances in documentaries, and attendance at photo shoots have increased dramatically over the past two decades. In that time period Maria herself has made appearances in four documentaries, and has lost count of the number of interviews and photo shoots she has done. She made a point of emphasizing that her community's relationship with media workers has changed dramatically in this time period:

> It used to be that they would tell us where to meet and a few of us would show up to talk while they invited us to some refreshments ... [but now] people with money show up, and they tell us "I need ten muxes for a photo shoot, I want them to show up dressed in *tehuana* attire at X location at X time in the morning and we'll pay 500 or 1000 pesos per head."

Maria and two other muxe people visiting her salon during our interview, who had also ostensibly appeared in documentaries and photo shoots, commented on the absurdity and repetitive nature of the scenes that photographers are fond of staging: one stated "they walk us around town, here and there—to show how we are accepted in broader society— asking every time for the same scene of us standing in a crowd." "Or they make us sit at some damn sewing machine!" another called out from across the room to the laughter of everyone else. When I raised the question of whether an "ancient transgender tradition" is simply an invention of foreign journalists, Juan Ramirez reasoned,

> There's a real openness here, but if they're buying it, someone's selling it ... I had a masculine-presenting [*masculinizada*] friend—a flamboyant [*loca*] muxe, a big old bald queen—she always complained "how come nobody ever takes photos of me?" One day I told her to give them the exoticness [*lo exótico*] that they were asking for, to dress up as a *tehuana*, and sure enough she made a few dollars taking pictures with foreigners at the next *vela*.

This is all to illustrate that mass mediated representations of muxe indigeneity are oftentimes staged, constructed, and couched in drastically unequal economic relations, *and that many muxe people understand this and act accordingly*.

I do not present this information to set up an all too common anthropological variant of the "gotcha" moment, wherein some social phenomenon is triumphantly revealed to be constructed, or "fake," nor to replicate the older but related anthropological tradition of obsessively trying to discern the degree zero of "real," indigenous practices from "diluted" ones (Povinelli 2002, 4). I have no interest here in making an ontological claim on what muxe indigeneity is and is not. But I can offer up that muxe indigeneity, "every inch a relationship and not a thing in itself" (Taussig 1993, 129), is both the radically constructed object of external desire, and an earnestly felt dimension of personal subjectivity. When I asked if someone could be muxe but not *istemeño* Zapotec, Maria, two of the muxe visitors in her salon, and (later) one of the muxe workers in the office of Sexual Diversity, responded with a resounding "no." This was a surprising response in some respects, since all the other questions that I had asked about gender presentation, sexuality, and choices of profession elicited elaborately hedged, occasionally internally contradictory responses.

Although indigeneity seems to be the aspect of muxe presentation that most captures the imaginations of politicians, development bureaucrats, and journalists alike, its most seductive quality is its couching in an uncanny sexual modernity—and *vice versa*, the sexual modernity of the muxe community is at its most compelling when it is couched in the trappings of a palatable indigeneity. At no point in the elaboration of a muxe, indigenist claim to the public sphere is their equally visible claim to a national and international sexual commons cancelled out or eclipsed. Rather, a discourse on sexual modernity that is already grounded in the frustrated dialectics of nature and culture, man and woman, straight and gay, defers its excess material, its latent contradictions, into a discourse and aesthetics of indigeneity. Indigeneity then grounds muxe identity—especially its public manifestation as an earnest claim to resources and rights—where ambivalence and translation errors pervade elsewhere. But, similar to the aesthetics of sexual citizenship, the aesthetic markers of muxe indigeneity, like the *traje tejuana*, retain a contradictory element; they remain that inscribed surface that paradoxically constitutes an authentic, essential core.

Conclusions

This chapter, as part of an ongoing and larger ethnographic project, provides more questions than answers in many respects. I have referenced manifold histories—particularly those of the broader LGBT movement in Mexico, of muxe activism in the Isthmus, of a national politics of indigenous recognition from the revolution to the present, and of the emergence of neoliberalism in Mexico—that have been well-analyzed separately, but remain unconnected in much of the scholarly literature.

This case complicates and adds nuance to existing critical ways of understanding cosmopolitan sexual citizenship as it is articulated in the milieu of that civilizing project that its overseers so fondly refer to as "development." A muxe politics of representation does and does not fit into an existing critical understanding of the hegemonic global discourse on sexual citizenship as a compulsion to assimilate to western forms of knowing the body.

Yet the case of muxe politics is not merely a counterpoint or an added nuance. I have attempted to read the points at which permutations occur as elaborations of the contradictory fissures already existing in the object of critique. This means reading the puzzle of a muxe politics of recognition as produced by (and generative of) existing contradictions in the material reality of global institutions of sexual citizenship. This materiality can register as a kind of political economy and a corresponding form of immanent critique that one might characterize as "materialist"—but it also consists of elaborate micro economies of affect, fetishes, and objects of desire that constitute sexual subjects as *embodied* subjects, and political representation as personal identity.

Notes

1 Statement translated from Spanish. All translations are mine unless otherwise noted.
2 For further reading on processes of neoliberalization and commodity production in Mexico in general, see Weaver (2012). For further scholarly reading on wind farm projects in Oaxaca, see Howe (2014) and Altamirano-Jiménez (2017).
3 Two organizations actually fall under the banner of *Las Intrépidas*: *Las Intrépidas Buscadoras del Peligro* (The Intrepid Women in Search of Danger) and *Las Intrépidas Contra el SIDA* (The Intrepid Women against AIDS), an offshoot advocacy group (run by the same core group of people) that is dedicated to the prevention of HIV/AIDS in the Isthmus.
4 Pseudonyms are used for all interviewees and people mentioned in interviews.
5 Muxe people's use of gendered pronouns often varies by context. In situations where an interviewee and their acquaintances use a particular gendered pronoun consistently (as Maria did), I use that pronoun.
6 Although originally applied to gay men in Latin America, Mirandé here is deploying the *activo/pasivo* model of sexual identification—a model that has been taken up as a general heuristic by scholars of Latin American sexuality (Carrier 1995; Murray 1995; Lancaster 2002). Murray defines the *activo/pasivo* model of sexual identification as characteristic of "cultures with gender stratified organizations of homosexuality" (Murray 1995, 11), wherein the conventionally passive feminine partner (regardless of their designated sex at birth) is (1) always the passive partner and (2) considered to a certain degree to have a gender distinct from the more masculine partner, reminiscent of Don Kulick's category of "not-men" (Kulick 1998, 229). In this structure of sexual identification, there is little trace of the contemporary distinction (often mobilized by activists in the global north) between sexuality and gender—indeed the form of expression of sexual desire often defines (but not necessarily determines) the subject's gender. This is in contradistinction to a model wherein ones "biological" (designated at birth) sex and the sex of the subject's preferred partner defines the subject's sexuality.

References

Agencia Presentes. 2016. *Las muxes, una identidad transgénero milenaria*. http://agenciapresentes. org/2016/11/24/las-muxes-una-identidad-transgenero-milenaria/ (accessed April 5, 2017).
Altamirano-Jiménez, I. 2017. "'The Sea is Our Bread': Interrupting Green Neoliberalism in Mexico." *Marine Policy* 80, no. 28: 28–34.

BBC. 2016. "Making noise about machismo in Mexico." http://www.bbc.com/news/world-36324570 (accessed March 5, 2017).

BID. 2017. *Lo que hacemos*. http://www.iadb.org/es/acerca-del-bid/departamentos/lo-que-hacemos,1342. html?dept_id=IFD (accessed February 26, 2017).

Bosia, M. and Weiss, M. 2013. "Political Homophobia." In *Global Homophobia*, edited by Weiss, M. and Bosia, M., pp. 1–29. University of Illinois: Urbana, IL.

Buzzfeed. 2013. "One photographer showcases Mexico's gender-defying indigenous community." https://www.buzzfeed.com/skarlan/one-photographer-showcases-mexicos-gender-defying-indigenous?utm_term=.pkYYVvQPw3#.rh3b0VnrqD (accessed March 17, 2017).

Carrier, J. 1995. *De Los Otros: Intimacy and Homosexuality among Mexican Men*. New York: Columbia University Press.

Chassen-López, F. 2014. "The *Traje Tehuana* as National Icon: Gender Ethnicity, and Fashion in Mexico." *The Americas* 71, no. 2: 281–314.

Coffey, M.K. 2012. "'All Mexico on A Wall': Diego Rivera's Murals at the Ministry of Public Education." In *Mexican Muralism*, edited by Anreus, A., Folgarait, L. and Greeley, R.A., pp. 56–74. Berkeley, CA: University of California Press.

Covarrubias, M. 1946. *Mexico South: The Isthmus of Tehuantepec*. New York: Alfred A. Knopf.

De la Dehesa, R. 2010. *Queering the Public Sphere in Mexico and Brazil*. Duke Durham, NC: University Press.

Driver, A. 2015. *More or Less Dead: Feminicide, Haunting, and the Ethics of Representation in Mexico*. Tuscon, AZ: University of Arizona Press.

El Universal. 2016. *Feminicidio en Mexico*. http://www.eluniversal.com.mx/entrada-de-opinion/articulo/arnoldo-kraus/nacion/2016/03/13/feminicidio-en-mexico (accessed March 5, 2017).

Excelsior. 2016a. *Atacan a candidate del PRD en Oaxaca, muere una persona*. http://www.excelsior.com.mx/nacional/2016/05/14/1092615 (accessed February 26, 2017).

Excelsior. 2016b. *Baile, cerveza y alegría, fueron protagonistas de la vela muxe en Oaxaca*. http://www.excelsior.com.mx/nacional/2016/11/20/1129349 (accessed March 15, 2017).

Ferguson J. 1994. "The Anti-Politics Machine: 'Development' and Bureaucratic Power in Lesotho." *The Ecologist* 24: 176–181.

Fusion. 2015. "Meet the muxes." http://interactive.fusion.net/meet-the-muxes/ (accessed March 8, 2017).

GobApp. 2014. *La fascinante historia de los muxhes*. https://www.youtube.com/watch?v=D2XyrHfKhas (accessed February 17, 2017).

Howe, C. 2013. *Intimate Activism: The Struggle for Sexual Rights in Postrevolutionary Nicaragua*. Durham, NC: Duke University Press.

Howe, C. 2014. "Anthropocenic Ecoauthority: The Winds of Oaxaca." *Anthropological Quarterly* 87, no. 2: 381–404.

Howell, J. 2006. "Constructions and Commodifications of Isthmus Zapotec Women." *Studies in Latin American Popular Culture* 25, no. 1: 1-23.

Juchitán, Queer Paradise. 2002. Film. Directed by Patricio Henriquez. New York: Filmakers Library.

Kipling, R. 1899. "The White Man's Burden." *MuClure's Magazine* 8, no. 4: 290–291.

Kulick, D. 1998. *Travesti: Sex, Gender and Culture among Brazilian Transgendered Prostitutes*. Chicago, IL: University of Chicago Press.

La Jornada. 2012. *Amenazan presuntos paramilitares a opositores a parquet eólico en Oaxaca*. http://www.jornada.unam.mx/2012/09/19/estados/046n1est (accessed February 26, 2017).

Lancaster, R. 2002. "Subject Honor and Object Shame: The Construction of Male Homosexuality and Stigma in Nicaragua." In *Sexuality and Gender*, edited by Williams, C. and Stein, A., pp. 87–99. Blackwell: Oxford.

Laskar, P. 2014. "The Illiberal Turn: Aid Conditionalis and the Queering of Sexual Citizenship." *Lambda Nordica* 1: 87–100.

Miano Borruso, M. 2010. "Muxe: 'Nuevos Liderazgos' y Fenómenos Mediáticos'." *Revista Digital Universitaria* 11, no. 9: 3–15.

Mirandé, A. 2016. "Hombres Mujeres: An Indigenous Third Gender." *Men and Masculinities* 19, no. 4: 384–409.

Murray, S.O. 1995. "Homosexual Categorization in Cross-Cultural Perspective." In *Latin American Male Homosexualities*, edited by Murray, S.O., pp. 3–32. Albuquerque, NM: University of New Mexico Press.

National Geographic. 2017. "Third gender, an entrancing look at Mexico's Muxes." https://www.youtube.com/watch?v=S1ZvDRxZlb0 (accessed February 26, 2017).

The New York Times. 2016. "Los Parques eólicos generan prosperidad en Oaxaca, pero no para todos." https://www.nytimes.com/es/2016/08/01/los-parques-eolicos-generan-prosperidad-en-oaxaca-pero-no-para-todos/ (accessed February 26, 2017).

NPR. 2012. "In Mexico, mixed genders and 'muxes'." http://www.npr.org/sections/pictureshow/2012/05/30/153990125/in-mexico-mixed-genders-and-muxes (accessed March 15, 2017).

Povinelli, E. 2002. *The Cunning of Recognition: Indigenous Alterities and the Making of Australian Multiculturalism*. Durham, NC: Duke University Press.

Puar, J. 2007. *Terrorist Assemblages: Homonationalism in Queer Times*. Durham, NC: Duke University Press.

Schaefer, C. 1992. *Textured Lives: Women, Art and Representation in Modern Mexico*. Tucson, AZ: University of Arizona Press.

Sinembargo. 2015. *Parques Eólicos: la cara de despojo en el istmo de Tehuantepec*. http://www.sinembargo.mx/01-04-2015/1298234 (accessed February 26, 2017).

Taussig, M. 1993. *Mimesis and Alterity: A Particular History of the Senses*. New York: Routledge.

The Guardian. 2010. "My Travels: Isabella Tree Meets the Glorious Matriarchs of A Mexican Town" https://www.theguardian.com/travel/2010/nov/13/isabella-tree-mexico-juchitan-oaxaca (accessed March 10, 2017).

Tönnies, F.1988. *Community and Society*. Routledge: New York.

Vice. 2013. *Las Intrépidas Buscadoras del Peligro*. https://www.vice.com/es_mx/article/las-intrepidas-buscadoras-de-peligro-video (accessed March 15, 2017).

Waites, M. 2009. "Critique of 'Sexual Orientation' and 'Gender Identity' in Human Rights Discourse: Global Queer Politics beyond the Yogyakarta Principles." *Contemporary Politics* 15, no. 1: 137–156.

Weaver, T. 2012. *Neoliberalism and Commodity Production Mexico*. Boulder, CO: University of Colorado Press.

Weber, M. 2015. *Rationalism and Modern Society*. New York: Palgrave Macmillan.

Wright, M. 2011. "Necropolitics, Narcopolitics and Femicide: Gendered Violence on the Mexico-US Border." *Signs: Journal of Women in Culture and Society* 36, no. 3: 707–731.

14

QUEER DILEMMAS

LGBT activism and international funding

Julie Moreau and Ashley Currier

Since 2011, the global funding landscape for development aid has shifted. After Hillary Clinton's speech at the United Nations in which she declared, "Gay rights are human rights," development aid has increasingly been tied to support for lesbian, gay, bisexual, and transgender (LGBT) rights (Bergenfield and Miller 2014). As studies of transnational sexualities have examined, Western sexualities travel transnationally and local constructions of sexuality modify, reject, and supplant them (Blackwood 2005; Grewal and Kaplan 2001; Morgan and Wieringa 2005). One way that Western identities have circulated transnationally is through Northern donors' funding of LGBT movements (Lind and Share 2003; Wright 2005). Due to the economic, political, and social threat that HIV/AIDS has posed worldwide, development agencies in the North have funded HIV/AIDS education and prevention programs in the global South. As some HIV/AIDS programs have included gender and sexually diverse persons, development agencies have contributed to the transnational diffusion of LGBT identities in and movements in Latin America, Asia, and sub-Saharan Africa (Lind 2010; Lind and Share 2003; Lorway 2014; Wright 2005). Within the past twenty years, Northern donors have begun to fund LGBT movement organizations in different African nations directly (Currier 2012; Hoad 2007). Although some donors primarily fund HIV/AIDS projects that serve African LGBT people, other donors earmark funds for projects on enhancing LGBT rights or on reducing African gender and sexual minorities' exposure to harm. Hivos, a donor agency based in the Netherlands, has historically funded LGBT rights non-governmental organizations (NGOs) in different African nations; most recently, their funding has supported South African lesbian activist organizations fighting antilesbian rape and violence and transgender organizing in Kenya.

Scholars have critiqued the heteronormativity, or the presumption of heterosexuality, of development theory and practice (Lind 2009, 2010; Lind and Share 2003). However, despite scrutiny of Northern funding of LGBT movement organizations in the global South (Blessol 2013; Gosine 2013; Hoad 2007; Seckinelgin 2009), there is little understanding about new forms of normativity among LGBT movements in the global South that arise in relation to Northern funding. In this chapter, we argue that African LGBT activists face a "queer dilemma" with respect to Northern funding. The benefits Northern funding affords make it difficult for African LGBT activists to refuse, although accepting funding renders LGBT groups vulnerable to both heteronormative and homonormative pressures that buttress neocolonial power relations. Some organizations experience antigay hostility cast as efforts to decolonize the country, while others experience expectations to replicate Northern LGBT organizational forms and practices.

This essay draws on original research conducted in Malawi and South Africa. Currier interviewed 51 activists involved with HIV/AIDS, human rights, women's rights, and LGBT rights NGOs in Malawi in 2012 and 80 Malawian gender and sexual minorities about their experiences with politicized, religious, and social homophobias in 2014. Moreau interviewed 36 activists from 21 different organizations in Cape Town, Pretoria, Johannesburg and the surrounding townships in 2011 and 2012 about the movement's direction after lawmakers enshrined a sexual-orientation nondiscrimination clause in the constitution in 1996 and passed marriage-equality legislation in 2006.

The NGOization of feminist and LGBT movements

Transnational feminist scholars have documented a trend toward "NGOization" among some feminist movements—the tendency of feminist activists to form funded, specialized and professional bureaucratic organizations after the 1995 United Nations Fourth World Conference on Women in Beijing (Alvarez 1998, 306; Bernal and Grewal 2014; Jad 2007). Drawing on their knowledge of and experience with economic, social, and political development projects initiated by the West, many feminist activists throughout Africa, Asia, and Latin America have sought funding for specialized projects. "[S]tability and visibility" may accompany the foreign funding and NGOization of feminist activism, but these perquisites may put feminist movement organizations in the path of the "'tyranny of funders'" (Yuval-Davis 2006, 287). In particular, feminists skeptical of NGOization assert,

> NGOs have enabled the depoliticization of social and women's movements, their appropriation by donor-driven agendas, and a neoliberal co-optation of feminist practice. They understand NGOs as a fall from Eden—a teleological decline from an idealized age of revolutionary feminist activism to the contemporary era of professionalized organizations that function as donors' peons.
>
> *(Hodžić 2014, 221)*

Feminist scholarship shows how international support can positively impact feminist organizing within democratizing nations (Viterna and Fallon 2008, 672), although some feminists urge caution with respect to international influence and funding (Bulbeck 2007; Mindry 2001). First, they are concerned that African, Asian, Eastern European, Middle Eastern, and Latin American feminists may become too dependent on funding from Northern donors, thus reproducing global inequalities between more and less affluent nations (Markowitz and Tice 2002; Nzegwu 2002). This dependency can derail activists' projects as they spend too much time trying to satisfy funders' demands, which siphons time, resources, and attention away from critical political projects and erodes their accountability to their constituents (Britton 2006; Hassim 2005). Often, organizations that become dependent on foreign funding are "left without the necessary resources to survive," if donors suspend their funding (Espinoza 2007, 18). Such NGOs become vulnerable to changing Northern donor priorities. Second, because organizations become so reliant on foreign funding, they may tailor their projects for specific donors, even revising organizational structures to please donors. Hannah Britton (2006, 157) observes that South African feminist movement organizations fighting domestic violence put their "long-term programmatic needs" on hold or at risk "to create new, eye-catching, pilot programmes to attract international funding agencies." She likens this process to "a form of commercialization" in which feminist movement organizations do their best to "remain attractive, interesting, if not titillating, to an international audience" (Britton 2006, 157). Queer women activists in Kenya adopted the NGO structure at the behest of international donors; they also framed sexuality-based demands in terms of human rights (Dearham 2013). Embracing an NGO structure and human-rights framework reveals a normalizing impulse among LGBT NGOs that "mirror[s] approaches and practices taken by 'mainstream' NGOs" (Dearham 2013, 191). In such instances, LGBT NGOs internalize donor priorities and work to ensure that other LGBT NGOs in the movement behave according to mainstream LGBT NGOs' expectations (Currier 2010, 2012). In these ways, leaders of feminist and LGBT movement organizations may come to put donors' priorities ahead of constituents' needs and movement priorities.

Some feminist scholars criticize the internal and external competition that can emerge as feminist and LGBT movement organizations vie for limited donor funding (Britton 2006; Hrycak 2007; Sperling, Ferree, and Risman 2001). In her study of Ghanaian women's organizing in the late 1990s, Kathleen M. Fallon (2008) shows how well-meaning Northern donors fostered rivalry among women's movement organizations that were competing for limited funding. Northern funding of the controversial 31st December Women's Movement, which was affiliated with President Jerry Rawlings' authoritarian regime, meant that some autonomous women's organizations had to scrape together funding to keep operating or scale back their projects. Donor staff eventually became aware of the contradiction in funding a state-affiliated women's organization, but they still did not "view women's organizations as directly taking on formal politics" (Fallon 2008, 67). Even when organizations obtain external funding, not all programs or project may receive funding, which can lead to internal friction among staff and activists about funding priorities (Ward 2008).

Queer development studies and emergent normativities

Although feminist theorizing has generated important criticisms about new forms of domination symptomatic of inequality between the global North and South, little is understood about the new forms of normativity and vulnerability that accompany Northern funding of feminist and LGBT organizing in the global South. The dawn of queer development studies has facilitated scholarly understandings of the complicated dynamics associated specifically with Northern funding of Southern LGBT activism. For example, Susie Jolly (2000, 83) contends that while activists are wary of foreign "imperialist" influence and support, international funding as been instrumental to the development of the Chinese *tongzhi*[1] movement. Similarly, Amy Lind and Jessica Share (2003) argue that development funding is an important mechanism for the flow of knowledge about gender and sexual diversity. The NGOization of the LGBT movement in Latin America has meant the construction of "a strong, growing network of local, regional and international organizations, many of which are connected to the international development field in one way or anther" (Lind and Share 2003, 64). In her examination of the NGOization of the Kenyan lesbian, gay, bisexual, transgender, and intersex (LGBTI) movement, Kaitlin Dearham (2013) discusses how queer women formed organizations in response to their under-representation in the movement. Development funding has helped to diffuse identity politics and institutionalize LGBT movements.

Seemingly paradoxical, the expansion in funding to groups that deal with issues of sexuality can increase heteronormative pressures for organizations in the global South. For example, funding is still distributed according to heteronormative standards, and therefore not reaching all NGOs. Susana T. Fried and Shannon Kowalski-Morton (2008) lament that Global Fund dollars are not reaching men who have sex with men (MSM), and sex-worker communities, even in places where HIV prevalence is high among these groups. They explain that these communities are barred from accessing the funding due to stigma and exclusion at the national level. Even when LGBT NGOs receive funding, movement practices can reproduce heteronormativities, including masculine dominance. There is a gender gap in the leadership of African LGBT organizations with gay and MSM-identified people outnumbering queer women and transgender people (Theron, McAllister, and Armisen 2016).

In the postcolonial African context, the link between nationalism and normative heteromasculinity allows African leaders to cast international funding as a corrupting outside influence (Currier 2012; Hoad 1999). Therefore, international funding of LGBT activist organizations also authorizes leaders of African countries to engage in political homophobia upon receipt, as well as withdrawal, of funding. Scapegoating of gender and sexual minorities occurred in Malawi in 2010, after the conviction of Tiwonge Chimbalanga and Steven Monjeza for violating the antisodomy law in Malawi. Rumors circulated that the UK would suspend donor aid to the country, if the government did not release the couple (Somanje 2010, 2). Then-President Bingu wa Mutharika claimed that some foreign donors were displeased with his "development initiatives" and capitalized on the "gay issue to prevent donor funding [from coming] to Malawi" (Khunga 2010, 1). Ultimately, Mutharika pardoned the couple days after the magistrate sentenced them to fourteen years in prison. In Mutharika's view, the pardon allowed him to regain control of the national narrative about morality so that "the two gays" could not "taint Malawi's democratic image to the outside world" (Khunga 2010, 1, 3). This statement confirmed Mutharika's concern about Malawi's international reputation. Implicit in his formulation is the association of democracy and national sovereignty with heteronormative morality, an equation out of step with international norms linking LGBT rights with democratic engagement.

African activists have not remained silent about Northern countries that use LGBT rights as an aid conditionality with African countries like Malawi and Uganda. "Donor sanctions," they write, "are by their nature coercive and reinforce the disproportionate power dynamics between donor countries and recipients" (African Statement 2013, 93). Aid conditionalities ignore African activists' agency and can exacerbate the divide between LGBT movements and other social movements such as women's and labor movements by increasing the heteronormative pressure on these other types of social movements.

Through the concept of homonormativity, queer theorizing offers another way to understand emerging normativities within and among LGBT movement organizations. Homonormativity consists of a "politics that does not contest dominant heteronormative assumptions and institutions, but upholds and sustains them, while promising the possibility of a demobilized gay constituency and a privatized, depoliticized gay culture anchored in domesticity and consumption" (Duggan 2003, 50). In Lisa Duggan's (2003) usage, homonormativity buoys neoliberal lesbian and gay subjectivities that mesh with and do not challenge heteronormative social and political arrangements. Homonormativity also creates new hierarchies in which "some queers are better than others" (Puar 2007, 48). Some queer theorists treat the professionalization and external funding of LGBT movement organizations as indicative of the rise of homonormativity of LGBT activism (Andrucki and Elder 2007; Richardson 2005). Diane Richardson (2005, 524, emphasis removed) notes that "some lesbian and gay social movements" are "no longer troubling to mainstream society." Professional movement organizations have mainstreamed and normalized certain images of lesbians and gay men who "conform to mainstream standards of middle-class respectability" (Doyle 2008, 210). These political strategies often leave queer persons who are not white, middle class, and gender normative behind (Oswin 2007). Additionally, theorists observe that homonormalizing LGBT movement organizations can spell the demise of independent spaces from which queer activists and individuals can criticize heteronormativity. In their study of disappearing, autonomous queer spaces in Vermont in the United States, Max J. Andrucki and Glen S. Elder (2007, 100) contend that nonprofit LGBT organizations may find themselves engulfed by homonormativity because the "regulatory environment into which [they] are born ensures that these voluntary-sector spaces are always already incorporated into state projects, neoliberal or not."

If homonormativity is at work in North–South funding relations, what forms does Northern donors' regulation of LGBT movement organizations in the global South take? And how does homonormativity influence internal movement dynamics? Rachel Bergenfield and Alice M. Miller (2014) examine the increase in funding tied to LGBT rights from international donors, such as the United Nations Development Programme (UNDP) and World Bank, and countries such as the United States through US Agency for International Development (USAID). They highlight issues that arise with this shift in funding priorities toward LGBT issues, including inadequate consultation with local LGBT activists, the isolation of "LGBT specific" interventions from other programs, and the reification of single-axis identities (Bergenfield and Miller 2014, 4).

The reification of single-axis identities occurs when Northern donors determine and narrow parameters for what constitute LGBT identities and through the use of donor language itself. Liesl Theron, John McAllister, and Mariam Armisen (2016) explain that activists must usually interact with donors in either English or French:

> As in African societies as a whole, colonial languages are associated with modernity, progress, authority, and "universal" values. Their supremacy in the official, documented work of African queer/LGBTIA+ activism inevitably imposes a Northern, universalizing (or homogenizing) point of view on the work. In particular, it means that the concepts and terminologies used to understand and express queer/LGBTIA+ identities have to be borrowed from the North, even when here and there an indigenous term is adopted for cosmetic effect (as with kuchu in East Africa). Specifically Northern cultural and political artifacts, especially connected to Northern gayness, are "naturalized" into African queer/LGBTIA+ cultures and activism. In the process, developing (or preserving) authentic, grassroots-based African queer/LGBTIA+ self-understandings, cultural expressions, and political agendas is stifled.

Colonial languages not only normalize certain concepts around gender and sexual identity, but also serve as "vehicles for Northern concepts of what development means, not just economically but also politically and culturally" (Theron, McAllister, and Armisen 2016). In this way, LGBT movement organizations can become absorbed by neoliberal, heteronormative structures and come to promote a restrictive vision of feminist and LGBT organizing (Oswin 2007; Richardson 2005).

Research concerning pitfalls of feminist and LGBT movements in the global South receiving Northern donor funding informs how scholars approach understanding the perils of Northern aid; how are we to reconcile this with its potential benefits? Apart from clearly affecting the economic wellbeing of Africans generally (African Statement 2013), what happens when donors turn off the funding spigot? Fluctuations in Northern donor funding for LGBT organizing in the global South suggest that financial support for LGBT organizing may be supplanted by other pressing injustices. How does the withdrawal of Northern funding impact not only LGBT NGOs but also sexual norms in countries in the global South? To recall the often-quoted phrase from Gayatri Spivak (2009, 50), is funding something global Southern NGOs "cannot not want"?

In the following sections of this chapter, we explore funding as posing "queer dilemmas" for global Southern activists. Our first case study examines how skepticism about Northern funding constrained LGBT activism in Malawi. LGBT rights activists understood supposedly tainted resources as enabling their work, whereas political elites and ordinary Malawians regarded LGBT NGOs as catering exclusively to Northern donors. The availability of Northern funding also seemed to exacerbate tensions among NGOs, as some NGO representatives envied the resources that flowed to LGBT NGOs. Northern funding rendered Malawian LGBT NGOs vulnerable to criticism and harassment from state actors and other civil society organizations. Our second case study looks at the departure of donor funding from the LGBT sector in South Africa and the dilemmas activists faced. Acceptance of Northern funding came with normative expectations. However, the withdrawal of funding did not eliminate this normative pressure but created new obstacles for activists to manage.

Tainted funding: perceptions about Northern donor-LGBT activist ties in Malawi

The perception that African LGBT NGOs existed primarily to serve Northern donors that funded their efforts constrained LGBT activism by increasing heteronormative pressure on organizations in two ways. First, LGBT NGOs were vulnerable to homophobic public attacks on their credibility, due in large part to Northern funding they received and to the LGBT-rights aid conditionalities that Northern governments threatened to attach to development aid they gave to Malawi (Biruk 2014). The perceived cozy relationship between Malawian NGOs and Northern donors put organizations advocating for LGBT rights, specifically the Centre for the Development of People (CEDEP) and Centre for Human Rights and Rehabilitation (CHRR), in an awkward bind. They struggled not only to promote LGBT rights in a country in which politicized homophobia began escalating in 2010, after the prosecution of Tiwonge Chimbalanga and Steven Monjeza for violating the antisodomy law, but also to garner respect for work funded in large part by Northern donors. The perception that Northern donor funding was tainted put LGBT rights NGOs in a bind. On the one hand, CEDEP and CHRR needed donor funding to keep projects supporting gender and sexual minority health and rights active. On the other hand, accepting Northern donor funding rendered these NGOs morally and nationally suspect in the eyes of the government. As antigay critics associated LGBT rights advocacy exclusively with donor funding, the negative link between Northern meddling and LGBT rights organizing became normative.

Second, because of increased heteronormative pressures in the form of homophobic threats, many NGO leaders were wary of portraying LGBT rights publicly, although it could be a way to procure donor funding. Supporting LGBT rights could backfire for such NGOs, making them the targets of politicized homophobia. As a result, very few NGOs were willing to lend support publicly for LGBT rights in Malawi. In addition, some NGO leaders yearned for the resources that LGBT rights NGOs had amassed, resulting in friction between some NGOs. As a result, LGBT NGOs became vulnerable to criticism from some NGO leaders.

State antipathy toward specific NGOs in Malawi encouraged media, citizens, politicians, and religious leaders to vilify NGOs, particularly those critical of Mutharika's leadership. Although political elites did not uniformly disapprove of all NGOs, there seemed to be widespread skepticism of NGOs perceived to have close ties to Northern donors and their representatives. Without foreign donor funding, most NGOs would not exist (Watkins, Swidler, and Hannan 2012). Although foreign-funded NGO activities can and do benefit ordinary Malawians, NGOs' reputations as currying favor with Northern donors enhance widespread misgivings about these organizations. "North-to-South aid has made Southern NGOs both prominent and vulnerable, presenting a tempting target for attack" (Dupuy, Ron, and Prakash 2015, 420). As in other African countries, "[r]elationships between contemporary … governments and civil society organizations [in Malawi] … have been largely adversarial and imbued with mutual mistrust" (Chikoto-Schulz and Uzochukwu 2016, 1). NGOs "working on proscribed issues," such as LGBT rights, are particularly susceptible to state repression, if they depend on Northern funding (Dupuy, Ron, and Prakash 2015, 428).

HIV/AIDS, human rights, women's rights, and LGBT rights activists in Malawi recognized how Mutharika's administration exploited the divisive issue of LGBT rights to discredit NGOs critical of his regime. Isaac, a human rights activist, pointed to warning signs in Mutharika's leadership, evidenced by how "he also progressively trampled on fundamental freedoms slowly, by criticizing the press, by deriding civil society for their actions, for what he called spearheading a gay agenda. So he wanted to … cultivate a mood of criticism" that turned "local communities" against a civil society that Mutharika portrayed as "protect[ing] the gay agenda in order to trample on Malawi's traditional values" (Interview with Ashley Currier, July 11, 2012, Lilongwe, Malawi). Mutharika's administration positioned LGBT rights as an unwelcome development in Malawi. The ruling party wielded politicized homophobia to turn public opinion against NGOs and to engender irreconcilable divisions within civil society.

The government used nationwide NGO-sponsored protests demanding that Mutharika take steps to improve the faltering economy and honor human rights on July 20, 2011—dubbed the July 20 protests—to smear NGOs' reputations. Unhappy with Mutharika's refusal to listen to alternative viewpoints, Davis, a human rights activist, explained that activists developed a "20-point petition because we felt that … having failed to dialogue with the president, [it] was important to … come up with a position that speaks to the concerns of Malawians" (Interview with Ashley Currier, July 10, 2012, Lilongwe, Malawi). As NGO leaders failed to persuade Mutharika to respond to their demands, they planned nationwide protests. In May 2011, representatives from the Council for Non-Governmental Organisations (CONGOMA) advised Mutharika not to use homophobia "to divert attention from real issues affecting the country" (Munthali 2011, 2). Mutharika reproached NGO leaders for "selling the country by getting money to champion foreign cultures" and for promoting gender and sexual diversity; he deplored LGBT rights as an aid conditionality, stating,

> Yes, we rely on donors but what is happening is like giving a beggar more money than he or she usually gets and spit[ting] on him or her. Sometimes it is fair to tell them to take their money so that we keep our culture.
>
> *(Nyirongo 2011, 4)*

With vivid imagery, Mutharika painted LGBT-rights aid conditionalities as requiring Malawians to prostrate themselves as beggars on a world stage. Asserting national sovereignty, Mutharika repudiated the notion of recognizing LGBT rights in favor of securing donor aid.

Leading LGBT rights NGOs participated in planning the July 20 protests, but demanding that the government recognize and respect LGBT rights was not a central demand made by NGOs. NGOs demanded that the government correct shortages of fuel, electricity, and foreign currency, address financial mismanagement and political corruption, and obey the rule of law. However, Mutharika's administration portrayed the July 20 protests as advocating for gay rights. Hetherwick Ntaba, Mutharika's spokesperson, implored protest organizers to reveal whether funding they had received from Northern donors was "funding … the July 20 demonstrations." According to Ntaba, this admission would "assure Malawians that one of the issues Malawians will be demonstrating for will not be the advancement of gay rights in the country" (Sonani 2011, 3). Repudiating Ntaba's insinuation that activists' demands motivating the July 20 protests were in any way illegitimate, Reverend Macdonald Sembereka characterized the government's "gimmick" of deploying politicized homophobia as "distracting Malawians from real issues that rob them of their hard-won democracy and rights" (Sonani 2011, 3). An LGBT rights supporter, Sembereka also demanded that the government furnish evidence that activist organizations had received "'huge' sums of money from gay rights bodies outside the country" (Sonani 2011, 3).

Malawian politicians constructed Northern donors as sponsoring LGBT rights organizing in the country. NGOs that received donor funding became morally and politically suspect in statements politicians made. Jeremiah, a human rights activist explained that politicians' message was: "Let us get rid of the donors because they're giving money to these few NGOs to advance their goal of homosexuality.… [P]eople should represent our government against the donors because the NGOs are supporting homosexuality" (Interview with Ashley Currier, July 14, 2012, Lilongwe, Malawi). While organizations, politicians, and religious leaders were "running away from the civil rights organizations," according to Jeremiah, Malawians were

> looking at us as if we [were] enemies of the state and enemies of the citizenry. So that is the way the government was manipulating, using the agenda of those few NGOs that were fighting for rights of these people we call [sexual] minorities.

Political elites and ordinary Malawians were not the only ones who regarded LGBT NGOs warily. Some leaders of less well-resourced NGOs envied LGBT NGOs like CEDEP and CHRR that received Northern donor funding. Funding does not trickle down to all organizations in a social movement or across movements. Therefore, resource inequalities between social movement organizations can generate enmity among activists who begrudge other NGOs' good fortunes. Gideon, a former human rights activist, observed such jealousy among activist leaders of NGOs that were "grossly underfunded. So, participating in a gay rights campaign would expose an NGO to readily available channels of funds" (Interview with Ashley Currier, July 12, 2012, Lilongwe, Malawi). The "readily available" funds flowing to organizations like CEDEP and CHRR frustrated the "struggling civil society sector. Even today as we speak, civil society is so grossly underfunded it will talk about anything that comes its way" in the hope that the organization will receive external funding. Gideon implied that despite the unpopularity of LGBT rights, activist organizations desperate for external funding would endorse LGBT rights publicly. Yet the "dilemma is … if an NGO is seen to be advancing same-sex relationships in Malawi, it's going to be disowned by the people." In other words, supporting LGBT rights as a way to procure donor funding could backfire for NGOs, making organizations the subject of antigay vitriol nationally. Benjamin, a staff member at CEDEP, observed this dynamic in other human rights NGOs. Speaking of an organization that worked in villages in the northern region, Benjamin narrated how staff at this organization expressed their disgust at the thought of working with CEDEP. Staff viewed CEDEP as a "human rights organization ... [that] is advocating for same-sex relationships. As much as we want human rights, we do not want such rights." For some civil society workers, LGBT rights sullied the category of "human rights," making organizations that championed human rights suspect in the eyes of antigay opponents.

Staff at other NGOs coveted the resources that CEDEP and other NGOs supporting LGBT rights could marshal, according to some LGBT rights activists. Despite the risks associated with endorsing LGBT rights and staff members' personal prejudices, the reality was that "there is a lot of money ... around" LGBT rights, according to Gideon. Benjamin related that some NGO leaders envied CEDEP's ability to garner "more resources." Benjamin recognized the problems donor funding overlap caused and thought it was odd that "five organizations ... have been funded by one donor." Citing Hivos, a Dutch donor agency that supports "equal advantages for all people regardless of their sexual orientation," Benjamin pointed to the possibility that one of the five Malawian organizations funded by Hivos did not "sympathize" with CEDEP "on the MSM issues." Donor funding overlap could generate infighting among such funded NGOs.

Although Northern donor funding afforded material resources to Malawian LGBT NGOs, the specter of Northern donors' involvement in local LGBT organizing constrained LGBT organizing when political elites deployed heteronormative, "homosexuality-is-un-African" discourses to undermine LGBT NGOs' standing in Malawi. Malawian LGBT activists faced the queer dilemma that the resources flowing from Northern donors rendered them vulnerable to state and social scrutiny and even hostility from other NGOs. After accepting Northern donor funding, "LGBT activists contended with the implication that their organizations were racially, culturally, and nationally inauthentic" (Currier 2012, 148). LGBT activists also found themselves at odds with NGO leaders who envied their funding or sided with the government's campaign of politicized homophobia. Many NGO leaders were unwilling to consider publicly supporting LGBT rights because it could make them susceptible to state-sponsored homophobic harassment. Northern donor funding certainly flowed to other Malawian NGOs besides LGBT NGOs. However, within Malawi, the perception that Northern donors favored funding LGBT NGOs over other organizations was powerful. This perception also reveals a growing normative regime in which Northern donor funding pits more well-resourced NGOs against less well-resourced NGOs. In such environments, solidarity across social movements becomes difficult to forge and sustain when activists eye each other with suspicion and envy the resources other groups possess.

The South African LGBT movement and the withdrawal of Northern funding

In 2011 and 2012, the South African LGBT movement was grappling with the departure of major funders, including Atlantic Philanthropies, after the global recession that began in 2008. South Africa is one of the eight countries where Atlantic Philanthropies has funded development programs since the early 1980s.[2] Activists' anxieties over diminishing financial support reveal several "queer dilemmas" for development work. In informal conversations with Moreau, activists explained the departure of funding for LGBT activities and organizations resulted from the perception among Northern funders that South Africa is now "gay friendly" due to passage of pro-LGBT legislation and increased regional awareness of LGBT issues; therefore, South African LGBT movement organizations no longer required funding. For example, the organization Behind the Mask, whose mission it was to disseminate LGBT news across the continent, was no longer considered necessary because of advances in social media and mainstream dissemination of queer news. The organization had achieved its mandate of normalizing media coverage of LGBT issues within South Africa and throughout Africa. Thuli, a representative of the organization, stated, "at the last board meeting … we really actually had to address the question of whether Behind the Mask has actually met its purpose … I think we've done that, you know, with the stories that we carry on our website in different countries" (Interview with Julie Moreau, March 5, 2012, Johannesburg, South Africa). Success in improving media visibility of queer issues justified closing the organization.

Dwindling resources for salaries and programs associated community outreach that address social intolerance and homophobia have increasingly become a movement reality (Phindi, Forum for the Empowerment of Women (FEW), Interview with Julie Moreau, March 5, 2012, Johannesburg, South Africa). To merit donor funding, activists demonstrate in their funding applications a violent social homophobia that reinforces the idea that Africa suffers from a kind of propensity for cultural violence (Wahab 2016). South Africa must collectively perform a particular kind of LGBT progressivity that then backfires at the level of organizations and individuals who lose their incomes. In this way, Northern funding compels the LGBT movement to reproduce homonormative ideas about queer (African) identities and experiences.

Ironically, it was the imperative to acquire donor funding in the first place that created an economic dependence on Northern resources and diverted activists' attention away from grassroots organizing. Theron, McAllister, and Armisen (2016) describe how the professionalization of LGBT organizing took organizers away from their base. Juan, a former member of OUT LGBT Wellbeing in Pretoria, explained the dilemma between a more inclusive, volunteer-based organization and one with a more formalized structure. Volunteer organizations can be more inclusive, but in the context of widespread poverty and lack of reliable employment, it is difficult to attract committed volunteers. As a result, organizations formalize but adopt new priorities. Juan said that before OUT formalized,

> Meetings were always very open, also to the public at large, not just to those that were volunteers or service users. [It remained that way] until it became a formal NGO, because then you have to have a formal board, formal portfolios, etc., etc. And at that stage, because there was no more, let's call it a member-driven organization, and because it was professionalizing, it changed in quite a lot aspects, which some of us resisted throughout, because in some ways, having volunteers participate and having ownership remains for me a very important process for me, otherwise logistically it became more and more difficult.
>
> *(Interview with Julie Moreau, March 8, 2012, Pretoria, South Africa)*

Juan described how the professionalization of OUT divested ownership of the organization and its mission from the local community. Logistically, retaining the involvement and voice of grassroots volunteers became harder to sustain.

Activists considered the relative benefits and drawbacks of this changing funding landscape, specifically international sources of funding and/versus domestic sources of funding. Activists found themselves in the queer bind of resenting the departure of hegemonic Northern funding but wary of approaching a government with a track record of homophobia. For example, prominent politicians such as President Jacob Zuma, the Minister of Arts and Culture Lulu Xingwana, and Jon Qwelane, Ambassador to Uganda, have all made public homophobic remarks (Distiller 2011). Moreau met up with Phindi Malaza in the lobby of a nearby hotel across the street from Forum for the Empowerment of Women's new location. They had to move out of the Constitution Hill complex that houses the Constitutional Court of South Africa because the rent was too expensive after major funders had withdrawn their support. Phindi discussed the need to look for new sources of funding and difficulty finding support in the homophobic government: "When you look at the current financial situation that we're in, it's not a nice situation, to be quite honest. Because a lot of government departments are homophobic. A lot of government people are very homophobic" (Interview with Julie Moreau, March 5, 2012, Johannesburg, South Africa). Phindi described how civil society organizations designed a workshop to educate government officials on the task team on LGBTI issues. According to Phindi,

> There was a workshop that was planned to do some awareness raising, educate government around LGBTI. Because they're very clueless, the ones that claim to know [about LGBTI issues]. They know nothing. So you find that even the way they talk, you know, they're not aware that they're being offensive, but they are.

Activists found themselves unsatisfied with the conditions of Northern funding, but likewise unable to interact with the national government to obtain resources for their work.

As evident in the case of Behind the Mask, an organization that lost Northern funding because the organization had fulfilled its original mission, retraction of Northern funding pressures NGOs to demonstrate their relevance to donor priorities. Leaders of professionalized, urban LGBT NGOs come disproportionately from privileged social strata, meaning they have tended to be white, male, and middle class (Cock 2003). In contrast, leaders of LGBT community-based organizations (CBOs) usually live in the communities they served. To appear legitimate in this new funding landscape, urban NGOs need to perform "outreach" that appears to support "poor, black gays and lesbians" (Oswin 2007, 660) who are understood by NGOs and foreign donors to be in need of resources and support. Several activists from CBOs mentioned receiving financial support from better-funded urban NGOs only when these NGOs "want their members" at events, thus proving the ongoing relevance of the NGO to its funders. Small amounts of funding trickle down from better-resourced NGOs to less-well-resourced NGOs. Ntsupe from the Ekurhuleni Pride Organising Committee (EPOC), located in the Gauteng township of KwaThema, explained that, as a small organization, maintaining relationships with urban NGOs is a must in order to access resources. Ntsupe said,

> They want our members … That's when they would send transport and pay for a bus, because they need our members to go somewhere. But when it comes to day-to-day running and other issues, they are not interested. They're not interested at all.
> *(Interview with Julie Moreau, March 10, 2012, KwaThema, South Africa)*

The power dynamic at work between NGOs and CBOs in the sector illustrates new forms of domination and homonormative regulation among LGBT movement organizations in the global South.

Several activists discussed intra-movement dynamics among better-funded NGOs and smaller CBOs. Jill at the Triangle Project, the oldest LGBT NGO in South Africa, discusses what she called the "funding crisis" in the sector and the problems that it has created for "working collectively" with CBOs. She said, "You find that people just don't have the resources to participate." Jill explained that because of the uneven resources between NGOs and CBOs and the gulf between urban NGOs and most affected communities, it could be difficult for NGOs and CBOs to engage in coordinated efforts. According to Jill, after becoming "NGO-ized," the funding "rug has been pulled out" from beneath LGBT NGOs. She said, "We're so dependent on funding and then we end up—our priorities become determined by funding. It's almost like we compete to get people to participate in our processes rather than being collective. And so there's this continual tension" (Interview with Julie Moreau, April 23, 2012, Cape Town, South Africa). The "tension" to which Jill referred is how NGO officers feel obligated to demonstrate the organization's relevance and to reflect funder priorities in NGO activities. Yet all organizations in the LGBT movement sector are behaving the same way, resulting in duplicate activities and organizations competing to serve the local LGBT community.

Both the receipt and withdrawal of Northern donor funding produce difficulties for African LGBT activists. Activists confront dilemmas regarding the perception that they have completed their mandate of eliminating anti-LGBT injustices and whether to replace Northern funding with state sources of funding, which often involves interacting with homophobic politicians. They also confront dilemmas regarding professionalization and the desire to earn a living for themselves, at the expense of breaking with LGBT communities and other NGOs. Although donor funding may be something that African activists "cannot not want" (Spivak 2009, 50), it creates a context in which activists are forced to compromise, sometimes in ways that radically depart from activists' original intentions.

Conclusion

As African activists contemplate the future of gender and sexual diversity organizing in relation to the queer dilemmas posed by Northern donor funding, Theron, McAllister, and Armisen (2016) ask, "Where do we go from here?" Their critiques of the current movement landscape stem from concerns about Western organizational models that emphasize "managerialism" and about the imposition of donor agendas that aim narrowly to enact legal reform and policy change through state engagement. This strategy excludes more grassroots, base-building activist work. This "top-down model of organizing" prioritizes donor agendas making donors "virtual members of the leadership teams" (Theron, McAllister, and Armisen 2016).

The opportunity to gain organizing skills and earn a living as an activist also disconnects professional activists from the grassroots and fosters an elitist LGBT movement. Acquiring these skills, including language and accounting expertise, makes movement leaders "foreign" to their local communities (Theron, McAllister, and Armisen 2016). As their livelihoods come to depend on this professional activism in a context where jobs may be scarce, they

> may be more vulnerable to outside pressures and demands, particularly from donors, at the expense of the needs of our communities. Stories abound of donor pressure to change priorities and strategies or risk losing support. Such pressures, though usually subtle, can be difficult for activists to resist when our own livelihoods depend on donor goodwill.
>
> *(Theron, McAllister, and Armisen 2016)*

Along with African critiques of Northern supremacy in continental LGBT organizing, transnational feminist and queer theorists have generated important critiques of the racial, gender, and sexual hierarchies that accompany the circulation of capital, people, and ideologies transnationally (Bhaskaran 2004; Grewal and Kaplan 2001; Hoad 2007). These hierarchies accompany Northern funding and categorization of African LGBT activism and are evident in how well-meaning donors work with queer activists. Future studies are needed to document how macro-level racial, gender, and sexual hierarchies affect the distribution and availability of political opportunities and choices to queer Africans and how they particularly impact LGBT activism in Africa. For example, donors define some African LGBT movement organizations as "bad" organizations because they are not Westernized enough, meaning that their staff and volunteers lack Western cultural competencies. Yet if poor or working-class African activists have not completed high school because their families lacked the money to pay for their school fees, a feature of structural adjustment policies introduced and enforced by international funding agencies, or because their gender and sexual nonconformity kept them out of school (Muholi 2004), they may not know how to document how their organizations spent their money, which can lead to gaps in accounting. They also may not be proficient in English or French, the dominant languages of transnational gender and sexuality organizing, which may compromise the "professional" nature of the reports they submit to donors.

Northern donor funding creates obstacles for African LGBT activism (Oswin 2007). Not only does the perception that African LGBT activists do the bidding of Northern donor funding constrain LGBT organizing, but it also renders LGBT NGOs vulnerable to homophobic criticism and hostility from NGOs in other social movements under pressure to uphold dominant heterosexual norms. At the same time that African LGBT movement organizations run the risk of being coopted and controlled by Northern donors, as feminist and queer theorists have pointed out, African LGBT activism may be stymied by the process of homonormativity. As Duggan warns, homonormativity depoliticizes activism and prioritizes a narrow gay identity. Increasingly, fledgling African LGBT movement organizations are opting to apply for external funding from Northern donors and transform themselves into professional organizations. The process of professionalization may not be inherently problematic for queer activism in Africa. However, when professionalization overshadows other queer political strategies and suppresses indigenous forms of gender and sexual identification and practice, such that they no longer seem viable to African LGBT activists, it is possible that Northern modes of organizing will go unquestioned and unchallenged. Thankfully, African-generated criticisms of the supremacy of Western LGBT modes of organizing continue to gain strength (African Statement 2013; Massaquoi 2008; Theron, McAllister, and Armisen 2016).

Notes

1 *Tongzhi* is the "word for 'comrade', which many lesbian, bisexual, and gay people in mainland China, Hong Kong, and Taiwan now use to refer to themselves" (Jolly 2011, 82).
2 Other funding destinations include Australia, Bermuda, Cuba, Northern Ireland, Republic of Ireland, the United States and Vietnam. http://www.atlanticphilanthropies.org/our-story.

References

"African Statement in Response to British Government on Aid Conditionality." 2013. In *Queer African Reader*, edited by Sokari Ekine and Hakima Abbas, pp. 92–94. Dakar, Senegal: Pambazuka.

Alvarez, Sonia E. 1998. "Latin American Feminisms 'Go Global': Trends of the 1990s and Challenges for the New Millennium." In *Cultures of Politics, Politics of Cultures: Re-Visioning Latin American Social Movements*, edited by Sonia E. Alvarez, Evelina Dagnino, and Arturo Escobar, pp. 293–324. Boulder, CO: Westview.

Andrucki, Max J. and Glen S. Elder. 2007. "Locating the State in Queer Space: GLBT Non-profit Organizations in Vermont, USA." *Social & Cultural Geography* 8, no. 1: 90–104.

Bergenfield, Rachel and Alice M. Miller. 2014. "Queering International Development? An Examination of New 'LGBT Rights' Rhetoric, Policy, and Programming among International Development Agencies." *LGBTQ Policy Journal*. November 20. http://www.hkslgbtq.com/queering-international-development-an-examination-of-new-lgbt-rights-rhetoric-policy-and-programming-among-international-development-agencies/.

Bernal, Victoria and Inderpal Grewal. 2014. *Theorizing NGOs: States, Feminisms, and Neoliberalism*. Durham, NC: Duke University Press.

Bhaskaran, Suparna. 2004. *Made in India: Decolonizations, Queer Sexualities, Trans/National Projects*. New York: Palgrave Macmillan.

Biruk, Crystal. 2014. "'Aid for Gays': The Moral and the Material in 'African Homophobia' in Post-2009 Malawi." *Journal of Modern African Studies* 52, no. 3: 447–473.

Blackwood, Evelyn. 2005. "Transnational Sexualities in One Place: Indonesian Readings." *Gender & Society* 19, no. 2: 221–242.

Blessol, Gathoni. 2013. "LGBTI-Queer Struggles Like Other Struggles in Africa." In *Queer African Reader*, edited by Sokari Ekine and Hakima Abbas, pp. 220–228. Dakar, Senegal: Pambazuka.

Britton, Hannah. 2006. "Organising against Gender Violence in South Africa." *Journal of Southern African Studies* 32, no. 1: 145–163.

Bulbeck, Chilla. 2007. "Hailing the 'Authentic Other': Constructing the Third World Woman as Aid Recipient in Donor NGO Agendas." *Advances in Gender Research* 11: 59–73.

Chikoto-Schulz, Grace and Kelechi Uzochukwu. 2016. "Governing Civil Society in Nigeria and Zimbabwe: A Question of Policy Process and Non-state Actors' Involvement." *Nonprofit Policy Forum* 7 no 2. https://www.degruyter.com/view/j/npf.2016.7.issue-2/npf-2015-0051/npf-2015-0051.xml

Cock, Jacklyn. 2003. "Engendering Gay and Lesbian Rights: The Equality Clause in the South African Constitution." *Women's Studies International Forum* 26, no. 1: 35–45.

Currier, Ashley. 2010. "The Strategy of Normalization in the South African LGBT Movement." *Mobilization: An International Journal* 15, no. 1: 45–62.

Currier, Ashley. 2012. *Out in Africa: LGBT Organizing in Namibia and South Africa*. Minneapolis, MN: University of Minnesota Press.

Dearham, Kaitlin. 2013. "NGOs and Queer Women's Activism in Nairobi." In *Queer Africa Reader*, edited by Sokari Ekine and Hakima Abbas, pp. 186–202. Dakar, Senegal: Pambazuka.

Distiller, Natasha. 2011. "Am I That Name? Middle Class Lesbian Motherhood in Post-Apartheid South Africa." *Studies in the Maternal* 3, no. 1: 1–21.

Doyle, Vincent. 2008. "'But Joan! You're My Daughter!' The Gay and Lesbian Alliance against Defamation and the Politics of Amnesia." *Radical History Review* 100: 209–221.

Duggan, Lisa. 2003. *The Twilight of Equality? Neoliberalism, Cultural Politics, and the Attack on Democracy*. Boston, MA: Beacon Press.

Dupuy, Kendra E., James Ron, and Aseem Prakash. 2015. "Who Survived? Ethiopia's Regulatory Crackdown on Foreign-funded NGOs." *Review of International Political Economy* 22, no. 2: 419–456.

Espinoza, Robert. 2007. "A Global Gaze: Lesbian, Gay, Bisexual, Transgender, and Intersex Grantmaking in the Global South and East." Funders for Lesbian and Gay Issues. http://www.soros.org/initiatives/health/focus/sharp/articles_publications/publications/global_20070705/global_20070820.pdf.

Fallon, Kathleen M. 2008. *Democracy and the Rise of Women's Movements in Sub-Saharan Africa*. Baltimore, MD: The Johns Hopkins Press.

Fried, Susana T. and Shannon Kowalski-Morton. 2008. "Sex and the Global Fund: How Sex Workers, Lesbians, Gays, Bisexuals, Transgender People, and Men Who Have Sex With Men Are Benefiting from the Global Fund, Or Not." *Health and Human Rights Journal* 10, no. 2: 127–136.

Gosine, Andil. 2013. "Murderous Men: MSM and Risk-rights in the Caribbean." *International Feminist Journal of Politics* 15, no. 4: 477–493.

Grewal, Inderpal and Caren Kaplan. 2001. "Global Identities: Theorizing Transnational Studies of Sexuality." *GLQ* 7, no. 4: 663–679.

Hassim, Shireen. 2005. *Women's Organizations and Democracy in South Africa: Contesting Authority.* Madison, WI: University of Wisconsin Press.

Hoad, Neville. 1999. "Between the White Man's Burden and the White Man's Disease." *GLQ* 5, no. 4: 559–584.

Hoad, Neville. 2007. *African Intimacies: Race, Homosexuality, and Globalization.* Minneapolis, MN: University of Minnesota Press.

Hodžić, Saida. 2014. "Feminist Bastards: Toward a Posthumanist Critique of NGOization." In *Theorizing NGOs: States, Feminisms, and Neoliberalism,* edited by Victoria Bernal and Inderpal Grewal, pp. 221–247. Durham, NC: Duke University Press.

Hrycak, Alexandra. 2007. "From Global to Local Feminisms: Transnationalism, Foreign Aid, and the Women's Movement in Ukraine." *Advances in Gender Research* 11: 75–93.

Jad, Islah. 2007. "The NGO-ization of Arab Women's Movements." In *Feminisms in Development: Contradictions, Contestations, and Challenges,* edited by Andrea Cornwall, Elizabeth Harrison, and Ann Whitehead, pp. 177–190. New York: Zed Books.

Jolly, Susie. 2000. "'Queering' Development: Exploring the Links Between Same-Sex Sexualities, Gender, and Development." *Gender and Development* 8, no. 1: 78–88.

Khunga, Suzgo. 2010. "Bingu Stops Comments on Gays." *Daily Times,* June 3, p. 3.

Lind, Amy. 2009. "Governing Intimacy, Struggling for Sexual Rights: Challenging Heteronormativity in the Global Development Industry." *Development* 52, 1: 34–42.

Lind, Amy. 2010. "Introduction: Development, Global Governance, and Sexual Subjectivities." In *Development, Sexual Rights, and Global Governance,* edited by Amy Lind, pp. 1–20. New York: Routledge.

Lind, Amy and Jessica Share. 2003. "Queering Development: Institutionalized Heterosexuality in Development Theory, Practice and Politics in Latin America." In *Feminist Futures: Re-imagining Women, Culture and Development,* edited by Kum-Kum Bhavnani, John Foran, and Priya Kurian, pp. 55–73. New York: Zed Books.

Lorway, Robert. 2014. *Namibia's Rainbow Project: Gay Rights in an African Nation.* Bloomington, IN: Indiana University Press.

Markowitz, Lisa and Karen W. Tice. 2002. "Paradoxes of Professionalization: Parallel Dilemmas in Women's Organizations in the Americas." *Gender & Society* 16, no. 6: 941–958.

Massaquoi, Notisha. 2008. "The Continent as a Closet: The Making of an African Queer Theory." *Outliers* 1: 50–60.

Mindry, Deborah. 2001. "Nongovernmental Organizations, 'Grassroots,' and the Politics of Virtue." *Signs: Journal of Women in Culture and Society* 26, no. 4: 1187–1211.

Morgan, Ruth and Saskia Wieringa, 2005. *Tommy Boys, Lesbian Men, and Ancestral Wives: Female Same-sex Practices in Africa.* Johannesburg: Jacana.

Muholi, Zanele. 2004. "Thinking through Lesbian Rape." *Agenda* 61: 116–125.

Munthali, Kondwani. 2011. "Slow Down Mr. President—NGOs." *Nation,* May 6, p. 2.

Mwikya, Kenne. 2014. "Unnatural and Un-African: Contesting Queer-phobia by Africa's Political Leadership." *Feminist Africa* 19: 98–105.

Nyirongo, Edwin. 2011. "NGOs Selling Malawi for Money—Bingu." *Nation,* June 8, p. 4.

Nzegwu, Nkiru. 2002. "Questions of Agency: Development, Donors, and Women of the South." *Jenda: A Journal of Culture and African Women Studies* 2, no. 1: 1–28.

Oswin, Natalie. 2007. "Producing Homonormativity in Neoliberal South Africa: Recognition, Redistribution, and the Equality Project." *Signs* 32, no. 3: 649–669.

Puar, Jasbir K. 2007. *Terrorist Assemblages: Homonationalism in Queer Times.* Durham, NC: Duke University Press.

Richardson, Diane. 2005. "Desiring Sameness? The Rise of a Neoliberal Politics of Normalisation." *Antipode* 37, no. 3: 515–535.

Seckinelgin, Hakan. 2009. "Global Activism and Sexualities in the Time of HIV/AIDS." *Contemporary Politics* 15, no. 1: 103–118.

Somanje, Caroline. 2010. "Malawi's Aid under Threat after Gays' Conviction." *Nation,* May 24, p. 2.

Sonani, Bright. 2011. "Government Using Gay Issues to Distract Malawians—HRCC." *Nation,* July 14, p. 3.

Sperling, Valerie, Myra Marx Ferree, and Barbara Risman. 2001. "Constructing Global Feminism: Transnational Advocacy Networks and Russian Women's Activism." *Signs* 26, no. 4: 1155–1186.

Spivak, Gayatri. 2009. *Outside in the Teaching Machine.* New York: Routledge.

Theron, Liesl, John McAllister, and Mariam Armisen. 2016. "Where Do We Go from Here? A Call for Critical Reflection on Queer/LGBTIA+ Activism in Africa." *Pambazuka News*. May 12. http://www.pambazuka.org/gender-minorities/where-do-we-go-here.

Viterna, Jocelyn and Kathleen M. Fallon. 2008. "Democratization, Women's Movements, and Gender-equitable States: A Framework for Comparison." *American Sociological Review* 73, no. 4: 668–689.

Wahab, Amar. 2016. "'Homosexuality/Homophobia Is Un-African'? Un-mapping Transnational Discourses in the Context of Uganda's Anti-Homosexuality Bill/Act." *Journal of Homosexuality* 63, no. 5: 685–718.

Ward, Jane. 2008. *Respectably Queer: Diversity Culture in LGBT Activist Organizations*. Nashville, TN: Vanderbilt University Press.

Watkins, Susan Cotts, Ann Swidler, and Thomas Hannan. 2012. "Outsourcing Social Transformation: Development NGOs as Organizations." *Annual Review of Sociology* 38: 285–315.

Wright, Timothy. 2005. "Gay Organizations, NGOs, and the Globalization of Sexual Identity: The Case of Bolivia." In *Same-sex Cultures and Sexualities: An Anthropological Reader*, edited by Jennifer Robertson, pp. 279–294. Malden, MA: Blackwell.

Yuval-Davis, Nira. 2006. "Human/Women's Rights and Feminist Transversal Politics." In *Global Feminism: Transnational Women's Activism, Organizing, and Human Rights*, edited by Myra Marx Ferree and Aili Mari Tripp, pp. 275–295. New York: New York University Press.

15

POLITICIZED PRIORITIES

Critical implications for LGBTIQ movements

Nick J. Mulé

Although the formation and development of the lesbian, gay, bisexual, transsexual, transgender, 2-spirit, intersex and queer (LGBTIQ) movements take their own path in various nation states and regions of the world, there is no denying the influence of Western and other developed nations' LGBTIQ movements: from rights claims that at once can offer protection and stigmatizing identities to equality initiatives such as same-sex marriage that aspire to homonormative standards. Such developed initiatives stand in contrast to agendas of LGBTIQ decriminalization and protection from serious persecutions in many nation states in which LGBTIQs are not formally recognized. The latter extends itself in our transnational world regarding the plight of LGBTIQ asylum seekers and refugees. An uncritical look at the achievements of developed LGBTIQ movements can be perceived as 'progressive,' symbolizing societies that are 'inclusive' of LGBTIQs. In this chapter, such notions of progressiveness and safety will be problematized through a nuanced in-depth examination of political agendas that inform such priorities (i.e. same-sex marriage followed by adoption). In turn, this chapter will critically expose the implications of such homonormative agendas, not only on developed LGBTIQ movements,[1] but their influence on developing LGBTIQ movements[2] in various nation states and regions of the world. The implications of such 'developments' will be critiqued using a queer liberation perspective that seeks broader freedoms, beyond what cisgender and heterosexual society socially sanctions as 'acceptable' and 'respectable.'

When one considers development from a temporal perspective, particularly when considering international development, many factors are at play regarding growth and loss, progression and regression. There are numerous factors that play into development as a means of movement, such as time, resources, economics, political stability or instability, climate and social realities to name a few. Yet the notion of development as movement, should not be confused with the concept of a linear progressive action towards improvement for the better (McCaskell 2017). From the outset, I take the position that development can be positive as well as negative and when carefully nuanced usually both, with varying effects on varied peoples. The LGBTIQ movement is a prime example of such a paradigm in that there will be moments that some members of these diverse communities will benefit while at the same time others will not.

For the purposes of this chapter the terms lesbian, gay, bisexual, transsexual, transgender, two spirit, intersex and queer (LGBTIQ) are used as an identity umbrella term. It is acknowledged that terminology has its limitations, particularly with regard to gender and sexual diversity in actually capturing the diversity and fluidity of these 'communities' (Kugle 2014). This is also further complicated by the nonexistence of language to name or define such desires, identities and expressions in many cultures (Murray 2009). Nevertheless, in an attempt to capture same-sex desires and gender variance, as well as a degree of specificities therein, I will be referring to LGBTIQs recognizing this may not be adequate terminology in many societies. Crucial to a discussion of LGBTIQ social movement development at the international level are the social locations of culture, race and ethnicity and how they intersect with sexual orientation and gender identity and expression. Such intersections are noteworthy as they provide defining sites of difference that counter dominant White, Euro and Western-centred LGBTIQ culture and political priorities (Kapoor 2008; Wahab 2016).

At its most physical level social movements arise locally, then can go on to organize at mezzo, national and even international levels. Social movements represent a gathering of people to voice a viewpoint that often challenges hegemonic thinking of society at a given time. LGBTIQ movements have formed and asserted their views accordingly, challenging society's normative notions of sexuality and gender identity and its expression (Stychin 2004; Thiel 2014; Weber 2014). Beyond these basics, the unparalleled process with which LGBTIQ social movements develop can in turn affect the development of other LGBTIQ social movements (Picq and Thiel 2015). Hence, the views developed and embraced by one LGBTIQ social movement may in turn be imposed upon other LGBTIQ social movements as a measure of the latter's 'progress.' This form of socio-cultural influence has homonationalist undertones that risk disrespecting the realities of developing LGBTIQ social movements (Puar 2007).

A means of countering socio-cultural imposition is to carefully address LGBTIQ social movement activism from an international perspective (Lind 2010). Such a broadened perspective calls for an ethical approach that respects the socio-cultural-political location of any LGBTIQ social movement (Bergenfield and Miller 2014). An example of this are the Yogyakarta Principles (2007) that take a measured approach to addressing sexual orientation and gender identity and expression issues on a global scale. A high profile international arena at which LGBTIQ issues have been increasingly taken up is at the United Nations (UN), where LGBTIQ-identified human rights defenders and their allies have not only brought their voices forth from respective nation state perspectives, but importantly have strategized collaboratively with each other in the process (Vance, Mulé, Khan and McKenzie Forthcoming). It is this process that calls for a delicate balance between upholding emancipatory liberationist ideals and resorting to homonationalist, assimilationist aspirations. Although much promise can be found in the Yogyakarta Principles (2007) (which are currently being updated) and the LGBTIQ activism taking place at the UN (Mulé, Khan and McKenzie 2017), the heavy emphasis on rights claims and legal justice has the potential to undermine social justice, further taken up below.

Advancement in technology has played a major role in information sharing and connecting social movements internationally via the World Wide Web. As more and more people are able to access the Internet they can make use of various social media platforms to organize, provide and share resources, fundraise through crowdsourcing and solicit activist support on pressing issues. The Internet has become an essential tool for LGBTIQ people to find each other, connect, form contacts and organize into social movements, particularly for people in developing nations for which diverse sexualities and genders are less tolerated and/or criminalized as compared to the developed world where LGBTIQ social movements are more established. Save for countries in which the Internet is censored (i.e. China) or more difficult to access, it has served as a means for social movement development and activism with direct and instant international connections (Altman 2001). For those in Internet-censored nations, organizing develops via the underground or subversively through HIV/AIDS services. As much as the Internet provides a powerful tool for development, what is not to be overlooked is the power of developed LGBTIQ social movements (in mostly Australasian, European and Western countries) on the Web and their influence on LGBTIQ culture internationally (Altman and Symons 2016).

The intent of this chapter is to slow the rapid process of development many LGBTIQ social movements are engaged in, to carefully consider what is involved in that process, what the focus is increasingly becoming and to critically examine the implications of hegemonic notions of political priorities that ultimately form a 'gay agenda.' Described is a queer liberation perspective that is the premise of the discussion and arguments herein. Dominant hegemonic LGBTIQ movement themes are then contrasted with the harsh realities of those who are persecuted and/or criminalized. A form of transnationalism then develops in which some individuals become asylum seekers or refugee claimants, with minimal if any effects on diversifying host land LGBTIQ movements. The implications of such a process then risks the formation and development of LGBTIQ social movements that take on homonationalist political agendas.

Politicized divides: a queer liberation perspective

The premise of the arguments put forth in this chapter is based upon a queer liberation perspective (Mulé 2015, 2016) that draws from tenets and principles derived from the gay liberation movement of the late 1960s to early 1970s (Adam 1995; Smith 1999; Warner 2002). To begin it is important to identify and distinguish political differences at play within the LGBTIQ movement that in turn inform political initiatives pursued. For purposes of distinction, yet not to be overgeneralized, I define the LGBT segment of the movement as equality seekers usually within the confines of cisgender and heterosexual standards of acceptability. By contrast 'queers' politically define their lives as they choose unrestricted by cissexist and heterosexist norms. This often results in political motivations that diverge from each other, with LGBTs pursuing assimilation and queers social transformation. Hence this divergence often serves as sites of tension within the LGBTIQ movement, for like all social movements this too is non-monolithic, yet will have its implications on broader social agendas taken up.

Before proceeding further, it is important to emphasize the non-monolithic positionings of many in the LGBT segment and that by grouping them together for the purpose of this political analysis is not meant to generalize them. The intersex members of the movement, to date, have been the least organized as a group and so I resist including them as part of this political perspective as some of their members are still in the process of finding a place and politically positioning themselves within the broader LGBTIQ movement. I define 'queer' as having non-normative sexual orientations, gender identities and expressions with a political conscience. Regarding gender variations, 'gender queer' is terminology sometimes used to signify a departure from gender binary notions and restrictive bio-medical definitions of sex (Queer Ontario 2010a). Therefore, 'queer' is defined here politically as those of us who have reclaimed a label, once – and to some currently – seen as pejorative; believe in a distinct queer culture; do not aspire to the mainstream; take pride in and celebrate our differences; and possess politicized views that resist assimilation (Brown 2007; Mulé 2016).

Prior to delving into the divide that has and continues to exist in the LGBTIQ movement, worth noting is the fluidity and variance of language and the meanings associated with terminology such as 'LGBT' and 'queer.' Firstly, they are not fully agreed upon within broader LGBTIQ communities. Secondly and importantly, the use and meanings of such terminology varies based on communities, cultures and societies, if used at all. What I am positing in this chapter is very much based on my experiences as a queer activist in Toronto and Ontario's queer liberation movement, which in many ways parallels that of national and international LGBTIQ social movements and discourse. Also, so as not to be caught up in binary definitions of terminology and their relations to one another, it is important to note that such concepts as 'LGBTs' and 'queers' are not necessarily diametrically opposed. In reality, there is not always a fine line between the two. As is well known, depending on the issues at hand, individuals' experiences, values, mores and views will determine their political positions, which can be quite varied (Edelman 1998). For example, legalizing same-sex marriage is seen by some LGBTs as a radical change to the institution of marriage for its inclusion of same-sex couples, whereas viewed through a queer lens it is seen as assimilationist. Nevertheless, some queers opposed to same-sex marriage would stop short of limiting same-sex couples the choice of being able to marry. As with all political movements, a spectrum of political positions exists within the LGBTIQ movement. The focus in this section is more so on two perspectives that are not necessarily or explicitly distinct, yet have marked implications on LGBTIQ movement development.

By outlining these distinctions, my intent is to illustrate differing views that inform political agendas and the divergent goals that develop within the broad LGBTIQ movement. A major difference of perspective is maintaining and sustaining heteronormative and gender binary world views that align with heterosexual and cisgender expectations versus troubling, disrupting, challenging and ultimately recreating such notions as experienced by non-normative sexualities and genders. These divergent political motivations – assimilation for LGBTs and societal transformation for queers – not only have direct implications on local political initiatives but can also influence the agendas of larger LGBTIQ social movement development. For queer liberationists adhering to traditional gender binary and heteronormative constructs, LGBTs are in effect ascribing to socially controlling forces. The goal then is for LGBT lives and social relations to reflect the lives of cisgender heterosexuals, becoming palatable in the process with the goal of achieving 'respect' and 'acceptance' in mainstream society. Queer liberationists, on the other hand, contribute to the forces of social change by rejecting such forces and offering alternatives both for themselves and society in general by creating gender identities and forming social relations outside rigid gender roles and couplist constructs (Idems 2016). In activist work, this in effect results in two very different end goals based on these diverging social agendas. For the LGBT segment of the movement the focus is on acceptance and respect within cisnormative and heteronormative constructs, whereas for queers, the focus is on freedom and emancipation from these very constructs (Mulé 2015, 2016; Warner 2002).

Inevitably, one of the contingents emerges with a higher profile. I argue that for the most part it has tended to be the LGBT segments of the developed LGBTIQ movements, who, in their pursuit of acceptance and respectability based upon cisnormative and homonormative standards, are more easily understood by mainstream society. It is an endeavour of seeking equality and inclusion towards fitting in, which mainstream society can more easily tolerate, in effect mainstreaming the LGBTIQ movements (Rimmerman 2008). An example of this includes same-sex marriage, followed by having or adopting children (deemed more acceptable if in that order). Another is transitioning one's gender to the opposite gender along rigid binary traditions based on social expectation (i.e. old constructs of masculinity or femininity)[3] (Pyne 2016). Yet, the mobility of LGBTIQs, such as the diverse experiences of LGBTIQ asylum seekers and refugees have far less influence within the movement. The divergence of the social agendas of both contingents becomes apparent: LGBTs are fighting for equality with heterosexuals, whereas queers are struggling to more broadly transform society. A consequence of mainstreamed LGBTs' notions and goals becoming popularized is that they in effect push radical queers further to the margins.

Theoretically, the relationship, if one exists at all, between the gay liberationist perspective, which has since evolved into queer liberation (see Queer Ontario 2010b) and queer theory (Crosby et al. 2012; Jagose 2000) is a tensioned one. Queer liberation as a progression from gay liberation is based on modernist notions of self-defined sexual orientation, gender identity and expressions that celebrates its differences from the norm. The pursuit of civil rights by liberationists was seen as a means to an end, but not an end in and of itself, and its engagement with identity politics is clearly for collective purposes. A major mantra for liberationists is to live their lives as they choose, not as defined by a cisnormative and heteronormative society. Importantly, gay/queer liberationist perspectives are intended to extend towards the liberating of all of society from imposed social constraints and restrictions on sexual experiences and gender identity and expression (Altman 1971; Smith 1999; Warner 2002).

Today's queer-identified liberationists ascribe to a highly politicized meaning of the term 'queer' a pronounced identity deliberately distinguishing it from mainstream LGBTs (Brown 2007; Queer Ontario 2010a). Some queer theorists would label such a term/identity as essentialist (Jagose 1996), yet embracing such an identity inclusive of its vast variance across non-normative gender identities/expressions and sexual orientations holds meaning for liberationists in effecting material change. Outcomes can be clearly contrasted between those in the mainstream LGBT movement who think they have reached an end-point victory when achieving a rights claim that is equal to or mimics heteronormative models (i.e. same-sex marriage and adoption) versus queer liberationists who question the privileging of one kind of relationship (marriage) over others and adoption being limited to two parents or less. Depending on where one is positioned in the LGBTIQ movement will determine if 'progress' is really being made. For LGBTs striving to fit into a mainstream heteronormative model, progress is claimed by their very presence, which is acknowledged as a disruption to norms. Yet for queer liberationists who challenge heterosexual models, progression is taken to another level by striving to create alternative models toward living a more liberated existence (Mulé 2016). The problem that arises with this divergence is that LGBTs ascribe privileges by nature of becoming part of the mainstream, which, in turn, serves to further marginalize queers. In the absence of a resolution to this circumstance, it is best to acknowledge that 'progress' is non-linear, highly subjective and will be claimed by those who perceive it to be beneficial to their goals.

I would like to briefly return to the political positioning of the intersex segment of the LGBTIQ communities, as they are at an interesting juncture in their development as a social movement. As with all segments of the LGBTIQ movement, and social movements in general, the non-monolithic nature of groups extends itself to the most micro of levels. For the intersex community this is no different. Somewhat similar to trans issues regarding gender identity and expression, internal positions vary in the intersex community regarding alignment and identification with one particular gender or choosing to be non-gendered, with varying reasons for any of these decisions (Grabham 2007). It is within the reasoning that political differences arise. It is expected that as the intersex community becomes increasingly organized, it too will inevitably have members that will align with a mainstreaming assimilationist approach and others from a critical liberationist approach. If the intersex communities intend to work in alliance with the LGBTQ communities, it will most certainly bump up against this divide.

This split in the Australasian, European and Western LGBTIQ movements raises serious questions with regard to development. Higher profile LGBTs have premised their focus on a human rights agenda towards equality, utilizing the Internet and social media to spread their cisnormative and homonormative agenda worldwide. Yet, this assimilationist perspective does not necessarily represent the desires of all LGBTIQs, with potential culturally imperialistic influence. What exactly are the desires of the movement? Is it for us to seek inclusion and presumably respect and acceptance in mainstream society based on heteronormative and cisnormative terms? Is it to try to question, challenge and transform normative notions of mainstream society urging it to diversify to the benefit of all regardless of sexual orientation and gender identity and expression? Is it truly progress to achieve inclusion in socially sanctioned notions within existing institutional constructs? Can it be considered development when one segment of the LGBTIQ communities gains privileges over others? The answers to these questions have a direct impact on how political ideations are prioritized, strategized and pursued; how the public perceives them; who benefits and who does not; and ultimately what direction 'development' in the LGBTIQ movement takes.

Influential priorities: persecution and decriminalization of LGBTIQs

An example of the temporality and prioritization of political issues in the LGBTIQ movement is that of same-sex marriage. As numerous countries were in a race to legalize same-sex marriage, with a number actually beginning to achieve it, the concept quickly became an agenda item that movements the world over began to debate pursuing. This contrasted starkly with the fact that the death penalty is imposed on same-sex sexual activity in 12 of the following countries or parts of: Afghanistan, Iran, Iraq, Mauritania, Nigeria, Pakistan, Qatar, Saudi Arabia, Somalia, Syria, United Arab Emirates and Yemen (Carroll 2016). In 73 countries and 5 entities, same-sex sexual activity can result in imprisonment from 14 years to life, while 13 other states (or part of) carry prison sentences of up to 14 years. Forty-five states criminalize same-sex relationships by deeming relationships between females illegal and 73 states that deem the same for male relationships. Additionally, maximum sentencing can be imposed via promotion 'propaganda' laws (2 states), morality laws that prohibit LGB expression (7 states and some provinces), sexual act (11 states), sodomy (11 states), against nature (30 states) and buggery (13 states) (ILGA 2016a).

Given the harrowing realities in the aforementioned nation states in which decriminalization of same-sex desires becomes paramount, the juxtaposition with LGBTIQ movements in developed nation states is all the more apparent. In international human rights arenas, the legalization of same-sex marriage has become the bar of LGBTIQ social acceptance (ILGA 2016b). How does one justify the right to pursue same-sex marriage in the face of the persecution of LGBTIQs via arrests, detainments, imprisonment, torture and sometimes executions (Amnesty International 2015)? Indeed it can be argued that the progress of some nation states on LGBTIQ human rights can serve notice to other nation states regarding the equal treatment of all their citizens, an incremental approach per se that challenges ongoing discrimination against these populations. There is still no less a creeping cultural effect of Westernized initiatives and their negative implications via first world problems versus those of developing nations, homonormatively shaping and defining burgeoning LGBTIQ communities. Knowledge shared through the Internet plays a large role in this kind of agenda shaping with mainstreaming developmental effects, a form of cultural imperialism (Binnie 2004; Bosia 2015; Haritaworn, Erdem and Tauqir 2008).

Transnationalism: LGBTIQ asylum seekers and refugees

Because of such intense persecutions there are increasing numbers of LGBTIQ asylum seekers and refugees trying to escape and resettle. Forty-four countries in the world recognize persecution based on sexual orientation, gender identity and expression (United Nations 2011). Although these countries are sought after by those fleeing persecution, getting there presents serious challenges, from escaping homelands undetected to dealing with host country authorities without the language to declare one's sexual orientation and/or gender identity or expression. What these progressive host countries may offer in terms of protection may not be easy to respond to for an asylum seeker or refugee claimant who comes from a culture in which gender or sexual diversity was neither uttered nor culturally recognized (Envisioning 2015; Lennox and Waites 2013). Trying to resettle in the new homeland can be extremely difficult, from trying to attain basics such as housing, employment, food and clothing, to the deep psychological effects of coping with past experiences of persecution, leaving loved ones behind (including a love for their home country) and dealing with guilt for having escaped while leaving others behind still struggling. These experiences in the diaspora are considered mentally re-traumatizing. The lack of adequate resources to address these needs are twofold: mainstream social services lack the knowledge and resources to address the needs of LGBTIQ asylum seekers and refugees; and specialized LGBTIQ social services lack the funding and programming resources to accommodate them (Mulé and Gamble Forthcoming).

One of the difficulties LGBTIQ asylum seekers and refugees experience is trying to become integrated in the host country's or local area's LGBTIQ community. Whether through language or cultural barriers, minimal resources (usually due to unemployment) or simply lack of understanding of the local LGBTIQ culture, they often become isolated and feel alienated. Their journey of survival, in most cases forcibly so, is not included within part of local LGBTIQ community awareness and development (Envisioning 2015; Mulé and Gamble, Forthcoming). LGBTIQ communities are often presented as organisms of inclusion, but can be highly politicized sites of internalized hegemonic cultural norms that leave little room for expansion by those with diversified cultural perspectives, such as what LGBTIQ asylum seekers and refugees bring. What is lost in terms of what these asylum seekers and refugees left behind? What is lost in terms of trying to settle in a new developed LGBTIQ community that lacks resources or is unresponsive? The transnationalism that takes place via asylum seekers and refugees unfortunately does not get taken up in determining political goals and development. What this process reveals is a cultural privileging of those who are citizens with resources and most easily align with mainstream society – the assimilationist agenda of LGBTs whose political agenda continues to have transnational influence.

Cultural imperialism: LGBTIQ political agendas

As more and more LGBTIQ people organize in countries and various regions of the world they are ushering in the beginnings of their respective social movements. These courageous human rights defenders do so often with few resources and little support and protection in highly hostile environments. Nevertheless, their strength, passion and commitment to improve their own as well as the lives of others is a testament to their resilience. Increasingly these non-governmental organizations (NGOs) are connecting in the international arena of human rights activism, in places such as the UN and its various organs, to expose their realities and advocate for change (ARC International, n.d.; ILGA 2017). To carry out this level of international LGBTIQ human rights work requires the assistance and resources of Australasian, Euro and/or Western human rights NGOs that possess greater resources. To work effectively with the diverse LGBTIQ NGOs advocating in the international arena, the more resourced NGOs have had to develop a culturally sensitive approach that facilitates activism via the input and direction of the developing NGOs. This involves a careful dance that takes cultural, socio-political, economic, racialized and ethnicized differences into consideration. Even differences among the LGBTIQs of these NGOs need to be carefully reconciled.

A major thrust of LGBTIQ social movements is the pursuit of social justice. Social justice work involves the attempt to effect change in society in order to improve the material existences of the marginalized, disenfranchised and oppressed (Mullaly 2007). Social justice work is committed to both equality of treatment and opportunities for all but also and importantly that of equity, the recognition that some are far more disadvantaged systematically and systemically. Privileged groups often benefit from such inequities, therefore the disenfranchised require material responses that adequately address their specific needs. The employed LGBTIQ-identified person will have an easier time attaining a lawyer regarding discrimination than an LGBTIQ-identified person who is unemployed. All levels of social justice work usually engages in advocacy, raising consciousness regarding an issue and its history, educating the public, naming and articulating the issues clearly, and positing a critical analysis and proposed solution for social change towards emancipation (Hoefer 2012) of, in this case, LGBTIQ communities.

Because gay liberationists saw human rights as a means to an end, not an end in and of itself, it was clear that pursuing legal justice on specific focused issues was a viable means of attracting people to the movement, yet social justice work would be ongoing (Warner 2002). This is also the place at which mainstream LGBTs and queer liberationists part. The former are content settling with legal justice under the belief they have achieved equality (see Berger, Searles and Neuman 1988 for a feminist perspective on this), whereas the latter are discontented with legal justice alone, recognizing the real work will involve an ongoing fight for social justice. Liberationists hold a clear understanding that social justice involves making changes on the ground level in order to ensure both attitudes and behaviours towards queers change for the better far beyond what is iterated in human rights legislation. Legal justice and social justice may have a dialectical relationship, but they are not necessarily one and the same, as their outcomes are quite differentiated. Whereas legal justice often operates within conservative, equality-based constraints, by comparison the vastness of social justice operates in an equity-based, liberationist, emancipatory modality (Mulé 2016). The latter exposes differences on the ground, for legal justice on the part of the socially marginalized or disenfranchised is often inaccessible.

There is also a paradoxical outcome of rights claims (Smith 2005; Smith and Grundy 2007), that at once provides needed protection and produces 'othered' identities that can contribute to stigmatization. It is understood that minority and disenfranchised groups seek and need to be enumerated in human rights legislation, for their omission was the source of society's ignorance of their plight. Named representation in legislation and social policy is to ensure a degree of recognition that these groups often encounter unique discriminatory experiences due to not being part of the dominant culture, qualitatively and/or power-wise. Yet, by naming particular groups for specific attention in legislation and social policy can inadvertently single them out as the 'other,' who are minoritized, disenfranchised, vulnerable and less than. Because both the law and policies tend to work in categories, such groups become slotted. Although LGBTs see inclusion in legislation and social policy as a somewhat finite victory, queer liberationists understand that such 'development' at the legal justice level needs to be parsed and nuanced at the social justice level.

International LGBTIQ human rights work, particularly at the UN, operates under legal structures. Relatedly, guidelines for this kind of work such as the Yogyakarta Principles (2007), place a heavier emphasis on legal justice over social justice (Waites 2009). Although many LGBTIQ NGOs attain UN member status via the UN Economic and Social Development Committee (ECOSOC) and do much of their work through the UN Human Rights Council (UNHRC) (ARC International n.d.; ILGA 2017), their involvement is guided by the legalistic system of the UN, limiting their focus primarily to legal justice issues over social justice issues. This is more of a critique of how the UN operates. Nevertheless, the collaborations between these international LGBTIQ NGOs, which involve meetings, strategizing sessions and conferences outside the UN, not to mention advocacy and side presentations within the UN, are extremely valuable. Consciousness is raised and supportive strategies are developed within this collaborative effort and education is shared and mindsets challenged beyond these NGOs.

What is being cautioned is the importance of a socio-political, culturally sensitive approach to LGBTIQ movement and community development. Whether at the international human rights arena level, or more importantly at all other levels, Australasian, Euro and Western LGBTIQ activists need firstly to be careful about the political issues they are prioritizing and for what purposes. The emphasis on mainstreaming and assimilation on the part of LGBTs has served to widen the divides within the movement and further marginalize queers in the process. Becoming impassioned about those mainstreamed issues to the point of imposing similar expectations on other nation states risks replicating such processes internationally.

Therefore, what is called for is for LGBTIQ activists to rise to a higher level of development that seeks to address the needs and desires of both those who seek acceptance in mainstream society and those who hope to transform mainstream society to make room for how they choose to live their lives. Failure to do so will result in continued homonormative developments that will further marginalize and alienate progressives who seek structural and systemic change. It is this latter form of development that will better serve international LGBTIQ NGOs whose home countries are in desperate need of this level of change. Thus responsibility lies with both Australasian, Euro and Western LGBTIQ activists to be cognizant of their political agendas and for under-resourced LGBTIQ activists to resist being influenced by mainstreaming assimilationist initiatives.

Conclusion

In this chapter I have pointed out the influence Australasian, Euro and Western LGBTIQ movements have on developing LGBTIQ social movements, particularly as we are now connected more than ever before due to technological advancements. Divides within the developed LGBTIQ movement were outlined regarding the differing political prioritizing on the part of mainstreaming, assimilationist LGBTs and critical liberationist queers. Same-sex marriage and two-parent, same-sex adoptions were both offered as prime examples of homonormative initiatives promulgated by assimilationist, mainstreaming LGBTs and how such initiatives contrast with the stark realities of persecution and criminalization of LGBTIQs in numerous nation states. Regarding the ongoing development of the LGBTIQ movement, little room is made for the contribution of LGBTIQs in the diaspora, those seeking asylum or refugee claims. Developed LGBTIQ movements are urged to address their internal divides so as not to continue to marginalize and alienate a liberationist perspective that both the movement and society could gain from. Developing LGBTIQ movements are similarly urged to resist being influenced by mainstreamed assimilationist developed LGBTIQ movements. Both can begin to do so by placing as much emphasis on social justice as is being placed on legal justice, if not more. I argue LGBTIQ development needs to go far beyond mere respectability and acceptability.

Notes

1 Developed LGBTIQ movements are organized social movements with a history of activism and have acquired support and resources to have a public and influential presence.
2 Developing LGBTIQ movements are fledgling organized social movements early in their development with little or no support and resources and at the beginning stages of influential presence in unsupportive and sometimes hostile environments.
3 See also trans theory that argues gender transitions across the binary contributes to the undoing of the binary in Julia Serano's *Whipping Girl* (2007).

References

Adam, B.D. 1995. *The Rise of a Gay and Lesbian Movement*, New York: Twayne Publishers.
Altman, D. 1971. *Homosexual Oppression and Liberation*, New York: Outerbridge and Deinstfrey.
Altman, D. 2001. *Global Sex*, Chicago, IL: University of Chicago Press.
Altman, D. and Symons, J. 2016. *Queer Wars: The New Global Polarization over Gay Rights*, Cambridge, UK: Polity.
Amnesty International Canada. 2015. "LGBTI rights." Retrieved from www.amnesty.ca/our-work/issues/lgbti-rights
ARC International. (n.d.) "Background." Retrieved from http://arc-international.net/about/background/
Bergenfield, R. and Miller, A. 2014. "Queering International Development? An Examination of New 'LGBT Rights' Rhetoric, Policy, and Programming among International Development Agencies." *Harvard Kennedy School LGBT Policy Journal*. Retrieved from http://www.hkslgbtq.com/wp-content/uploads/2014/11/Queering-InternationalDevelopment_-An-Examination-of-New-_LGBT-Rights_-Rhetoric-Policy-andProgramming-among-International-Development-Agencies-1.pdf
Berger, R.J., Searles, P. and Neuman, L. 1988. "The Dimension of Rape Reform Legislation." *Law and Society Review* 22, no. 2. Retrieved from http://search.proquest.com.ezproxy.library.yorku.ca/docview/1297914211?accountid=15182
Binnie, J. 2004. *The Globalization of Sexuality*, London: SAGE.
Bosia, M. 2015. "To Love or to Loathe: Modernity, Homophobia, and LGBT Rights." In *Sexualities in World Politics: How LGBTQ Claims Shape International Relations*, edited by M.L. Picq and M. Thiel, pp. 38–53. New York: Routledge.
Brown, G. 2007. "Mutinous Eruptions: Autonomous Spaces of Radical Queer Activism." *Environment and Planning* 39, no. 11: 2685–2698.
Carroll, A. 2016. *State-Sponsored Homophobia: A World Survey of Sexual Orientation Laws: Criminalisation, Protection and Recognition*. (11th edn). Geneva, Switzerland: International Lesbian, Gay, Bisexual, Trans and Intersex Association (ILGA). Retrieved from http://ilga.org/downloads/02_ILGA_State_Sponsored_Homophobia_2016_ENG_WEB_150516.pdf
Crosby, C., Duggan, L., Ferguson, R., Floyd, K., Joseph, M., Love, H., McRuer, R., Moten, F., Nyong'o, T., Rofel, L., Rosenberg, J., Salamon, G., Spade, D. and Villarejo, A. 2012. "Queer Studies, Materialism and Crisis: A Roundtable Discussion." *GLQ: A Journal of Lesbian and Gay Studies* 18, no. 1: 127–147.

Edelman, L. 1998. "The Future is Kid Stuff: Queer Theory, Disidentification, and the Death Drive." *Narrative* 6, no. 1: 18–30.

Envisioning Global LGBT Human Rights. 2015. "Is Canada a Safe Haven?" Retrieved from http://envisioninglgbt.blogspot.ca/p/publicationsresources.html.

Grabham, E. 2007. "Citizen Bodies, Intersex Citizenship." *Sexualities* 10, no. 1: 29–48.

Haritaworn, J., Erdem, E. and Tauqir, T. 2008. "Gay Imperialism. The Role of Gender and Sexuality Discourses in the War on Terror." In *Out of Place: Interrogating Silences in Queerness/Raciality*, edited by Adi Kuntsman and Esperanza Miyake, pp. 9–34. New York: Raw Nerve Book.

Hoefer, R. 2012. *Advocacy Practice for Social Justice* (2nd edn), Chicago, IL: Lyceum Books Inc.

Idems, B. 2016. "Opening Theory: Polyamorous Ethics as a Queering Inquiry in the Social Work Classroom." In *Queering Social Work Education*, edited by S. Hillock and N.J. Mulé, pp. 185–204. Vancouver: University of British Columbia Press.

International Lesbian, Gay, Bisexual, Trans and Intersex Association (ILGA). 2016a. "Sexual Orientation Laws in the World – Criminalisation." Retrieved from http://ilga.org/downloads/04_ILGA_WorldMap_ENGLISH_Crime_May2016.pdf

International Lesbian, Gay, Bisexual, Trans and Intersex Association (ILGA). 2016b. "Sexual Orientation Laws in the World – Recognition." Retrieved from http://ilga.org/downloads/06_ILGA_WorldMap_ENGLISH_Recognition_May2016.pdf

International Lesbian, Gay, Bisexual, Trans and Intersex Association (ILGA). 2017. "What We Do – United Nations." Retrieved from http://ilga.org/what-we-do/united-nations/

Jagose, A. 1996. *Queer Theory: An Introduction*, New York: New York University Press.

Jagose, A. 2000. "Queer World-Making." *Genders*, 31, Retrieved from http://www.genders.org/g31/g31_jagose.html

Kapoor, I. 2008. *The Postcolonial Politics of Development*, London: Routledge.

Kugle, S. 2014. *Living Out Islam: Voices of Gay, Lesbian, and Transgender Muslims*, New York: New York University Press.

Lennox, C. and Waites, M. 2013. *Human Rights, Sexual Orientation and Gender Identity in the Commonwealth: Struggles for Decriminalisation and Change*, London: Institute of Commonwealth Studies.

Lind, A. 2010. *Development, Sexual Rights and Global Governance*, London: Routledge.

McCaskell, T. 2017. *Queer Progress: From Homophobia to Homonationalism*, Toronto: Between the Lines Press.

Mulé, N.J. 2015. "The Politicized Queer, the Informed Social Worker: Dis/Re-Ordering the Social Order." In *LGBTQ People and Social Work: Intersectional Perspectives*. edited by B.J. O'Neill, T.A. Swan and N.J. Mulé, pp. 17–35. Toronto: Canadian Scholars' Press.

Mulé, N.J. 2016. "Broadening Theoretical Horizons: Liberating Queer in Social Work." In *Queering Social Work Education*, edited by S. Hillock and N.J. Mulé, pp. 36–53. Vancouver: University of British Columbia Press.

Mulé, N.J. and Gamble, K. Forthcoming. "Haven or Precarity: The Mental Health of LGBT Asylum Seekers and Refugees." In *Envisioning: Global LGBT Human Rights*, edited by N. Nicol, R. Lusimbo, N.J. Mulé, S. Ursell, A. Wahab and P. Waugh. London: Institute of Commonwealth Studies/Human Rights Consortium.

Mulé, N.J., Khan, M. and McKenzie, C. 2017. "The Growing Presence of LGBTQIs at the UN: Arguments and Counter-Arguments." *International Social Work*. Online First. http://journals.sagepub.com/doi/abs/10.1177/0020872817702706

Mullaly, B. 2007. *The New Structural Social Work* (4th edn), Don Mills, ON: Oxford University Press.

Murray, D. 2009. *Homophobias: Lust and Loathing across Time and Space*. Durham, NC: Duke University Press.

Picq, M.L. and Thiel, M. 2015. *Sexualities in World Politics. How LGBTQ Claims Shape International Relations*, London: Routledge.

Puar J. 2007. *Terrorist Assemblages: Homonationalism in Queer Times*, Durham, NC: Duke University Press.

Pyne, J. 2016. "Queer and Trans Collisions in the Classroom: A Call to Throw Open Theoretical Doors in Social Work Education." In *Queering Social Work Education*, edited by S. Hillock and N.J. Mulé, pp. 54–72. Vancouver: University of British Columbia Press.

Queer Ontario. 2010a. "'Queer' in Name." Toronto: Queer Ontario. Retrieved from http://queerontario.org/about-us/foundational-ideas/queer-in-name/

Queer Ontario. 2010b. "Queer Liberation." Queer Ontario. Retrieved from http://queerontario.org/about-us/foundational-ideas/queer-liberation/

Rimmerman, C.A. 2008. "The Assimilationist and Liberationist Strategies in Historical Context." In *Lesbian and Gay Movements: Assimilation or Liberation?*, edited by C.A. Rimmerman, pp. 11–29. New York: Basic Books.

Serano, J. 2007. *Whipping Girl: A Transsexual Woman on Sexism and the Scapegoating of Feminity*. Berkeley, CA: Seal Press.

Smith, M. 1999. *Lesbian and Gay Rights in Canada: Social Movements and Equality-Seeking, 1971–1995*, Toronto: University of Toronto Press.

Smith, M. 2005. "Social Movements and Judicial Empowerment: Courts, Public Policy and Lesbian and Gay Organizing in Canada." *Politics and Society* 33, no. 2: 327–353.

Smith, M. and Grundy, J. 2007 "Activist Knowledges in Queer Politics." *Economy and Society* 36, no. 2: 295–318.

Stychin, C.F. 2004. "Same-Sex Sexualities and the Globalization of Human Rights Discourse." *McGill Law Journal* 49: 951–968.

Thiel, M. 2014. "LGBTIQ Politics and International Relations: Here? Queer? Used To It?" *International Politics Review* 2: 51–60.

United Nations – Human Rights Council. 2011. "Discriminatory Laws and Practices and Acts of Violence against Individuals Based on Their Sexual Orientation and Gender Identity." Retrieved from http://www.ohchr.org/Documents/Issues/Discrimination/A.HRC.19.41_English.pdf

Vance, K., Mulé, N.J., Khan, M. and McKenzie, C. Forthcoming. "The Rise of SOGI: Human Rights for LGBT People at the United Nations." In *Envisioning: Global LGBT Human Rights*, edited by N. Nicol, R. Lusimbo, N.J. Mulé, A.S. Ursell, A. Wahab and P. Waugh. London: Institute of Commonwealth Studies/Human Rights Consortium.

Wahab, A. 2016. "Homosexuality/Homophobia is Un/African?: Un/Mapping Transnational Discourses in the Context of Uganda's Anti-Homosexuality Bill/Act." *Journal of Homosexuality* 63, no. 5: 685–718.

Waites, M. 2009. "Critique of 'Sexual Orienation' and 'Gender Identity' in Human Rights Discourse: Global Queer Politics beyond the Yogyakarta Principles." *Journal of Human Rights* 8, no. 4: 137–156.

Warner, T. 2002. *Never Going Back: A History of Queer Activism in Canada*. Toronto: University of Toronto.

Weber, C. 2014. "Queer International Relations. From Queer to Queer IR." *International Studies Review* 16: 596–622.

Yogyakarta Principles. 2007. "The Yogyakarta Principles on the Application of International Human Rights Law in Relation to Sexual Orientation and Gender Identity." Retrieved from: http://www.yogyakartaprinciples.org/index.php?item=25

16

CIRCUMSCRIBED RECOGNITION

Creating a space for young queer people in Delhi

Maria Tonini

In recent years, the status of sexual minorities in India has been the focus of significant contestations: same-sex sexuality was decriminalized in 2009, only to be recriminalized in 2013. These changes have generated intense debates, in India and beyond, on the importance and meaning of recognition in connection to sexual minorities in postcolonial societies (Kapur 2012; Puri 2016). In this chapter, my aim is to illuminate how recognition is experienced by young queer people (16–25 years old) living in Delhi. In particular, I focus on Niral Club, a grassroots queer youth group based in Delhi whose activities I followed during a three-month ethnographic fieldwork period in 2012. Run by students from various universities in Delhi, Niral Club was a meeting point for young queer people who looked for recognition and peer solidarity, while not fully subscribing to activist-inspired discourses about sexual rights and socio-legal equality. The recognition these young people desired and valued was intertwined with a desire to feel 'normal' and 'safe'. Through the narratives and experiences of young queer people, I aim to offer a counterpoint to wider discourses about sexual rights in the Global South (Cruz and Manalansan 2002; Lind 2010; Sabsay 2013) by suggesting ways to look at recognition that move beyond the dichotomy between resistance and oppression.

To provide context, Section 377 of the Indian Penal Code, which criminalizes sexual acts 'against the order of nature', had been in place since 1861 and had been repealed by the Delhi High court in 2009 (Gupta and Narrain 2011). The first few years after this landmark judgment were marked by a sense of hope and possibility for sexual and gender minorities in India, who for the first time could be recognized as rights-bearing citizens entitled to equality and non-discrimination; at the same time, however, it was a period of uncertainty, since the positive judgment had immediately been appealed and has been reinstated in full through a much-criticized verdict by the Supreme Court of India at the end of 2013. In the four years between the two judgments, many people within India's lesbian, gay, bisexual, transgender, and queer (LGBTQ) communities knew that, even though they had won an important legal battle, they still faced stigma and discrimination in society.

My fieldwork with Niral Club, founded in 2010 by two college students who realized that there were no support groups for queer students in Delhi, encapsulates many of the tensions felt and experienced by young queer people in a time of hope mixed with uncertainty. By zooming in on the vision and practices of this queer youth collective, my chapter expands the ways in which we can understand concepts of recognition, sexual subjectivity, and normality. Specifically, I argue for the need for a situated analysis of 'other' queer subjects, who are neither inherently radical, nor passively assimilated (Brown 2012; Podmore 2013).

Queer sexuality and recognition

Since the issue of gender and sexual rights in India has been in the spotlight for a number of years, several claims made by the Indian LGBTQ community have been framed in terms of a struggle for recognition. The travails of Section 377 and the centrality attributed to the role of the law both by the media and by scholarly critiques have contributed to the construction of a discourse that sees the precarious status of queer sexuality in India principally as a matter of recognition, or lack thereof (Gupta and Narrain 2011).

Recognition can be defined as the acknowledgment of the existence of another individual, group, or entity. Being recognized means being validated in one's own existence and granted respect (Honneth 1996); focusing on the relationship between identity categories and social equality, Nancy Fraser defines recognition as 'participatory parity' (Fraser 2001, 25).

Here, I am interested in exploring the intricacies of the concept of recognition from the vantage point of situated, contingent practices and behaviours such as those of the people frequenting Niral Club who, while wanting to be recognized, also desired to be 'normal'. Two theoretical questions inform my chapter: How do we account for the ambivalences in people's experiences and narratives vis-à-vis a discourse that places recognition as an unquestionable goal? How else might it be possible to understand the notion of recognition?

Illustrated by the narratives of queer youth presented in this chapter, recognition is experienced as a set of practices and negotiations effected within relations of reciprocity (Young 1997). Recognition must be understood as a perpetually shifting cluster of desires, affective attachments, and demands, in which queer individuals invest in different and uneven ways in an effort to adjust asymmetrical relations of reciprocity with the people, groups, and institutions with which they interact in their daily lives (Berlant 2007, 2011; Butler 1997, 2004).

Inspired by these theoretical considerations, the objective of this chapter is to examine the tensions felt by young queer 'others', who do not easily immediately fit within narratives of politicized queerness or its binary opposite of subservient homonormativity.

First, I introduce Niral Club within the spectrum of LGBTQ organizations in India and in Delhi; I then explore the meaning of safety; afterwards, I examine how Niral Club rejects a radical agenda, following a vision according to which sexual identity should not be a totalizing element of subjectivity. Finally I analyse how Niral Club members articulate the quest for recognition and normality.

LGBTQ organizations in India

The Naz Foundation, a non-governmental organzsation (NGO) founded in 1990 to support vulnerable groups at risk of HIV/AIDS, has become one of the most prominent LGBTQ organizations in India, partially thanks to the petition they filed in 2001 against Section 377 of the Indian Penal Code (Horton, Rydstrøm and Tonini 2015). Many other organizations and support groups for LGBTQ people, including Niral Club, are connected to Naz. However, such groups have been present in the subcontinent since the 1980s, but back then they were more like small networks of friends rather than formally structured organizations (see Dave 2012).

Not all the groups forming in the 1990s had sexual rights as an explicit agenda. Some gay and lesbian groups were mainly focused on meeting up and creating a space (physical and virtual) for homosexual people; others provided information and resources about sexuality and health; others still were more vocal in fighting AIDS-related discrimination (Ramasubban 2004; Ranade 2015). The organizing around issues such as decriminalization and legalization became more explicit around the period when the Naz petition was filed.

ABVA, a Delhi-based collective founded by activist Siddhart Gautam, was the first organization to openly protest against the damages of Section 377, when in 1992 they staged a demonstration in front of the Delhi police headquarters. ABVA also compiled a seminal report on the condition of homosexuals in India (ABVA 1991), and were the first to file a petition for the repeal of Section 377 in 1994. One of the key people who pioneered the LGBTQ movement in India is Ashok Row Kavi, who came out publicly in the 1980s and in 1989 started *Bombay Dost*, the first Indian gay magazine. In 1991, he then moved on to found the Humsafar Trust in Mumbai, an NGO focusing on health advice and counselling for male homosexuals. A different kind of network – also catering to male homosexuals – based in Mumbai was the Gay Bombay group, started in 1998 and consisting of a website, a mailing list, cultural and leisure events held in the city, and fortnightly meetings (see Shahani 2008).

With respect to lesbian movements, in 1990 Giti Thadani founded the Sakhi Collective in Delhi, the first lesbian organization in India; she opened a Post Office box to which women could write and reach out to each other. Thadani's house became the physical meeting point, where women could stay for short periods, accessing resources and sharing experiences. In 1997, Betu Singh, a lesbian activist and friend of Thadani's went on to start Sangini, another organization focusing on lesbian issues which is still operational. The Mumbai answer to Sakhi and Sangini was Aanchal, founded by Geeta Kumana; Aanchal was the first lesbian organization employing professional counsellors in order to provide support to women in difficult situations.

In the 1990s, LGBTQ issues were beginning to be discussed at conferences and similar events as well; the Humsafar Trust and Naz Foundation organized the first meeting of LGBTQ activists in Mumbai in 1995; in 1997, the Bangalore National Law School of India authorized a conference on gay rights; and since the beginning of the new millennium such events and conferences have grown in size and international scope. The 1990s saw the beginning of LGBTQ public demonstrations and pride parades as well. The first Indian pride march took place in Calcutta in 1999; as of 2017, pride parades are held in tens of cities all over India.

Since the turn of the century, and particularly after the Naz Foundation filed the petition to repeal Section 377, India's LGBTQ activist movements have consolidated their presence in the country and increased their collaboration with respect to issues of LGBTQ rights. One of the most important moments was the joining of forces in 2006 and forming the collective 'Voices Against 377' (grouping several grassroots organizations, NGOs and civil society organizations working with rights, sexuality, health and gender issues; see Misra 2009), which supported the Naz petition and contributed by organizing awareness campaigns and workshops, as well as gathering favourable media coverage, all over India.

Niral Club: a background

While Niral Club was part of a larger movement of LGBTQ organizations operating in Delhi, there are a number of factors that marked it as a unique kind of space: first, at the time of fieldwork, it was the only organization founded after the 2009 partial repealing of

Section 377; second, it specifically targeted youth; third, contrary to most other LGBTQ organizations, it was not tied to only one sexual identity (i.e. it aimed to reach gays, lesbians, transgender people, bisexuals, and even heterosexual people who wanted to question prevalent sexual norms); fourth, it was the only organization to hold frequent and regular meetings as well as having a continuing online presence though Facebook; fifth, Niral Club did not engage in activism or political mobilization. These characteristics, taken together, marked Niral Club as unique within the spectrum of LGBTQ organizations in Delhi.

It was Alok (22) and Shobha (24) who came up with the initial idea of starting a group in 2010, when they were both engineering students. As young queer students, they had no places to go to meet other people and envisioned a 'support centre for youngsters, for campus issues, campus ideas', as Alok explained. The club should target students because the campus environments, and especially engineering colleges, were places where a queer person could not come out and had no one to talk to for support. India's campuses have been described as spaces of silence and invisibility (D'Penha and Tarun 2005) where 'coming out' or 'being out' was not an option for most people. For those who worked, the office was not a place where one could share details about sexual preferences. This cultural logic of silence, coupled with the impossibility of coming out to the parents at home, characterized the daily life of young queer people as one of isolation and 'closeted-ness', most of the time.

The first Niral Club meeting took place in June 2010, with about eight people present. At that point, they were the first campus-youth-specific group existing in Delhi. They relied on each other for getting the Niral Club up and running, since they had no funding and no administrative support from other organizations. In particular, they lacked a physical space to meet, so in the first six months they asked around for available spaces and met at a bookstore, a café or one of the city's cultural centres. Eventually, they got in touch with the Naz Foundation, which allowed them to use one of their properties called the Jhansi Centre for their meetings. They advertised their presence through the Naz Foundation, by distributing leaflets during LGBTQ events in the city, and on the Internet through blogs. Later on the Jhansi Centre was suddenly closed and Niral Club went back to having itinerant meetings, often in a central Delhi café.

Despite relying only on volunteers and lacking a clear organizational structure, Niral Club managed to hold regular meetings, which took place twice a month on Saturdays or Sundays, between 3 and 6 pm. The timing of the meetings was scheduled so that young people could attend with ease; young women did not have to worry about being out after sunset which, as discussed by Phadke (2013) and Viswanath and Mehrotra (2007), might compromise their safety; students staying in hostels did not need special permission. In short, people could come to the meetings without anyone knowing about it.

People came to Niral Club with different motivations and different attitudes. Since they wanted to provide a safe space without imposing any obligations, Niral Club administrators did not require that anyone attended the face-to-face meetings with regularity. This meant that the composition of the group at any given face-to-face meeting was different every time. On average, any meeting would have about twenty people attending, but beside a core group of five or six regulars, all others were new. Some people would return now and then, while others remained connected only through Facebook. The constant presence of new people meant that the topics of discussion were both varied and to a degree repetitive. While the administrators tried to structure the meetings so that there would be a variety of topics discussed, the presence of several new people meant that a large part of the meeting would be spent trying to get to know the new people. The round of introductions was enough to get the debate going; while explaining why they had come to Niral Club, new people talked about problems at home, at work or at college; some were struggling with accepting their sexuality and had questions; others were curious to meet other gay people for the first time. Other times the topic of a meeting was set and advertised beforehand on Facebook – for example: bullying, the importance of physical appearances and beauty ideals, queer romantic relationships. The people moderating the meeting were good at keeping the atmosphere comfortable and uplifting by encouraging people to also talk about entertaining anecdotes, Bollywood-related gossip and similar 'lighter' topics. After meetings, they would go out for a meal or a snack. Often these socializing moments stretched to the evening, and those who did not have to go back home would stay on, ending up at Prem's place for improvised parties that went on till the morning hours.

A safe space

The first thing people told me when I asked them to describe Niral Club was that it was a safe space. Alok, one of the founding members, elaborated:

> [Niral Club] is a safe space, it is like the space where queer people can just be, they don't need to talk, they don't need to express, they don't need to go out and, you know, shout slogans or something – it is just a safe space where if you want you can just listen, if you want to just be around queer people you can just be around queer people. You want to ask, you want to help someone…totally…we do not say that, you know, you need to go out and, you know, campaign with us or something. It's a personal thing…it's a safe space.

As will be explained in the course of this chapter, safety is to be understood as the desired outcome of practices of recognition that rely on circuits of reciprocity rather than overt resistance against heteronormativity. Safety thus means being comfortable about one's own sexuality through the presence of other queer people in particular spaces at particular times. Within Niral Club, queer sexuality was recognized not as coextensive with someone's individuality, but only as one of its aspects, and one that didn't need to be expressed, talked about, or revealed in the 'outside world'. In responding to the needs of young queer people for emotional safety, peer solidarity, and a sense of normality (Berlant 2007, 287), a space like Niral Club addressed the needs of young people whose desire for recognition is fraught with ambivalences.

These ambivalent desires for recognition and normality need to be projected against the specific life circumstances of participants. Young people who are studying and whose lifestyle choices are limited by material and symbolic constraints because of their age and lack of economic self-sufficiency are particularly exposed to normative institutions like family, school and workplace and their attendant pressures, from family expectations, to peer pressure, to academic performance, and career anxieties.

For them, deciding to be 'openly queer' would be a risk, understood here following Mary Douglas as 'not only the probability of an event, but also the probable magnitude of its outcome' where 'everything depends on the value that is set on the outcome' (Douglas 1992, 31). The outcome of being an 'out' queer includes open threats as well as subtler forms of discrimination, blackmailing, and stereotyping that might undermine their opportunities. The young members of Niral Club grew up when (metropolitan) India was already significantly integrated in the circuits of globalization; in cultural terms, this means that they have grown up surrounded by images, ideas, information, and cultural references coming from everywhere.

The rapid economic growth of India since the 1990s has brought them opportunities of professional and personal fulfilment unknown to previous generations (Nisbett 2007).

Yet teenagers and people in their early twenties have not gained a socially or financially independent status; whether they live with their parents or not, they largely depend on the family's economic support. Being unmarried, they are expected to fulfil parental expectations regarding partner choice while at the same time working hard to build the foundations of a successful professional life (Lukose 2009; Mankekar 2015). Young men and women thus are not only caught between several dependencies, but also not 'taken seriously', having to justify and defend their choices before family, peers, and colleagues.

The people in my study had come of age after the repeal of Section 377; they benefited from activist struggles but did not take part in them; they could look things up on the Internet, learn about LGBTQ movements in the US, make friends with other gay people abroad before they even knew another gay person in their own city. Yet the advantages brought by being legally recognized (albeit temporarily) had not dispelled the stigma associated with homosexuality. The young queer people of Niral Club were caught in a conflicted predicament where they needed to find a way of expressing their sexuality that did not expose them to further marginalization. Niral Club emerged as a space where such circumscribed, 'safe' recognition became possible.

Normalizing queerness

Niral Club addressed the needs of a generation of young queer people who benefited from the victories of the Indian LGBTQ activist movement (above all, the repeal of Section 377) without needing to be part of it. Before the Supreme Court recriminalized homosexuality in 2013, the recognition of same-sex relationships was at least legally a reality, and queer people had high hopes for the future. These hopes did not, however, translate into activist political engagement.

In its first months of existence, Niral Club relied on renowned and experienced activists for its meetings and events; these activists were invited to share their experience and insight, inform people and provide theoretical foundations to the claims for LGBTQ equality. This activist 'imprint' did not vanish, since people like Alok, Shobha (24) and Nikhil (20) were also engaged in other queer activist circles; but it remained confined to a few people, not the majority of Niral Club regular members. While other organizations in Delhi aimed at visibilizing non-heterosexual sexuality and making space for it within broader socio-political debates, Niral Club eschewed such a vision.

Two of the first Niral Club members I met were Prem (30) and Harsh (21). I had noticed their joviality during the first meeting I attended, and we had agreed to meet a few days later. We met at a large shopping mall in South Delhi and wandered for a while trying to find a quiet place to talk. In the end we decided to sit on the floor between the shelves of a bookstore. I had left my first meeting with the impression that the Club promoted an open and positive vision of queer identity, and I asked them whether my impression was correct. Prem answered:

> Ah, there has to be something more to life than being gay. You can't just pour all your energy into being gay. Being just one single part of who you are and ignore everything else, and that's the problem! I come across people [who are] either in the closet and they are married and they're having you know, sex on the side, which – NO!...or they're so completely involved with the lifestyle that they...

Harsh filled in by saying: 'They have no room for other things' and Prem concluded: 'there's no growth anywhere, they're just gay'.

Having studied in the USA for a few years, Prem recalled how things were different there, where no one paid special attention to his sexuality. He found Niral Club people easier to be friends with, since they did not frame their sexual identity as the totalizing aspect of their personality. I asked him what he and Niral Club were trying to achieve, in terms of equality.

> A positive outcome would be that people see you for who you are. And then being gay is incidental. As: 'Oh! You have all of these things and there's the little quirk that you're gay!' How cool is that? That means you can be all of these other things and gay at the same time, that's what's going to change people's minds. … In the ideal society you wouldn't even need to come out, you'd just be like, 'Oh I'm dating a guy, I'm dating a girl, I'm experimenting' and nobody's saying 'Oh, you belong to this part.' There's no distinction.

Harsh joined the conversation and highlighted how a neutral opinion on homosexuality could be the key to equality:

> The coolest thing would be for me when our society would be in a state when the relatives are coming [and saying] 'Your son has grown, he's 29, let's look for a girl…', then the parents say 'Oh no, but he is gay'; 'Uh-oh, let's look for a guy then.'

For Harsh, the high visibility of LGBTQ issues in mainstream media was a double-edged sword that had divided people. He wished people would stop caring so much about homosexuality so that gay people could 'move on' without needing others' approval 'except for parents, probably'. In the end, they summed up their shared views:

> Harsh. We don't want a gay community.

> Prem. We want a community.

> Harsh: We want a society, and then you can have communities based on literature, music, arts, whatever, but please don't have a community based on sexuality. That's just stupid.

Harsh and Prem voiced an important concern when they spoke of wanting not a gay community, but a community. Same-sex preference becomes a detail of little relevance when gay people are recognized as being much more than their sexuality and, as such, can be part of different communities not necessarily based on sexuality. Such statements recall a point made by Judith Butler, who has discussed how an identity marker like homosexuality is a term 'which not only names, but forms and frames the subject' (Butler 1997, 93), so that anything that the subject says or does will be 'read back as an overt or subtle manifestation of [its] homosexuality' (1997, 93). In participants' accounts of what it would mean to be equal, an awareness transpired of the stigmatizing character of homosexuality, whereby, as Goffman has argued, the whole identity of a person carrying the 'deeply discrediting attribute' (Goffman 1963, 3) is reduced to only that attribute, despised, and separated from the 'normals' (i.e. people not carrying the stigma, in Goffman's use of the term). Thus, in wanting 'a community' without the 'gay' qualifier, young queer people acknowledged the ways in which their sexuality worked as an impediment to social inclusion and social recognition; and the most successful way to overcome the exclusions produced by a heteronormative matrix would be to 'trade' one's sexual difference in exchange for the possibility of a broader social acceptance. Young queers' willingness to downplay the assertion of their sexuality can be seen as a way of bargaining with a complex of social norms that continue to exclude queers; a strategy enacted to carve out spaces where it is possible not only to survive, but also to interact and participate to social life.

Against a sexual identity that was seen as reductive ('They're just gay'), Prem and Harsh preferred the possibility to be normalized to the point of going unnoticed. They argued that only when gays are recognized for more than their sexuality, then people (i.e. the straight majority) will accept them, and even include them in social practices like arranged marriages. Wishing to see relatives suggesting prospective grooms instead of brides can be seen as a sign of what Lauren Berlant calls 'aspirational normativity' (Berlant 2007), and it is indeed an assertion of the desire to access normality and social value which, in the Indian context, are best accessed through the institution of marriage (Palriwala and Kaur 2013). However, such normative desires have to be evaluated while keeping in mind the scarcity of alternative recognized forms of social belonging. Moreover, the utopic prospect of having relatives accept a spouse of the same gender would certainly involve a fair amount of work for young queers, given the difficulties they experience even just in communicating their sexuality to their parents. Yet, the possibility of a same-sex arranged marriage was imagined as an ideal future scenario, which leads me to argue that 'desiring sameness' (Richardson 2005) is not necessarily the easiest way. Young queer people such as Harsh and Prem would rather work to stretch the boundaries of existing social norms than call themselves out by proclaiming their radical alterity; their vision is one where queerness can find a place within established systems of reciprocity, and where participating in those systems is essential for further practices of recognition to take place.

The struggle is real

Rejecting a radical agenda and refusing to promote 'outness' at all costs were framed as success factors for Niral Club. Prem remembered how a prominent Indian queer activist had been positively surprised by the fact that Niral Club had managed to reach out to engineering students; engineering students were considered the hardest to reach because of their isolation from other students and campuses. The reason for this wide appeal was, according to Prem, that in order to join Niral Club 'you don't have to be *gay* gay! You just have to be "Oh, I just want a place where I can be a full afternoon".' Niral Club did not demand an assertion of sexual identity as political subjectivity from its members, nor did Niral Club members judge people for their views, even when such views were not in line with the shared belief about accepting oneself. An incident that occurred during one of the club meetings I attended is illustrative.

As we were completing a round of introductions, Amar, a young man who was attending for the first time, all of a sudden burst out saying that he could not accept his homosexuality. Unable to come out to anyone, he said he felt disgusted by himself. Amidst a stunned silence, he asked all of us present whether homosexuality could in fact be unnatural: how could it be otherwise, if it was the source of so much pain? The twenty or so people in the room were moved and seemed shocked. After a few seconds, several people started to react, wanting to counter Amar's opinion, but Harsh stepped in to the centre of the room, telling everyone to be silent and let Amar finish what he had to say. Amar continued, in a lower voice, staring at the floor. He wanted to find a cure; he wanted to know if everyone else at the meeting was really, actually happy about being gay; he didn't think it was possible.

The discussion that followed was gentle. Everyone shared their own doubts and struggles. Amar's confession was valued by the meeting participants for its honesty, and many people said they could relate to his feelings. It also led to a discussion about the detrimental effects of homophobia and isolation, with several people admitting to also feeling scared, isolated and 'wrong' from time to time. Amar in a way represented the young person Niral Club tried to reach out to: a person who was still confused and conflicted, who felt isolated and had not reached a sense of stability in relation to her/his sexuality.

When I later discussed the incident with Harsh and Prem, they explained to me that with people like Amar, a more radical/political approach where sexual recognition was predicated as a *sine qua non* could be perceived as alienating, even as a form of 'bullying'. Thus the avoidance of queer politics and activist discourse became important as a way to reach out to people without silencing them or discounting the feelings of inadequacy and self-abjection generated by the stigma surrounding homosexuality. Acknowledging the realness of stigma and its effects without expressing moral judgments was a shared practice within Niral Club meetings, a practice that, I argue, had the effect of fostering a sense of safety. Niral Club was a 'safe space' because it allowed people to recognize their own ambivalence toward being queer.

Commenting on Amar's confession and the long discussion it generated, Harsh told me plainly: 'Let's face it, no one in their right mind would choose to be gay at this point in history.' Harsh's admission might sound paradoxical if we consider that the time we had this conversation (the early spring of 2012) was, at least officially, a good 'point in history' for people like him and groups like Niral Club, who could exist and operate without fearing criminal punishment. What Harsh was referring to was the state of confusion, hesitation and fear that he encountered in many people who approached Niral Club. Hence, he and others chose to tackle the sense of precariousness from within, trying to normalize the ambivalence with which many young queers viewed their sexual identity. In this light, the way in which Niral Club enabled people to 'just be themselves' does not refer to solid, liberated, 'proud' queer identity, but rather a place where self doubt, insecurity and even fear are recognized as central aspects of what it means to be young and queer in India.

Are there any normal gays out there?

All the young people who joined Niral Club had one thing in common: they had been looking for other young queer people for a while. Being able to browse the Internet for signs of gay communities was a significant help, and yet, since the majority of LGBTQ online communities were based abroad, young queer people had a hard time believing that there could be other gay people living in the same city. Shobha recalled how she was startled when she met a gay man from Mumbai on a US-based gay Internet forum: 'I thought he must be the only other gay person in my country.' Testifying to the role of the Internet and social media, the majority of Niral Club members found out about it online, through forums or Facebook connections.

The difficulties experienced in reaching out and finding communities of peers do not mean that participants were unaware of the existence of an underground world of sex and dating opportunities. They knew about, and used, gay dating sites such as the popular Planet Romeo (called 'PR'); but these connections remained sporadic, and they were kept private. I often heard jokes about Planet Romeo during meetings and other social occasions, but people were reluctant to reveal details about their encounters to me. When I meet Varun, a

16-year-old transwoman and one of the few people to be open about her sexuality, she told me that Planet Romeo was the 'open secret' of gays all over India. 'No one wants to admit they use it but they are all there looking for a sex partner', she said with a hint of humour. Varun thought that Niral Club was a very different kind of group:

> [Niral Club] is for your sexuality from scratch, so it's about realizing your sexuality, it's about talking to people, who have the same sort of views about sexuality – it's about realizing that you're not the only one, there are more people like this, there are more intelligent people like this and it's not that difficult.

Dhruv (21) voiced a common feeling about the Niral Club by stating that it was 'the best, loveliest thing' that happened to him. Although he was initially wary of what kind of people he would meet and he hoped the Club was not another gay dating service, upon his first meeting he felt immediately comfortable, stressing the fact that he felt treated very differently from what he referred to as 'the other world', meaning his home, school, or neighbourhood. Ravi (21) shared Dhruv's curiosity about finding other gay people:

> I was apprehensive about stuff, what are the people like, are they like for real or whatever? Because … I hardly knew anyone like other people, normal people who were homosexual; because I always thought, you know, people with alternate sexuality exist, but they are all in the shade and hidden and doing all this – you know – not openly, but hiding from their families or whatever. So I did join Niral Club to really observe people, and how are they, and are they normal people and all that?

When saying that he wanted to meet 'normal people who were homosexual' Ravi makes a point that emerges as a central element in my participants' narratives about Niral Club. The quest for what might be called 'normal queerness' was especially urgent for young people who felt that they lacked the connections and the experience that older LGBTQ people might have. Perpetually being interpellated, or hailed (Althusser 1971; Butler 1997, 2004) as homosexuals by a variety of sources such as the law, the family, other people, and media's narratives about homosexuality, young queer people had an awareness of the negative social consequences of occupying the queer subject position. To respond to the ways in which they were interpellated as queer would mean to take on the stigma that came with it; and yet it was impossible not to hear the hailing. Hence, they looked for references to the existence of spaces of 'normal queerness' and circumscribed recognition, where sexual subjectivity did not preclude social existence (Butler 2015). In participants' accounts, gay dating sites offered instant gratification, but they did not offer the possibility to talk, share, and develop a common understanding of one's sexuality, when the process of defining it was still in progress. Nor did more established communities of older queer people, as Chandra's experience shows.

Chandra (22) was a college student living in a rented apartment with another girl. She had participated in every Delhi Pride parade since the first in 2008, but had not been impressed by the people she met there. Describing the atmosphere at the first pride parade, she said: 'it left me with a bad taste, it left me with the idea that I don't want to belong to this kind of people'. She had a hard time finding a space where she felt she belonged:

> It is a little difficult for me to really fit myself into an identity role because I see few people like me. There are a lot of gay men – I don't see young women like me

who simply don't – for example – who don't identify as heterosexual but live by it anyway. … But I've seen very few people like me, they're either very academic, la-di-da [i.e. pretentious, snobbish] type people, or people who identify as a certain type of lesbian and I've often felt like I don't quite fit, that's all … I have never felt that sense of belonging – it's always been either a little inaccessible or just no other people like me, and so then you feel insecure or you don't care.

Chandra referred to herself as 'queer', but it was only thanks to space like Niral Club that she felt safe to do so. She was out to her closest friends and to her brother, but not to her parents or her roommate. Conscious of the ways people looked down on homosexuals, she was afraid of facing discrimination if she were more open about her sexuality:

As a young person, my choices are somehow less legitimate so even if I, for example – I see that people with more accomplished or more – even just older than me, are more secure in their identities … and I'm sure that comes with a lot of what one does and goes to, but I don't know if I am supposed to arrive at a more fixed identity … but I see that other people seem to get it more so I don't really know. What I want to do is just to be open to more things, more questions.

Chandra expressed in clear terms a discomfort that many other participants also had experienced: a disconnection between the available sexual identity categories and their own ability to recognize themselves in them. This disconnect has been explored by Paul Boyce (2014) who argues that the project of recognition on the basis of sexuality might obscure other ways in which people establish relations of affect, identity, and belonging. According to Boyce, marginalized sexual subjects might even feel limited by the identification with a given identity category, since the everyday processes through which they negotiate stability and social existence escape and exceed the limits of categorical definitions.

The majority of people approaching Niral Club were searching tentatively for a community of peers who also shared the doubts and insecurities of a young person who is coming to terms with her/his own sexuality. The confession from Amar I described above is a case in point. This search was punctuated by ambivalent feelings: on the one hand, young people yearned for their sexuality to be recognized and not judged negatively. On the other hand, they feared the judgment that they knew to be inherent to the recognition they sought. To remain hidden and isolated was to yield to the subordinating power of institutionalized heterosexuality in which they lived their daily lives. But to decide to be 'out and proud' would be to accept the full burden of the subject identity they were assigned, and all its consequences.

Ambivalence lies at the core of the process of subject formation where, for Butler (1997), the power that subordinates the subject is also the power that constitutes it. Agency, thus, is always partially constituted by the power, which it tries to challenge (Butler 1997). Our ability to resist the oppressive aspect of power is thus undercut by the fact that it is the very same power that constitutes us as subjects in the first place. In an attempt to deal with subordination, Niral Club members thus have to act within dominant social categories because, as Butler points out:

Bound to seek recognition of its own existence in categories, terms and names that are not of its own making, the subject seeks the sign of its own existence outside itself, in a discourse that is at once dominant and indifferent. Social categories signify subordination and existence at once. In other words, within subjection the price of existence is subordination.

(Butler 1997, 20)

In this light, there is no possibility for total resistance, nor for unconditional, unambiguous recognition. By acknowledging that subordination is the price of social existence, the desire to be recognized will invariably be confronted with the pragmatics of survival: recognition then needs to be located in and understood as an ambiguous set of practices, rather than assumed as an unfailing goal.

Conclusion

In this chapter I have tried to highlight the spaces of recognition created by queer subjects whose desire for recognition is ambivalent and intertwined with a desire to feel 'normal'. Their narratives and experiences speak to the need to make room for a conceptualization of queer subjectivity that is not immediately radical, not merely oppressed and silenced. Niral Club, as I have shown, enabled its members to experience moments of circumscribed recognition by rendering queerness an inconspicuous 'quirk', as Prem said, rather than a totalizing aspect of one's personhood. This act of relativization and normalization of queer sexuality produced a sense of safety. However, the normalization of queerness was only possible within Niral Club; the remaining social spaces which young queer people navigated, by and large marked queer sexuality as abnormal, and this contrast was ever present not only in members' narratives and experiences, but also in the club's very methodology.

What was accessible through Niral Club was not the hegemonic heterosexually defined 'normality', but a sense of normality (Berlant 2007, 287). This distinction marks the predicament of sexual minorities in today's India, whose inclusion into the dominant heterosexual sociality remains conditioned and dependent on their affective bargains, thanks to which young queers can carve out spaces of recognition as they inhabit exclusionary wider social worlds.

References

ABVA. 1991. *Less Than Gay: A Citizens' Report on the Status of Homosexuality in India*. New Delhi: AIDS Bhedbhav Virodhi Andolan.

Althusser, L. 1971. *Lenin and Philosophy, and Other Essays*. New York: Monthly Review Press.

Berlant, L. 2007. 'Nearly Utopian, Nearly Normal: Post-Fordist Affect in La Promesse and Rosetta.' *Public Culture* 19, no. 2: 273–301.

Berlant, L. 2011. *Cruel Optimism*. Durham, NC: Duke University Press.

Boyce, P. 2014. 'Desirable Rights: Same-Sex Sexual Subjectivities, Socio-economic Transformations, Global Flows and Boundaries – in India and Beyond.' *Culture, Health & Sexuality* 16, no. 10: 1201–1215.

Brown, G. 2012. 'Homonormativity: A Metropolitan Concept that Denigrates "Ordinary" Gay Lives,' *Journal of Homosexuality* 59, no.7: 1065–1072.

Butler, J. 1997. *The Psychic Life of Power: Theories in Subjection*. Stanford, CA: Stanford University Press.

Butler, J. 2004. *Undoing Gender*. New York and London: Routledge.

Butler, J. 2015. *Senses of the Subject*. New York: Fordham University Press.

Cruz, A. and Manalansan, M. (eds) 2002. *Queer Globalizations: Citizenship and the Afterlife of Colonialism*. New York: New York University Press.

Dave, N. 2012. *Queer Activism in India: A Story in the Anthropology of Ethics*. Durham, NC: Duke University Press.

Douglas, M. 1992. *Risk and Blame: Essays in Cultural Theory*. New York: Routledge.

D'Penha, M. and Tarun. 2005. 'Queering the Campus.' In *Because I Have a Voice: Queer Politics in India*, edited by A. Narrain and G. Bhan, pp. 205–216. New Delhi: Yoda Press.

Fraser, N. 2001. 'Recognition without Ethics?' *Theory, Culture & Society* 18, no. 2–3: 21–42.

Goffman, E. 1963. *Stigma: Notes on the Management of Spoiled Identity*. Upper Saddle River, NJ: Prentice-Hall.

Gupta, A. and Narrain, A. 2011. *Law like Love: Queer Perspectives on Law*. New Delhi: Yoda Press.

Honneth, A. 1996. *The Struggle for Recognition: The Moral Grammar of Social Conflicts*. Cambridge, MA: MIT Press.

Horton, P., Rydstrøm, H. and Tonini, M. 2015. 'Contesting Heteronormativity: The Fight for Lesbian, Gay, Bisexual and Transgender Recognition in India and Vietnam.' *Culture, Health & Sexuality* 17, no. 9: 1–15.

Kapur, R. 2012. 'Multitasking Queer: Reflections on the Possibilities of Homosexual Dissidence in Law.' *Jindal Global Law Review* 4, no. 1: 36–59.

Lind, A. 2010. *Development, Sexual Rights, and Global Governance*. London: Routledge.

Lukose, R. A. 2009. *Liberalization's Children: Gender, Youth, and Citizenship in Globalizing India*. Durham, NC: Duke University Press.

Mankekar, P. 2015. *Unsettling India: Affect, Temporality, Transnationality*. Durham, NC: Duke University Press.

Misra, G. 2009. 'Decriminalising Homosexuality in India.' *Reproductive Health Matters*, 17, no. 34: 20–28.

Nisbett, N. 2007. 'Friendship, Consumption, Morality: Practising Identity, Negotiating Hierarchy in Middle-class Bangalore.' *Journal of the Royal Anthropological Institute* 13, no. 4: 935–950.

Palriwala, R. and Kaur, R. 2013. *Marrying in South Asia: Shifting Concepts, Changing Practices in a Globalising World*. New Delhi: Orient Blackswan.

Phadke, S. 2013. 'Unfriendly Bodies, Hostile Cities: Reflections of Loitering and Gendered Public Space.' *Economic and Political Weekly* 158, no. 39: 50–59.

Podmore, J. 2013. 'Critical Commentary: Sexualities Landscapes beyond Homonormativity'. *Geoforum* 49: 263–267.

Puri, J. 2016. *Sexual States: Governance and the Struggle over the Antisodomy Law in India*. Durham, NC: Duke University Press.

Ramasubban, R. 2004. 'Culture, Politics and Discourse on Sexuality: A History of Resistance to the Anti-Sodomy Law in India.' In *Sex/Politics: Reports from the Frontlines*, edited by R. Parker, R. Petchesky and R. Sember, pp. 91–125. Rio de Janeiro: Sexuality Policy Watch. http://www.sxpolitics.org/frontlines/book/index.php

Ranade, K. 2015. 'Queering the Pitch: A Need for Mainstreaming LGBTQ Issues in Professional Social Work Education and Practice in India.' In *Lesbian, Gay, Bisexual and Trans Health Inequalities: International Perspectives in Social Work*, edited by J. Fish and K. Karban, pp. 63–78. Bristol: Policy Press.

Richardson, D. 2005. 'Desiring Sameness? The Rise of a Neoliberal Politics of Normalisation.' *Antipode* 37, no. 3: 515–535.

Sabsay, L. 2013. 'Queering the Politics of Sexual Rights?' *Studies in Ethnicity and Nationalism* 13, no. 1: 80–90.

Shahani, P. 2008. *Gay Bombay: Globalization, Love and (Be)longing in Contemporary India*. Thousand Oaks, CA: SAGE Publications.

Viswanath, K. and Mehrotra, S. T. 2007. 'Shall We Go Out?: Women's Safety in Public Spaces in Delhi.' *Economic and Political Weekly*, 42, no. 17: 1542–1548. http://safedelhi.jagori.org/wp-content/uploads/shall-we-go-out-epw-apr-28-2007.pdf

Young, I. M. 1997. 'Asymmetrical Reciprocity: on Moral Respect, Wonder, and Enlarged Thought.' *Constellations* 3, no. 3: 340–363.

17

DISRUPTING
JOBURG PRIDE

Exploring the depoliticisation of
Africa's first Pride march

Nyx McLean

Pride parades are "public carnivalesque festivals, culturally shared rites of passage" which are also "forms of politically motivated consumption-related resistance, and magnets for commercialisation within the context of the festival" (Kates and Belk 2001, 393). In their research on Toronto Pride Kates and Belk found that members of the lesbian, gay, bisexual, transgender, intersex, asexual, and queer (LGBTIAQ) community felt that Pride had become too commercialised and had lost its historical and political meaning undermining Pride's original purpose of making visible and politicising LGBTIAQ identities, and thus "weakening the integrity" of the political movement (2001, 419). This is one of the arguments made by the One in Nine Campaign's[1] activists in their disruption of the 2012 Joburg Pride[2] parade. They disrupted Pride in order "to protest both systemic violence targeting black lesbians in South Africa and the commercialization of the Pride event itself," and felt that the commercialization of Joburg Pride had moved it away from its political roots (Hengeveld and Tallie 2012). The disruption was a protest, "calling for one minute of silence for black queer victims of violence," and it was "met by animosity and additional violence from the predominantly white attendees" (Hengeveld and Tallie 2012). This is the point of interest of this chapter: the moment of disruption, and Joburg Pride's loss of political edge through becoming increasingly commercialised and violent in the manner through which it excluded some LGBTIAQ identities based on apartheid-borne racism and discrimination (One in Nine Campaign 2012).

Research design

The research informing this chapter is qualitative and interpretivist employing archival research and oral history to explore the depoliticisation of Pride throughout the research period of 1990 to 2013. It positions itself within the interpretivist paradigm which places emphasis on the meanings that people assign to their lives and how they construct their social world through interactions and shared meanings, by investigating them within their social contexts (Nieuwenhuis 2011). Data collection was divided into two stages: stage one consisted of archive research and stage two consisted of the oral history interviews. Research data was collected from the Gay and Lesbians Archives (GALA), based at the University of the Witwatersrand and the content they had available on Joburg Pride from 1990 to 2013, sourcing primarily from *Exit* newspaper, South Africa's longest running "gay" publication (Davidson and Nerio 1994, 225). GALA houses and captures gay and lesbian history in South Africa, serving to "preserve materials excluded from the mainstream repositories" because marginalised identities, such as LGBTIAQ identities, are excluded from the archive (Hamilton et al. 2002, 11). This is either because they are deemed to not be significant to the national archives or because the archivist judges the content irrelevant (Reid 2002; Mbembe 2002). Key stakeholders were identified from Pride articles featured in *Exit* from 1990 to 2013, and oral history interviews were conducted with them. Oral history places the individual's telling within the context of "collective memory, political culture, social power" (Hesse-Biber 2005, 189). A textual analysis was applied to the archival contents and interview transcripts and consisted of a thematic and discourse analysis informed by the work of Fairclough (1995; 1992; 1989), and Jorgensen and Phillips (2002).

With regards to the language that emerged during the thematic analysis, it is important to note a few word and language choices made throughout this chapter. Wherever possible the letters LGBTIAQ – lesbian, gay, bisexual, transgender, intersex, asexual and queer – are used in order to be as inclusive of the LGBTIAQ community as possible. There are times when only a few letters will be employed such as LGBTI, LGBT, LGB or simply "lesbian and gay" or "gay." When this occurs it will be as a result of the texts provided by *Exit* articles, interview subjects or other sources that have been analysed and the historical context of the LGBTIAQ movement or community. "Gay" or "lesbian and gay" are often used as the catch-all terms for the community which speaks to a broader issue of assimilation and homonormativity. Where queer is used in the writing it is used in the political sense of the term and queer as understood within Queer Theory, employed for the purposes of deconstructing, interrogating and capsizing that which is read as "normal" or "natural" (Payne and Davies 2012; Oswin 2008; Browne 2006; Jagose 1996; Halperin 1995).

Context

Joburg Pride is the annual celebration held by the (LGBTIAQ) community and has taken place since 1990. It is South Africa's longest running Pride event, and is unique in that it was the first LGBTIAQ Pride in South Africa (and on the continent of Africa) at a time before there were legal protections in South Africa for LGBT South Africans. It is often described as having a history that "runs alongside the history of the transition to democracy in South Africa" (Craven 2011: III). There are several contestations that exist around Joburg Pride that are not unique to South Africa, but what makes it worthy of noting is "the context of the apartheid regime and the post-apartheid era" (Craven 2011, 61). The post-apartheid era saw the LGBTIAQ community granted legal protections under the South African Constitution, and integrated into the country's multicultural project, the Rainbow Nation. While the rest of the world often celebrates South Africa as the champion of LGBTIAQ rights with the country's constitution (1996) being the first in the world to protect people regardless of sexual orientation, as well South Africa's 2006 passing of the Civil Union Act, there is still reason to protest. Many LGBTIAQ South Africans continue to face homophobic and transphobic harassment and violence within their communities (McLean 2015). In addition to this, there is the added complexity of residual apartheid-borne racism within the LGBTIAQ community, which results in many LGBTIAQ South Africans of colour being excluded from predominantly white social LGBTIAQ spaces. For this reason, as Tucker writes, it is important to "acknowledg[e] local histories of discrimination" in addition to the community's "affinity with a 'Western' queer history of exclusivity and exclusion" when writing about LGBTIAQ South Africans (Tucker 2009, 192). Much of this racism, discrimination, and exclusion came to the fore with the disruption of Joburg Pride in 2012.

On 6 October 2012, approximately "20 black lesbians and gender non-conforming feminists" from the One in Nine Campaign, a campaign advocating for the rights of survivors of sexual violence including members of the LGBTIAQ community, staged a "die-in"[3] and halted the annual Joburg Pride parade (One in Nine Campaign 2012). Campaign members gave out "leaflets to explain why they were there," the leaflets contained information as to why they were staging the die-in, calling for "one minute of silence for the dead" and listing the names of 25 LGBTIAQ members of the community who had died as a result of hate crimes (One in Nine Campaign 2012).

The activists demanded a minute of silence from the parade, and lay down in the middle of the road with life-sized dolls that represented members of the LGBTIAQ community who had been raped and murdered because of their sexual orientation or gender identity and expression. Included in this was the agenda of bringing attention to how "pride has ceased to be a space for charting new futures" and highlighting that "the de-politicisation of most prides has allowed the old, racial apartheid to be translated into a new, economic apartheid, which is clearly evident in many pride celebrations" (One in Nine Campaign 2012). Continuing, "Capitalist consumerism and individualistic rights claims now characterise many prides in South Africa, as they characterise most other spaces for the LGBT community" (One in Nine Campaign 2012). Their disruption made clear that they felt there were links between Joburg Pride's depoliticisation and the increased commercialisation of Pride.

In response to this action, Joburg Pride parade organisers and marshals threatened to drive over the One in Nine Campaign activists, who were predominantly black lesbians and gender non-conforming people, with their vehicles while telling the activists they "had no right to be at the parade"(Valenza 2012). Members of the organising committee dragged One in Nine Campaign members out of the road, handling them roughly as can be seen in the footage, "Gay Pride March interrupted by activists" that circulated after the moment.[4] Following this, the Pride organising committee, One in Nine Campaign members and Pride participants became involved in a physically aggressive clash.[5] The clash between Joburg Pride organisers and parade participants with activists from the One in Nine Campaign highlighted tensions around racism, discrimination and exclusion that have surrounded the Joburg Pride event since its beginning in 1990 (Craven 2011; De Waal and Manion 2006).

The eruption in 2012 could simply have passed as an event in Pride history receiving a mention in *Exit*[6] as every Pride event had in years before (*Exit* 2012). However, it is the violence of the event, and the making visible of the tensions between Pride organisers and privileged participants and marginalised members of the community, that has brought about a sense of urgency to understanding what had happened and its larger implications. What emerged from this violent incident were several moments in 2013 where the LGBTIAQ community actively attempted to interrogate what it meant to hold a Pride event that represented all members of the South African LGBTIAQ community. Following the 2012 clash at Joburg Pride, social media emerged as an important site through which people could relive and explore what happened. Both the Joburg Pride organising committee and the One in Nine Campaign made statements via their Facebook pages. One such announcement by the Joburg Pride organising committee on 3 April 2013 resulted in a series of events offline that began to change the face of Joburg Pride. Firstly, the organising committee announced their dissolution[7] (DeBarros 2013; Nathan 2013). Following this,

LGBTIAQ organisations, members and individuals held events in Johannesburg to discuss a way forward. Events included a meeting on 7 April 2013 at a restaurant in Melville, Johannesburg, and another in the Johannesburg central business district (CBD) at the House of Movements entitled "Reclaim our Pride" on 13 April 2013, as well as a meeting at the University of the Witwatersrand (Mambagirl 2013). The Reclaim our Pride meeting organised by the Forum for the Empowerment of Women and the One in Nine Campaign was called to "discuss strategy for rejecting the commercialization and de-politicisation of Joburg Pride in recent years," and for "imagining ways forward for reclaiming our pride" (One in Nine Campaign 2013). Follow-up meetings saw the emergence of new groups such as Johannesburg People's Pride who would go on to organise the Joburg Pride events of 2013.

A key issue raised by the One in Nine Campaign in their disruption of Joburg Pride was that Joburg Pride had become increasingly depoliticised and commericalised, thereby deviating from the political roots of earlier Prides. Initially the liberation struggle, the Equality Clause[8] and HIV/AIDS were major issues that the LGBTIAQ community mobilised around at the Pride marches and parades. After 2000, hate crimes became a major issue affecting the LGBTIAQ community: primary targets were, and still are, "sex workers, single women, HIV positive women and women with non-normative gender expression, lesbians, transgender men, and bisexual women" (One in Nine Campaign 2012). Hate crimes were not viewed with the same seriousness and attention as previous issues had been. The reason is thought to be that Joburg Pride had been treated "as a business" and "the activist part" had not been considered or taken up by the organisers.' Instead, Pride continued as an entertainment-focused event. This shift from political movement to depoliticised celebration was made evident by *Exit* newspaper articles which covered the transitions, as well as critical academic discussions published around Pride in South Africa and internationally (Craven 2011; De Waal and Manion 2006; Kates and Belk 2001; Gevisser and Cameron 1994). In becoming increasingly commercialised, focusing on attracting sponsors and being driven by financial need over political need, Pride, and social movements at large, become depoliticised and lose their potential to be transgressive spaces because they would like to be "appealing" for sponsors and funders who would be happy to associate their brand with the event (Stella 2013; Ghaziani 2011; Ghaziani and Fine 2008; Bernstein 1997). This "desiring" to be appealing and to be presented as "safe" for brands and companies, such as Coca-Cola, South African Breweries and Mango Airlines, speaks to assimilationist politics or endeavours where those on the margins are ignored and obscured by the formation of a collective and "safe" identity that has no space for the nuanced ways of being that each identity may bring to the space. As Nath (2012) writes, "the commericalisation of Pride," and the formation of a "gay market" results in the "homogenising [of] diverse communities and their needs and concealing the poverty and marginalisation faced by the majority of the black LGBT population in South Africa" (Nath 2012).

The One in Nine Campaign protest made visible the assimilationist politics within the community, where "the urge to fit into this normalisation is so high, that a minor deviance from the course is a violent threat" (Huber 2014, 2), while acknowledging that the South African LGBTIAQ community is not equal: that "some gays consume 'luxury items' while others cannot afford three meals a day is just a detail that does not rhyme well with 'open happiness'" – the slogan of Coca-Cola, one of Joburg Pride's sponsors (Nath 2012). Nath concludes with, "it is not news that capitalism is inherently opposed to diversity and equity, and that a politics based on identity seeks to flatten difference among us and erase those of us who are not gay in the approved way" (Nath 2012).

Making visible the depoliticisation of Joburg Pride

Ishtar Lakhani, one of the One in Nine Campaign protestors, explained that "the idea was to disrupt Pride" because it "had morphed into this thing that was nothing like the reason why Pride started" (Lakhani 2016). Pride "had turned into this whole, kind of, gay white male extravaganza that completely overshadowed the fact that all the things they were celebrating was actually not real for [the] majority of the population" (Lakhani 2016).

The protest action was "performed by about 20 queer, feminist One in Nine Campaign members" who were dressed in purple T-shirts with messages such as "Lesbian," "Dyke," "Stabane," and "Sex worker" on the front and "Solidarity with women who speak out" on the back (One in Nine Campaign 2013). They

> held banners reading "Dying for Justice" and "No Cause for Celebration" and carried life-sized mannequins also dressed in purple t-shirts. Two of our members handed out leaflets explaining the direct action, a few held the banners, and the rest of us lay down on the road along with the mannequins in front of the banner that read "Dying for Justice."
>
> *(One in Nine Campaign 2013)*

One activist "was calling out on a loudhailer such slogans as 'Down with homophobia!' and 'Down with the killing of black lesbians!'" (One in Nine Campaign 2013). The Joburg Pride organising committee described this moment as

> a group of protestors ran out into the road and formed a human blockade across the Pride route. This consisted of two banners, dummies and the actual protestors who laid [*sic*] down on the road. This caused a major safety hazard.
>
> *(Joburg Gay Pride Festival Company 2012)*

They go on to write that, "One of the banners said 'NO CAUSE FOR CELEBRATION'. It was unclear as to whether this was an anti-gay protest by a homophobic group, which raised safety concerns even more" (Joburg Gay Pride Festival Company 2012).

In *Exit* the One in Nine Campaign disruption was described as "someone decided that the time for polite criticism was over, and action needed" (Exit 2012, 1). Gavin Hayward, the editor of *Exit*, said that the publication had "for years…criticised the depoliticisation of Pride, the lack of gay and allied signage on its stages, the lack of a significant speaker to send marchers on their way with a purpose" (Exit 2012, 1). Timothy Trengove-Jones, a regular contributor to *Exit*, wrote that he had "argued too many times for the comfort of myself and others that it is a 'crying shame' that Pride has become so depoliticised." He further claimed that through the One in Nine intervention, "the point about the politicisation of Pride came to the fore, at last" and that it had "redeemed the event from absolute triviality" (Trengove-Jones 2012, 4). Tanya Harford, the chairperson of the Joburg Pride organising committee, was criticised for her "decision not to give the Parade a political focus" because as Trengove-Jones explains

> one cannot depoliticise an inherently political event. But you can stand in the way of those who wish to emphasise its political nature. And that, as far as I can see, is what Harford and her Committee have done over the last several years. In that decision lie the roots of what happened this year.
>
> *(Trengove-Jones 2012, 4)*

As Trengove-Jones continues

the action from 1 in 9 can be "seen as stemming from considerable anger at the (non) direction Pride has taken" and that the 2012 moment "exposed the fault lines that exist in the 'chimerical community'"

(Trengove-Jones 2012, 4)

As made clear by *Exit*, although the disruption to 2012 Joburg Pride and the subsequent dissolution of the organising committee was heralded by some as "shocking" a closer examination of the history of Joburg Pride from 1990 to 2013 shows the manner in which the event had become increasingly depoliticised and commercialised.

The movement away from the political

Joburg Pride had once had a very strong political rooting in the early drive for legal recognition, in "wanting the Equality Clause," and some members of the community, such as Hayward, believed that "once that was achieved it just fell away" (Hayward 2016). The 1990 march was an "an avowedly political gathering" (De Waal and Manion 2006, 7), one through which Pride participants marched to "demand our rights as full, proud, productive participants in a fully equal society" (Cameron 2006, 4). Pride is an integral part of LGBTIAQ history by making the community visible, placing it firmly in the "public gaze," and in doing so works to counter the shame, "concealment and disavowal" that the community experiences (De Waal and Manion 2006, 9). It is a tool for a minority group to "challenge the status quo, fight for social change" (Ratcliff et al. 2013, 472), as well as occupy space in society (Matebeni 2011). Gevisser and Reid described the march as "simultaneously angry and carnivalesque; both deeply earnest in its call for lesbian and gay rights and wildly subversive in its challenge to heterosexual stereotyping" and as having a "strangely dual character" (1994, 278). The early marches "invoke[d] the tradition of human rights protest marches in South Africa, from the Women's March on Pretoria in 1956 through to the marches of the defiance campaigns of the 1980s that signified the collapse of apartheid," while also adopting "its style and indeed its name from the carnivalesque tradition of the pride march, initiated in North America after the Stonewall uprising of 1969" (Gevisser and Reid 1994, 278). De Waal and Manion writing on the 25-year anniversary of Joburg Pride wrote "Pride has changed, for better or for worse; it may be that the commercialisation of Pride ensured its survival as an annual event, but it also contributed to its depoliticisation and estrangement from black gay and lesbian people" (De Waal and Manion 2006, 8).

A key criticism that has emerged in the years following 1990, is that Pride has increasingly moved from the political to the commercial, with Pride being described as "serv[ing] no discernible purpose at all," "nudging away from anything 'political' towards some kind of carnival" (*Exit* 2002, 4). Some South Africans hold that simply having a Pride event is already a political act in that LGBTIAQ individuals take up space at the time of a Pride event: "a sexual minority, reviled by many, takes to the streets to demonstrate its existence, and its right to exist" (*Exit* 2000, 13). Moreover, an *Exit* staff journalist writes, "That when you put 10000 gay people in a park, by its sheer existence – it is political, especially in Africa" (*Exit* 2004, 1). For Mbhele (2016), "the mere fact of projecting and increasing LGBT visibility in itself is a political act because it is countering and challenging the attempt by heterosexist mainstream culture in many ways to make LGBT people invisible." However, there are moments throughout the analysis period where there is a push to interrogate and assess the purpose of Pride, "to stop pretending that nothing is wrong, and for Pride to have a political message" (*Exit* 2003a, 5). That for Pride to not have a political message would result in "the event defect[ing] from any and all political responsibility... We live in a country facing enormous challenges... Any 'gay' event that does not show an awareness of these political and economic realities is a waste of talent, energy and intelligence" (*Exit* 2010, 13).

Sharon Cooper, a member of the Pride organising committee in 1996 when Joburg Pride was called Lesbian and Gay Pride, suggests that the pull away from a political agenda is due to the loss of leadership in the movement. That when individuals like Zackie Achmat, Edward Cameron, Kevin Botha and Phumi Mtetwa, the "political think tank minds" had left for other movements; this resulted in there being "nothing to guide Pride, or even refresh the strategy" (Cooper 2016). Cooper said that as soon as they left "it [Pride] was a different space; it no longer has the minds behind it" (Cooper 2016). This absence of political leadership and a political motivating factor (such as the Equality Clause) could very well be the reason for the move away from the political. Pride has "got to be a vehicle for something slightly more important" (Cooper 2016); is one such possibility by placing Joburg Pride within the context of "larger social forces pertinent to South Africa today?" (*Exit* 2003b, 4). By not acknowledging the lived experiences of many LGBTIAQ South Africans, Pride becomes a "gross misinterpretation of who we are today," having "lost touch with reality and intention" (*Exit* 2009, 2).

For the sponsor: changing the name

A key moment to note in the depoliticisation of Pride is the removal of "gay" from Gay Pride and replacing it with "Joburg": "Joburg Pride is an altogether tamer name" (*Exit* 2011, 10). And that what lies at "the heart of the matter" is that being able to "take the gayness out of Pride and put[ting] the (Joburg) citizenry centre stage" is due to there being an "absence of any measurable political point" (*Exit* 2011, 10). Tanya Harford, the former chairperson of the Joburg Pride organising committee, in an interview with the author, said that they changed the name because they "had got to the point where we didn't have to define it as Gay Pride. Pride was Pride. It helped us quite a bit in our selling, sponsorships and how we positioned stuff on the radio" (Harford 2016). To need to make Joburg Pride less "gay" in order to gain sponsors is telling, and makes Harford's position clear, that "[Pride] needed to be run like a business" (Harford 2016). Joburg Pride under her leadership, she said, saw "everything [done] by the book. Correctly registered. Ran proper board meetings with minutes...we started running it correctly. And we ran it for six years, growing it" (Harford 2016). Harford described how they had "funded it ourselves"; "we didn't charge at the gate"; "we were having to make our money off the bar...in our last year, we took a million rand at the bar" (Harford 2016). Continuing on this topic, she stated "we understood that there was an activist part to pride and we created areas for it but our driving force was to make money to cover the costs which were extreme" (Harford 2016). This "activist part" is what Pride was founded upon, the need to advocate for recognition and protection of the LGBTIAQ community, but it is forgotten here in the desire for sponsorship, to cover costs, and to present a safe "gay event" to sponsor. As Nath (2012) writes, "Pride's politics...follow[ed] the money."

Zak Mbhele, former co-chairperson of the Joburg Pride organising committee, suggested that "the gayness" is "implied" in that "Pride means a gay orientated or LGBT oriented event" (Mbhele 2016). He said that "we also wanted to engender this notion that pride wasn't necessarily exclusively for LGBT people. It was an open community event. Maybe rather more centred round certain values and ideas around embracing diversity and...I suppose a 'rainbowism' of sorts" (Mbhele 2016). And that, "not having the name gay or LGBT in the brand name is a nod in that direction" (Mbhele 2016). In choosing this "nod in that direction" does Joburg Pride then not play into a politics of "sameness" instead of "difference"? (Einwohner, Reger and Myers 2008, 5). This endeavour to "emphasize their similarities to straights" serves to depoliticise Pride because a Pride driven by a politics of sameness does not necessarily allow for as much of a political edge that one would find through a politics of difference (Ghaziani 2011, 100). The desire to belong speaks to the "strong assimilationist streak in gay politics" that De Waal and Manion (2006) speak of, as well as others (Johnson 2002; Richardson 2000; Bernstein 1997). It is this desire to assimilate that possibly overrides the need to emphasise difference, to disrupt the status quo, and to call attention to the continued violence that many LGBTIAQ South Africans face (Milani 2013; De Waal and Manion 2006).

The yearning to belong and to be recognised as the "same" may be as a result of the legal rights and protections afforded to LGBTIAQ South Africans who have now come to believe "that it's all fine. That we're in South Africa and we've got the Equality Rights Bill and our rights are protected" (Hayward 2016). This is despite the "homophobic violence and 'corrective rape'" that many LGBTIAQ South Africans face, "who may be multiply marginalised by poverty, sexism and racism" and this occurs "despite legal gains" (Thoreson 2008, 695). The violence against the LGBTIAQ community in the way of hate crimes such as corrective rape and murder represents an opportunity to articulate a political direction but Pride organisers do not seize it and Pride fails to reignite its political nature. As leaders of the LGBTIAQ community in Johannesburg, the Joburg Pride organising committee can be seen as having the responsibility to direct the political focus of the community, but the concern with sponsorship and running Pride "like a business" directed their focus away from a cause-based approach and to a rather commercial approach – profits over politics. In not acknowledging the violence that many LGBTIAQ South Africans continue to face, Joburg Pride organisers "obscure the lived terror of less privileged members" of the community (Hengeveld and Tallie 2012).

In 2009, in an attempt to return to the political, *Exit* offered Phumi Mtetwa, one of South Africa's key LGBTIAQ activists in pushing for equal rights, the opportunity to write and publish a speech should she have been invited to address the Pride participants of that year. Mtetwa wrote in *Exit* that

> lesbian women and feminine gay men are being targeted for rape as a measure to "correct" their sexuality. We cannot lose sight of these realities. We should challenge all commercialisation of our identities and lives because these hide the struggles we are facing and will continue to face.
>
> *(Mtetwa 2009, 2)*

Despite this call, Pride organisers continue to not respond to these struggles beyond moments of silence. For example, *Exit* (2007) notes that a moment of silence was observed to "mark the recent brutal murder of two lesbians in Meadowlands, as well as acknowledging all victims of hate-crimes" which helps to politicise the event, but not in a manner or with a sense of urgency that a response to violence of this nature should receive (*Exit* 2007, 28). Pride has the potential to be a political vehicle to rally for real change for the majority of LGBTIAQ South Africans but continuously fails to step up into the role because of the direction those who lead and organise Joburg Pride continue to take: they perceive the political and "the activist part" as not integral parts of Pride.

As highlighted by the One in Nine Campaign, and evidenced by the presence of hate crimes against the LGBTIAQ community, there is no reason for Joburg Pride to be depoliticised and lacking in political direction. The reality is that many LGBTIAQ persons, primarily queers of colour who are more often than not lesbians and transgender persons, face physical and sexual violence, and are often murdered because of the homophobia and transphobia that persists. Rights on paper do not necessarily translate into protections, when little has been done to address cultures of homophobia and transphobia. In fact, if there is little public education happening at local, provincial or national levels, then the onus is on a major LGBTIAQ event such as Joburg Pride to drive the politicisation, education, and awareness of LGBTIAQ South Africans. Hate crimes and violence against queer bodies ought to be enough to motivate for dedicated organising and rallying to bring information from the margins into the centre, to make visible these identities and to strive for their recognition and protection in public and private spaces. But in a world where the desire is to belong, to present as "same," and where "pride events have to have a certain marketability," there is little awareness of those who are not the 'same' (Huber 2014, 1).

The predominantly white organisers of Joburg Pride in their organising of Pride events did not understand the need for the "activist" part, for the political focus of Pride, and for a returning to the political roots of Joburg Pride because of their commercial interests, and perhaps because their lens onto the world is informed by whiteness (Steyn 2005, 2001). White is, as Dyer writes, to be "normal" to have one's experience read as the default or standard experience (Dyer 1997). This is particularly pertinent when one looks to South Africa under apartheid, a nation governed by whiteness, the privileging of white experience, and the active project of othering all bodies queer to the white body (Falkof 2016; Steyn 2005, 2001). White South Africans under apartheid were taught to privilege the white body and the white experience, and this could be a core reason for the depoliticisation of Pride. White LGBTIAQ South Africans, while facing discrimination with regards to gender and sexual identity, still hold a position of privilege in South Africa, and as their rights are protected under the South African Constitution, and with access to legal protection, wealth and other privileges that come with being white and middle-class in South Africa, it is no surprise that many believe "it's all fine." It is, mostly, for those who occupy such a protected space in South Africa. As the One in Nine Campaign (2012) states, "in the absence of social and economic justice, rights only benefit social elites and a privileged few." Violence against members of the LGBTIAQ community who do not have access to such privileges persists, and thus to organise a Pride event such as Joburg Pride without a political focus and without interrogation, while ignoring the lived experiences of the majority of South Africans, is irresponsible.

Conclusion

Joburg Pride, Africa's first Pride event, and LGBTIAQ South Africa's key defiant moment in 1990, had its roots in the political. From the media analysis and interviews presented above it appears there were multiple opportunities to return to these roots, simply in turning to the community, observing and acknowledging the violence and hate crimes perpetrated against queer bodies. Joburg Pride had the potential to be driven by a clear politicised agenda, to take a political stance, but those in leadership, in their desire to gain sponsors and to make Pride financially viable, overrode this "activist part." As Huber writes, on the visibility of the LGBTIAQ collective through Pride, the assimilationist politics see it become "a visibility of normalisation within capitalist markets" and these markets are "not really interested in social change and emancipation" (Huber 2014, 1). It seems that these were key motivations for the One in Nine Campaign to disruption Joburg Pride 2012, as an attempt and to make visible its depoliticisation and its commercial interests.

Pride in South Africa can still do the work to make visible all LGBTIAQ individuals, their experiences, and to do the work to counter the shame and violence that many still experience. Pride events, be they Joburg Pride, or other pride events organised throughout the country, have the space to do the work to challenge the status quo, to claim space, and to contextualise the LGBTIAQ experience within the broader South African experience. Pride events, such as Soweto Pride, Johannesburg People's Pride and the Alternative Inclusive Pride, "push for the recognition and acknowledgement of the reality that the majority of LGBTIAQ individuals are faced with" and "attempt to strike the balance between celebration and protest" (McLean 2015).

In particular, it is worth mentioning the Johannesburg People's Pride, which One in Nine Campaign activist Ishtar Lakhani described as "very unmoving and unapologetic in that this [is] going to be collaborative" (Lakhani 2016). She described it as "such a beautiful process to watch" and that "what was powerful about it was the fact that they take on multiple issues and multiple struggles and the acknowledgement that 'yes, we're LGBTI people, but yes we want land, yes we want access to water'" (Lakhani 2016). Johannesburg People's Pride described themselves as

> a diverse group of people from suburbs and townships, queer and non-queer, workers and unemployed people, black and non-black, differently-abled and able-bodied activists, feminists, conscious and interested people. We come from economically advantaged and disadvantaged backgrounds, with competing interests and visions, yet joining in the call to Reclaim Our Pride.
>
> *(Exit 2013, 1)*

Johannesburg People's Pride shows that it is possible to organise a Pride event in South Africa in a collaborative manner, to do the work to "restore the traditions of activism, assertion and equality" while situating the organising of the event and the event itself within the context of the lived experiences of many South Africans (Heywood 2012). In a way they responded to the One in Nine Campaign's rallying call:

> It is time for everyone – queer, lesbian, femme, trans, gender resistant, straight, butch, bisexual, gender fluid, black and non-black – to bring back to pride the spirit of revolution. Not only an LGBT revolution but a sexual revolution, a workers' revolution, an anti-capitalist revolution, a revolution of unemployed people, a revolution of people living with HIV and AIDS, a revolution of immigrants, a revolution of sex workers, a revolution of single people, a revolution of students without textbooks, a queer feminist revolution.
>
> *(One in Nine Campaign 2012)*

Notes

1 The One in Nine Campaign is an organisation "grounded on a feminist critical analysis of the patriarchal nature of existing political arrangements" (Milani 2012: 20). The campaign was formed in 2006 in response to the Zuma rape trial in which South Africa's then deputy president, Jacob Zuma, was accused of rape. The campaign "supports survivors of sexual violence" and "apply

pressure on various branches of the criminal justice system through direct action and targeted advocacy." http://www.oneinnine.org.za/

2 Johannesburg Pride (Joburg Pride – Joburg is the shortened and colloquial name for Johannesburg).

3 A die-in is a form of protest where activists feign being dead. Die-ins were popular forms of protest among members of ACT UP in the 1980s (Taylor 2012).

4 The video, "Gay Pride March interrupted by activists" shows the clash between protesters and parade participants. http://www.youtube.com/watch?v=LYjp-xbdFS0)(accessed 6 February 2014).

5 Ibid.

6 Many articles in *Exit* are not attributed to an author. This usually occurs when the content has been produced by a staff reporter.

7 In a post, titled 'Joburg Gay Pride Festival Company board votes to stop production of annual Joburg Pride event,' Joburg Prides's organising committee announced their dissolution on 3 April 2013 (Joburg Gay Pride Festival Company 2013).

8 The Equality Clause forms part of the South African Constitution and affords protection to all South Africans, and states that "the state may not unfairly discriminate directly or indirectly against anyone on one or more grounds, including race, gender, sex, pregnancy, marital status, ethnic or social origin, colour, sexual orientation, age, disability, religion, conscience, belief, culture, language and birth" (Constitution of the Republic of South Africa 1996).

References

Bernstein, M. 1997. "Celebration and suppression: The strategic uses of identity by the lesbian and gay movement." *American Journal of Sociology* 103, no. 3: 531–565.

Browne, K. 2006. "Challenging queer geographies." *Antipode* 38: 885–893.

Cameron, E. 2006. "Foreword." In *Pride: Protest and Celebration*, edited by De Waal, S. and Manion, A., pp. 4–6. Johannesburg: Fanele.

Constitution of the Republic of South Africa. 1996. Act No. 108 of 1996.

Cooper, S. 2016. Interview with the researcher on 3 February 2016, Pietermaritzburg and Cape Town (Skype).

Craven, E. 2011. "Racial identity and racism in the gay and lesbian community in post-apartheid South Africa." Master of Arts thesis. University of the Witwatersrand, Johannesburg.

Davidson, G. and Nerio, R. 1994. "Exit: Gay publishing in South Africa." In *Defiant Desire: Gay and Lesbian lives in South Africa*, edited by Gevisser, Mark and Cameron, Edwin, pp. 225–231. Braamfontein; Ravan Press.

DeBarros, L. 2013. "Breaking: Shock as Joburg Pride shuts down." Mambaonline. www.mambaonline.com/article.asp?artid=8011 (accessed 15 April 2015).

De Waal, S. and Manion, A. 2006. *Pride: Protest and Celebration*. Johannesburg: Fanele.

Dyer, R. 1997. *White: Essays on Race and Culture*. London Routledge.

Einwohner, R.L., Reger, J., and Myers, D.L. 2008. "Introduction." In *Identity Work in Social Movements*, edited by Reger, Jo., Myers, Daniel L. and Einwohner, Rachel L., pp. 1–17. Minneapolis, MN: University of Minnesota Press.

Exit. 2000. "Pride and the party animal." November, Edition 129, page 13.

Exit. 2002. "What purpose did Pride 2002 serve?" November, Edition 153, page 4.

Exit. 2003a. "Has Pride become meaningless?" December/January, Edition 166, page 5.

Exit. 2003b. "Pride 2003: Benighted we fall." November, Edition 165, page 4.

Exit. 2004. "Equality project takes over Pride." November, Edition 176, page 1.

Exit. 2007. "Coming of age: Joburg Pride 2007: A new kind of Pride." September, Edition 207, page 28.

Exit. 2009. "You need Pride??" October, Edition 230, page 2.

Exit. 2010. "Make a point of Pride." October, Edition 241, page 13.

Exit. 2011. "Is Joburg's Pride mainly in vain?" October, Edition 252, page 10.

Exit. 2012. "Joburg Pride 2012: In the news for the wrong reasons." November, Edition 264, page 1.

Exit. 2013. "All the Pride events." September, Edition 274, page 1.

Fairclough, N. 1989. *Language and Power*. London: Longman.

Fairclough, N. 1992. *Discourse and Social Change*. Cambridge: Polity Press.

Fairclough, N. 1995. *Critical Discourse Analysis*. London: Longman.

Falkof, N. 2016. *The End of Whiteness: Satanism and Family Murder in Late Apartheid South Africa*. Johannesburg: Jacana.

Gevisser, M. and Cameron, E. 1994. *Defiant Desire: Gay and Lesbian Lives in South Africa*. Braamfontein: Ravan Press.

Gevisser, M. and Reid, G. 1994. "Pride or protest?: Drag queens, comrades, and the Lesbian and Gay Pride March." In *Defiant Desire: Gay and Lesbian Lives in South Africa*, edited by Gevisser, Mark and Cameron, Edwin, pp. 278–283. Braamfontein: Ravan Press.

Ghaziani, A. 2011. "Post-gay collective identity construction." *Social Problems* 58, no. 1: 99–125.

Ghaziani, A. and Fine, G.A. 2008. "Infighting and ideology: How conflict informs the local culture of the Chicago Dyke March." *International Journal of Politics, Culture, and Society* 20, no. 1: 51–67.

Halperin, D.M. 1995. *Saint Foucault: Towards a Gay Hagiography*. New York: Oxford University Press.

Hamilton, C., Harris, V., and Reid, G. 2002. "Introduction." In *Refiguring the Archive*, edited by Hamilton, Carolyn, Harris, Verne, Taylor, Jane, Pickover, Michele, Reid, Graeme, and Saleh, Razia, pp. 6–17. Cape Town: David Philip.

Harford, T. 2016. Interview with the researcher on 25 January 2016, Plettenberg Bay and Cape Town (Skype).

Hayward, G. 2016. Interview with the researcher on 24 March 2016, Johannesburg.

Hengeveld, M. and Tallie, T.J. 2012. "'This is my route!' Race, entitlement and Gay Pride in South Africa." 15 October. Africa's a Country. http://africasacountry.com/2012/10/this-is-my-route-race-entitlement-and-gay-pride-in-south-africa/ (accessed 20 October 2012).

Hesse-Biber, S.N. 2005. "Oral history: A collaborative method of (auto)biography interview." In *The Practice of Qualitative Research*, edited by Hesse-Biber, Sharlene and Leavy, Patricia, pp. 149–194. Thousand Oaks, CA: Sage Publications.

Heywood, M. 2012. "Go back to the townships – the shame of gay South Africa." *Daily Maverick*. 23 October. https://www.dailymaverick.co.za/opinionista/2012-10-23-go-back-to-the-townships-the-shame-of-gay-south-africa#.WSQJUJKGMdV (accessed 25 October 2012).

Huber, M. 2014. "Revisiting places of queer crisis." *Spheres: Journal for Digital Cultures* 1, no. 1: 1–3.

Jagose, A. 1996. *Queer Theory: An Introduction*. New York: New York University Press.

Joburg Gay Pride Festival Company. 2013. "Joburg Gay Pride Festival Company board votes to stop production of annual Joburg Pride event." 3 April. https://www.facebook.com/joburgpride/posts/615596805134764 (accessed 5 April 2013).

Joburg Gay Pride Festival Company. 2012. "Joburg Pride response to One in Nine protest." 8 October. https://www.facebook.com/joburgpride/posts/126936200787842 (accessed 9 October 2012).

Johnson, C. 2002. "Heteronormative citizenship and the politics of passing." *Sexualities* 5, no. 3: 317–36.

Jorgensen, M. and Phillips, L. 2002. *Discourse Analysis as Theory and Method*. London: Sage Publications.

Lakhani, I. 2016. Interview with the researcher on 9 February 2016, Cape Town.

Kates, S.M. and Belk, R.W. 2001. "The meanings of Lesbian and Gay Pride Day: Resistance through consumption and resistance to consumption." *Journal of Contemporary Ethnography* 30, no. 4: 392–429.

Mambagirl. 2013. "Joburg Pride crisis: Future still uncertain." Mambagirl. http://www.mambagirl.com/article.asp?artid=8070 (accessed 5 July 2016).

Matebeni, Z. 2011. "Exploring black lesbian sexualities and identities in Johannesburg." Doctor of Philosophy thesis. University of the Witwatersrand, Johannesburg.

Mbembe, A. 2002. "The power of the archive and its limits." In *Refiguring the Archive*, edited by Hamilton, Carolyn, Harris, Verne, Taylor, Jane, Pickover, Michele, Reid, Graeme, and Saleh, Razia, pp. 19–26. Cape Town: David Philip.

Mbhele, Z. 2016. Interview with the researcher on 18 November 2016, Cape Town.

McLean, N. 2015. "Zwischen Party und Protest." *Sudlink* no. 174: 17.

Milani, T.M. 2012. "Sexual citizenship: Discourses, spaces and bodies at Johannesburg Pride 2012". *Journal of Language and Politics* 14, no. 3: 431–454.

Milani, T.M. 2013. "Are 'queers' really 'queer'? Language, identity and same-sex desire in a South African online community." *Discourse & Society* 24, no. 5: 615–633.

Mtetwa, P. 2009. "The speech you didn't hear at Joburg Pride." *Exit*. November, Edition 231, page 2.

Nath, D. 2012. "Gay Pride is political." Mail and Guardian Thought Leader. 10 October. http://thoughtleader.co.za/dipikanath/2012/10/10/gay-pride/ (accessed 12 October 2012).

Nathan, M. 2013. "Johannesburg Gay Pride cancelled as board dissolves." O-blog-dee-o-blog-da. https://oblogdeeoblogda.me/2013/04/03/johannesburg-gay-pride-cancelled-as-board-dissolves/ (accessed 5 July 2016).

Nieuwenhuis, J. 2011. "Qualitative research designs and data gathering techniques." In *First Steps in Research*, edited by Maree, K., pp. 70–97. Pretoria: Van Schaik Publishers.

One in Nine Campaign. 2012. Leaflet distributed at Joburg Pride 2012. 8 October. www.facebook.com/groups/10123398375/ (accessed 9 October 2012).

One in Nine Campaign. 2013. "Now is the time to reclaim our pride: One in Nine statement on the dissolution of Joburg Gay Pride Festival Company." 4 April. Posted in an event, 'Reclaim our Pride.' https://www.facebook.com/events/377097409070969/?acontext=%7B%22ref%22%3A%224%22%2C%22feed_story_type%22%3A%22308%22%2C%22action_history%22%3A%22null%22%7D (accessed 4 April 2013).

Oswin. N. 2008. "Critical geographies and the uses of sexuality: Deconstructing queer space." *Progress in Human Geography* 32, no. 1: 89–103.

Payne, R. and Davies, C. 2012. "Introduction to the special section: Citizenship and queer critique." *Sexualities* 15, no. 3: 251–256.

Ratcliff, J.J., Miller, A.K., and Krolikowski, A.M. 2013. "Why pride displays elicit support from majority group members: The meditational role of perceived deservingness." *Group Process Intergroup Relations* 16, no. 4: 462–475.

Reid, G. 2002. "'The history of the past is the trust of the present': Preservation and excavation in the gay and lesbian archives of South Africa." In *Refiguring the Archive*, edited by Hamilton, Carolyn, Harris, Verne, Taylor, Jane, Pickover, Michele, Reid, Graeme, and Saleh, Razia, pp. 193–207. Cape Town: David Philip.

Richardson, D. 2000. "Claiming citizenship? Sexuality, citizenship and lesbian/feminist theory." *Sexualities* 3, no. 2: 255–272.

Stella, F. 2013. "Queer space, pride, and shame in Moscow." *Slavic Review* 72, no. 3: 458–480.

Steyn, M. 2001. *Whiteness Just Isn't What It Used To Be: White Identity in a Changing South Africa*. New York: State University of New York Press.

Steyn, M. 2005. "White talk: White South Africans and the management of diasporic whiteness." In *Postcolonial Whiteness: A Critical Reader on Race and Empire*, edited by Lopez, Alfred J., pp. 119–136. Albany NY: State University of New York Press.

Taylor, J. 2012. *Playing It Queer: Popular Music, Identity and Queer World-Making*. Bern: Peter Lang.

Thoreson. R.R. 2008. "Somewhere over the Rainbow Nation: Gay, lesbian and bisexual activism in South Africa." *Journal of Southern African Studies* 34, no. 3: 679–697.

Trengove-Jones, T. 2012. "Pride 2012: Fight those heinous pissers back." *Exit*. November, Edition 264, page 4.

Tucker, A. 2009. "Framing exclusion in Cape Town's gay village: The discursive and material perpetration of inequitable queer subjects." *Area* 41, no. 2: 186–197.

Valenza, A. 2012. "One in Nine Campaign." ILGA. http://ilga.org/one-in-nine-campaign/ (accessed 15 April 2015).

POSTSCRIPT

Heteronormative legacies, queer turns

Amy Lind

Routledge Handbook of Queer Development Studies is the first comprehensive reader of its kind to archive the research and the wide range of scholarly, political, and epistemological perspectives on "queering development," a term introduced in the early 2000s (Jolly 2000; Lind 2003). Contributors address a wide range of topics, from LGBTIQ policy and planning, forms of LGBTIQ mobilization, the politics of humanitarian aid, and expressions and notions of queerness in transnational contexts. Together, they demonstrate the legacy of institutionalized heterosexuality within development discourse, specifically, as central to modernization discourses that assume a linear, teleological path to economic prosperity and cultural modernity. Importantly, a heteronormative notion of the family as central to progress, civilization, and modernity has a much longer history: heteronormativity underlaid and fueled processes of colonization, postcolonial nation-building, international relations, and national and local planning initiatives. And, as this volume demonstrates, it also became central to the post-World War II geopolitical focus on the "war on poverty" in the Global South, with its modernization aim of combatting poverty and maintaining political and economic stability in poor regions. Since the 1940s, funds have been channeled to Global South development efforts for family planning, to control birthrates and plan "responsible" parenting as a way to improve national economies and "modernize" societies (Adams and Pigg 2005). In these ways, sexuality and gender have *always* been central to states' and global institutions' efforts to improve living conditions and "develop" poor communities, nations, and regions.

Given this broad set of histories, what makes the contemporary "sexuality turn" different? On one hand, acknowledging SOGI/SC/LGBTIQ people is arguably incorporating sexual and gender deviants into the respectable realm of modern development. Some argue that this in itself is "queering" development. Yet, of course, there are many ways in which this type of "queering" is simply the "add LGBTIQs and stir" approach. Let me give one recent example. In 2014, the World Bank held its first public forum focused on sexuality and development. Economist Lee Badgett, a lead researcher on sexual rights and economic development, presented the results of the World Bank's pilot study on India (Badgett 2014). Her argument is simple. If we take into account how discrimination hinders LGBT individuals from working, earning an income, and living a decent life, and address these issues, a country's economy is likely to improve. "Adding LGBT people" to economic analysis, according to Badgett, is a key solution to both addressing discrimination and combatting poverty. This sexual modernization approach dominates the "sexuality turn" in the global development industry, with some exceptions. As Corinne Mason explains in the Introduction, following this event, World Bank employee and event organizer Fabrice Houbart faced much scrutiny for his work on this topic (among other issues). In addition, World Bank employees in India were unhappy with the results of this study, as it implied they needed to address issues with which they themselves were uncomfortable. I spoke at this event as a "critic" and have wondered ever since whether it was worth it, or whether my words mattered.

The "sexuality turn" has thus occurred within the global development industry, and much of the original aims of activists have been repackaged and resignified in the language of sexual modernization. The bodies, movements, and ideas that have become intelligible within the industry, including to Global North donors, are sanitized, relatively (gender)normative, viewed as respectable, productive, and clean. LGBTI people who are "targeted" in development initiatives are viewed as worthy of rescue, leaving out any gender or sexual deviants who do not fit within this sexual modernization framing. As Jasbir Puar (2011) and Rahul Rao (2014) have articulated it, the "homosexual question" has replaced the "woman question" as a barometer of a nation's sovereignty and development, thus marking the good gay as worthy of rescue and humanitarian aid. Rather than learning from the spaces/identities in-between/outside Western/Northern binaries, temporalities, and logics, rather than rethinking hegemonic forms of heteronormativity or homophobias, LGBTI people have been integrated into this modernization practice. Importantly, the broader heteronormative, now also homonormative, narrative continues. I would argue that while this increased visibility within state and global apparatuses is important, neither is it enough nor does it represent a *queer* turn.

A queer(er) reading of, or turn in, development would entail a further questioning of the notions of queerness themselves, in their multiplicity, as understood and expressed in various linguistic and geopolitical contexts. Likewise, it would entail a further questioning of Western temporalities and rationalities as the basis for understanding the "queer questions" addressed in this volume. The Queer/Cuir Americas Workshop is one example of an attempt to decenter discussions about queerness as emanating from the North and reframing it (in this case) hemispherically, across geopolitical and linguistic borders, and temporally, in part by creating a living archive of "queer" interventions that originate in Spanish, Portuguese, French, Quichua, and languages other than English, from a wide range of starting points, many of which having nothing seemingly to do with sex, sexuality or gender but rather about other (colonial, racial, etc.) anxieties of their time and location (see Viteri 2017).

A queer(er) reading would also entail a more critical reading of development itself (see Hoad, Gosine, and Klapeer in this volume) and would further scrutinize how, for example, anti-capitalist projects often are also gender- and heteronormative, thus reinforcing homophobia and transphobia in more seemingly "progressive" contexts (e.g., Lind and Keating 2014). Further *querying* development also would involve rethinking the centrality of heteronormativity in global development frameworks such as the UN's Millennial Goals, and in national(ist) politics; asking how and why queerness is now a global terrain of dispute (see Altman, this volume); and literally following the money: examining how funding paths and agendas powerfully shape activist agendas in the Global South and North (see Moreau and Currier, this volume); and acknowledging how and why some LGBTI people benefit from legal and policy change, while many others do not.

As in the "queer wars" within (especially North American) academia, there is increasingly a clear epistemic, political split between liberal and more transgressive approaches to "queering development." Indeed, this split is reflected in this volume. As we work toward inclusivity within liberal institutions (those of us who do), let's not lose sight of the more radical potential of imagining a most just, sustainable, antiracist, feminist, and queer future. These chapters are working toward this imagined future.

Acknowledgement

Many thanks to Ashley Currier for her comments.

References

Adams, Vincanne and Stacy Leigh Pigg (eds) (2005). *Sex in Development: Science, Sexuality, and Morality in Global Perspective*, Durham, NC: Duke University Press.

Badgett, Lee (2014) "The Economic Cost of Stigma and the Exclusion of LGBT People: A Case Study of India." Washington, DC: World Bank Group. Available online at: http://documents.worldbank.org/curated/en/527261468035379692/The-economic-cost-of-stigma-and-the-exclusion-of-LGBT-people-a-case-study-of-India.

Jolly, Susie (2000) "What Use Is Queer Theory to Development?" Queering Development Seminar Series. IDS Discussion Paper. Brighton: Institute for Development Studies.

Lind, Amy (2003) "Queering Development: Institutionalized Heterosexuality in Development Theory, Practice, and Politics in Latin America," in Kum-Kum Bhavnani, John Foran, Priya A. Kurian and Debashish Munshi (eds) *Feminist Futures: Re-imagining Women, Culture and Development*, (pp. 55-73). London: Zed Books.

Lind, Amy and Christine Keating (2014) "Navigating the Left Turn: Sexual Justice and the Citizen Revolution in Ecuador," *International Feminist Journal of Politics* 15, no. 4: 515–533.

Puar, Jasbir (2011) "Citation and Censorship: The Politics of Talking About the Sexual Politics of Israel," *Feminist Legal Studies* 19, no. 2: 133–142.

Rao, Rahul (2014) "Queer Questions," *International Feminist Journal of Politics* 16, no. 2: 199–217.

Viteri, Maria Amelia (2017) "*Intensiones*: Tensions in Queer Agency and Activism in Latino América," *Feminist Studies* 43, no. 2: 405–417.

INDEX